RED HOT CHILI SAMURAI

D1227903

VOLUME 3

BY
YOSHITSUGU KATAGIRI

TOKYOPOP®

HAMBURG // LONDON // LOS ANGELES // TOKYO

Red Hot Chili Samurai Volume 3
Created By Yoshitsugu Katagiri

Translation - Ryan Peterson
English Adaptation - Bryce P. Coleman
Script Editor - Tim Leavey & Jordan Acosta
Retouch and Lettering - Star Print Brokers
Production Artist - Rui Kyo
Graphic Designer - Louis Csontos

Editor - Cindy Suzuki
Print Production Manager - Lucas Rivera
Managing Editor - Vy Nguyen
Senior Designer - Louis Csontos
Art Director - Al-Insan Lashley
Director of Sales and Manufacturing - Allyson De Simone
Associate Publisher - Marco F. Pavia
President and C.O.O. - John Parker
C.E.O. and Chief Creative Officer - Stu Levy

A TOKYOPOP® Manga

TOKYOPOP and [logo] are trademarks or registered trademarks of TOKYOPOP Inc.

TOKYOPOP Inc.
5900 Wilshire Blvd. Suite 2000
Los Angeles, CA 90036

E-mail: info@TOKYOPOP.com
Come visit us online at www.TOKYOPOP.com

KOKAKUTORIMONOCHO vol.3 © Yoshitsugu KATAGIRI 2008 First published in Japan in 2008 by KADOKAWA SHOTEN Publishing Co., Ltd., Tokyo. English translation rights arranged with KADOKAWA SHOTEN Publishing Co., Ltd., Tokyo through TUTTLE-MORI AGENCY, INC., Tokyo. English text copyright © 2010 TOKYOPOP Inc.

All rights reserved. No portion of this book may be reproduced or transmitted in any form or by any means without written permission from the copyright holders. This manga is a work of fiction. Any resemblance to actual events or locales or persons, living or dead, is entirely coincidental.

ISBN: 978-1-4278-1722-8

First TOKYOPOP printing: December 2010

10 9 8 7 6 5 4 3 2 1

Printed in the USA

ISBN
YA Anime
Red
vol 3

3

YOSHITSUGU
KATAGIRI

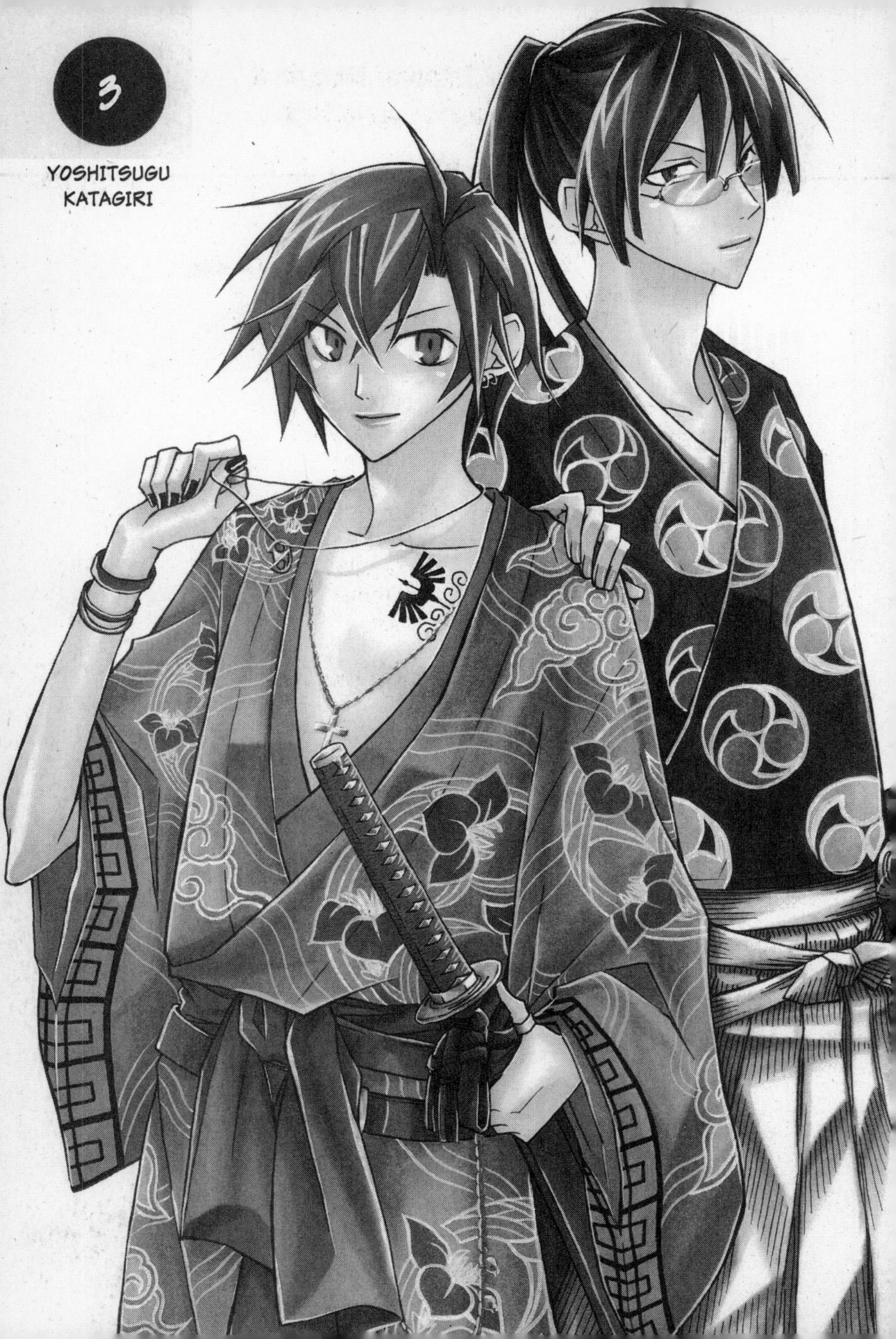

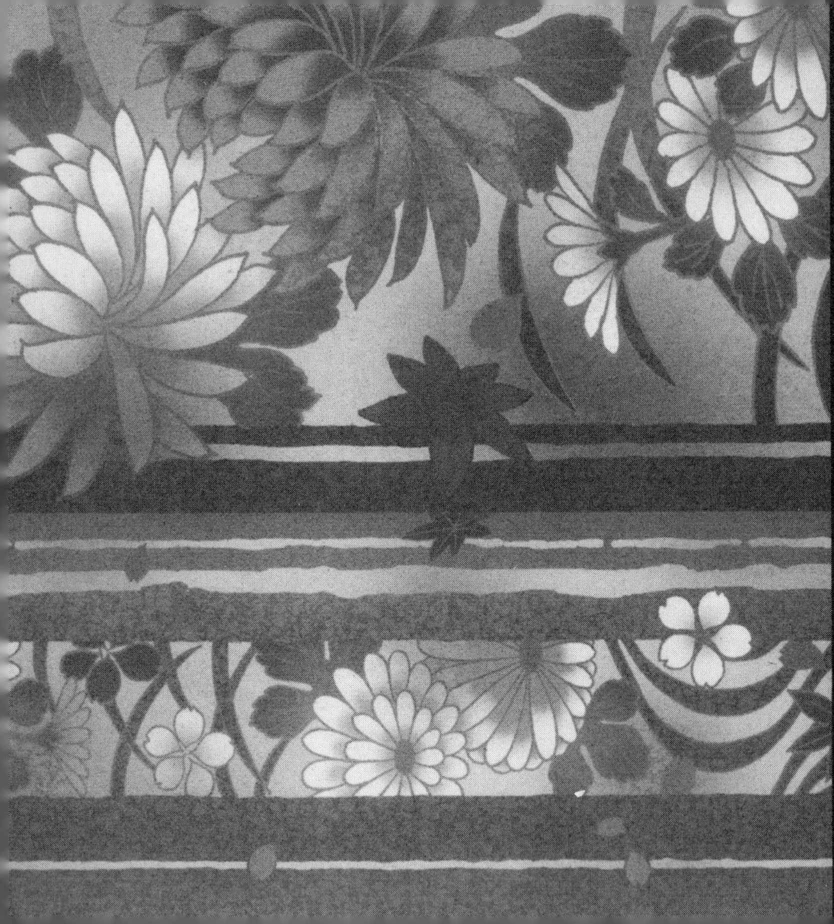

CONTENTS

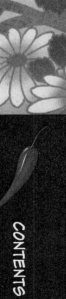

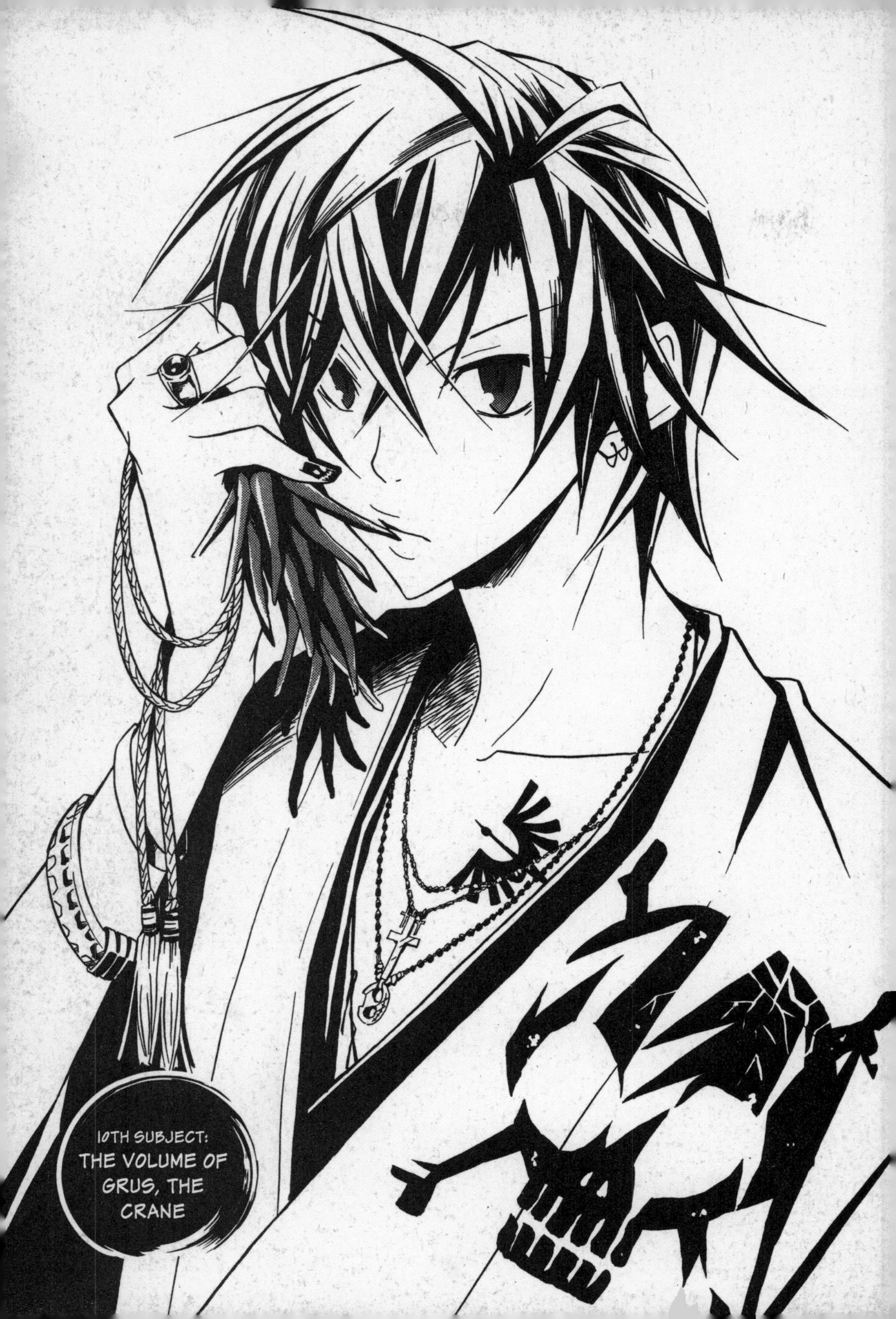
10TH SUBJECT:
THE VOLUME OF GRUS, THE CRANE

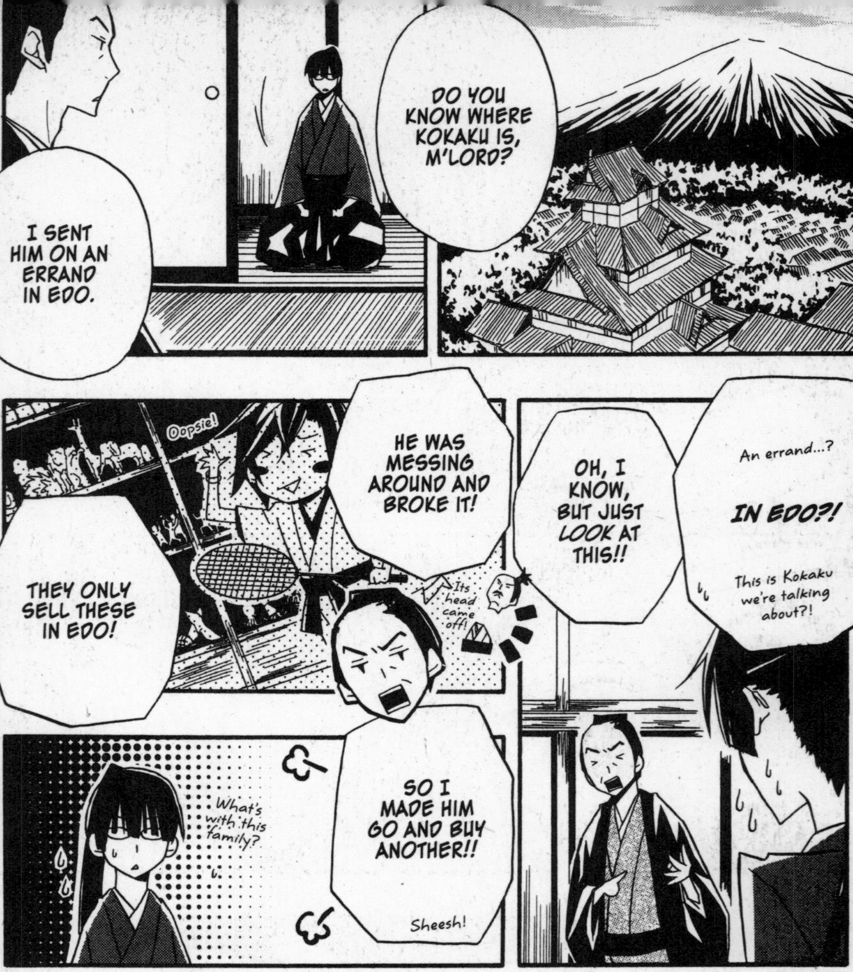
DO YOU KNOW WHERE KOKAKU IS, M'LORD?
I SENT HIM ON AN ERRAND IN EDO.
An errand...?
IN EDO?!
This is Kokaku we're talking about?!
OH, I KNOW, BUT JUST LOOK AT THIS!!
HE WAS MESSING AROUND AND BROKE IT!
Oopsie!
Its head came off!
THEY ONLY SELL THESE IN EDO!
SO I MADE HIM GO AND BUY ANOTHER!!
Sheesh!
What's with this family?

EGGPLANT FAMILY PEPPER TRIBE NUMBER 4

"YUZUKOSHŌ"
A SPECIALTY OF ŌITA PREFECTURE. MADE BY MIXING TOGETHER PEPPER, YUZU PEEL PASTE, AND SALT AND THEN FERMENTING. TYPICALLY MADE FROM GREEN CHILIES.

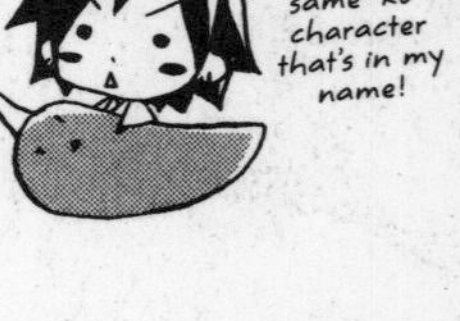
It uses the same "ko" character that's in my name!

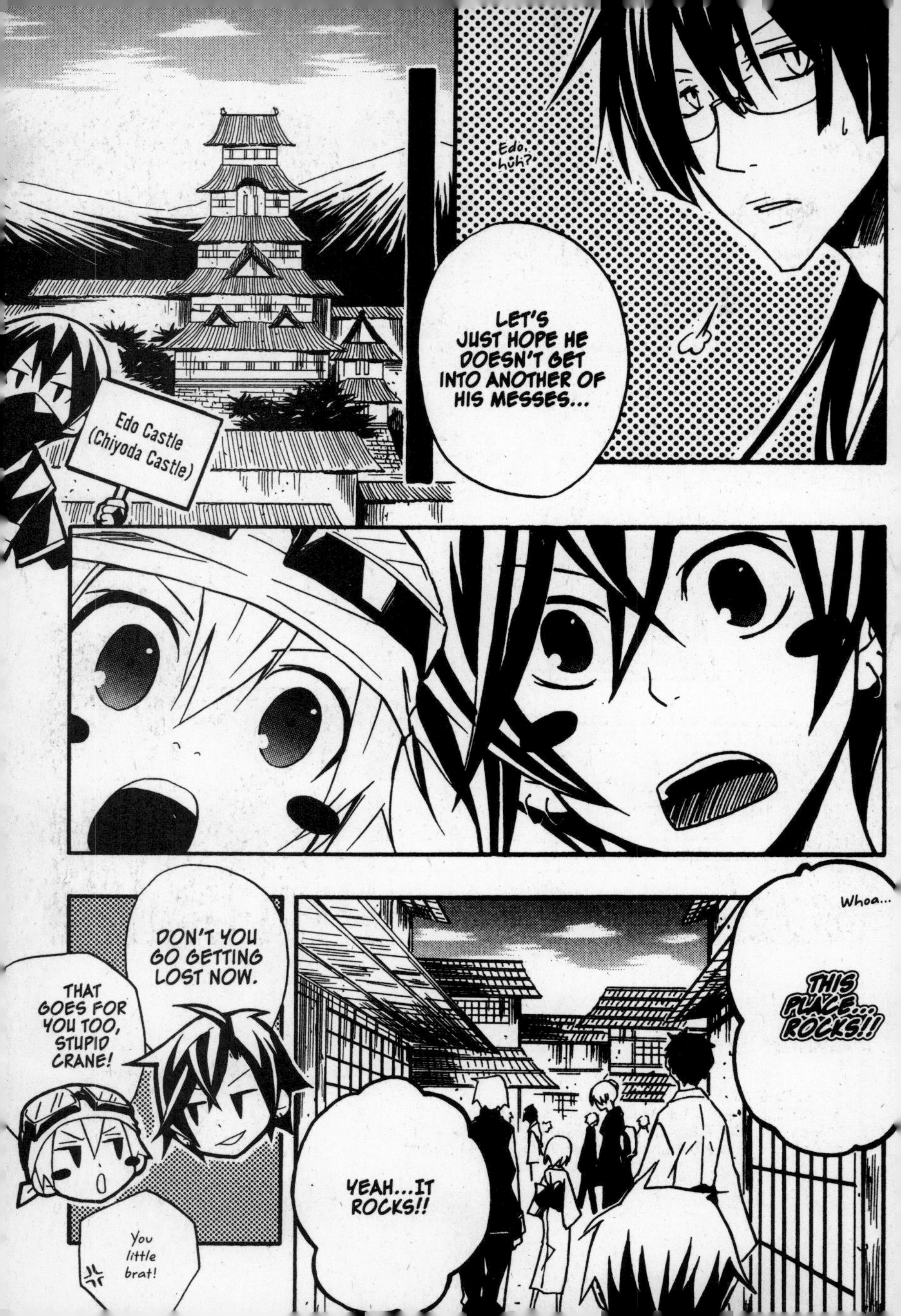
Edo, huh?
LET'S JUST HOPE HE DOESN'T GET INTO ANOTHER OF HIS MESSES...
Edo Castle (Chiyoda Castle)
Whoa...
THIS PLACE... ROCKS!!
YEAH...IT ROCKS!!
DON'T YOU GO GETTING LOST NOW.
THAT GOES FOR YOU TOO, STUPID CRANE!
You little brat!

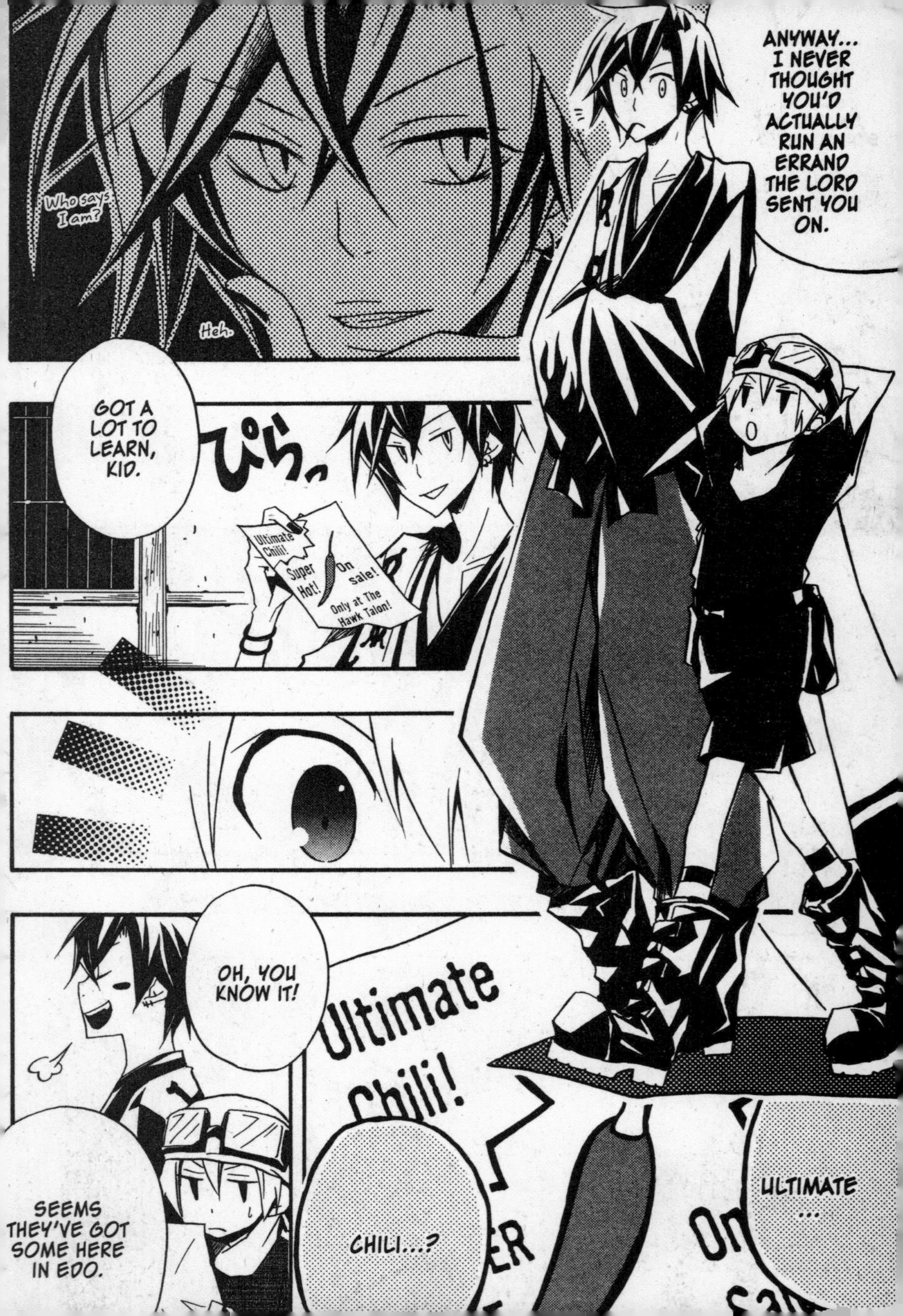
ANYWAY... I NEVER THOUGHT YOU'D ACTUALLY RUN AN ERRAND THE LORD SENT YOU ON.
Who says I am?
Heh.
GOT A LOT TO LEARN, KID.
ぴらっ
Ultimate Chili!
Super Hot!
On sale!
Only at The Hawk Talon!
Ultimate Chili!
ULTIMATE...
CHILI...?
On
OH, YOU KNOW IT!
SEEMS THEY'VE GOT SOME HERE IN EDO.

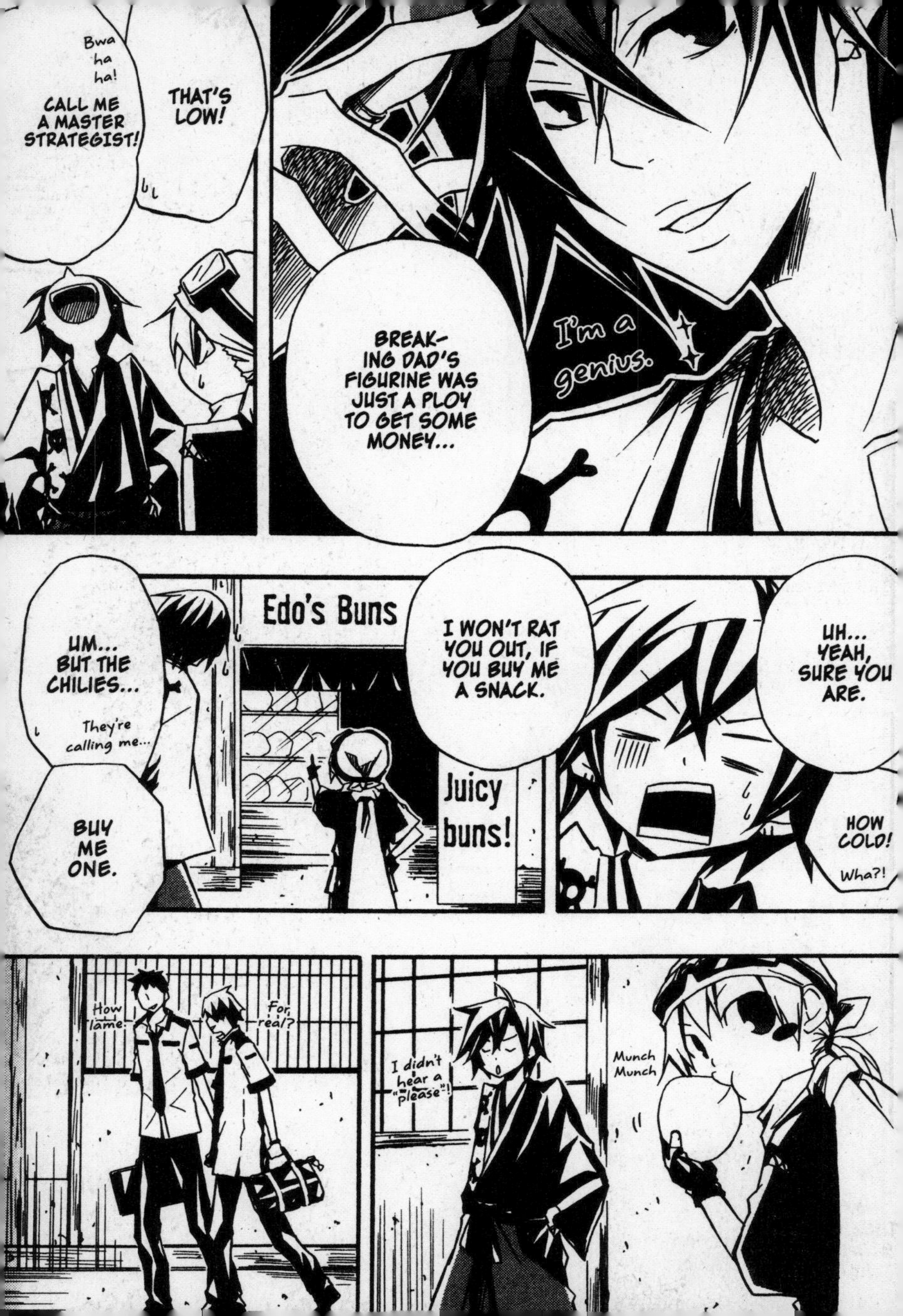

I'm a genius.
BREAKING DAD'S FIGURINE WAS JUST A PLOY TO GET SOME MONEY...
THAT'S LOW!
Bwa ha ha! CALL ME A MASTER STRATEGIST!
UH... YEAH, SURE YOU ARE.
HOW COLD!
Wha?!
I WON'T RAT YOU OUT, IF YOU BUY ME A SNACK.
Edo's Buns
Juicy buns!
UM... BUT THE CHILIES...
They're calling me...
BUY ME ONE.
Munch Munch
I didn't hear a "please"!
For real?
How lame.

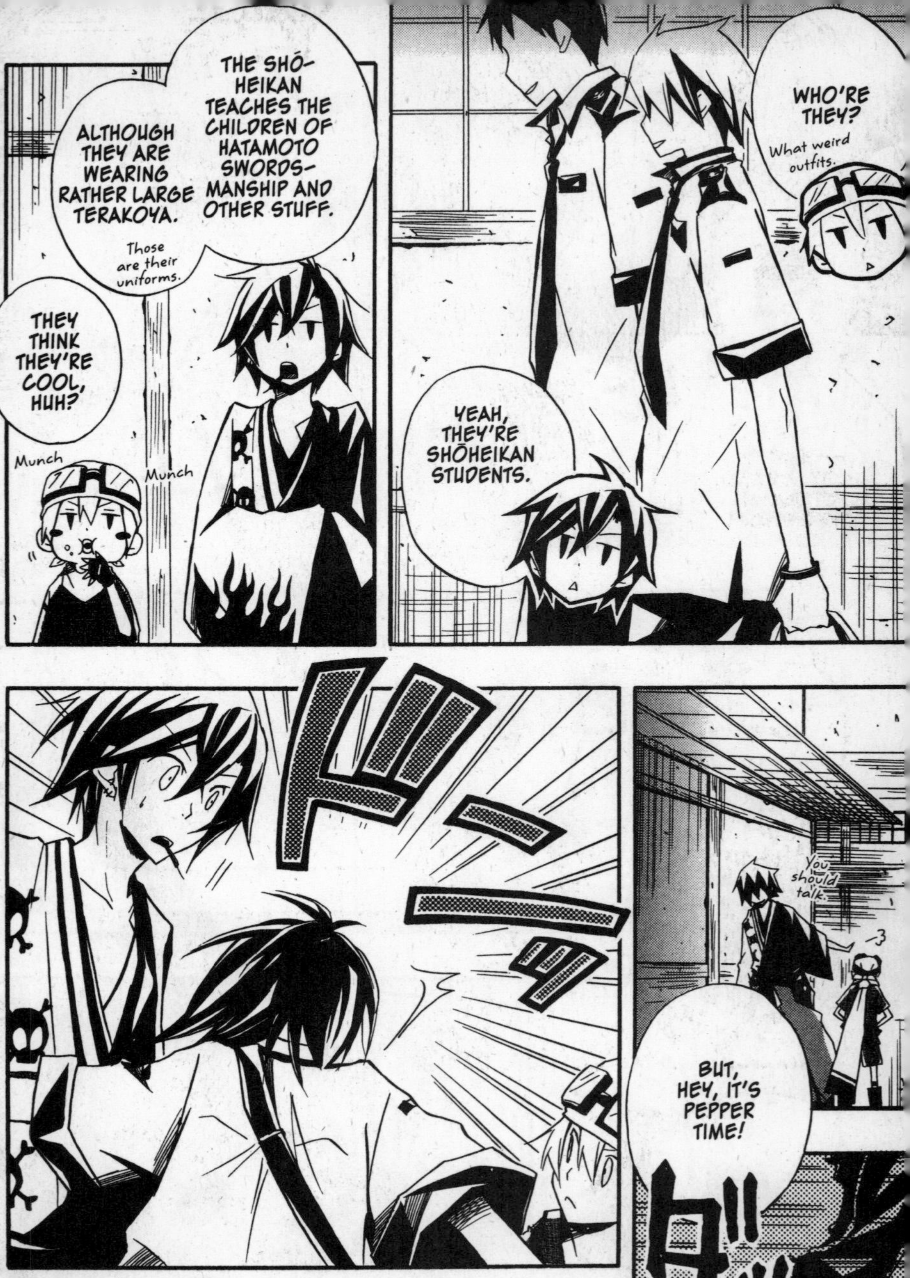
WHO'RE THEY?
What weird outfits.
YEAH, THEY'RE SHŌHEIKAN STUDENTS.
THE SHŌ-HEIKAN TEACHES THE CHILDREN OF HATAMOTO SWORDS-MANSHIP AND OTHER STUFF.
ALTHOUGH THEY ARE WEARING RATHER LARGE TERAKOYA.
Those are their uniforms.
THEY THINK THEY'RE COOL, HUH?
Munch
Munch
You should talk.
BUT, HEY, IT'S PEPPER TIME!

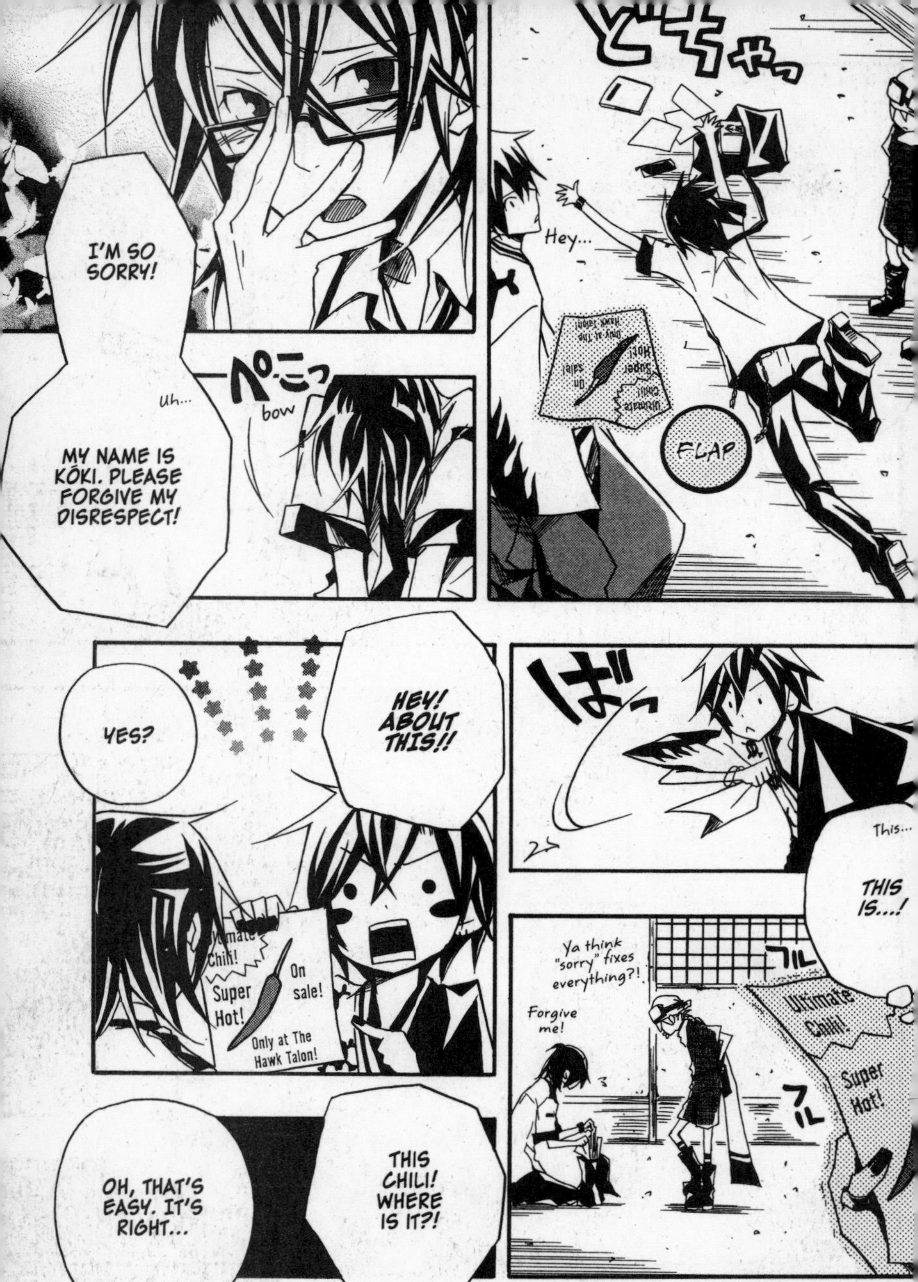
どちゃっ
Hey...
FLAP
I'M SO SORRY!
ぺこっ
bow
Uh...
MY NAME IS KŌKI. PLEASE FORGIVE MY DISRESPECT!
ばっ
This...
THIS IS...!
Ya think "sorry" fixes everything?!
Forgive me!
フル
フル
Ultimate Chili!
Super Hot!
YES?
HEY! ABOUT THIS!!
Ultimate Chili!
Super Hot!
On sale!
Only at The Hawk Talon!
THIS CHILI! WHERE IS IT?!
OH, THAT'S EASY. IT'S RIGHT...

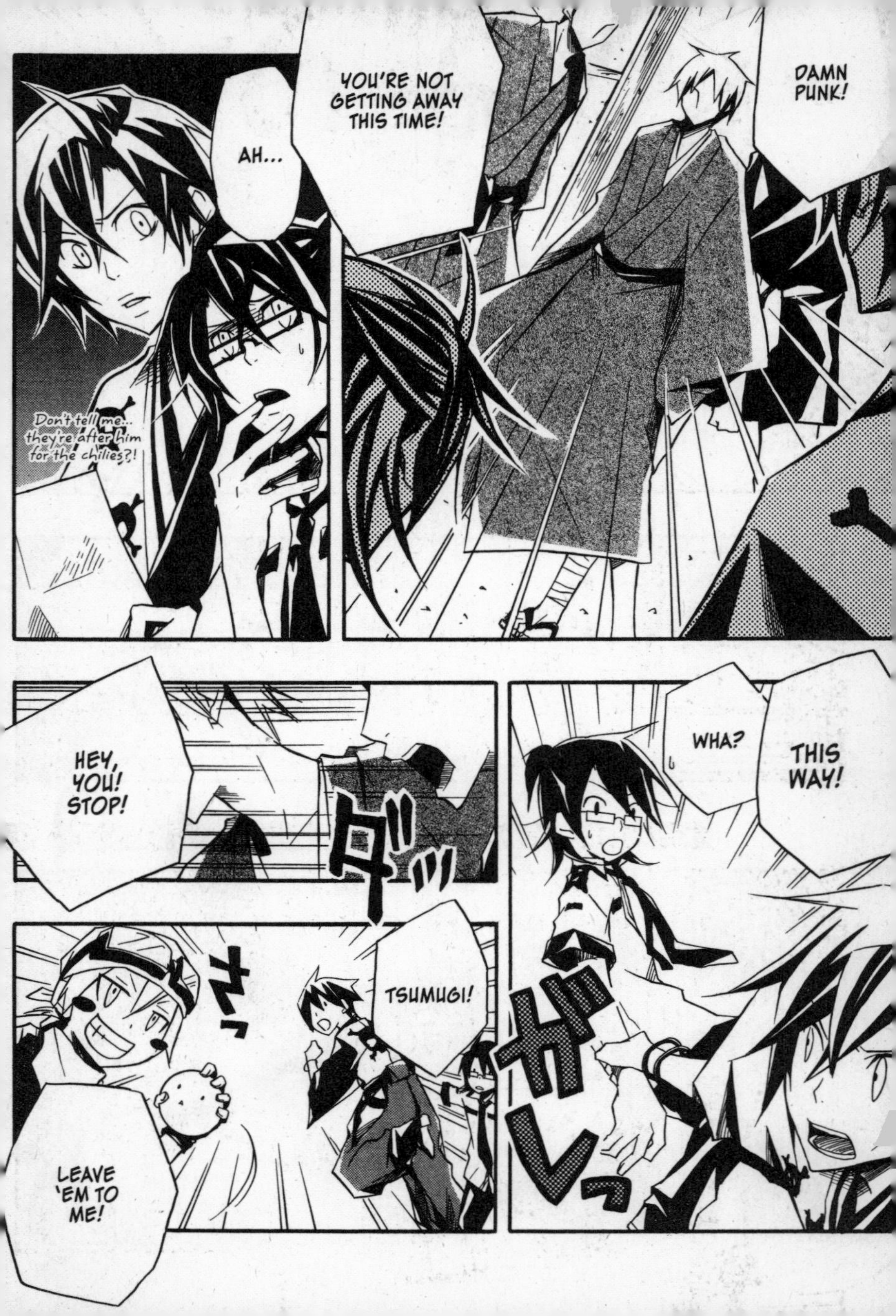

DAMN PUNK!
YOU'RE NOT GETTING AWAY THIS TIME!
AH...
Don't tell me... they're after him for the chilies?!
THIS WAY!
WHA?
HEY, YOU! STOP!
ダッ
TSUMUGI!
LEAVE 'EM TO ME!

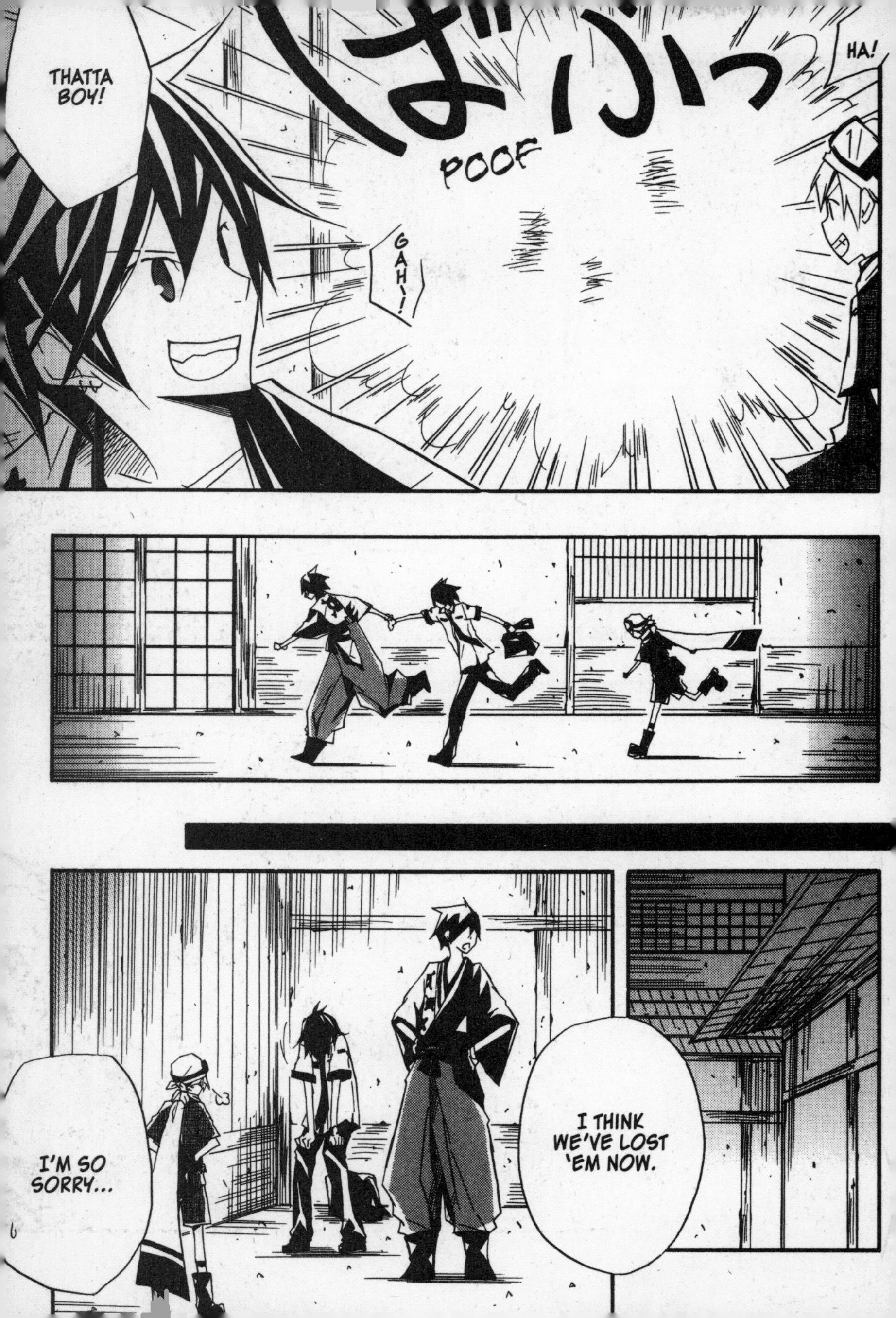
HA!
ばふっ
POOF
GAH-!
THATTA BOY!
I THINK WE'VE LOST 'EM NOW.
I'M SO SORRY...

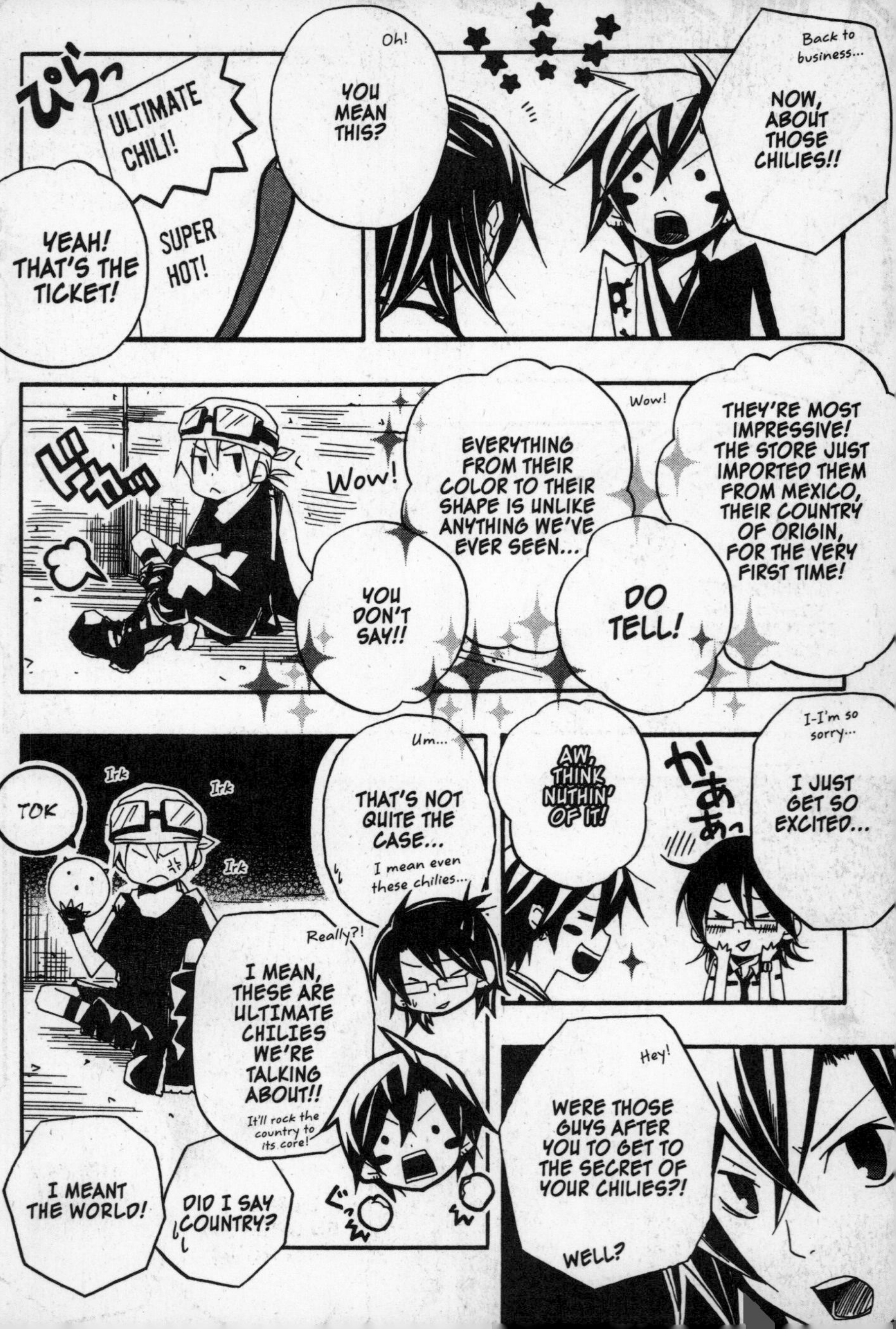
Back to business...
NOW, ABOUT THOSE CHILIES!!
Oh!
YOU MEAN THIS?
ぴらっ
ULTIMATE CHILI!
SUPER HOT!
YEAH! THAT'S THE TICKET!
THEY'RE MOST IMPRESSIVE! THE STORE JUST IMPORTED THEM FROM MEXICO, THEIR COUNTRY OF ORIGIN, FOR THE VERY FIRST TIME!
Wow!
EVERYTHING FROM THEIR COLOR TO THEIR SHAPE IS UNLIKE ANYTHING WE'VE EVER SEEN...
DO TELL!
YOU DON'T SAY!!
Wow!
I-I'm so sorry...
I JUST GET SO EXCITED...
かあぁっ
AW, THINK NUTHIN' OF IT!
Um...
THAT'S NOT QUITE THE CASE...
I mean even these chilies...
Really?!
I MEAN, THESE ARE ULTIMATE CHILIES WE'RE TALKING ABOUT!!
It'll rock the country to its core!
Irk
Irk
Irk
TOK
DID I SAY COUNTRY?
I MEANT THE WORLD!
Hey!
WERE THOSE GUYS AFTER YOU TO GET TO THE SECRET OF YOUR CHILIES?!
WELL?

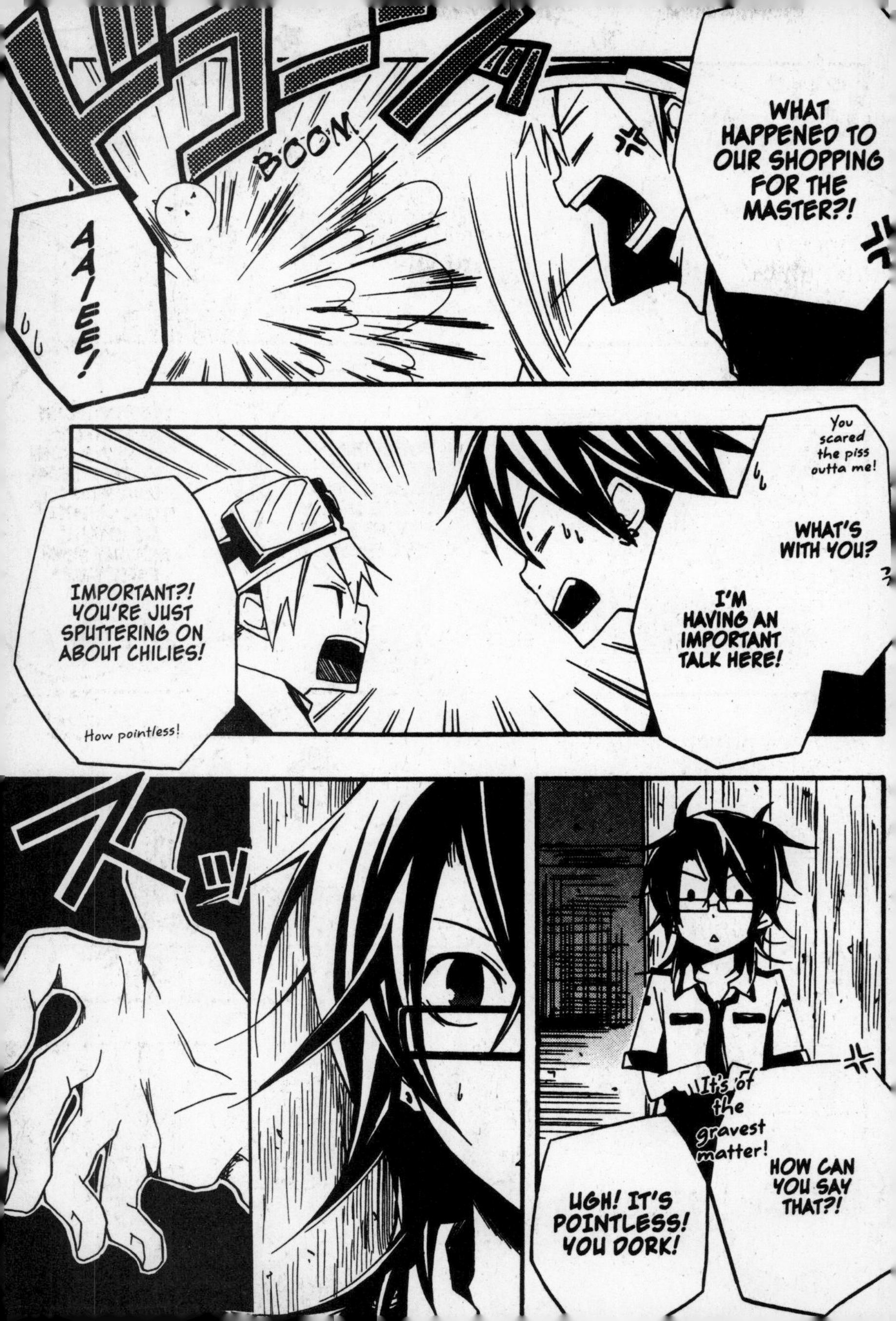
WHAT HAPPENED TO OUR SHOPPING FOR THE MASTER?!
BOOM
AAIEE!
You scared the piss outta me!
WHAT'S WITH YOU?
I'M HAVING AN IMPORTANT TALK HERE!
IMPORTANT?! YOU'RE JUST SPUTTERING ON ABOUT CHILIES!
How pointless!
It's of the gravest matter!
HOW CAN YOU SAY THAT?!
UGH! IT'S POINTLESS! YOU DORK!

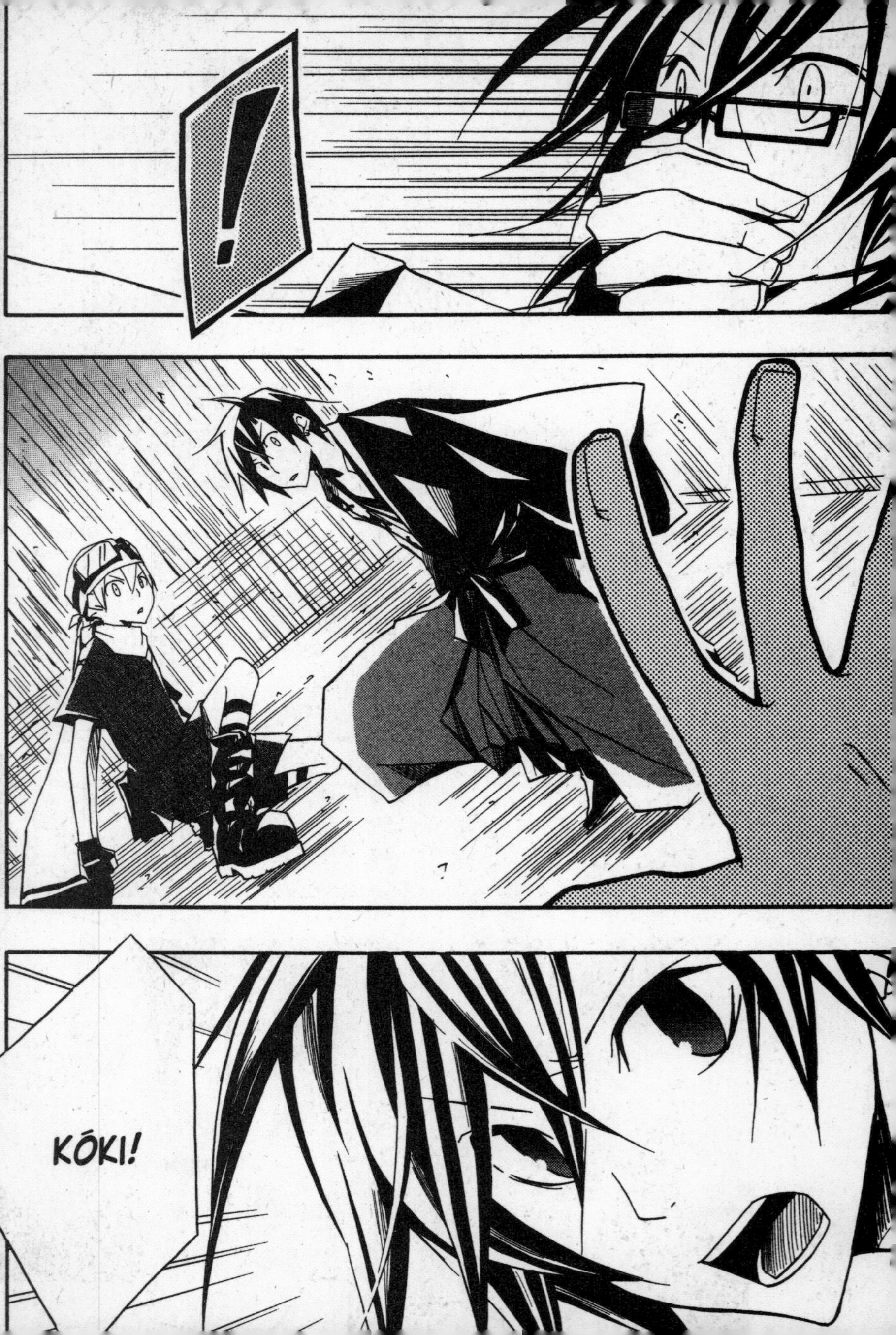
!
KŌKI!

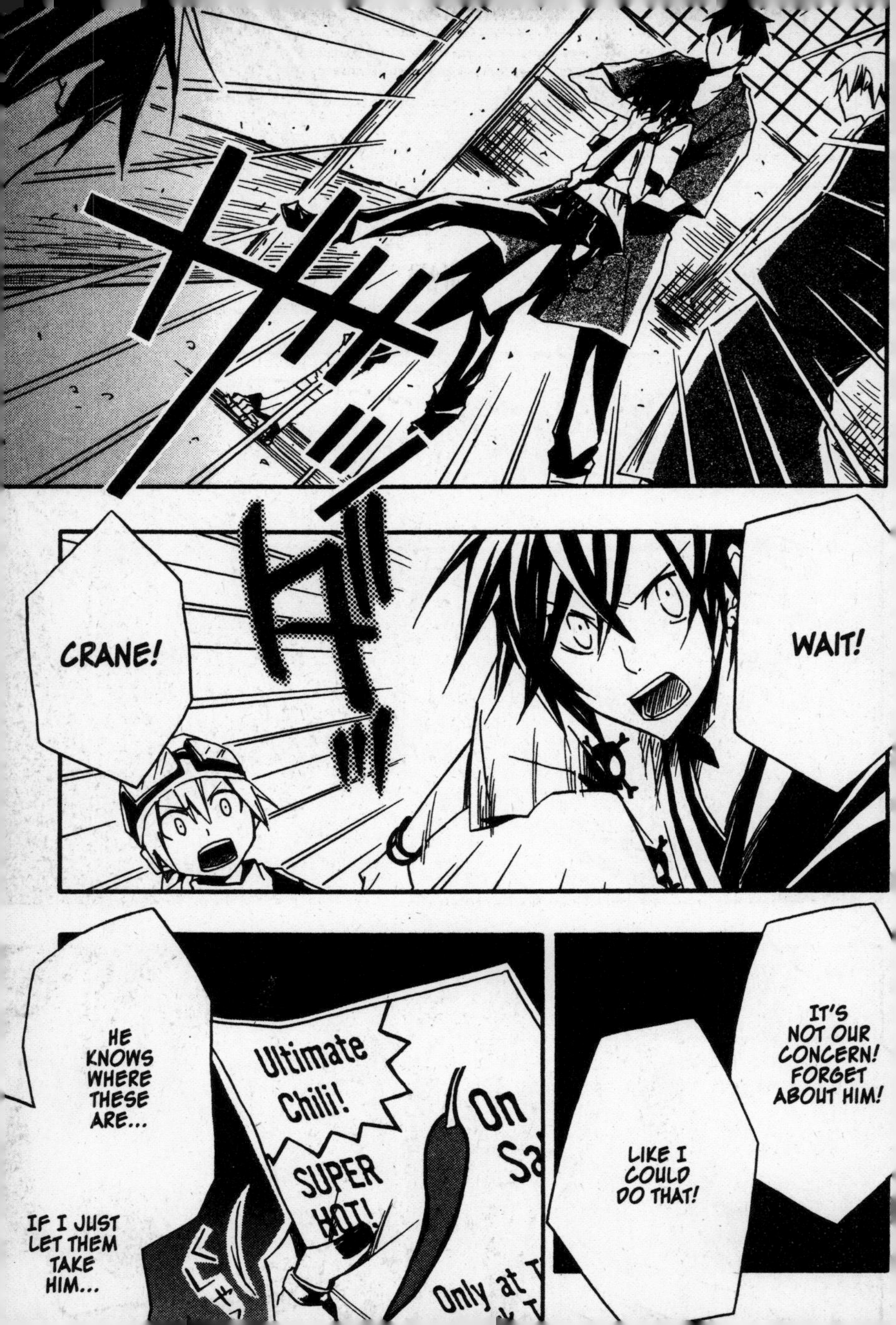
WAIT!
CRANE!
IT'S NOT OUR CONCERN! FORGET ABOUT HIM!
LIKE I COULD DO THAT!
Ultimate Chili!
SUPER HOT!
HE KNOWS WHERE THESE ARE...
IF I JUST LET THEM TAKE HIM...

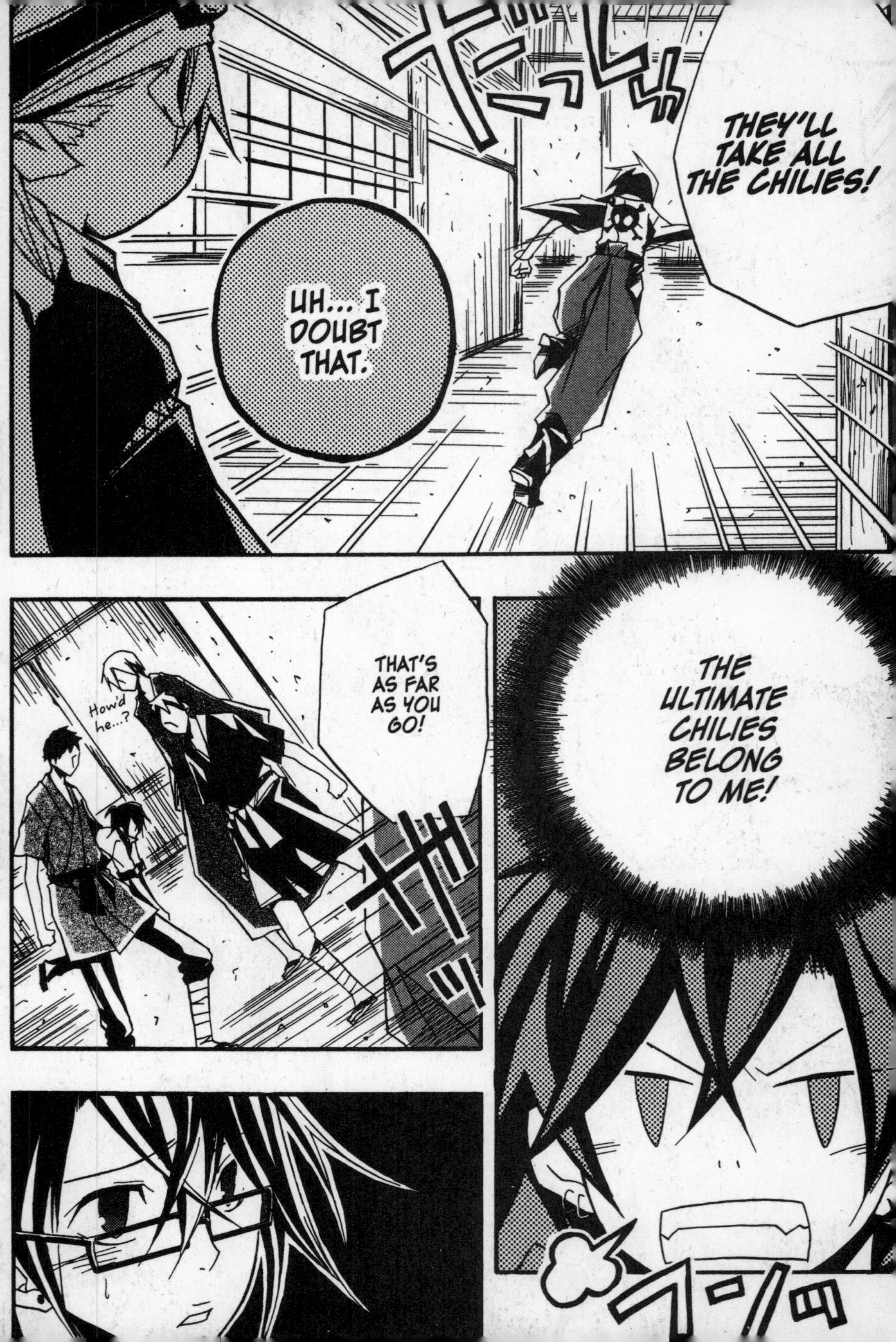
THEY'LL TAKE ALL THE CHILIES!
UH... I DOUBT THAT.
THE ULTIMATE CHILIES BELONG TO ME!
THAT'S AS FAR AS YOU GO!
How'd he...?

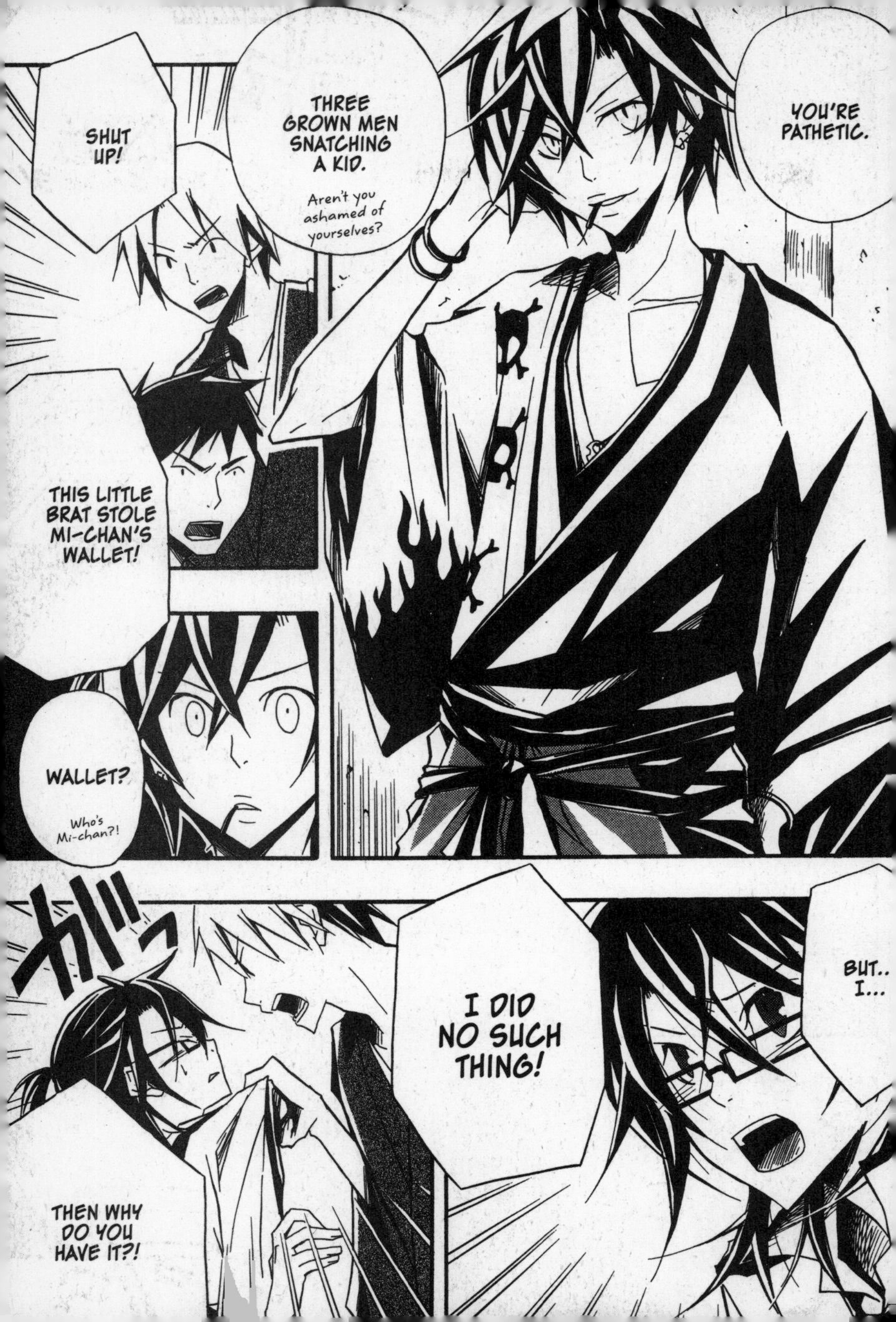
THREE GROWN MEN SNATCHING A KID.
Aren't you ashamed of yourselves?
YOU'RE PATHETIC.
SHUT UP!
THIS LITTLE BRAT STOLE MI-CHAN'S WALLET!
WALLET?
Who's Mi-chan?!
BUT.. I...
I DID NO SUCH THING!
THEN WHY DO YOU HAVE IT?!

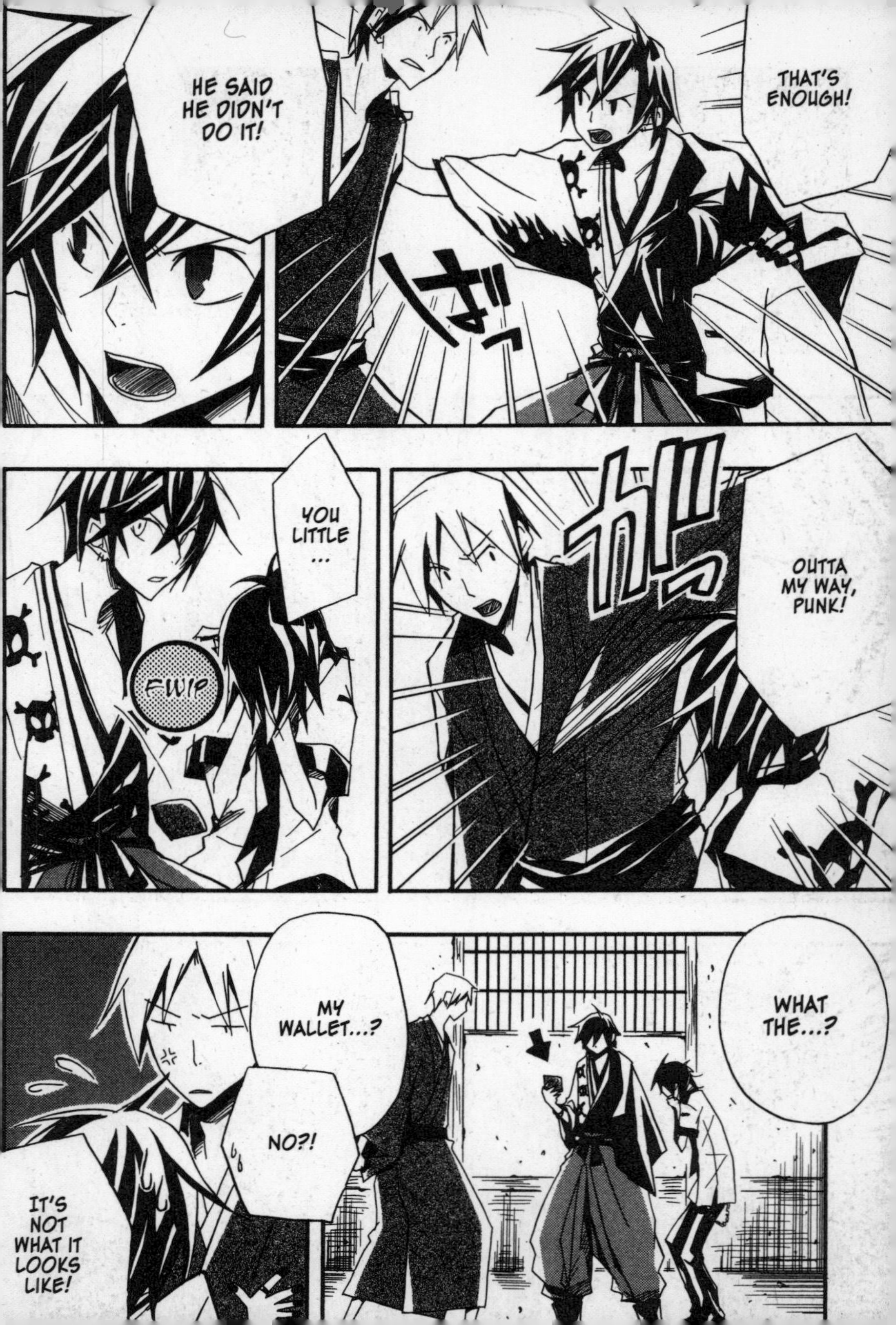
THAT'S ENOUGH!
ぎっ
HE SAID HE DIDN'T DO IT!
がっ
OUTTA MY WAY, PUNK!
YOU LITTLE ...
FWIP
WHAT THE...?
MY WALLET...?
NO?!
IT'S NOT WHAT IT LOOKS LIKE!

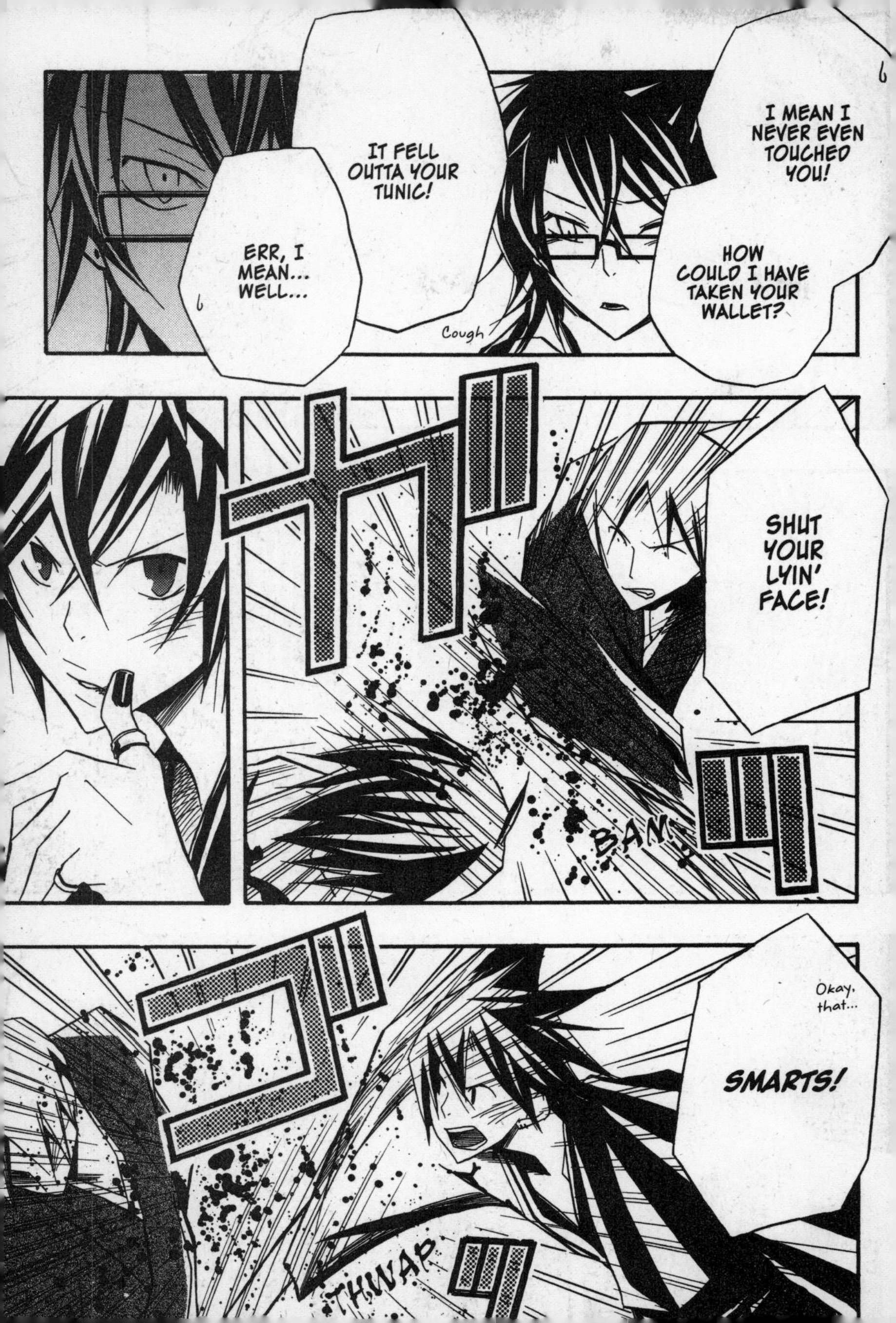
I MEAN I NEVER EVEN TOUCHED YOU!
HOW COULD I HAVE TAKEN YOUR WALLET?
IT FELL OUTTA YOUR TUNIC!
Cough
ERR, I MEAN... WELL...
SHUT YOUR LYIN' FACE!
BAN!
Okay, that...
SMARTS!
THWAP

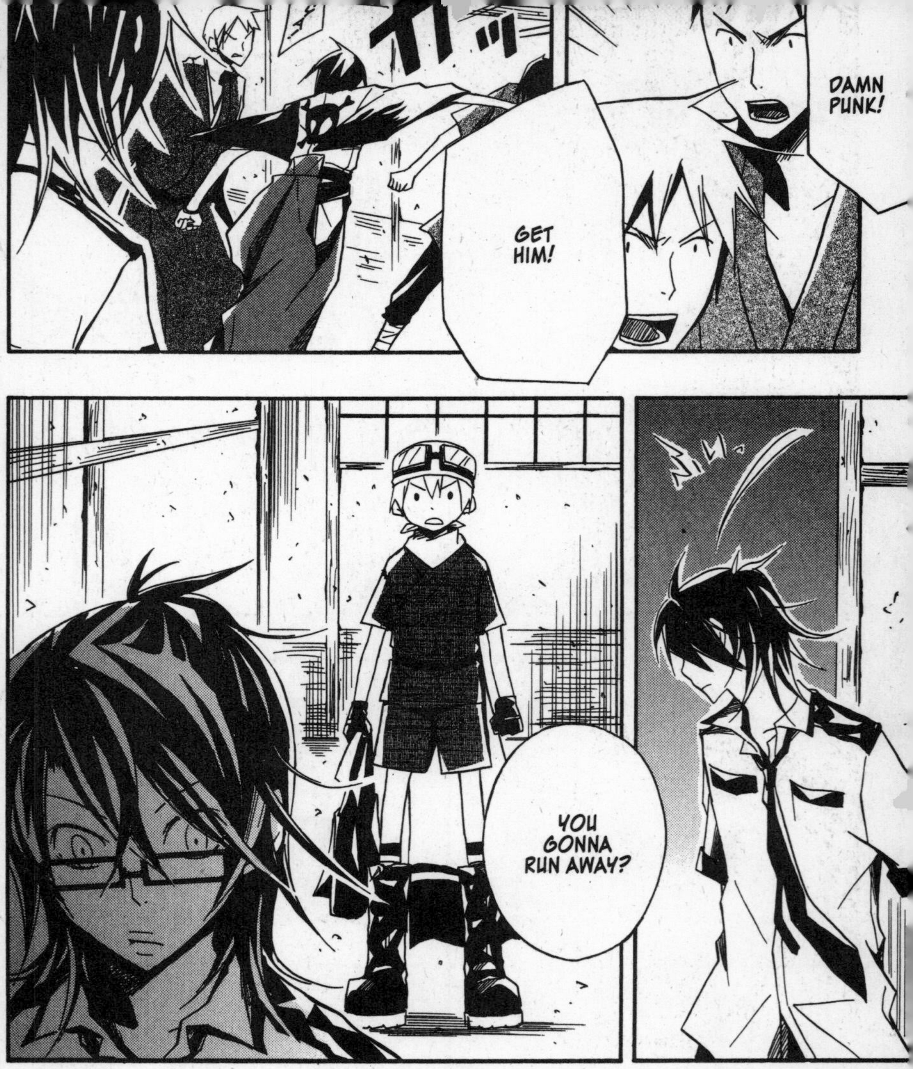
DAMN PUNK!
GET HIM!
YOU GONNA RUN AWAY?

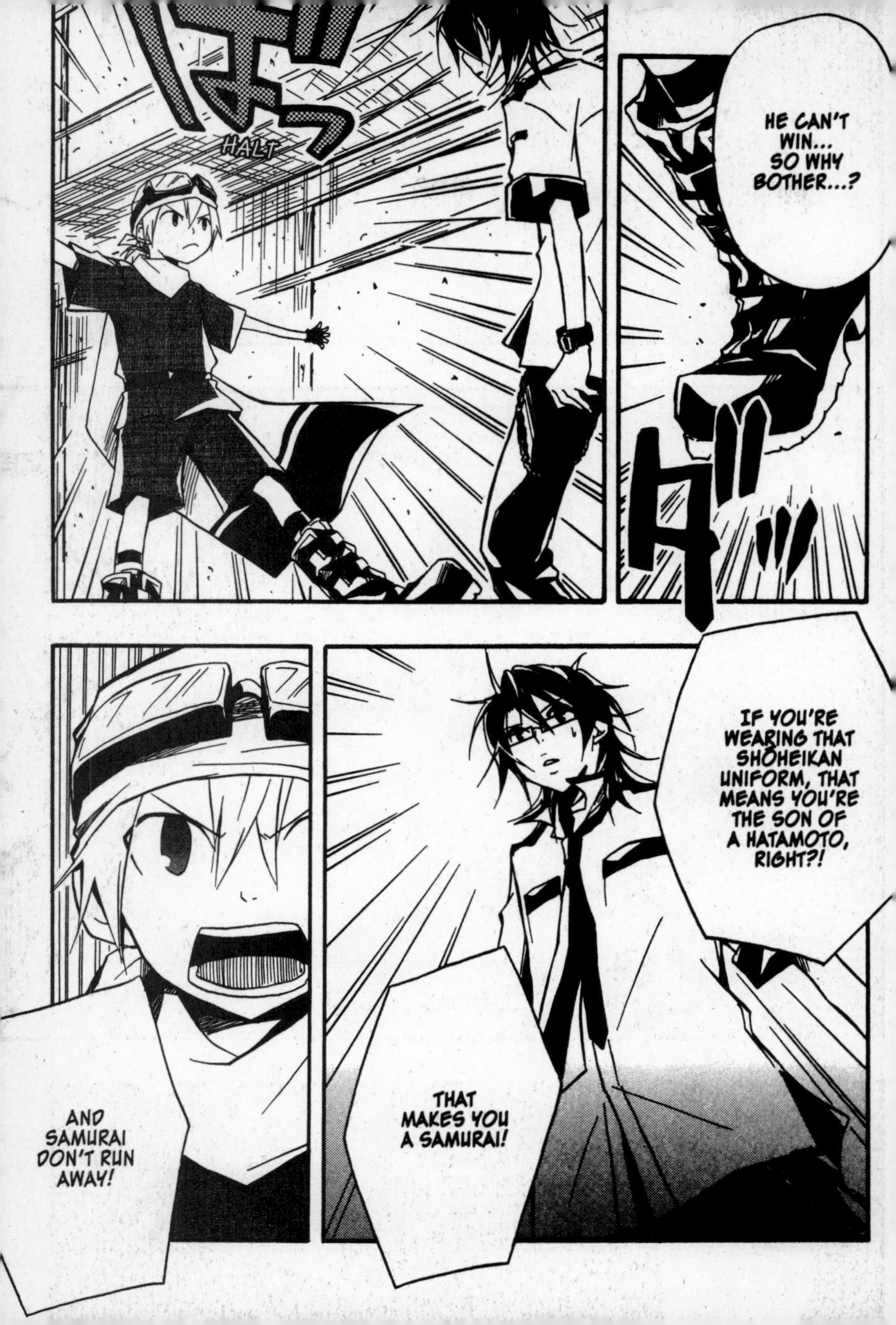
HE CAN'T WIN... SO WHY BOTHER...?
HALT
IF YOU'RE WEARING THAT SHŌHEIKAN UNIFORM, THAT MEANS YOU'RE THE SON OF A HATAMOTO, RIGHT?!
THAT MAKES YOU A SAMURAI!
AND SAMURAI DON'T RUN AWAY!

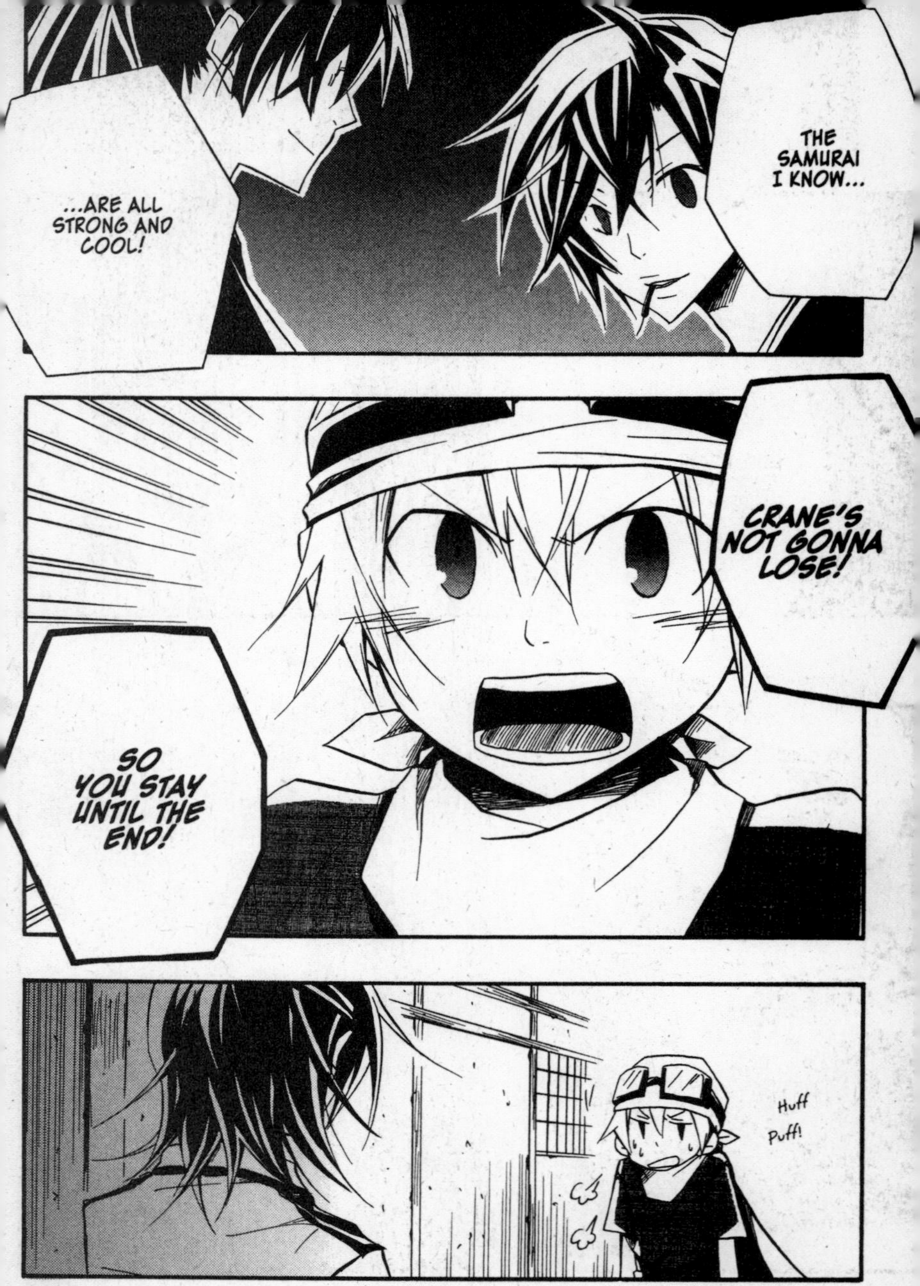
THE SAMURAI I KNOW...
...ARE ALL STRONG AND COOL!
CRANE'S NOT GONNA LOSE!
SO YOU STAY UNTIL THE END!
Huff
Puff!

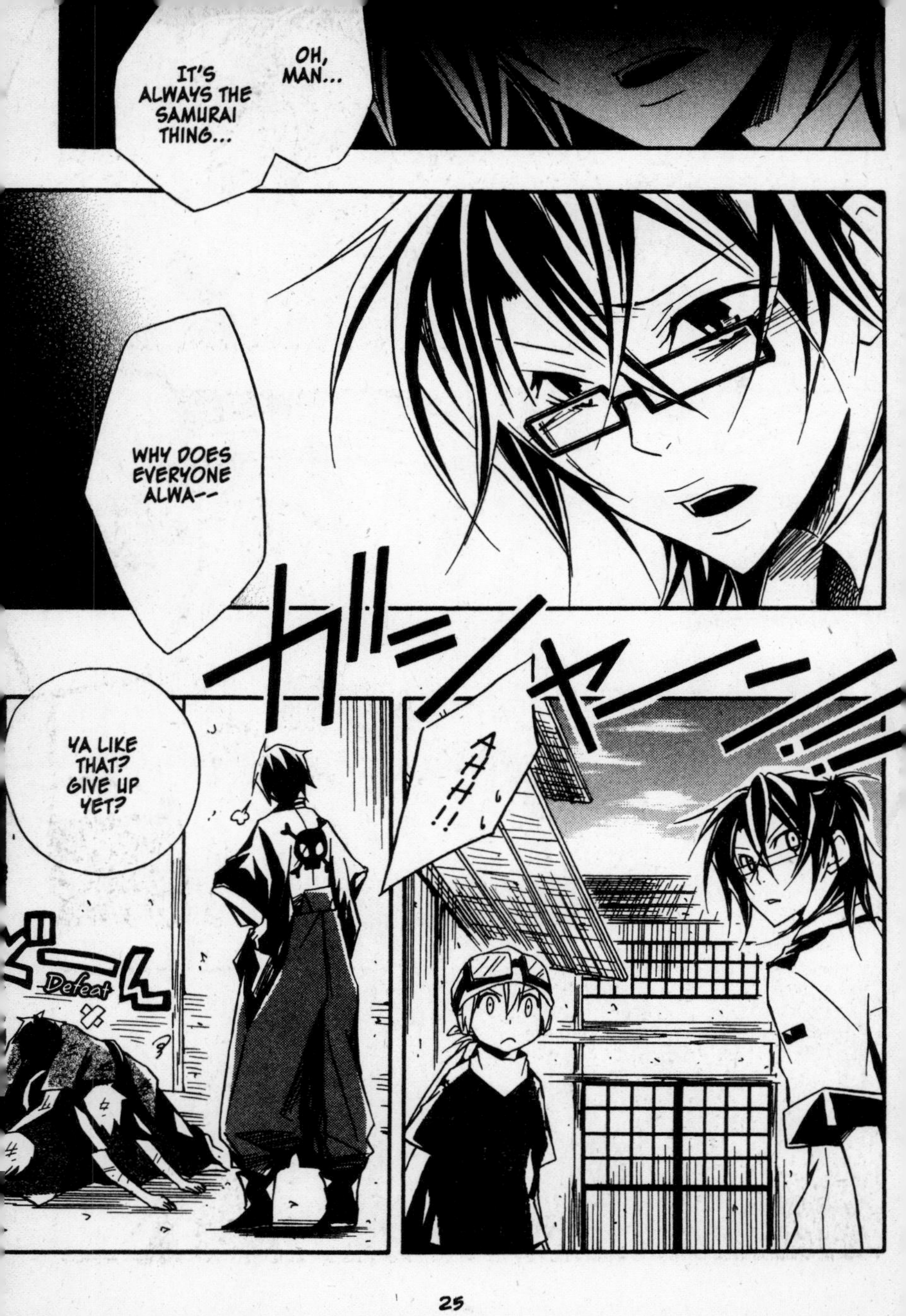
OH, MAN...
IT'S ALWAYS THE SAMURAI THING...
WHY DOES EVERYONE ALWA--
ガシャーン!!
AHH!!
YA LIKE THAT? GIVE UP YET?
Defeat

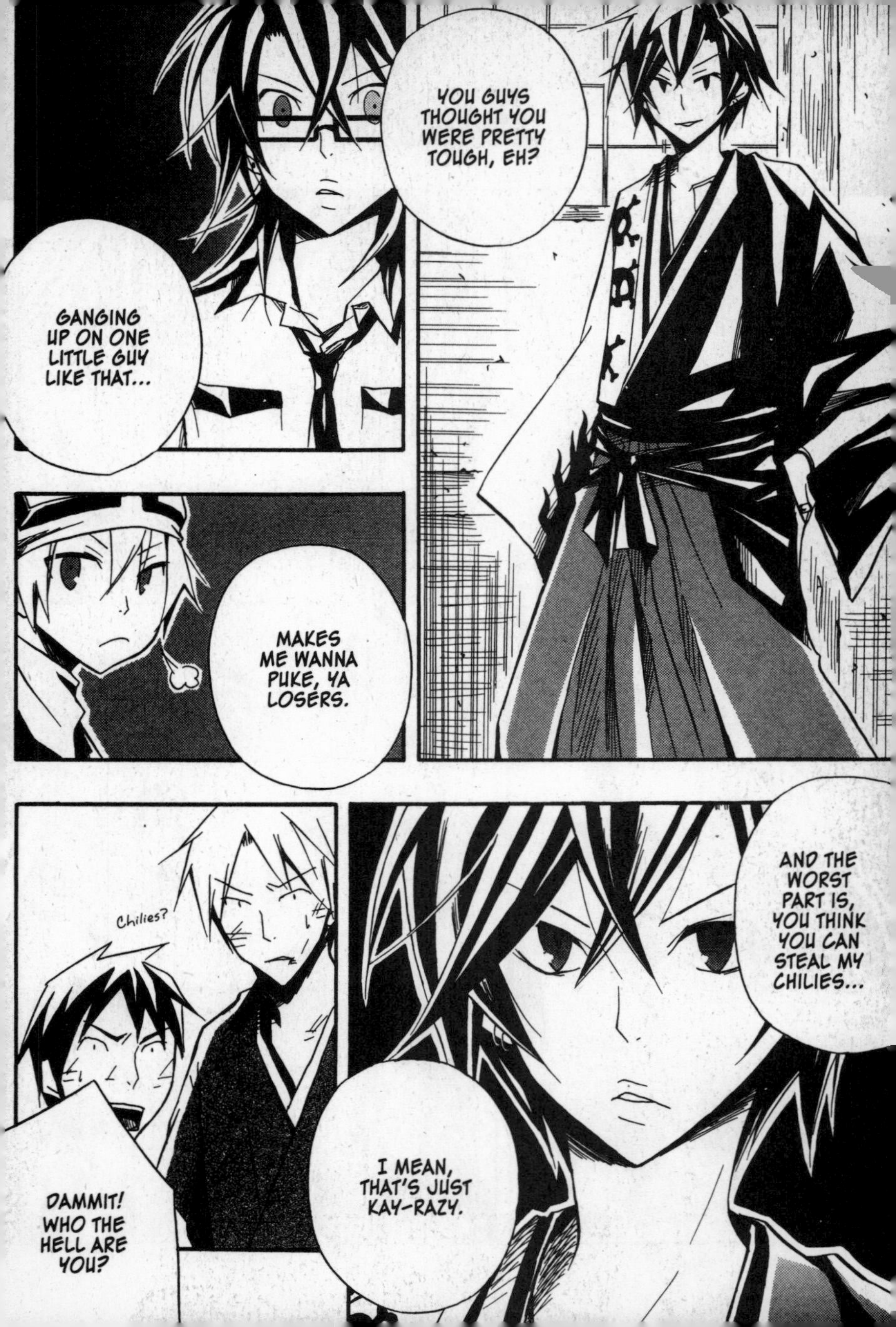
YOU GUYS THOUGHT YOU WERE PRETTY TOUGH, EH?
GANGING UP ON ONE LITTLE GUY LIKE THAT...
MAKES ME WANNA PUKE, YA LOSERS.
AND THE WORST PART IS, YOU THINK YOU CAN STEAL MY CHILIES...
I MEAN, THAT'S JUST KAY-RAZY.
Chilies?
DAMMIT! WHO THE HELL ARE YOU?

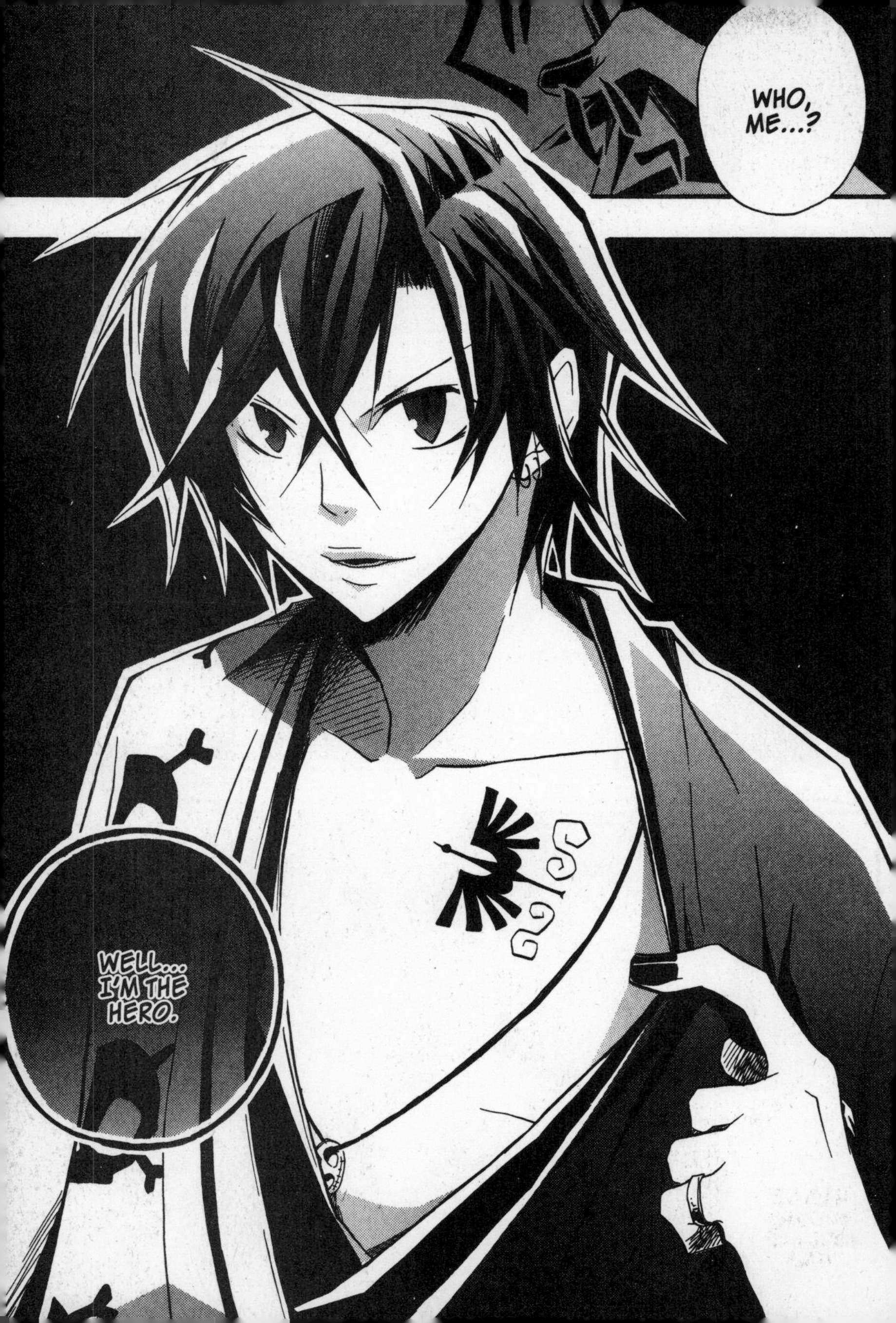
WHO, ME...?
WELL... I'M THE HERO.

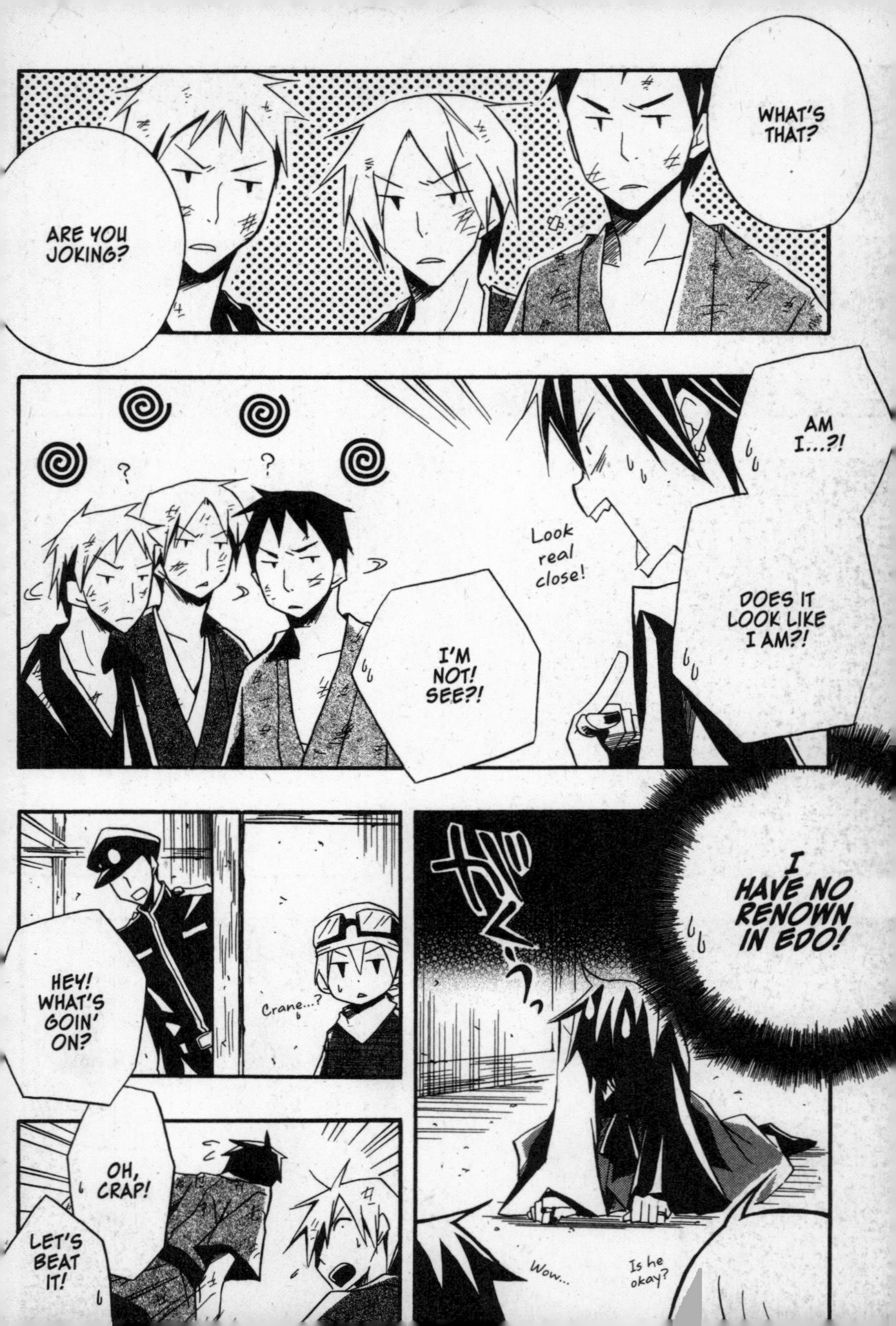
WHAT'S THAT?
ARE YOU JOKING?
AM I...?!
DOES IT LOOK LIKE I AM?!
Look real close!
I'M NOT! SEE?!
I HAVE NO RENOWN IN EDO!
Is he okay?
Wow...
HEY! WHAT'S GOIN' ON?
Crane...?
OH, CRAP!
LET'S BEAT IT!

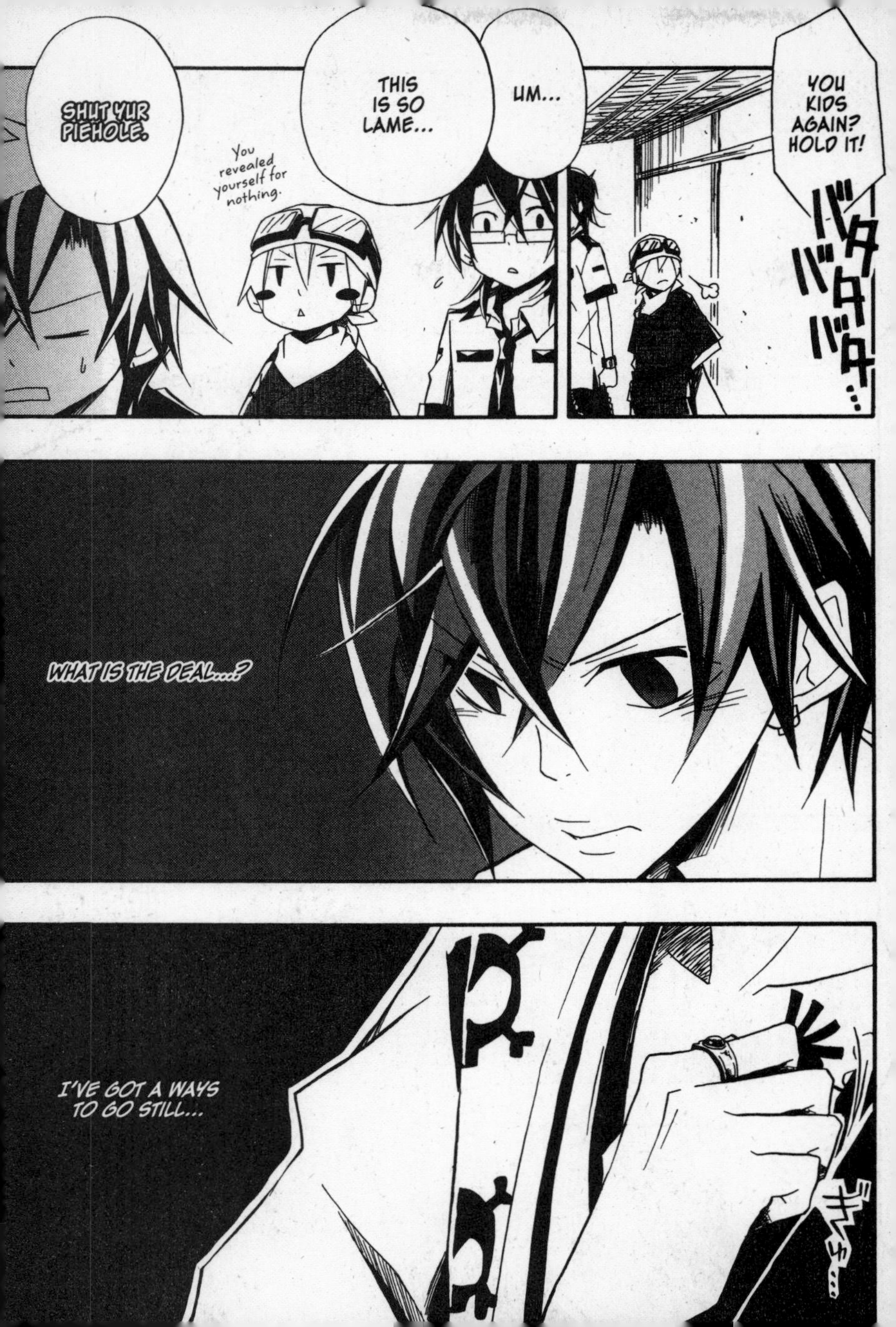
YOU KIDS AGAIN? HOLD IT!
バタバタバタ…
UM...
THIS IS SO LAME...
You revealed yourself for nothing.
SHUT YUR PIEHOLE.
WHAT IS THE DEAL...?
I'VE GOT A WAYS TO GO STILL...

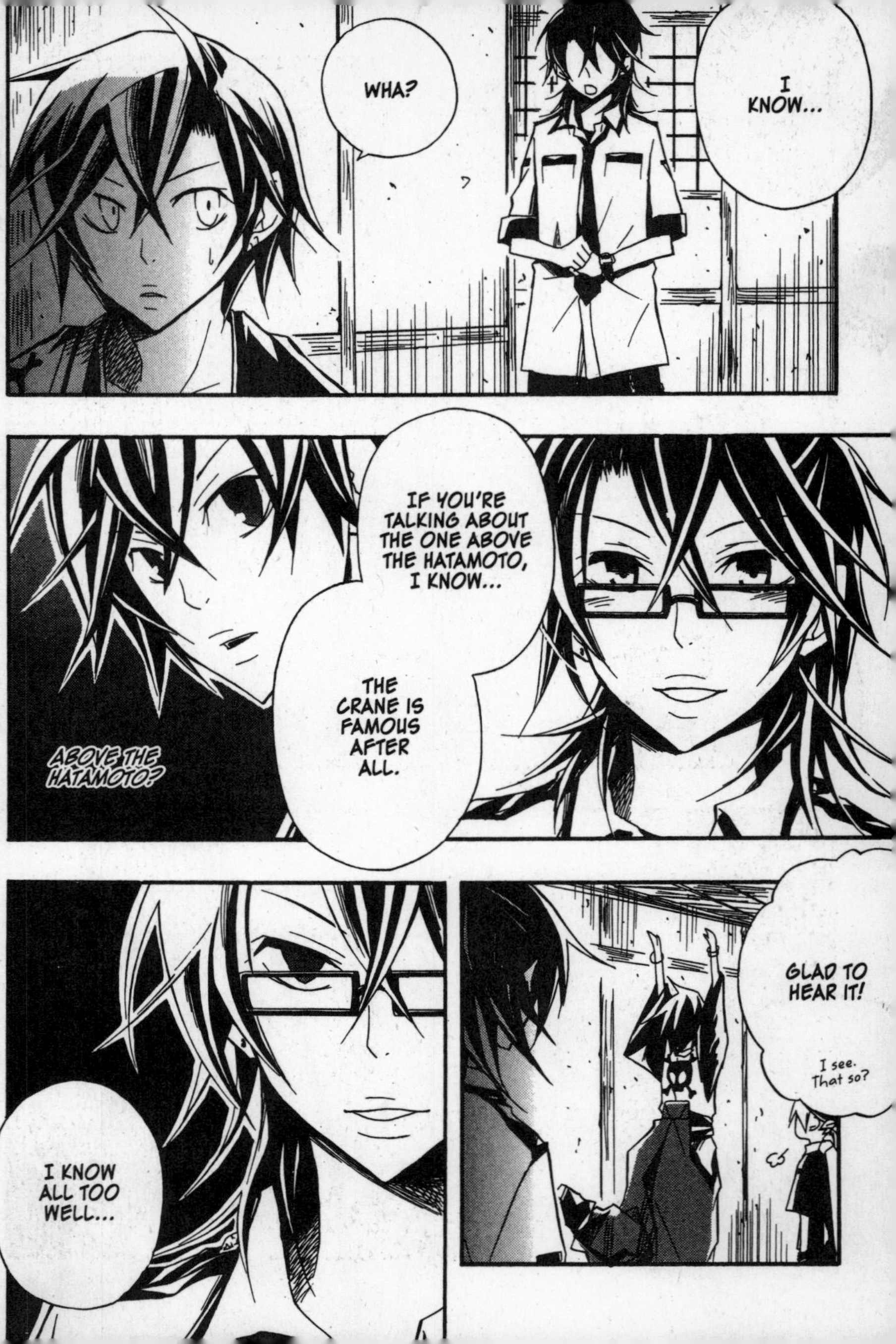
I KNOW...
WHA?
IF YOU'RE TALKING ABOUT THE ONE ABOVE THE HATAMOTO, I KNOW...
THE CRANE IS FAMOUS AFTER ALL.
ABOVE THE HATAMOTO?
GLAD TO HEAR IT!
I see. That so?
I KNOW ALL TOO WELL...

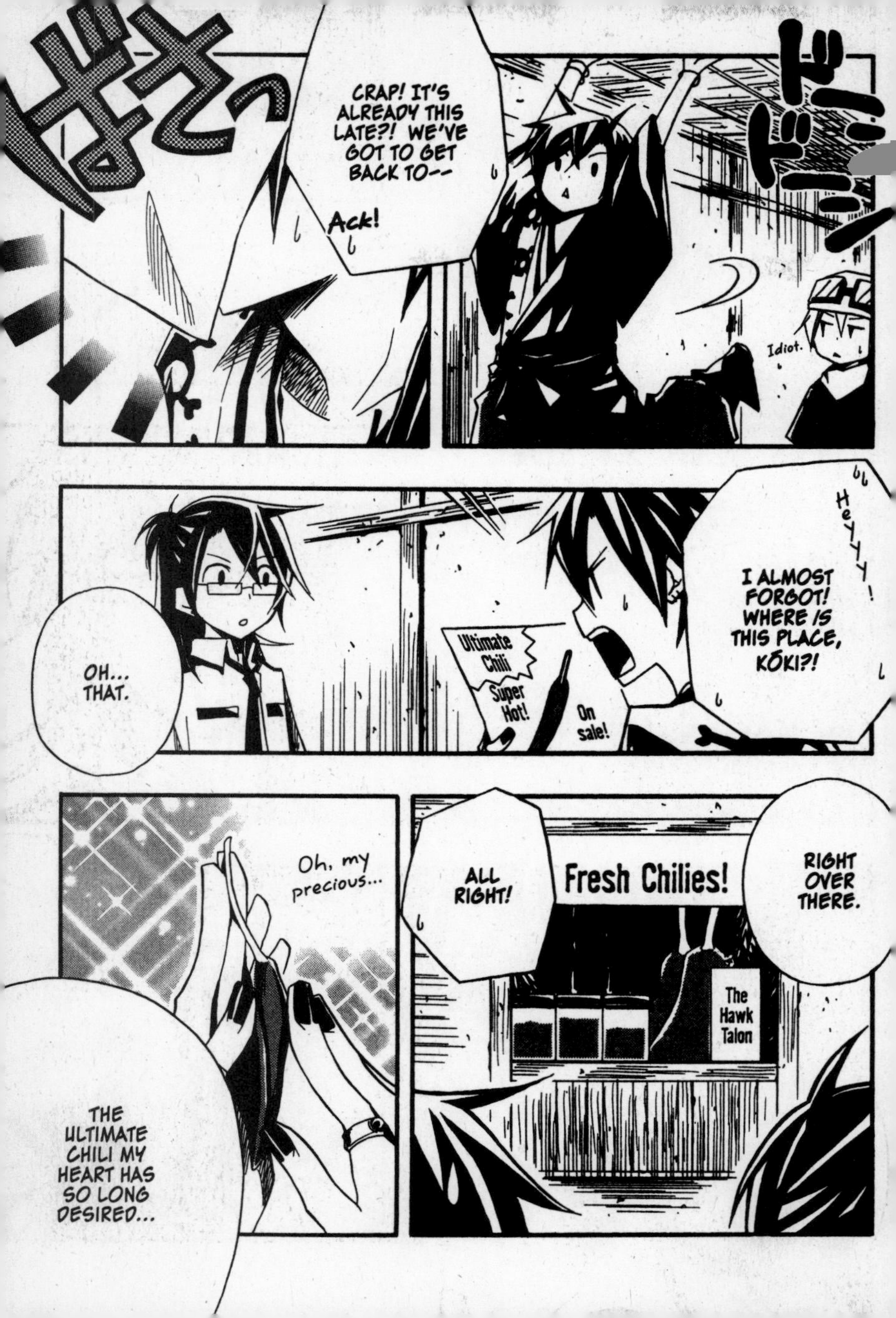

Idiot.
CRAP! IT'S ALREADY THIS LATE?! WE'VE GOT TO GET BACK TO--
Ack!
ばさっ
Heyyyy!
I ALMOST FORGOT! WHERE IS THIS PLACE, KŌKI?!
Ultimate Chili
Super Hot!
On sale!
OH... THAT.
RIGHT OVER THERE.
Fresh Chilies!
The Hawk Talon
ALL RIGHT!
Oh, my precious...
THE ULTIMATE CHILI MY HEART HAS SO LONG DESIRED...

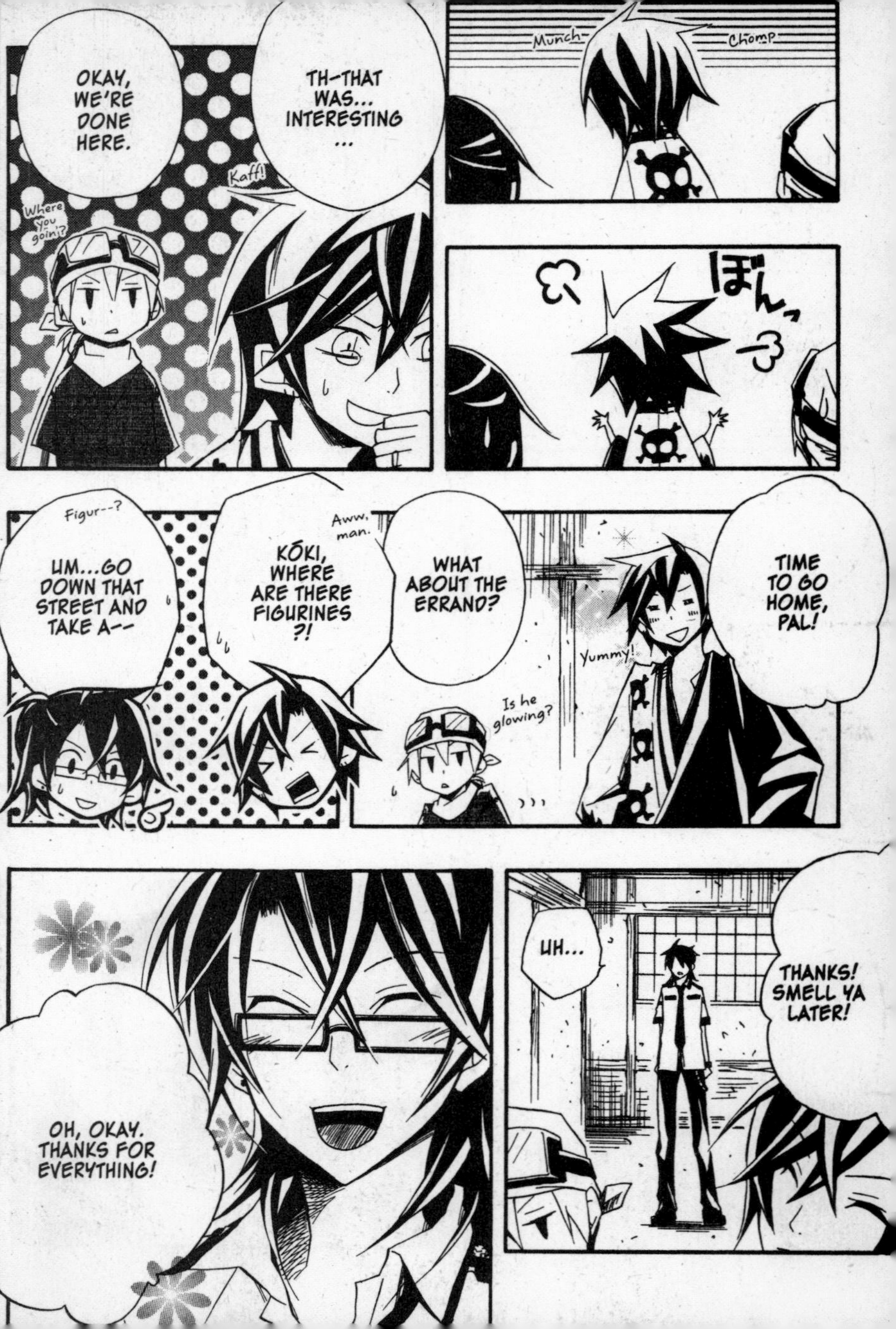
Munch
Chomp
ぼんっ
TH-THAT WAS... INTERESTING ...
Kaff!
OKAY, WE'RE DONE HERE.
Where you goin'?
TIME TO GO HOME, PAL!
Yummy!
Is he glowing?
WHAT ABOUT THE ERRAND?
Aww, man.
KŌKI, WHERE ARE THERE FIGURINES ?!
Figur--?
UM...GO DOWN THAT STREET AND TAKE A--
THANKS! SMELL YA LATER!
UH...
OH, OKAY. THANKS FOR EVERYTHING!

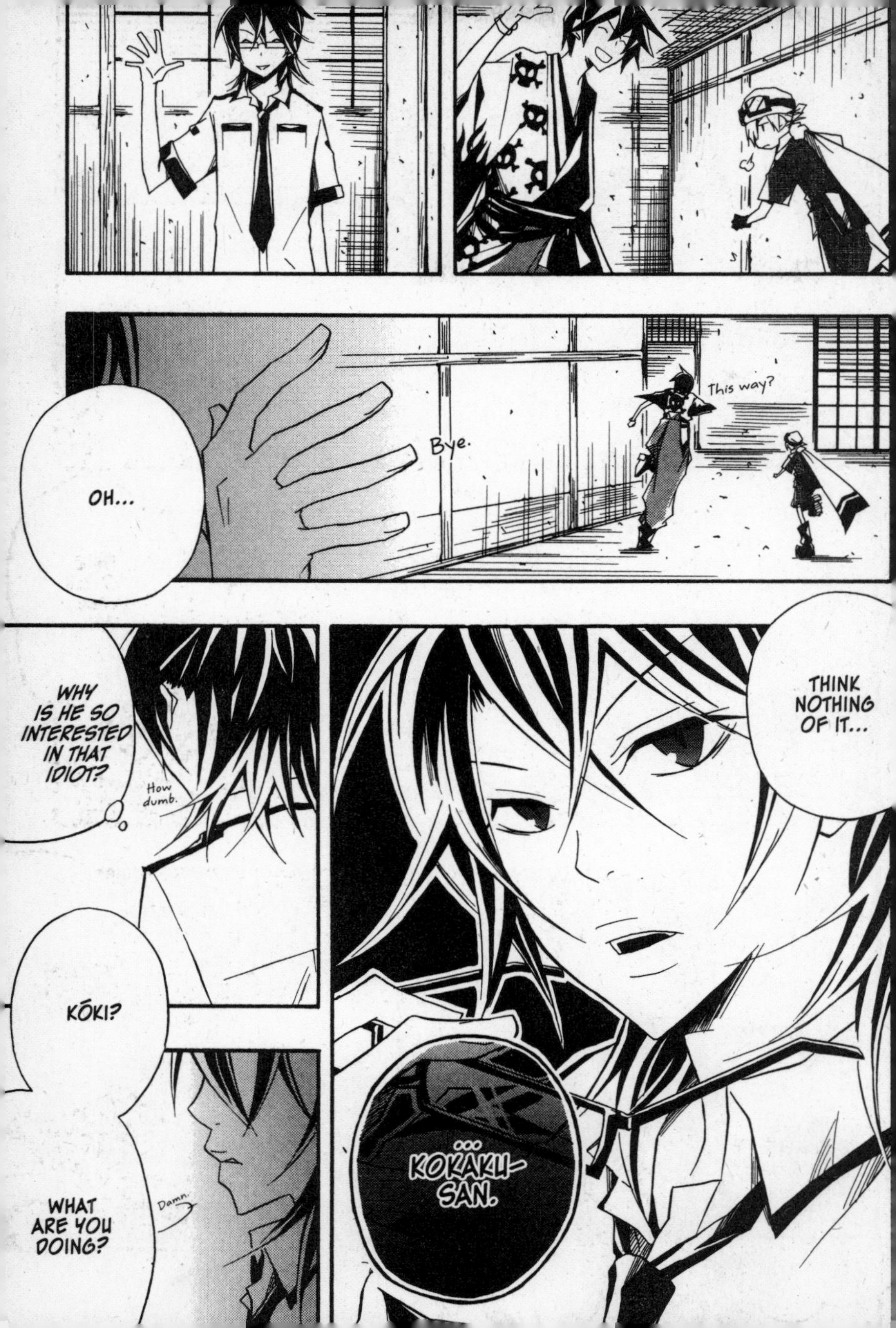
This way?
Bye.
OH...
THINK NOTHING OF IT...
... KOKĀKU-SAN.
WHY IS HE SO INTERESTED IN THAT IDIOT?
How dumb.
KŌKI?
WHAT ARE YOU DOING?
Damn.

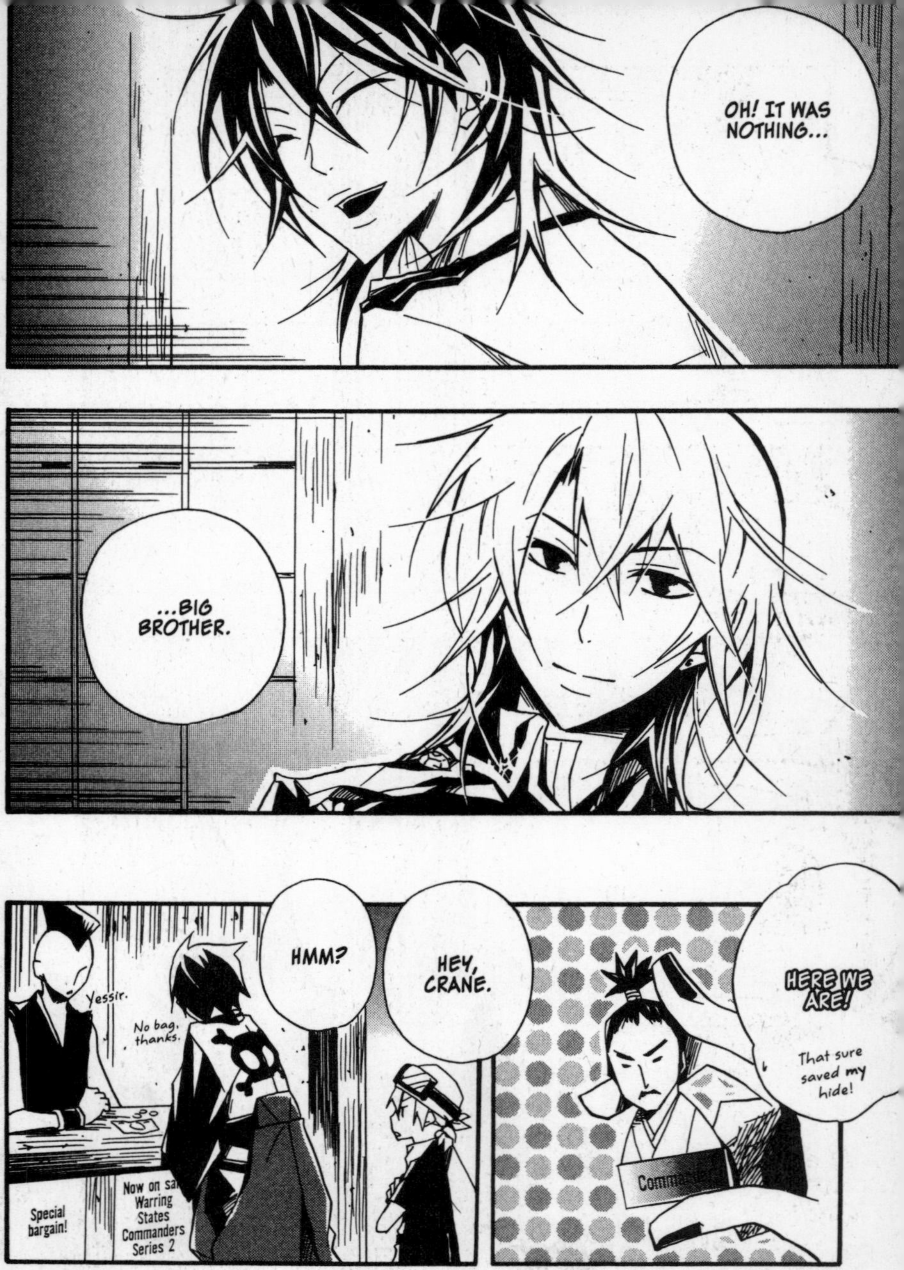
OH! IT WAS NOTHING...
...BIG BROTHER.
HERE WE ARE!
That sure saved my hide!
HEY, CRANE.
HMM?
No bag, thanks.
Yessir.
Now on sa
Warring States Commanders Series 2
Special bargain!

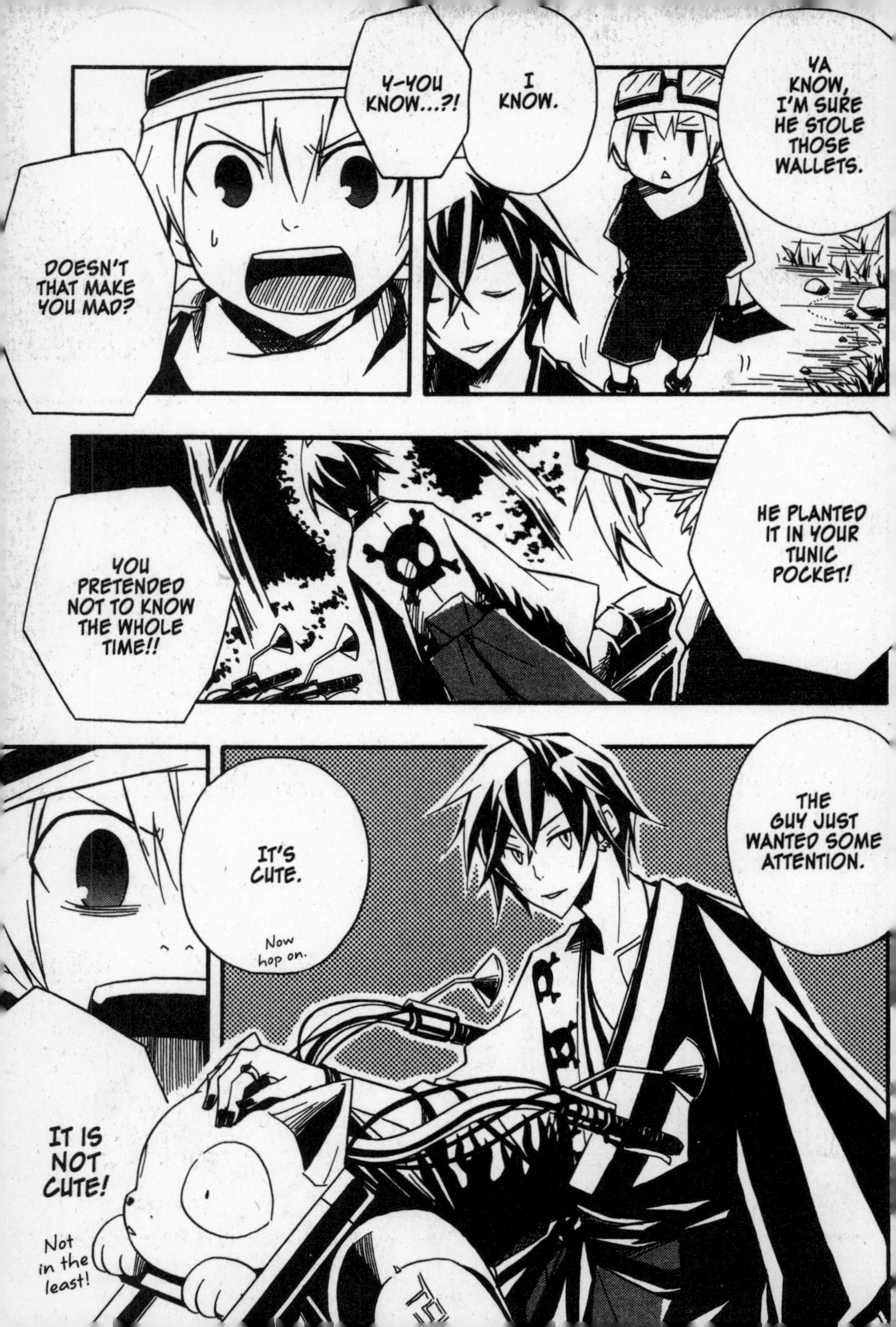
YA KNOW, I'M SURE HE STOLE THOSE WALLETS.
I KNOW.
Y-YOU KNOW...?!
DOESN'T THAT MAKE YOU MAD?
HE PLANTED IT IN YOUR TUNIC POCKET!
YOU PRETENDED NOT TO KNOW THE WHOLE TIME!!
THE GUY JUST WANTED SOME ATTENTION.
IT'S CUTE.
Now hop on.
IT IS NOT CUTE!
Not in the least!

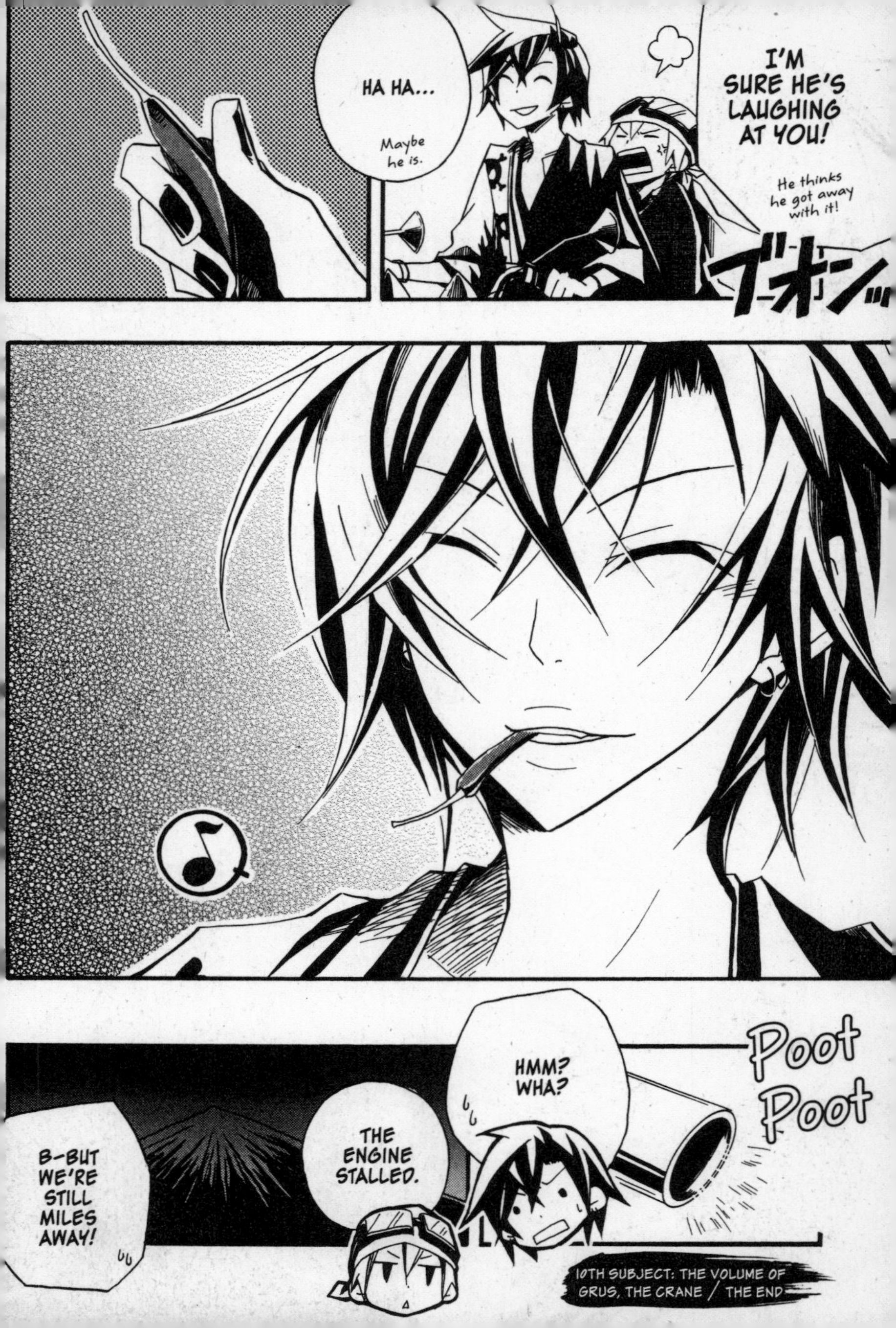
I'M SURE HE'S LAUGHING AT YOU!
He thinks he got away with it!
ブオーンッ
HA HA...
Maybe he is.
Poot Poot
HMM? WHA?
THE ENGINE STALLED.
B-BUT WE'RE STILL MILES AWAY!
10TH SUBJECT: THE VOLUME OF GRUS, THE CRANE / THE END

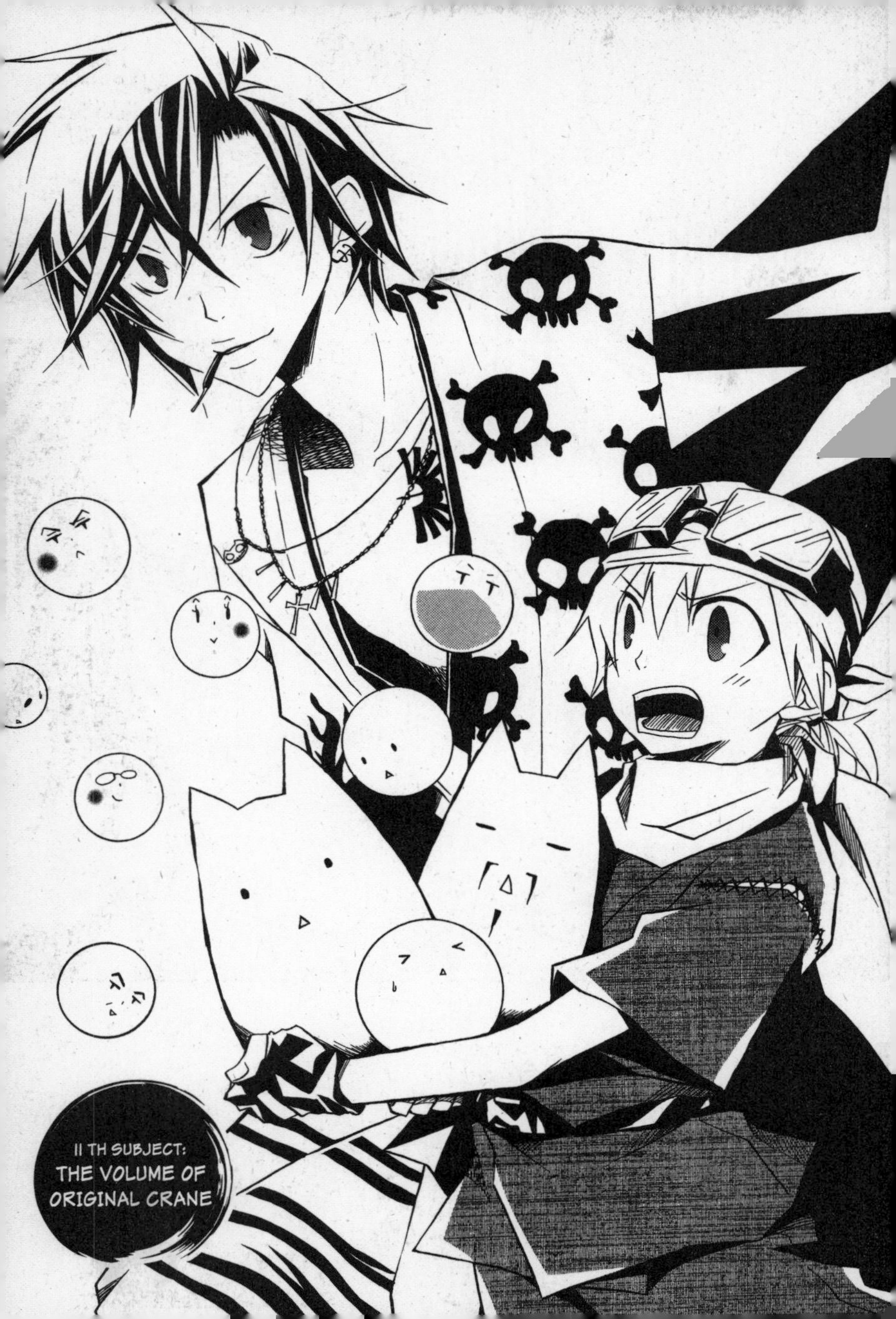
11 TH SUBJECT:
THE VOLUME OF
ORIGINAL CRANE

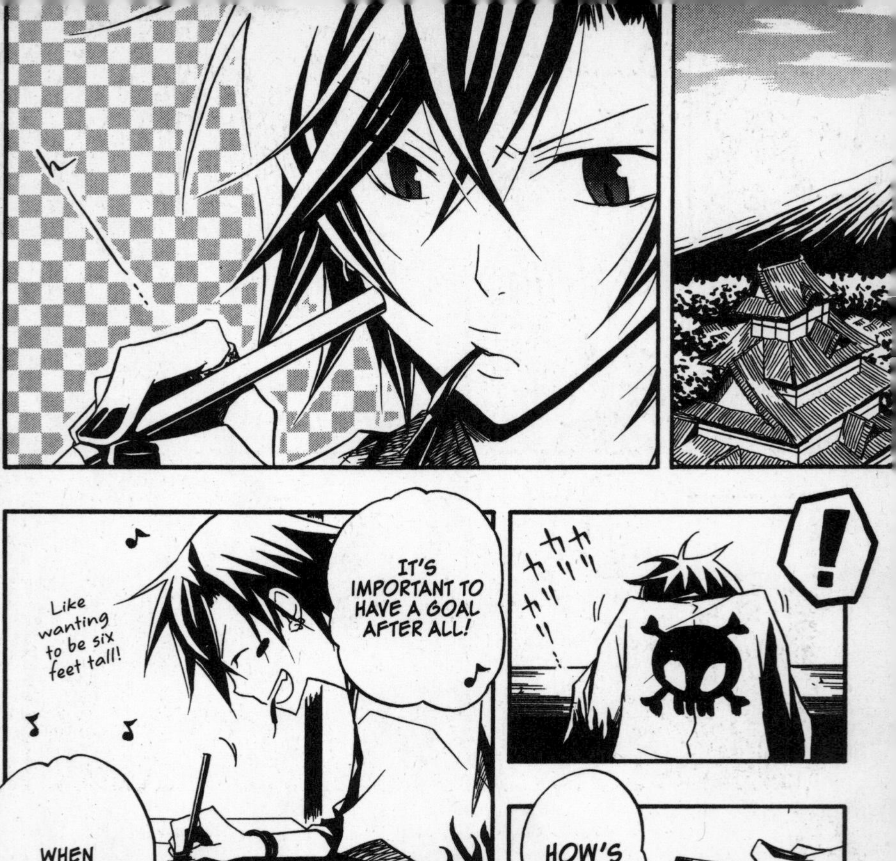
!
HOW'S THAT?
IT'S IMPORTANT TO HAVE A GOAL AFTER ALL!
Like wanting to be six feet tall!
WHEN I'M THE LORD...

EGGPLANT FAMILY PEPPER TRIBE NUMBER 5

"KOREEGUSU"
SPECIALTY OF OKINAWA PREFECTURE. AN OKINAWA-EXCLUSIVE CHILI; PICKLED IN POTENT LIQUOR. USED AS A CONDIMENT IN OKINAWA SOBA.

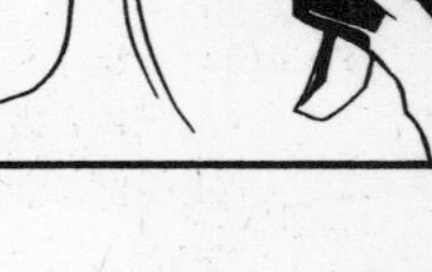
Spicier than I imagined...

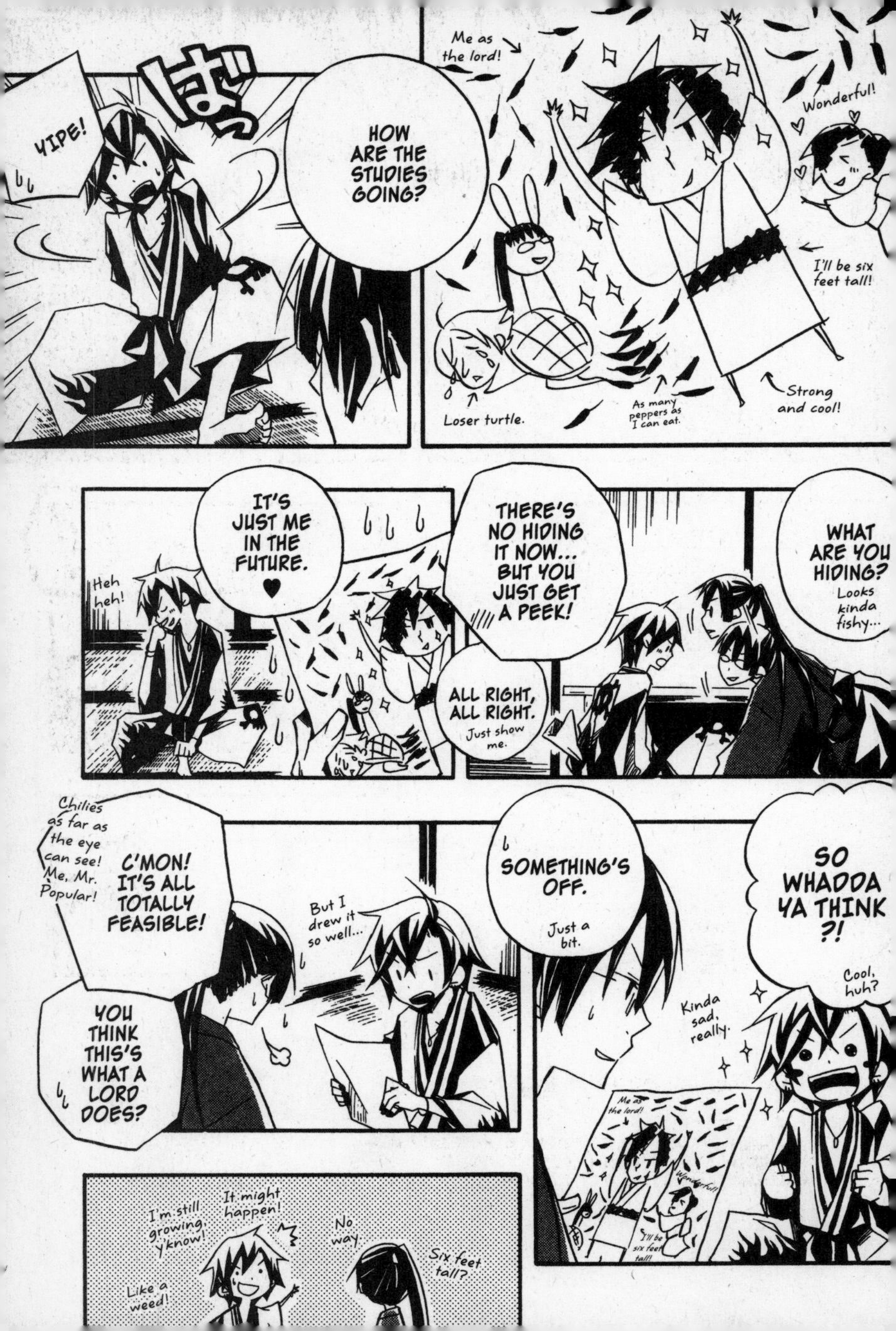

Me as the lord!
Wonderful!
I'll be six feet tall!
Strong and cool!
As many peppers as I can eat.
Loser turtle.
ばっ
YIPE!
HOW ARE THE STUDIES GOING?
WHAT ARE YOU HIDING?
Looks kinda fishy...
THERE'S NO HIDING IT NOW... BUT YOU JUST GET A PEEK!
ALL RIGHT, ALL RIGHT.
Just show me.
IT'S JUST ME IN THE FUTURE. ♥
Heh heh!
SO WHADDA YA THINK?!
Cool, huh?
Kinda sad, really.
SOMETHING'S OFF.
Just a bit.
Me as the lord!
Wonderful!
I'll be six feet tall!
But I drew it so well...
Chilies as far as the eye can see! Me, Mr. Popular!
C'MON! IT'S ALL TOTALLY FEASIBLE!
YOU THINK THIS'S WHAT A LORD DOES?
No way.
Six feet tall?
It might happen!
I'm still growing, y'know!
Like a weed!

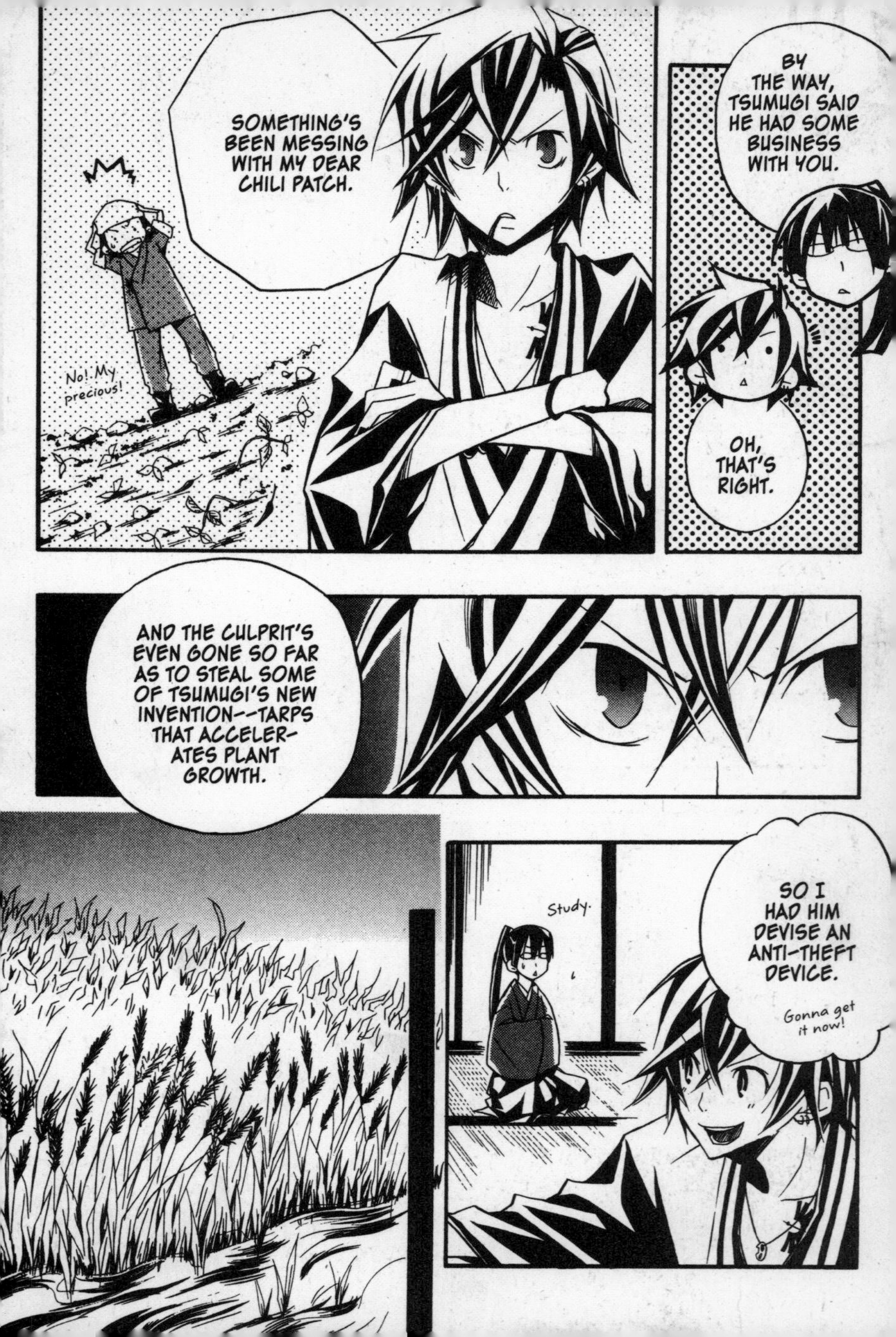
BY THE WAY, TSUMUGI SAID HE HAD SOME BUSINESS WITH YOU.
OH, THAT'S RIGHT.
SOMETHING'S BEEN MESSING WITH MY DEAR CHILI PATCH.
No! My precious!
AND THE CULPRIT'S EVEN GONE SO FAR AS TO STEAL SOME OF TSUMUGI'S NEW INVENTION--TARPS THAT ACCELER-ATES PLANT GROWTH.
SO I HAD HIM DEVISE AN ANTI-THEFT DEVICE.
Gonna get it now!
Study.

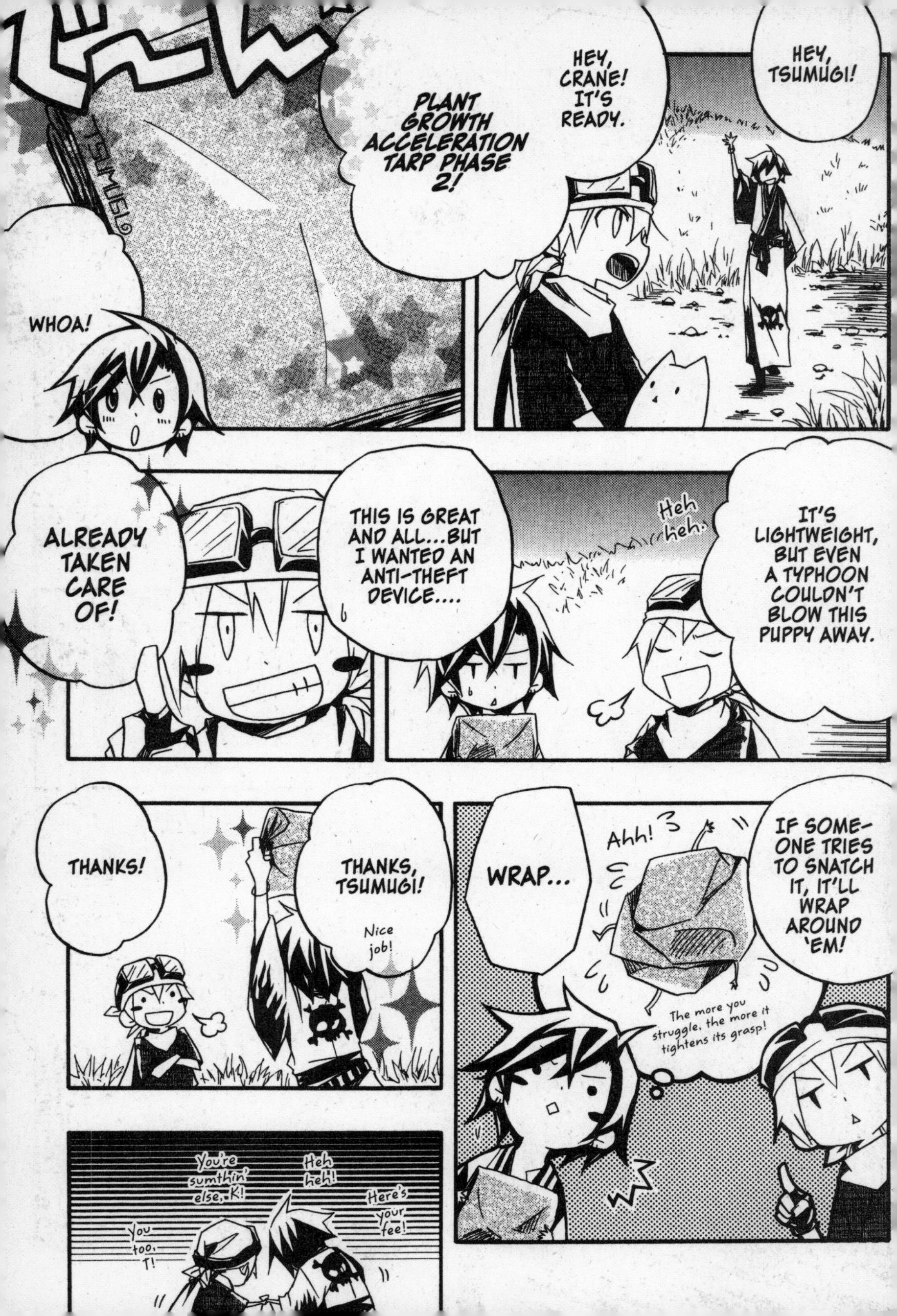
HEY, TSUMUGI!
HEY, CRANE! IT'S READY.
PLANT GROWTH ACCELERATION TARP PHASE 2!
TSUMUGI
WHOA!
IT'S LIGHTWEIGHT, BUT EVEN A TYPHOON COULDN'T BLOW THIS PUPPY AWAY.
Heh heh.
THIS IS GREAT AND ALL...BUT I WANTED AN ANTI-THEFT DEVICE....
ALREADY TAKEN CARE OF!
IF SOME-ONE TRIES TO SNATCH IT, IT'LL WRAP AROUND 'EM!
Ahh!
The more you struggle, the more it tightens its grasp!
WRAP...
THANKS, TSUMUGI!
Nice job!
THANKS!
Heh heh!
Here's your fee!
You're sumthin' else, K!
You too, T!

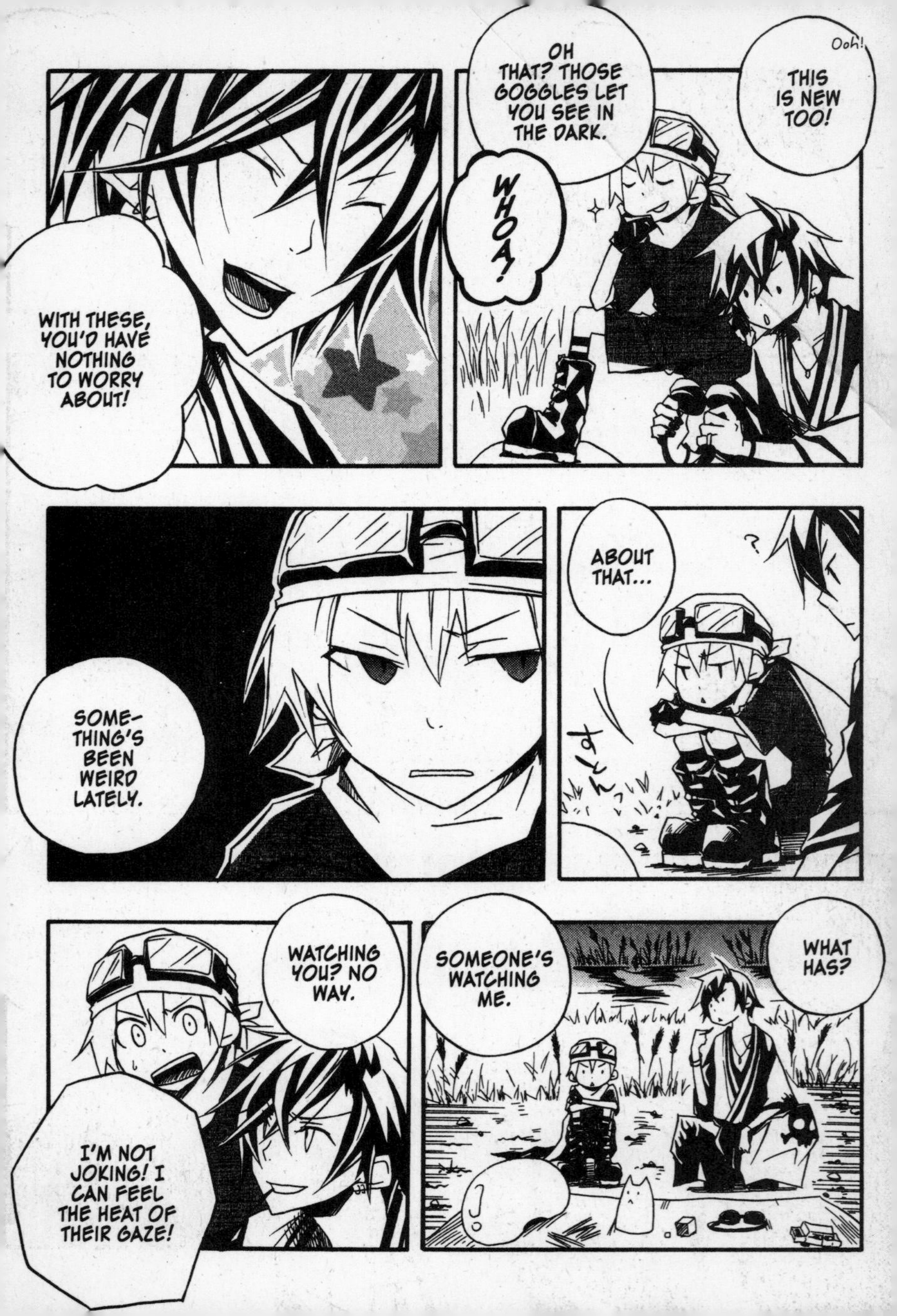
Ooh!
THIS IS NEW TOO!
OH THAT? THOSE GOGGLES LET YOU SEE IN THE DARK.
WHOA!
WITH THESE, YOU'D HAVE NOTHING TO WORRY ABOUT!
?
ABOUT THAT...
すとんっ
SOME-THING'S BEEN WEIRD LATELY.
WHAT HAS?
SOMEONE'S WATCHING ME.
WATCHING YOU? NO WAY.
I'M NOT JOKING! I CAN FEEL THE HEAT OF THEIR GAZE!

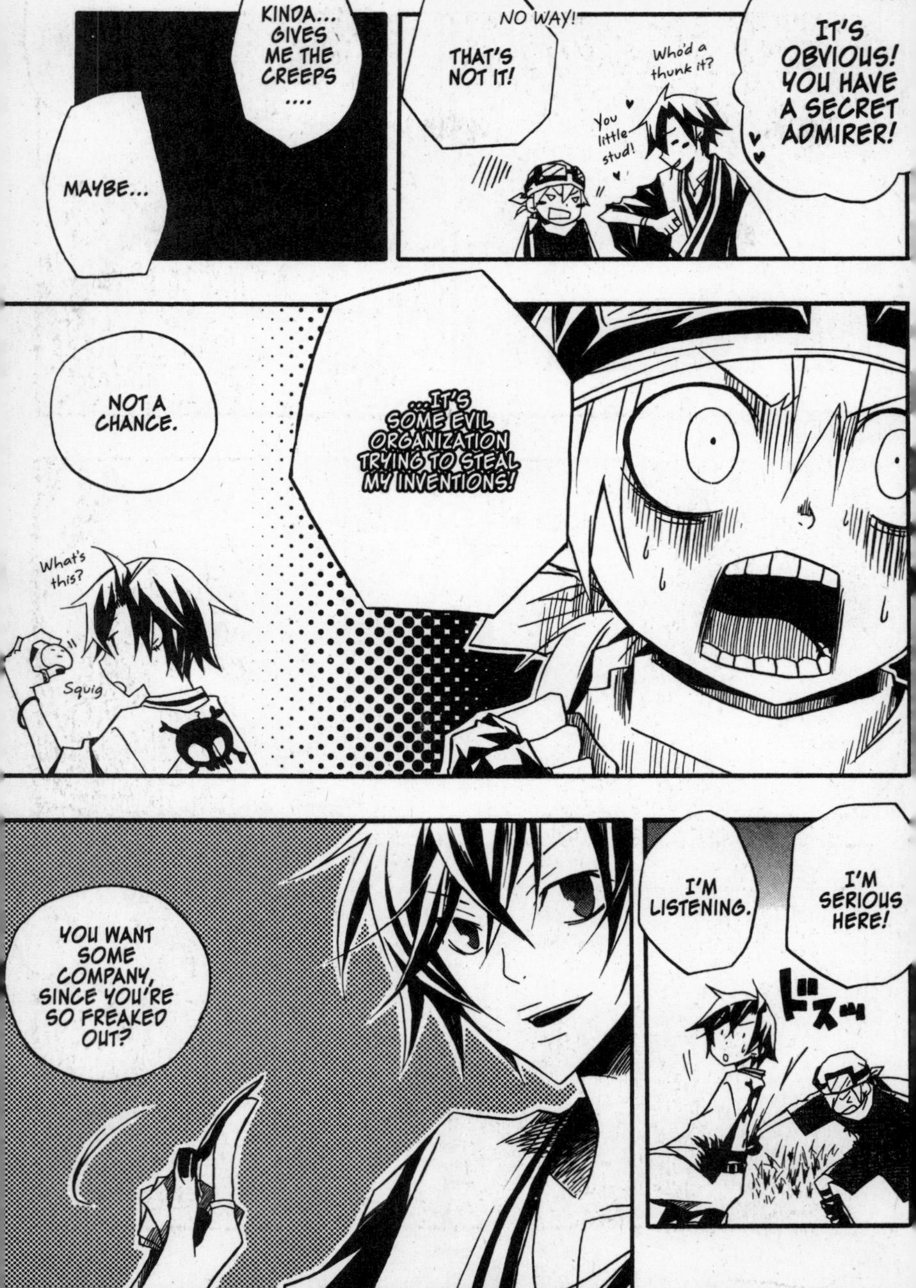
Aha!
IT'S OBVIOUS! YOU HAVE A SECRET ADMIRER!
Who'd a thunk it?
You little stud!
NO WAY!
THAT'S NOT IT!
KINDA... GIVES ME THE CREEPS ....
MAYBE...
...IT'S SOME EVIL ORGANIZATION TRYING TO STEAL MY INVENTIONS!
NOT A CHANCE.
What's this?
Squig
I'M SERIOUS HERE!
I'M LISTENING.
ドスッ
YOU WANT SOME COMPANY, SINCE YOU'RE SO FREAKED OUT?

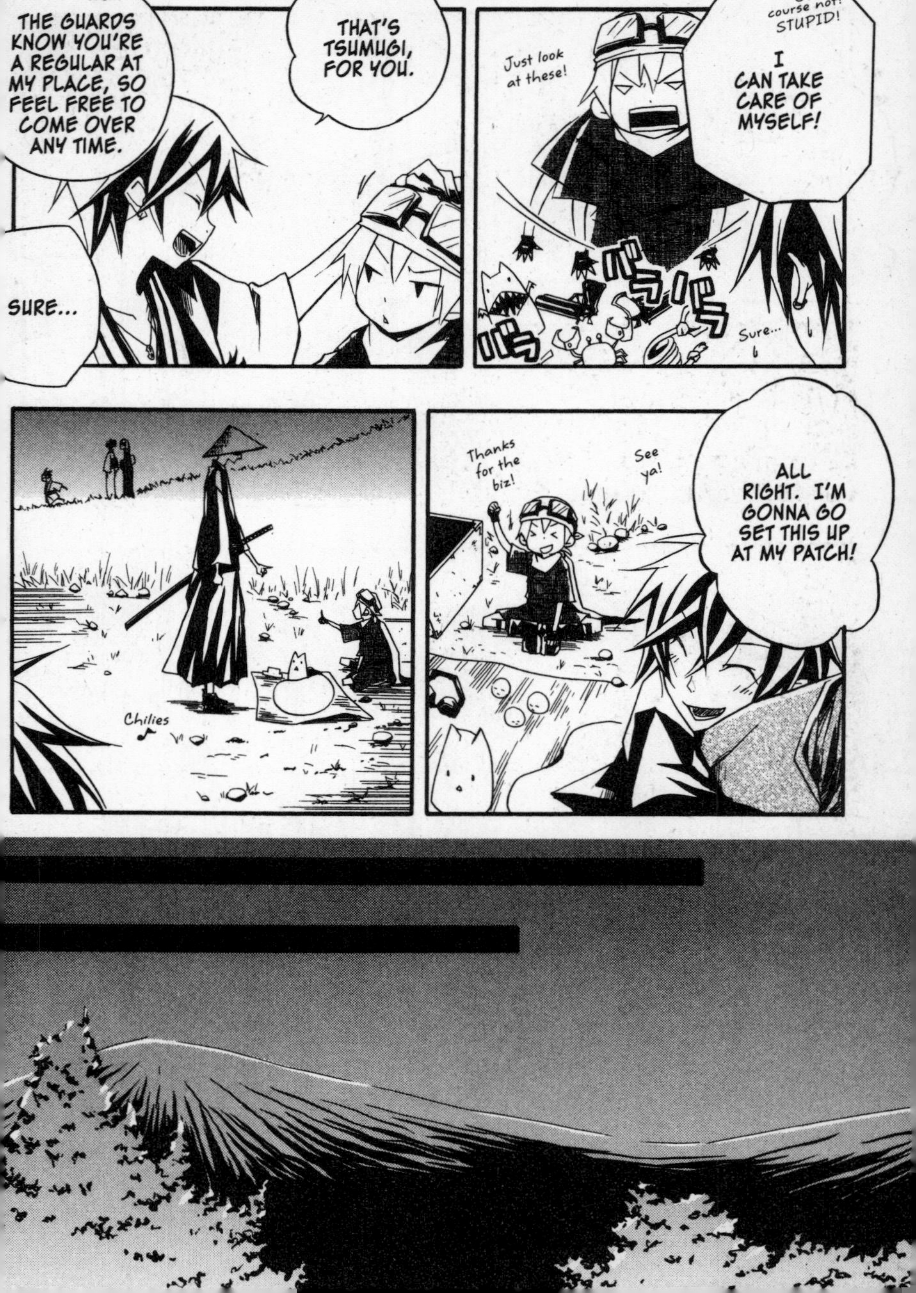
Of course not! STUPID!
I CAN TAKE CARE OF MYSELF!
Just look at these!
Sure...
Well!
THE GUARDS KNOW YOU'RE A REGULAR AT MY PLACE, SO FEEL FREE TO COME OVER ANY TIME.
THAT'S TSUMUGI, FOR YOU.
SURE...
ALL RIGHT. I'M GONNA GO SET THIS UP AT MY PATCH!
See ya!
Thanks for the biz!
Chilies
[redacted]

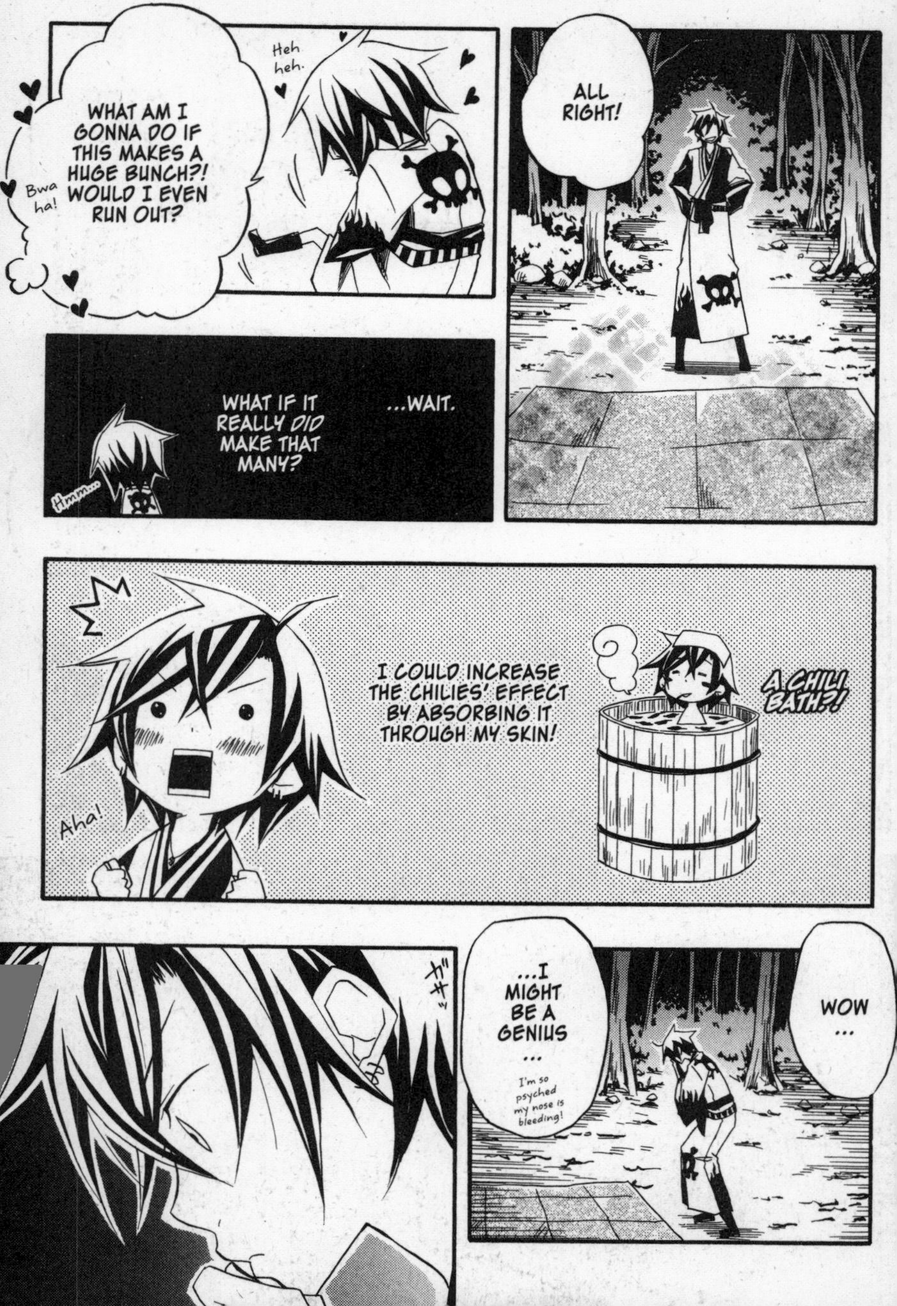
ALL RIGHT!
Heh heh.
WHAT AM I GONNA DO IF THIS MAKES A HUGE BUNCH?! WOULD I EVEN RUN OUT?
Bwa ha!
...WAIT.
WHAT IF IT REALLY *DID* MAKE THAT MANY?
Hmm...
A CHILI BATH?!
I COULD INCREASE THE CHILIES' EFFECT BY ABSORBING IT THROUGH MY SKIN!
Aha!
WOW ...
...I MIGHT BE A GENIUS ...
I'm so psyched my nose is bleeding!

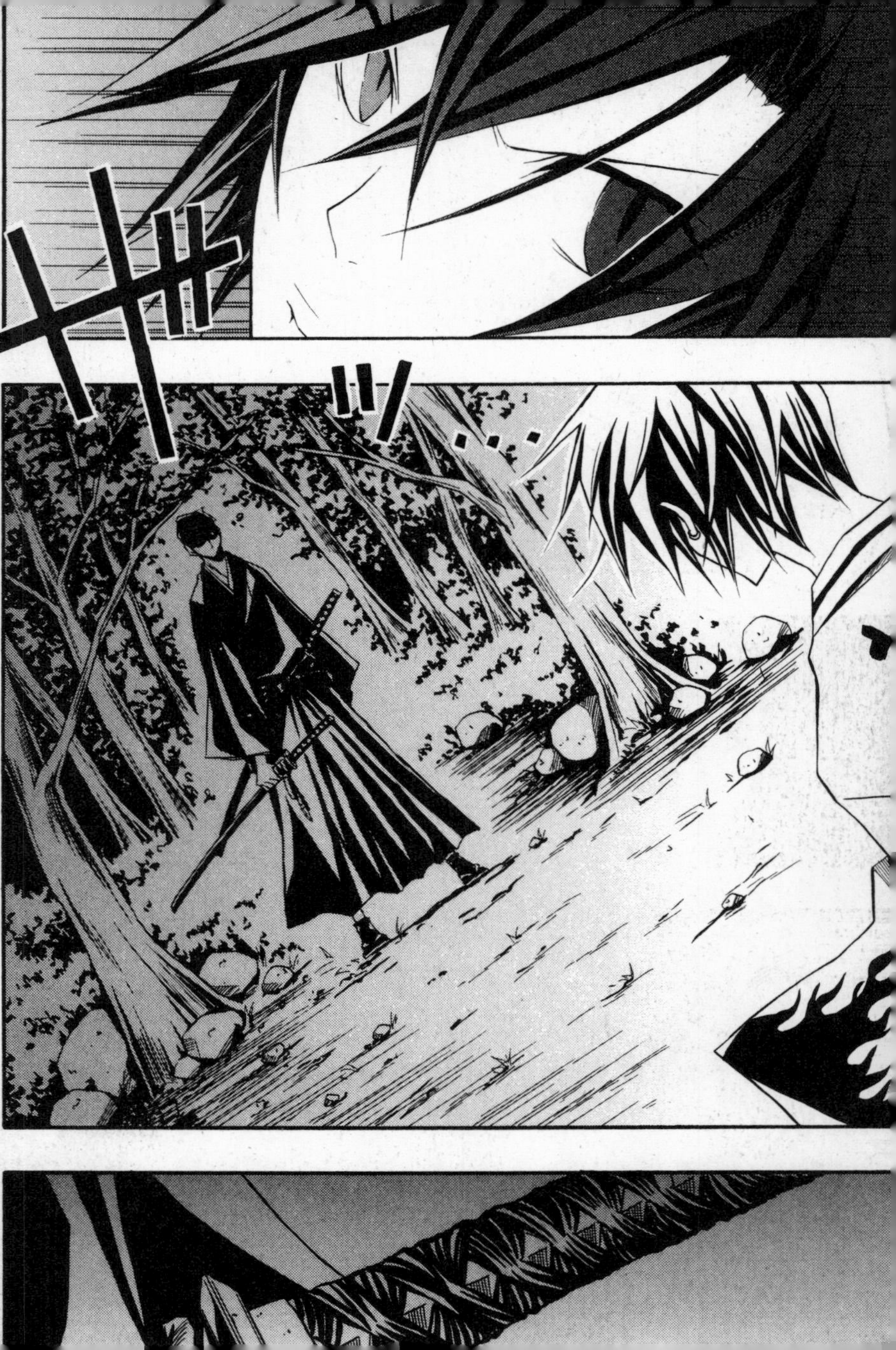
ザッ
...

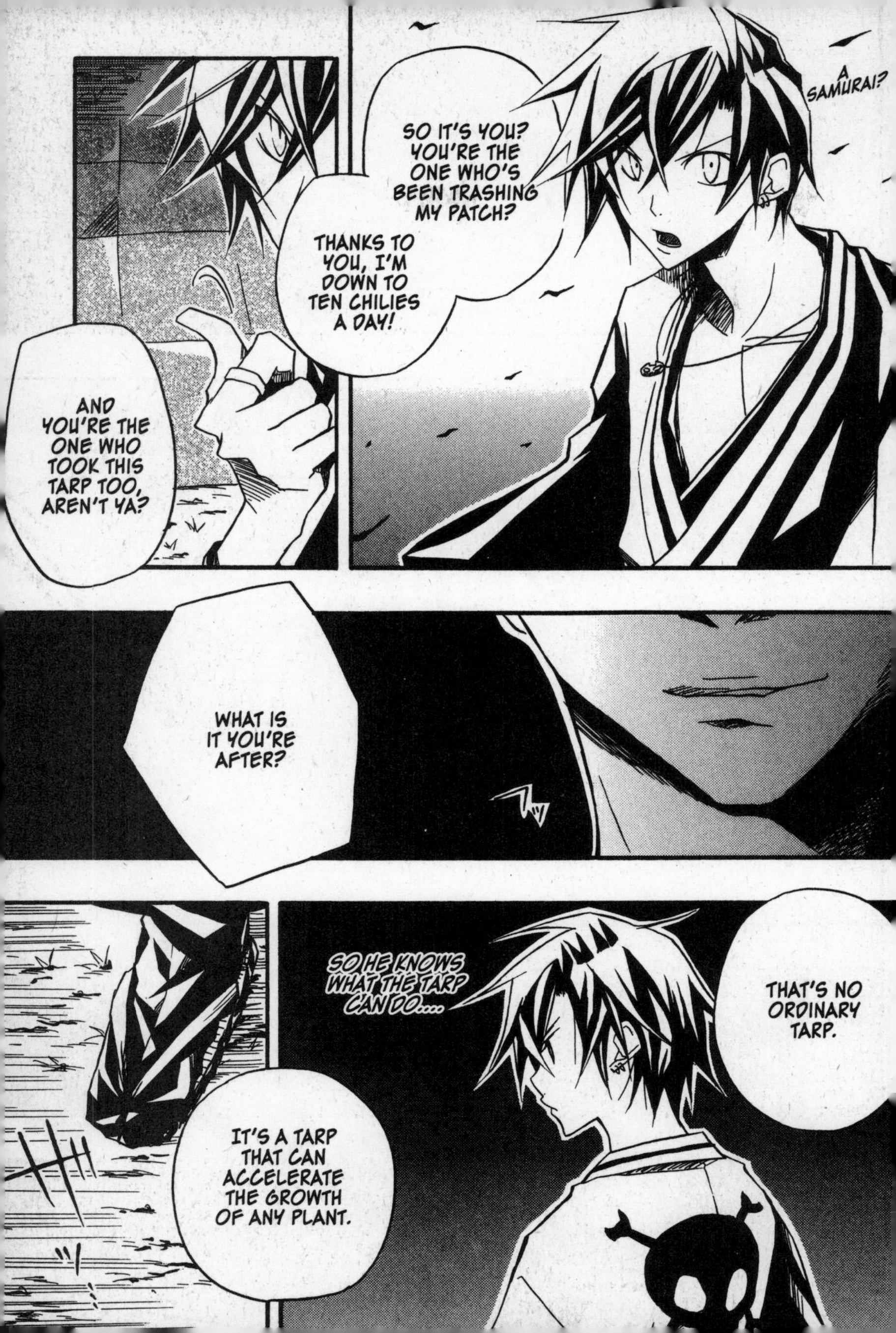
A SAMURAI?
SO IT'S YOU? YOU'RE THE ONE WHO'S BEEN TRASHING MY PATCH?
THANKS TO YOU, I'M DOWN TO TEN CHILIES A DAY!
AND YOU'RE THE ONE WHO TOOK THIS TARP TOO, AREN'T YA?
WHAT IS IT YOU'RE AFTER?
THAT'S NO ORDINARY TARP.
SO HE KNOWS WHAT THE TARP CAN DO....
IT'S A TARP THAT CAN ACCELERATE THE GROWTH OF ANY PLANT.

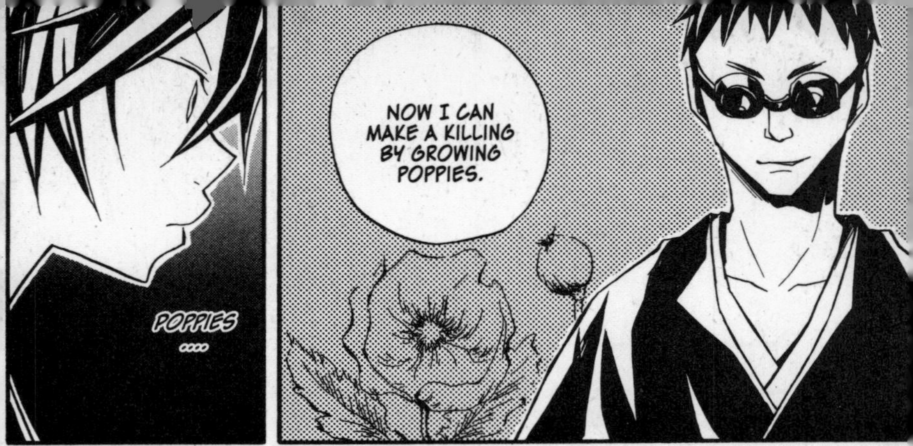
NOW I CAN MAKE A KILLING BY GROWING POPPIES.
POPPIES ....

※ Because their raw pods can be used as an ingredient for opium, its cultivation is generally prohibited in Japan.

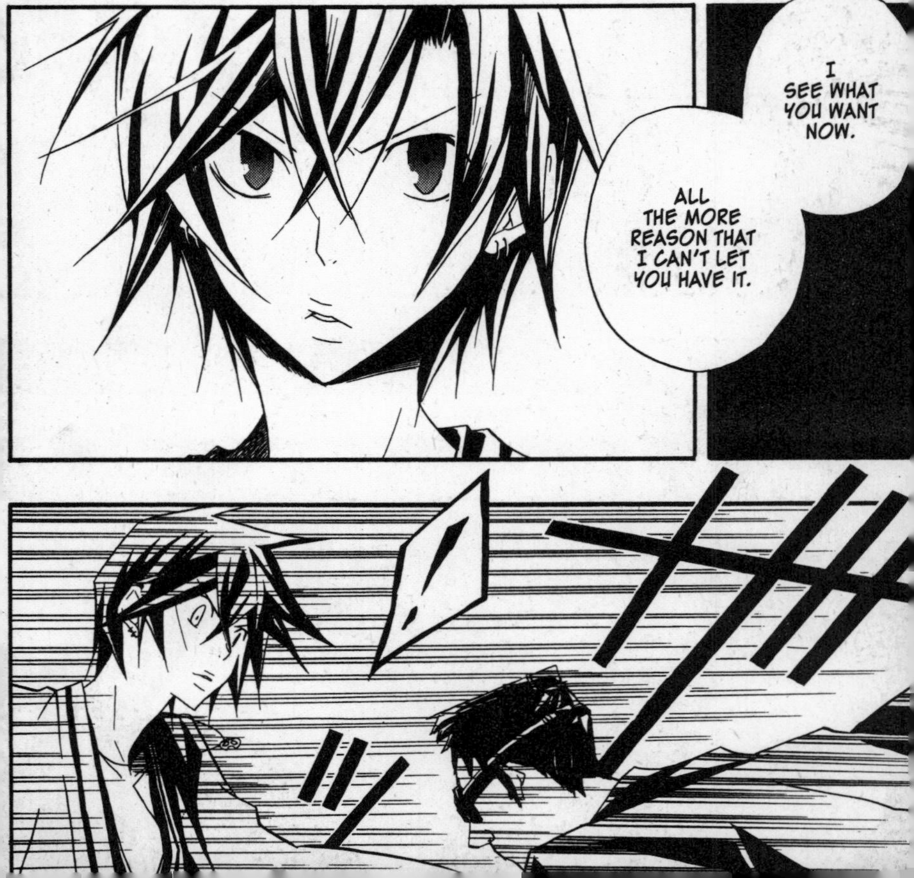
I SEE WHAT YOU WANT NOW.
ALL THE MORE REASON THAT I CAN'T LET YOU HAVE IT.

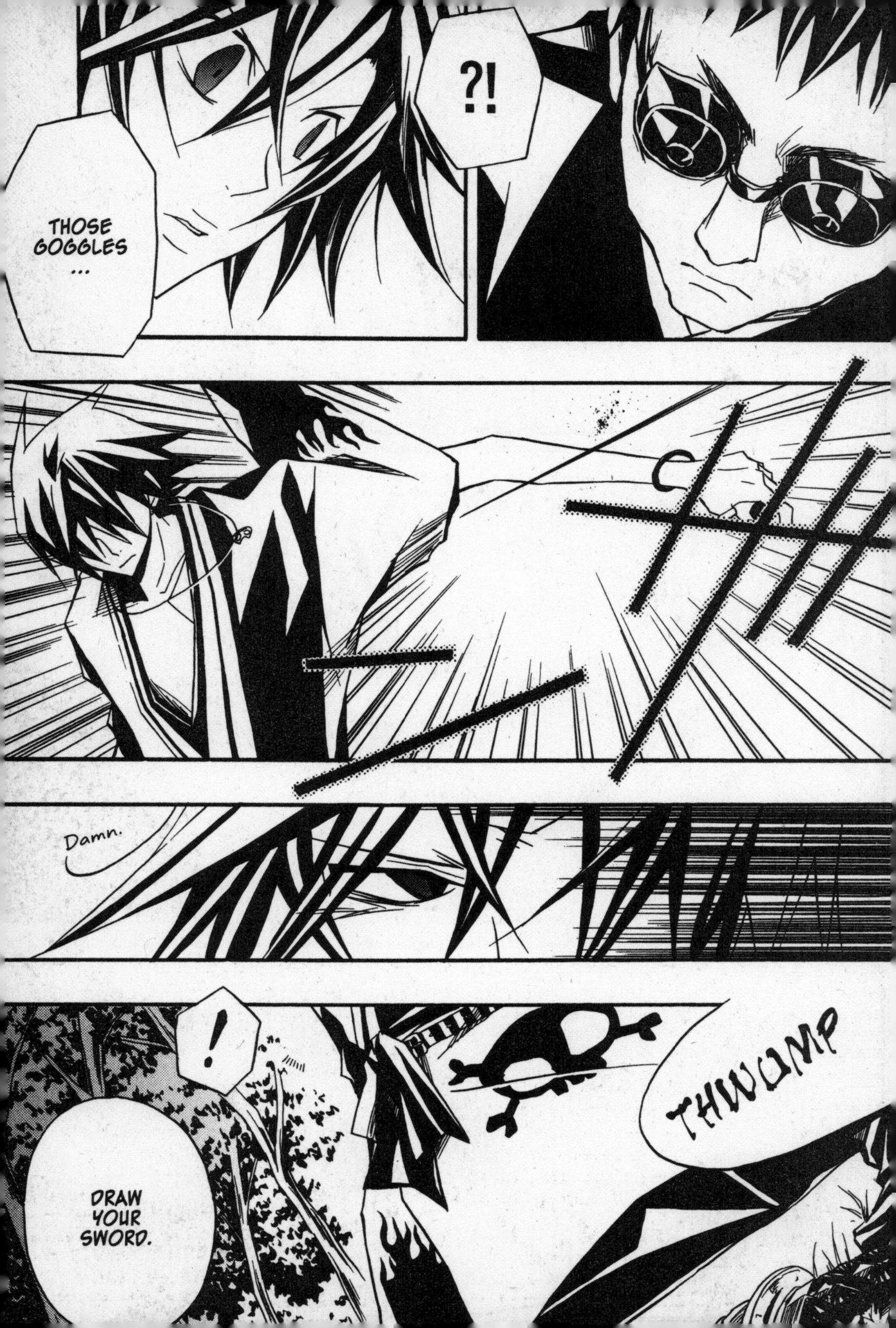
?!
THOSE GOGGLES ...
Damn.
THWUMP
!
DRAW YOUR SWORD.

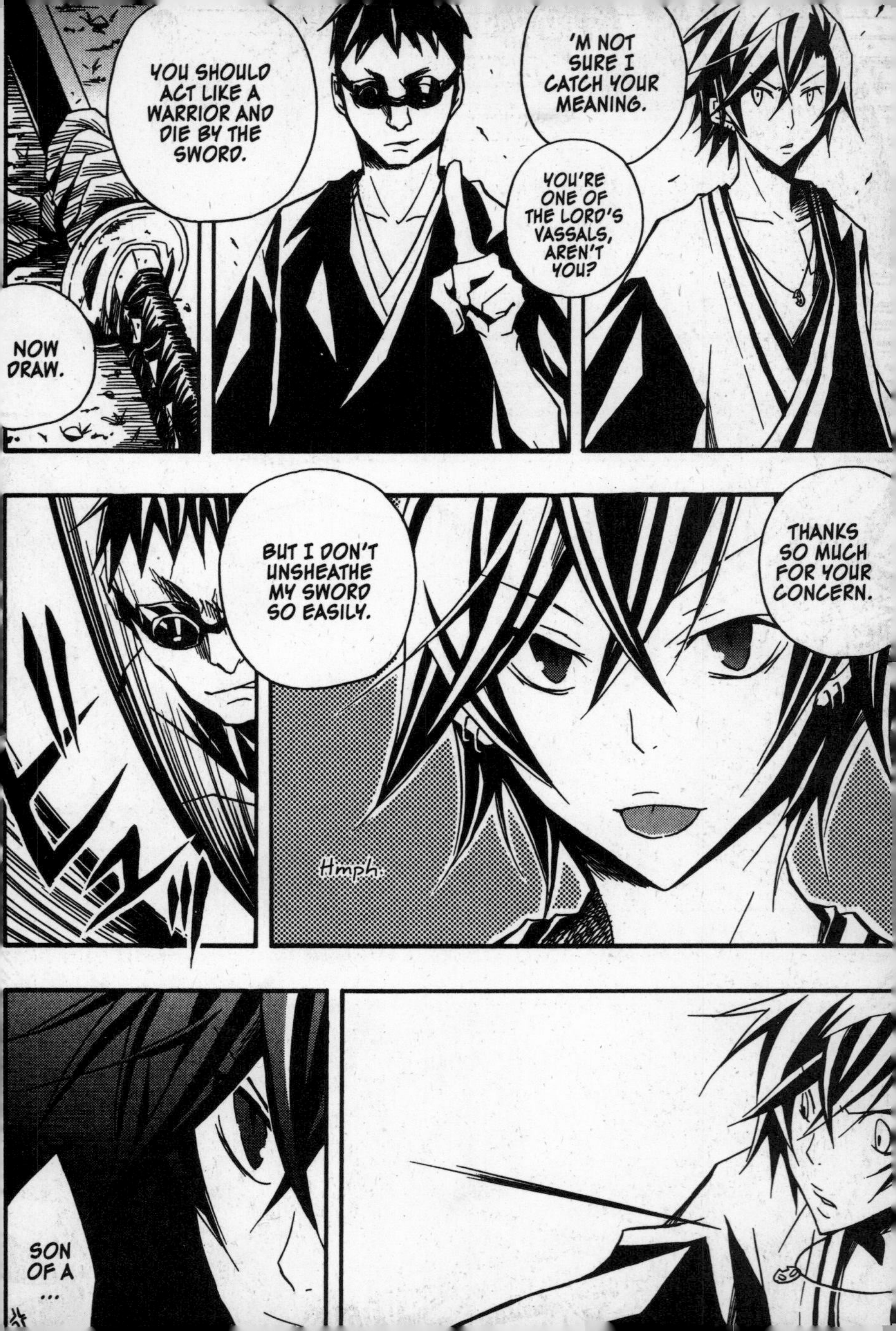
'M NOT SURE I CATCH YOUR MEANING.
YOU'RE ONE OF THE LORD'S VASSALS, AREN'T YOU?
YOU SHOULD ACT LIKE A WARRIOR AND DIE BY THE SWORD.
NOW DRAW.
THANKS SO MUCH FOR YOUR CONCERN.
Hmph.
BUT I DON'T UNSHEATHE MY SWORD SO EASILY.
SON OF A ...

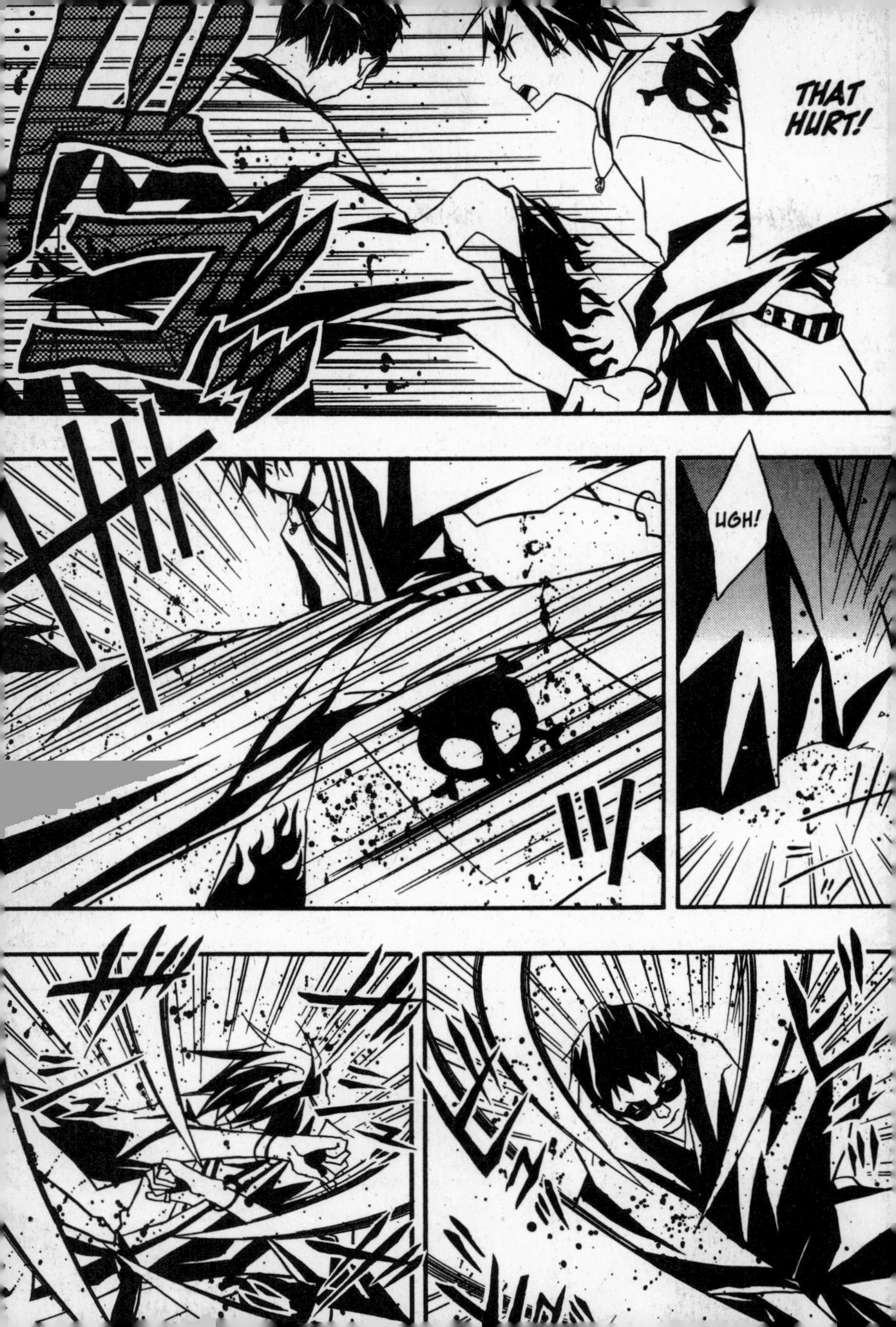
THAT HURT!
UGH!

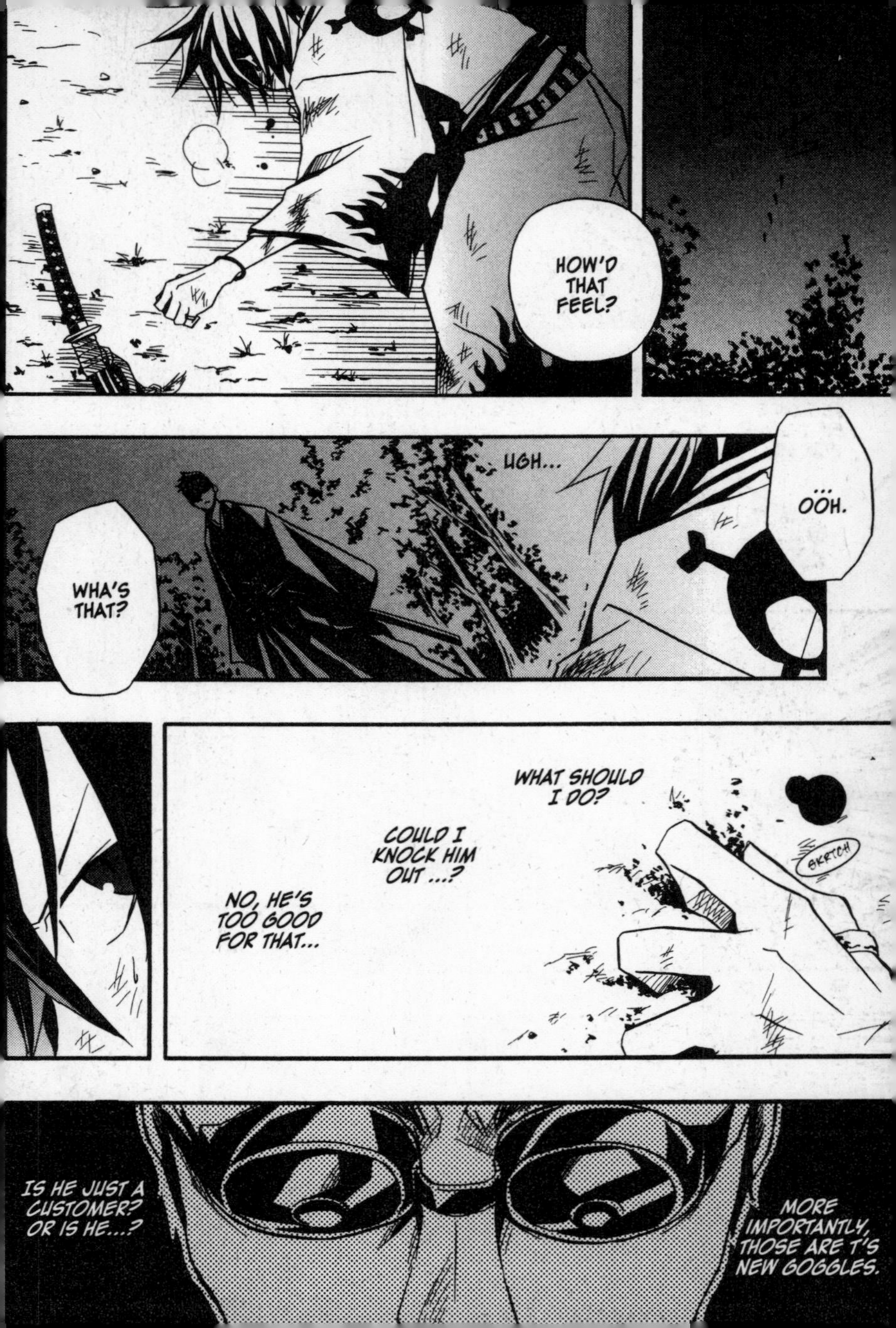
HOW'D THAT FEEL?
... OOH.
UGH...
WHA'S THAT?
WHAT SHOULD I DO?
SKRTCH
COULD I KNOCK HIM OUT ...?
NO, HE'S TOO GOOD FOR THAT...
MORE IMPORTANTLY, THOSE ARE T'S NEW GOGGLES.
IS HE JUST A CUSTOMER? OR IS HE...?

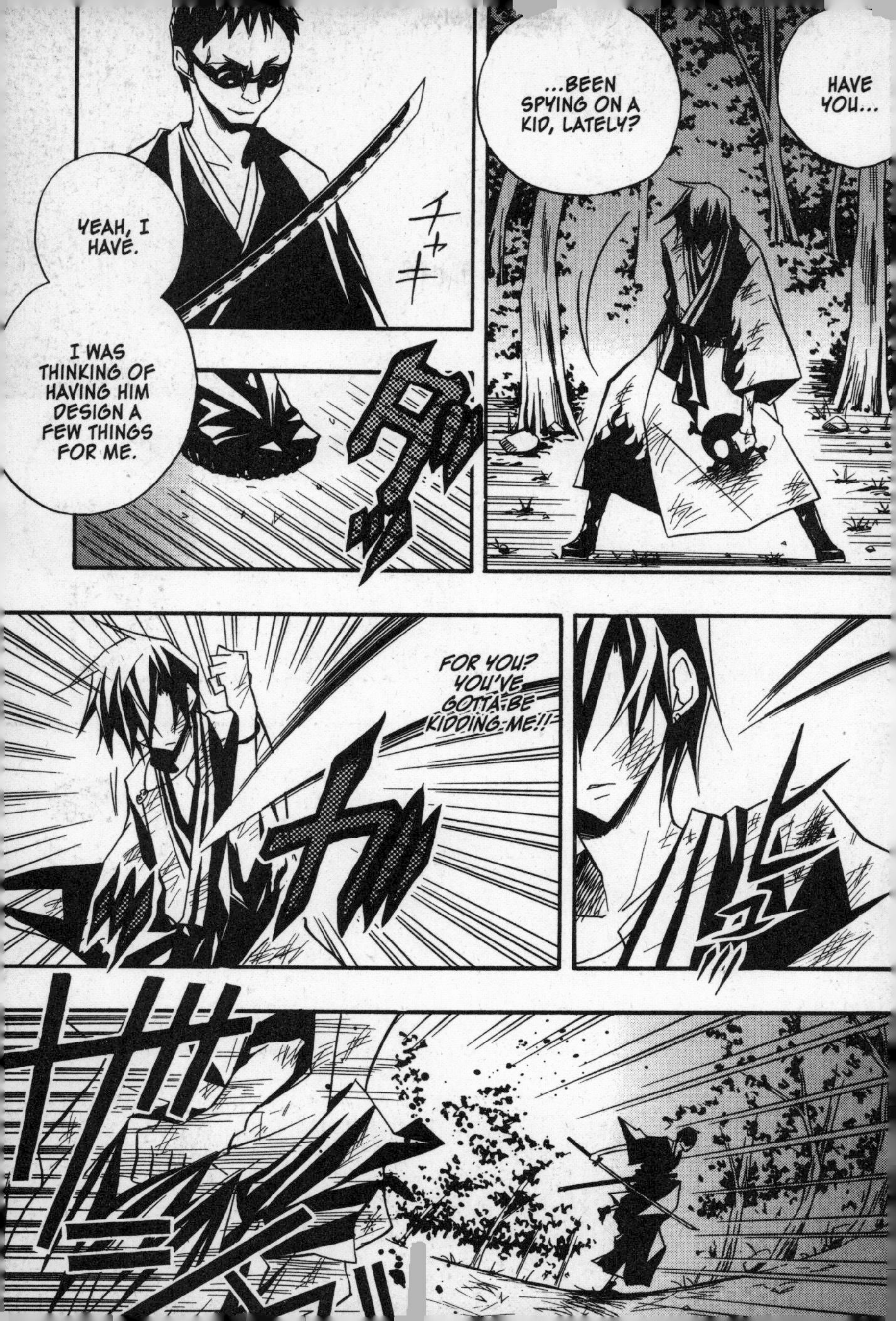
HAVE YOU...
...BEEN SPYING ON A KID, LATELY?
YEAH, I HAVE.
I WAS THINKING OF HAVING HIM DESIGN A FEW THINGS FOR ME.
チャキ
FOR YOU? YOU'VE GOTTA BE KIDDING ME!!

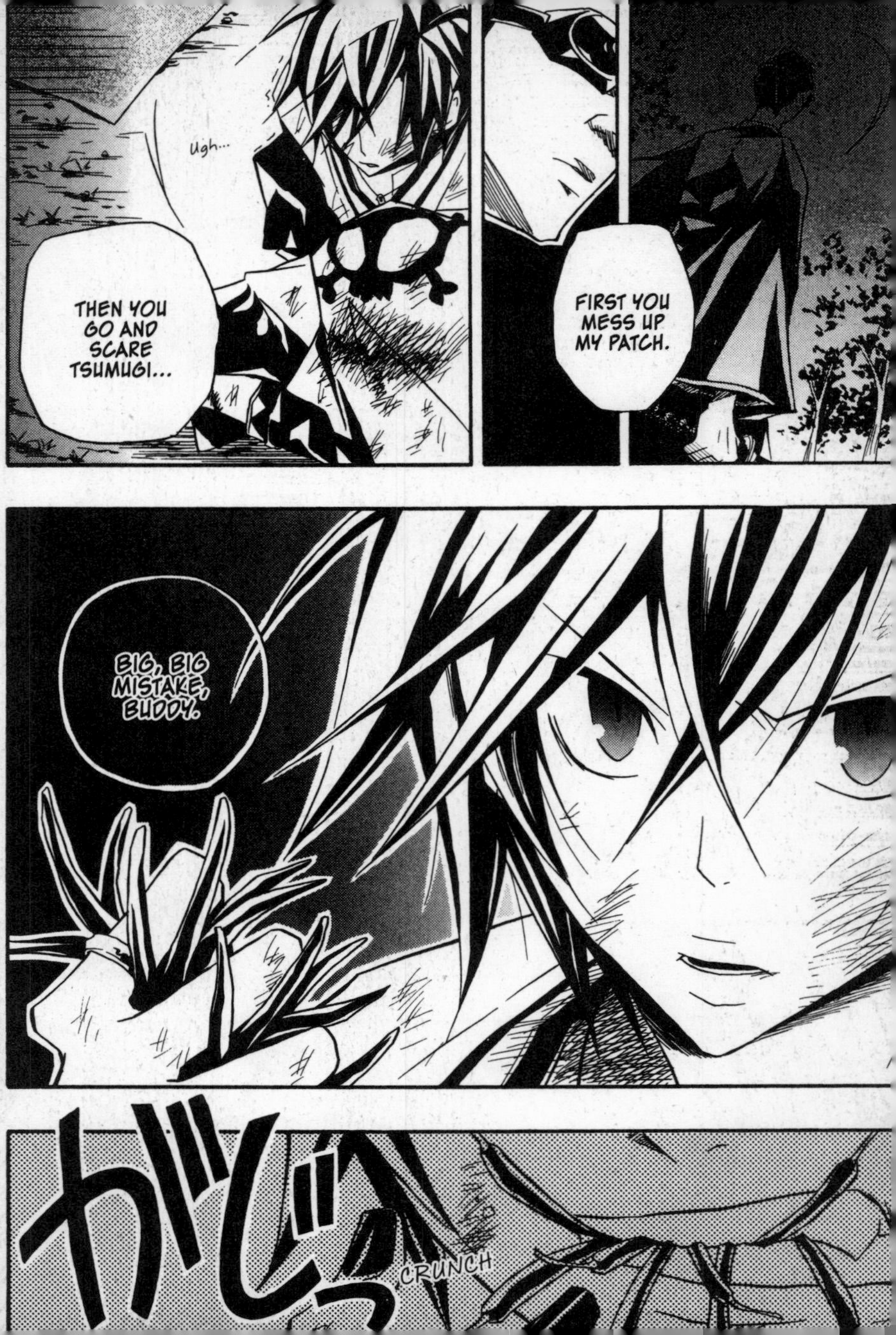
FIRST YOU MESS UP MY PATCH.
Ugh...
THEN YOU GO AND SCARE TSUMUGI...
BIG, BIG MISTAKE, BUDDY.
CRUNCH

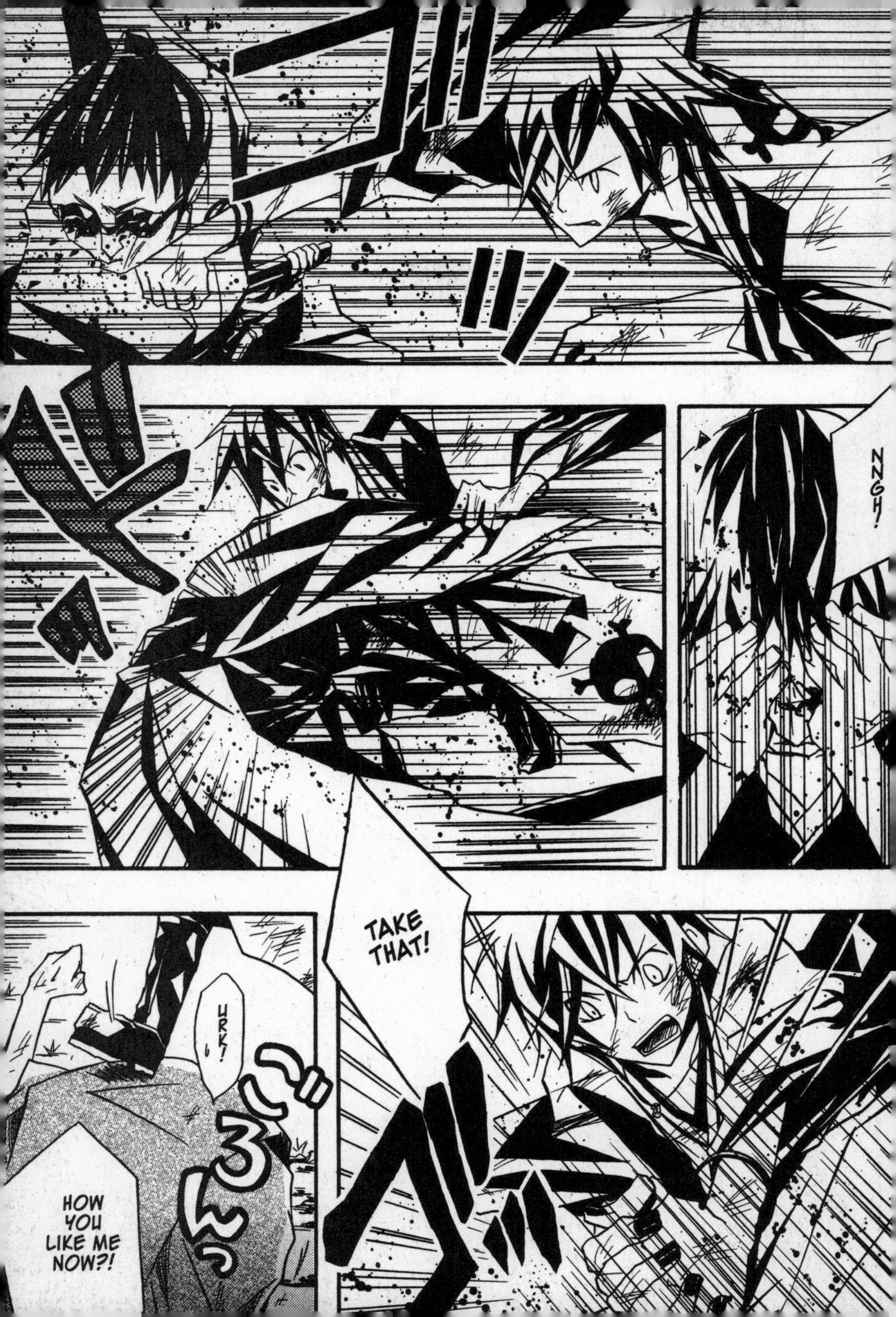
NNGH!
TAKE THAT!
URK!
HOW YOU LIKE ME NOW?!

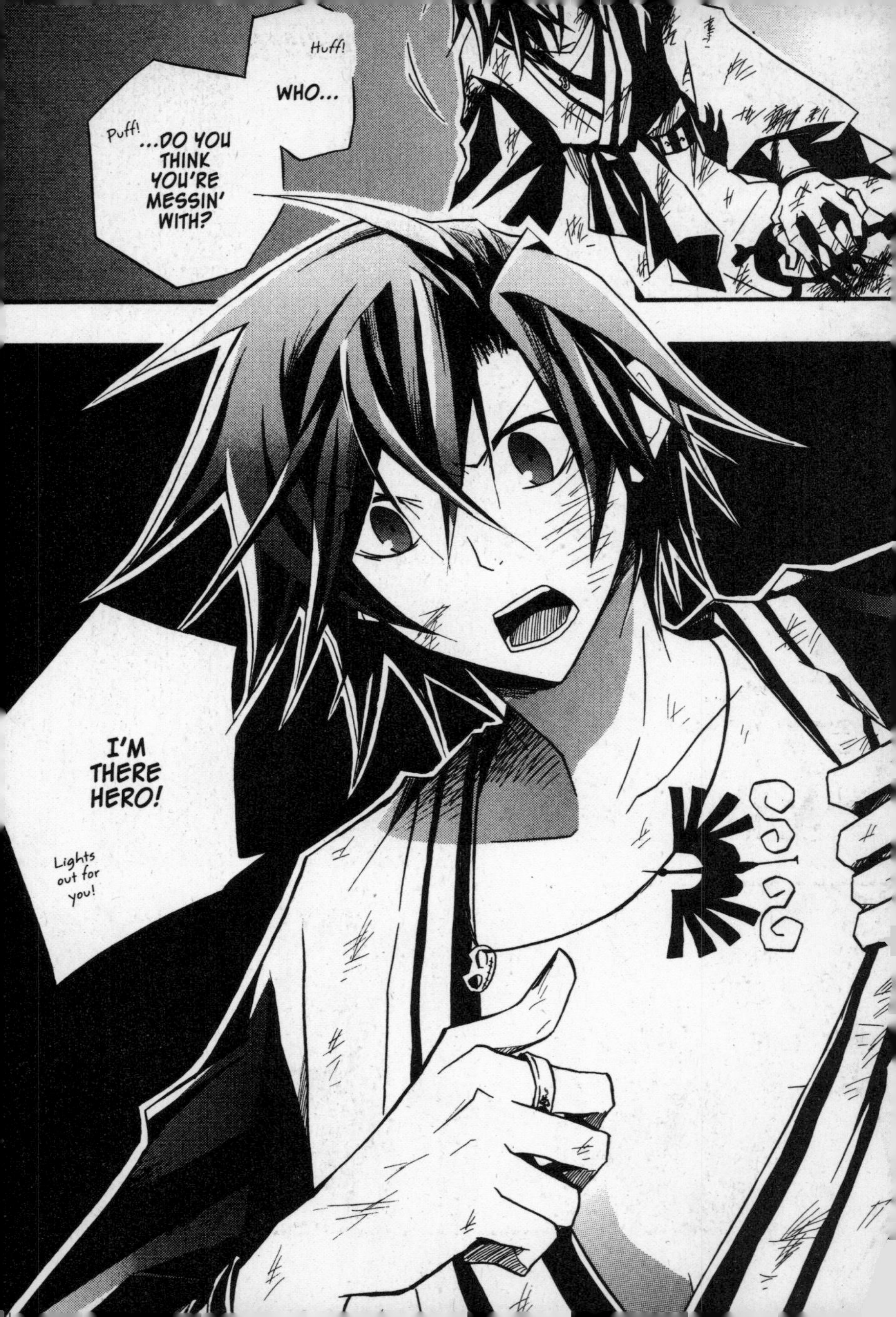
Huff!
WHO...
Puff!
...DO YOU THINK YOU'RE MESSIN' WITH?
I'M THERE HERO!
Lights out for you!

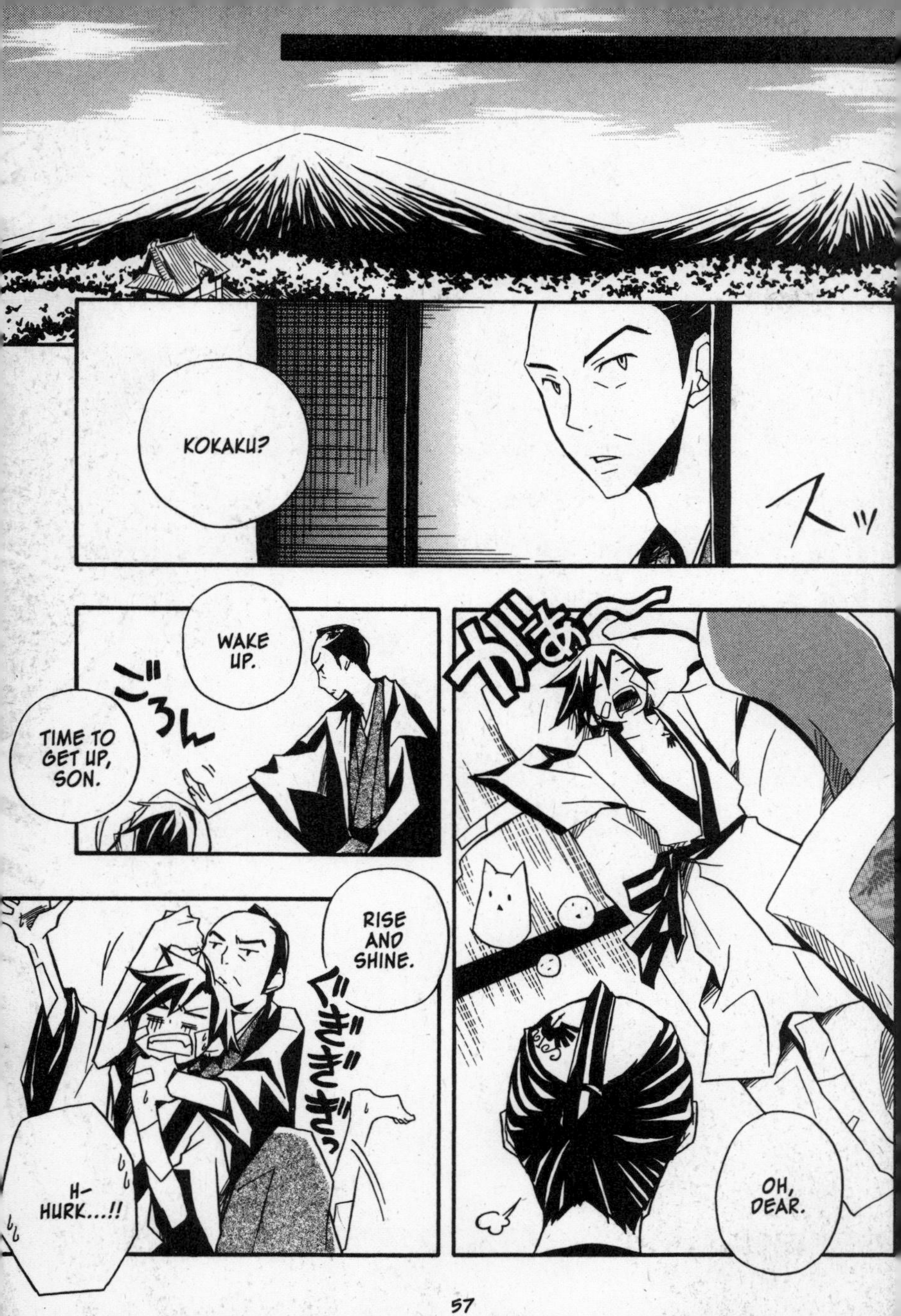

スッ
KOKAKU?
がばぁ〜
OH, DEAR.
WAKE UP.
ごろん
TIME TO GET UP, SON.
RISE AND SHINE.
ぐぎぎぎっ
H-HURK...!!

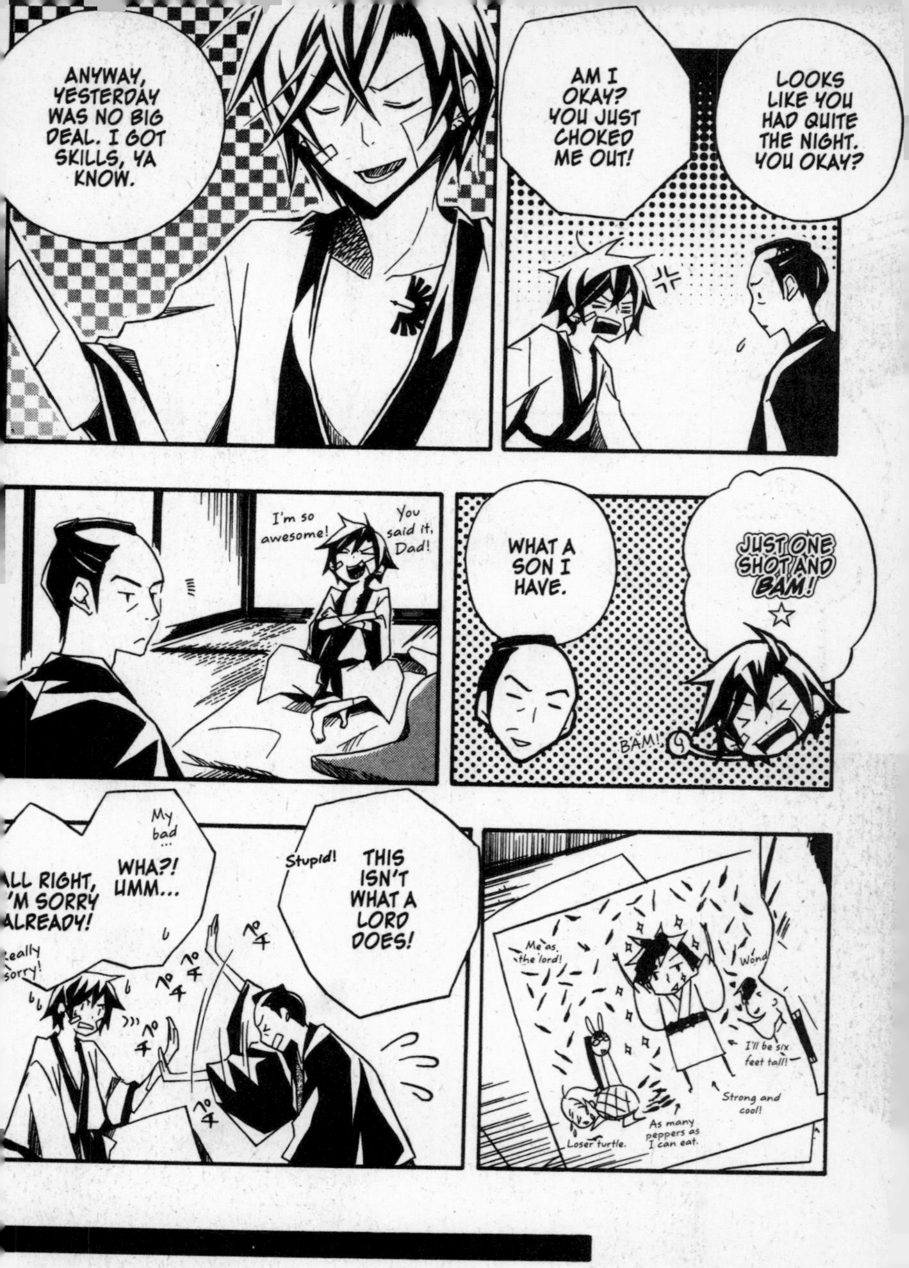
LOOKS LIKE YOU HAD QUITE THE NIGHT. YOU OKAY?
AM I OKAY? YOU JUST CHOKED ME OUT!
ANYWAY, YESTERDAY WAS NO BIG DEAL. I GOT SKILLS, YA KNOW.
JUST ONE SHOT AND BAM!
WHAT A SON I HAVE.
BAM!
You said it, Dad!
I'm so awesome!
Me as the lord!
Wond
I'll be six feet tall!
Strong and cool!
As many peppers as I can eat.
Loser turtle.
THIS ISN'T WHAT A LORD DOES!
Stupid!
My bad...
WHA?! UMM...
LL RIGHT, 'M SORRY LREADY!
eally sorry!

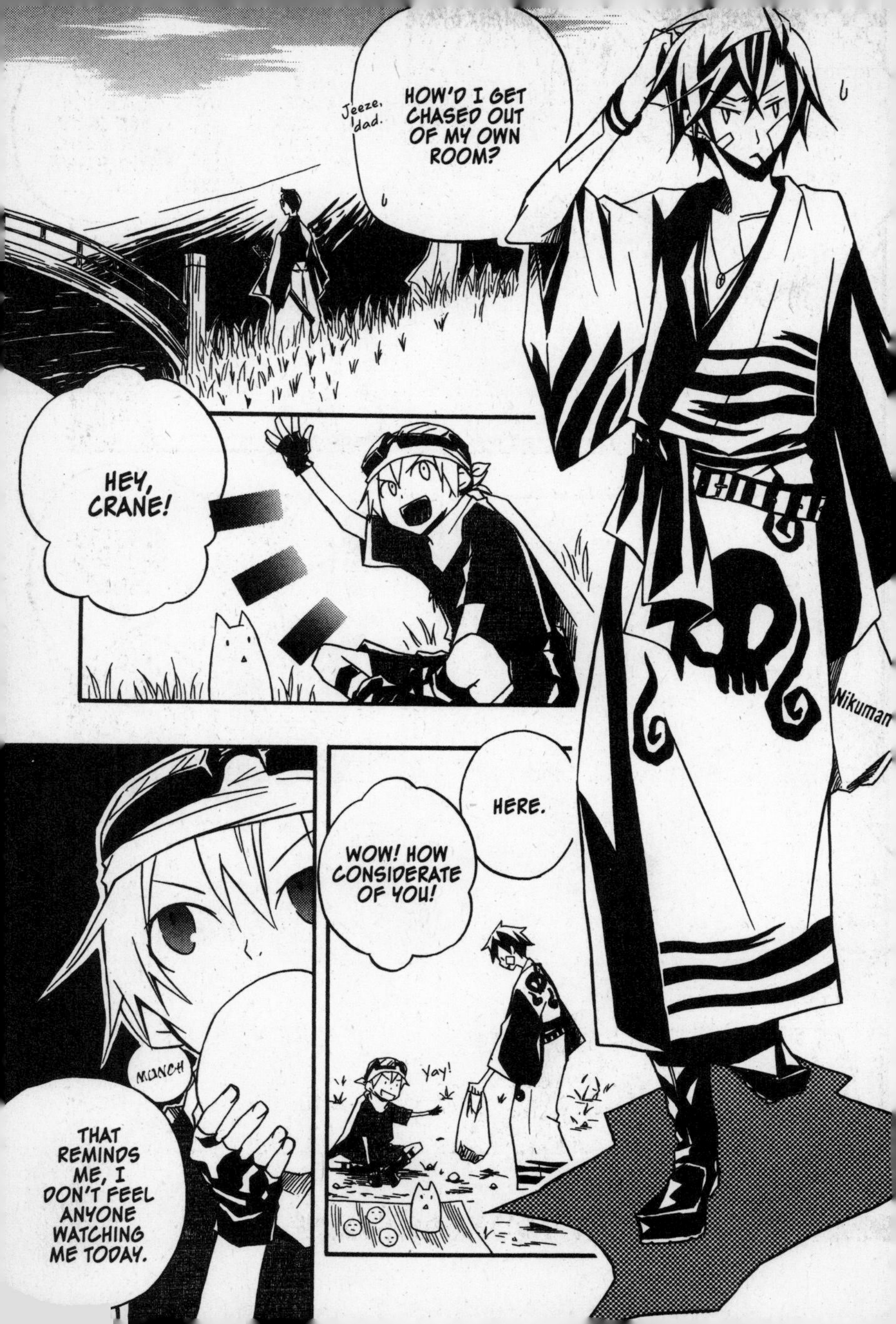
HOW'D I GET CHASED OUT OF MY OWN ROOM?
Jeeze, dad.
Nikuman
HEY, CRANE!
HERE.
WOW! HOW CONSIDERATE OF YOU!
Yay!
MUNCH
THAT REMINDS ME, I DON'T FEEL ANYONE WATCHING ME TODAY.

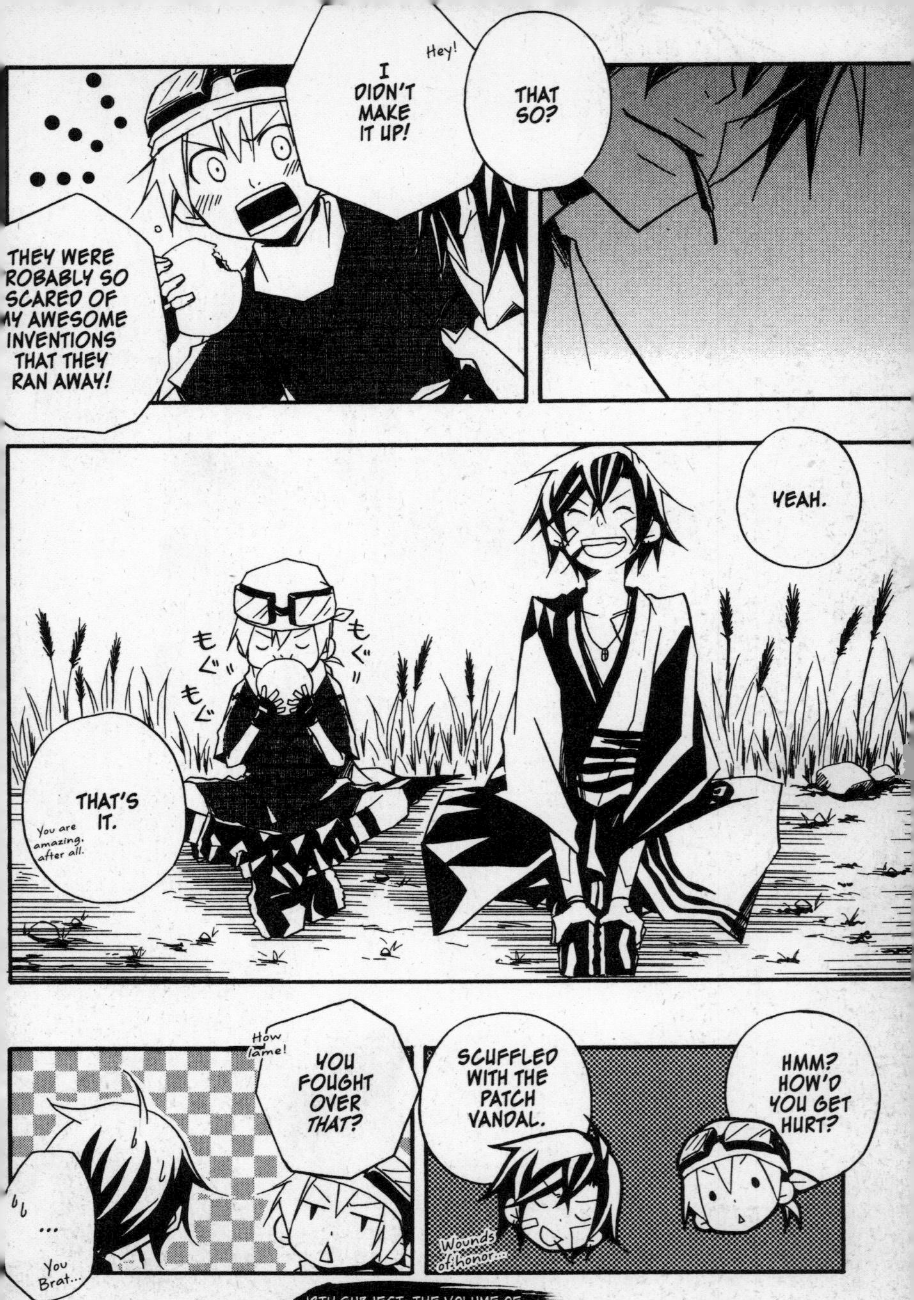
THAT SO?
I DIDN'T MAKE IT UP!
Hey!
• • • • • • • • •
THEY WERE ROBABLY SO SCARED OF MY AWESOME INVENTIONS THAT THEY RAN AWAY!
YEAH.
もぐ
もぐ
もぐ
THAT'S IT.
You are amazing, after all.
HMM? HOW'D YOU GET HURT?
SCUFFLED WITH THE PATCH VANDAL.
Wounds of honor...
YOU FOUGHT OVER THAT?
How lame!
...
You Brat...

12TH SUBJECT: THE VOLUME OF THE ORIENTAL CRANE / THE END

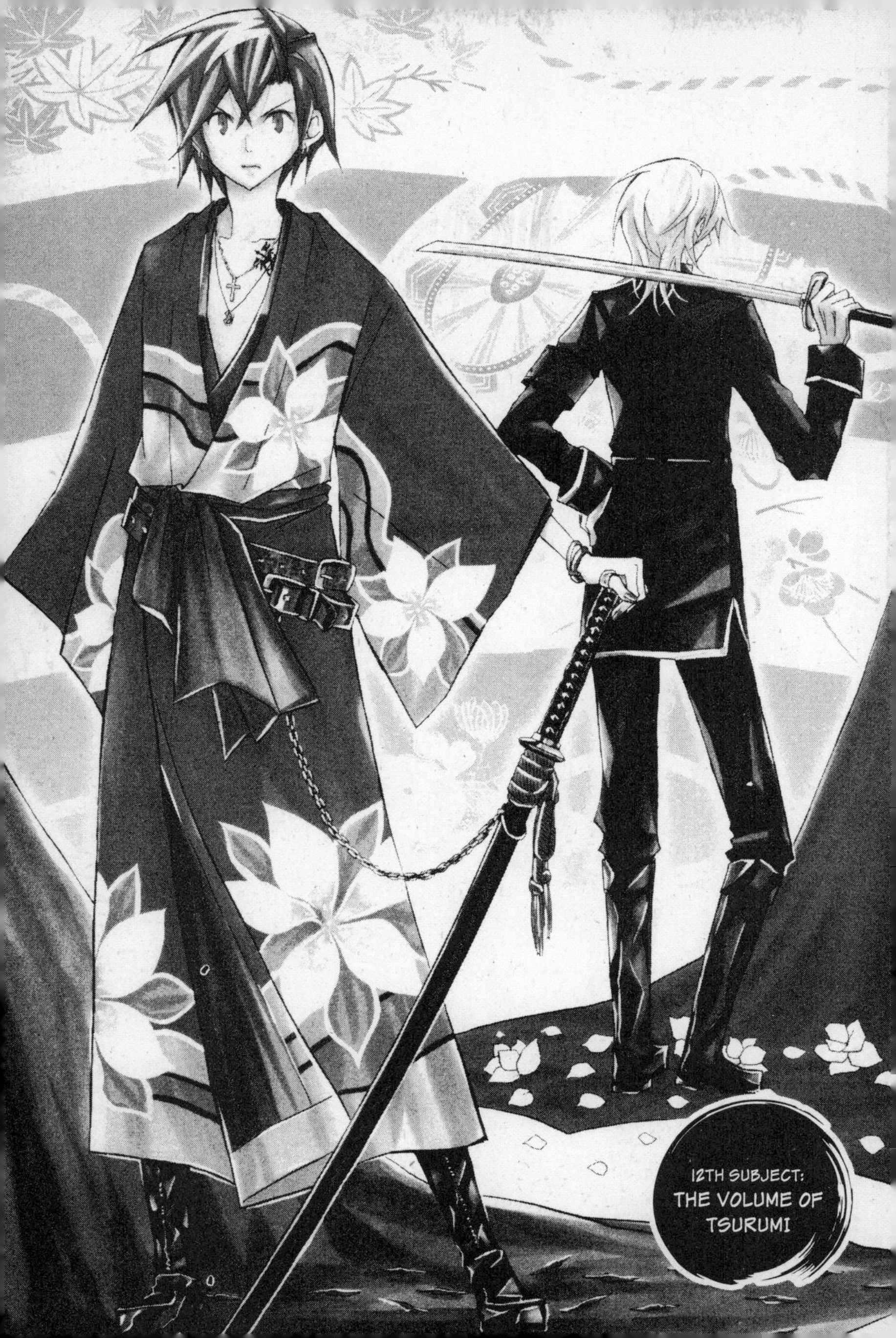
12TH SUBJECT:
THE VOLUME OF TSURUMI

The smiling perpetrator of the crime of conscience

Kōki Banka

Born February 5th / 14 years old

Sign: Aquarius / Blood Type: B

Favorite Food: Sushi

Hobbies: Kyūdō

(Japanese Archery)

Dislikes: Long creatures

without legs

Specialty: Quick response time

Has an earring matching Shikki's on his right ear (a keepsake of his mother's)

The "Kō" his name is derived from the term "Kōshitsu" using the same kanji "shi" that's in Shikki's name with the "ki" part meaning "turtle." This is an idiom that literally means glue (Ko) and lacquer (shitsu) which "like two peas in a pod" expresses how close the two substances are.

Has become rebellious due to his peerless elder brother. Occasionally wears glasses to be ostentatious. His image color is cerulean.

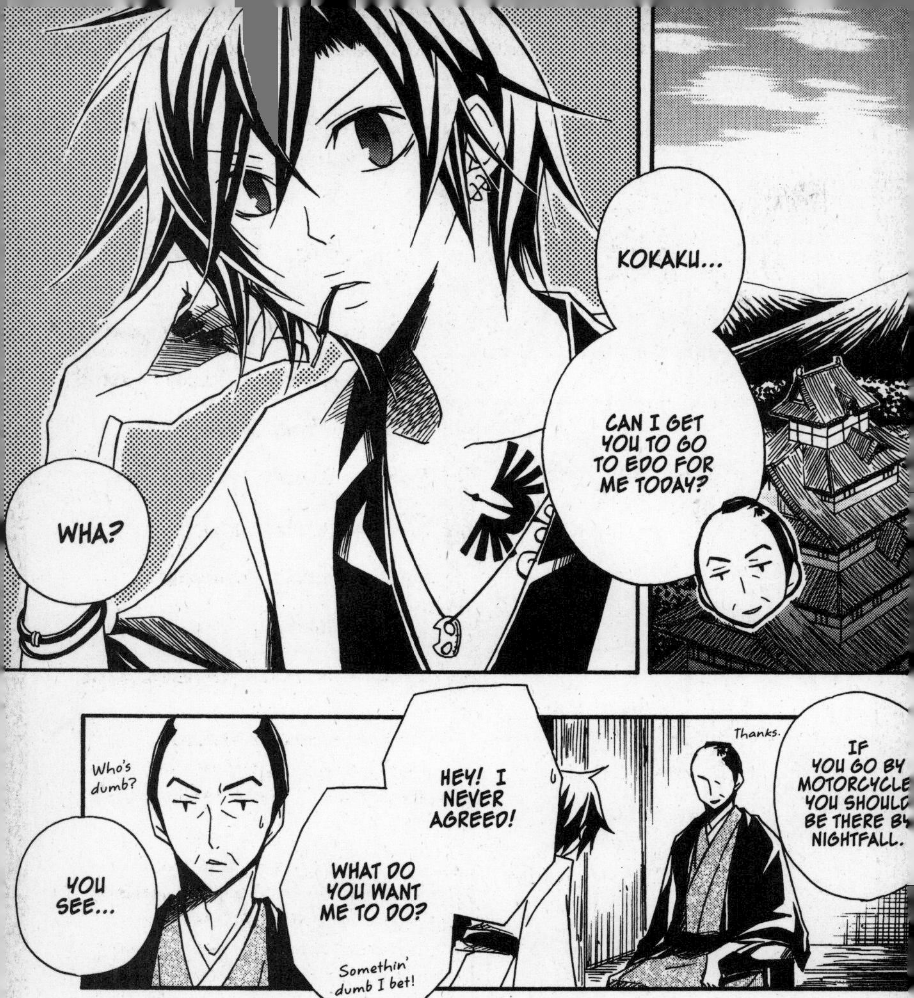
KOKAKU...
CAN I GET YOU TO GO TO EDO FOR ME TODAY?
WHA?
Thanks.
IF YOU GO BY MOTORCYCLE YOU SHOULD BE THERE BY NIGHTFALL.
HEY! I NEVER AGREED!
WHAT DO YOU WANT ME TO DO?
Somethin' dumb I bet!
Who's dumb?
YOU SEE...

EGGPLANT FAMILY PEPPER TRIBE NUMBER 6

"RĀYU" IS MADE BY HEATING A CHILI IN VEGETABLE OIL TO EXTRACT THE SPICY ELEMENT. A CONDIMENT OR SEASONING IN SZECHWAN CUISINE.

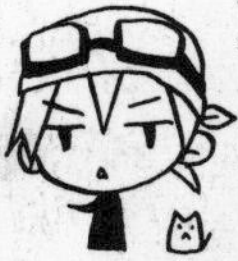
No matter how careful you are, the sauce always seems to get everywhere.

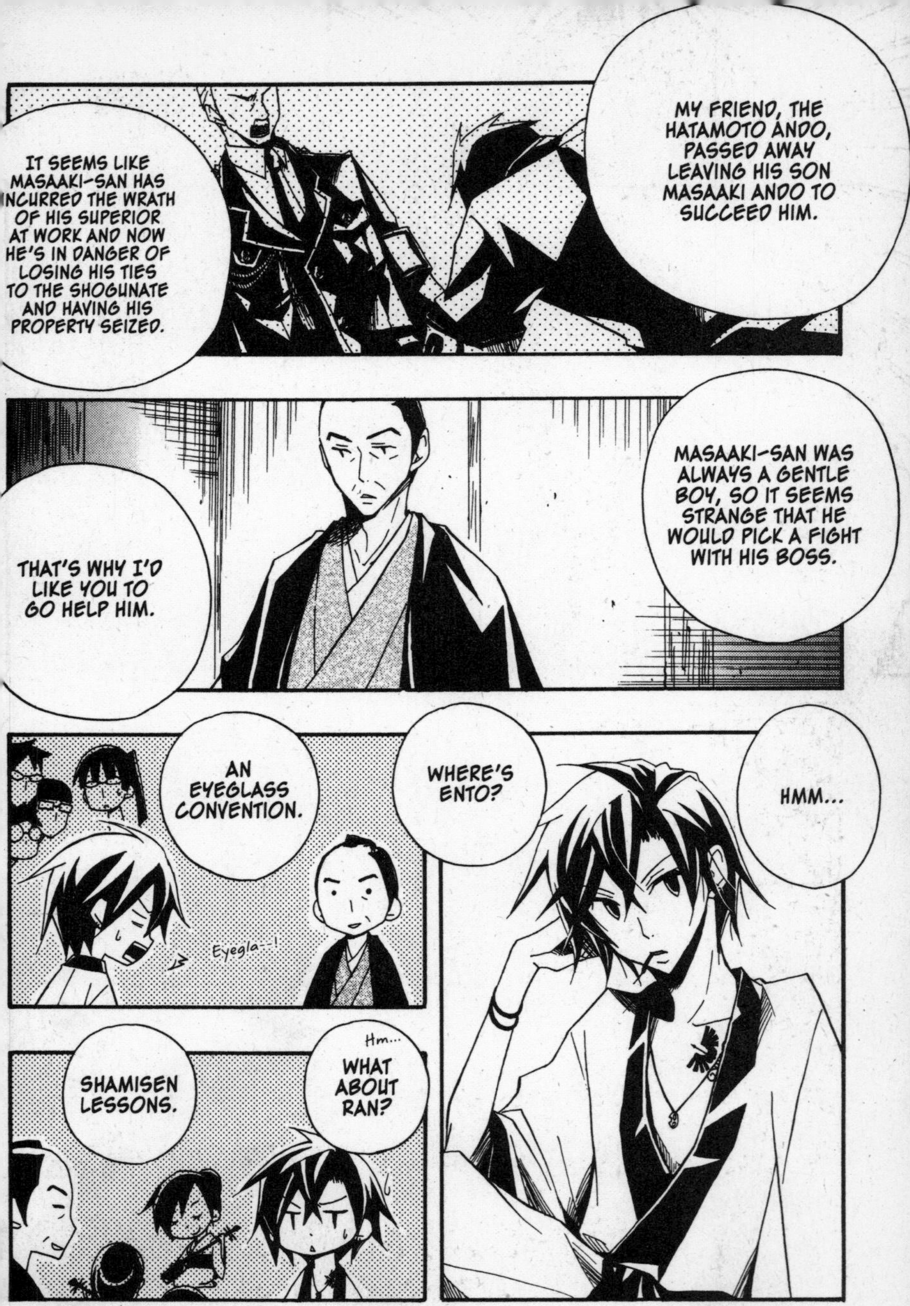
MY FRIEND, THE HATAMOTO ANDO, PASSED AWAY LEAVING HIS SON MASAAKI ANDO TO SUCCEED HIM.
IT SEEMS LIKE MASAAKI-SAN HAS INCURRED THE WRATH OF HIS SUPERIOR AT WORK AND NOW HE'S IN DANGER OF LOSING HIS TIES TO THE SHOGUNATE AND HAVING HIS PROPERTY SEIZED.
MASAAKI-SAN WAS ALWAYS A GENTLE BOY, SO IT SEEMS STRANGE THAT HE WOULD PICK A FIGHT WITH HIS BOSS.
THAT'S WHY I'D LIKE YOU TO GO HELP HIM.
HMM...
WHERE'S ENTO?
AN EYEGLASS CONVENTION.
Eyegla--!
Hm...
WHAT ABOUT RAN?
SHAMISEN LESSONS.

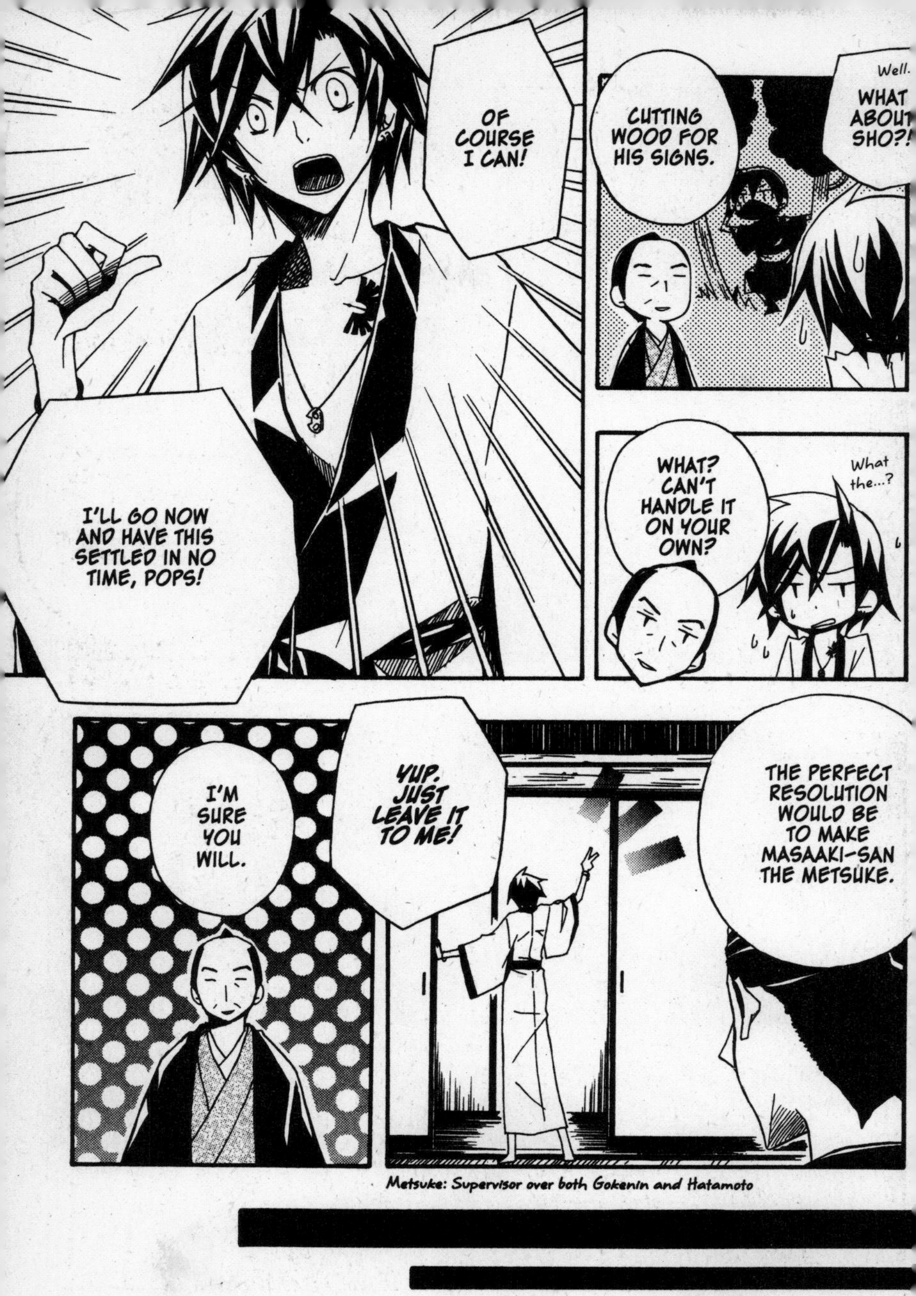
Well.
WHAT ABOUT SHO?!
CUTTING WOOD FOR HIS SIGNS.
WHAT? CAN'T HANDLE IT ON YOUR OWN?
What the...?
OF COURSE I CAN!
I'LL GO NOW AND HAVE THIS SETTLED IN NO TIME, POPS!
THE PERFECT RESOLUTION WOULD BE TO MAKE MASAAKI-SAN THE METSUKE.
YUP. JUST LEAVE IT TO ME!
I'M SURE YOU WILL.

Metsuke: Supervisor over both Gokenin and Hatamoto

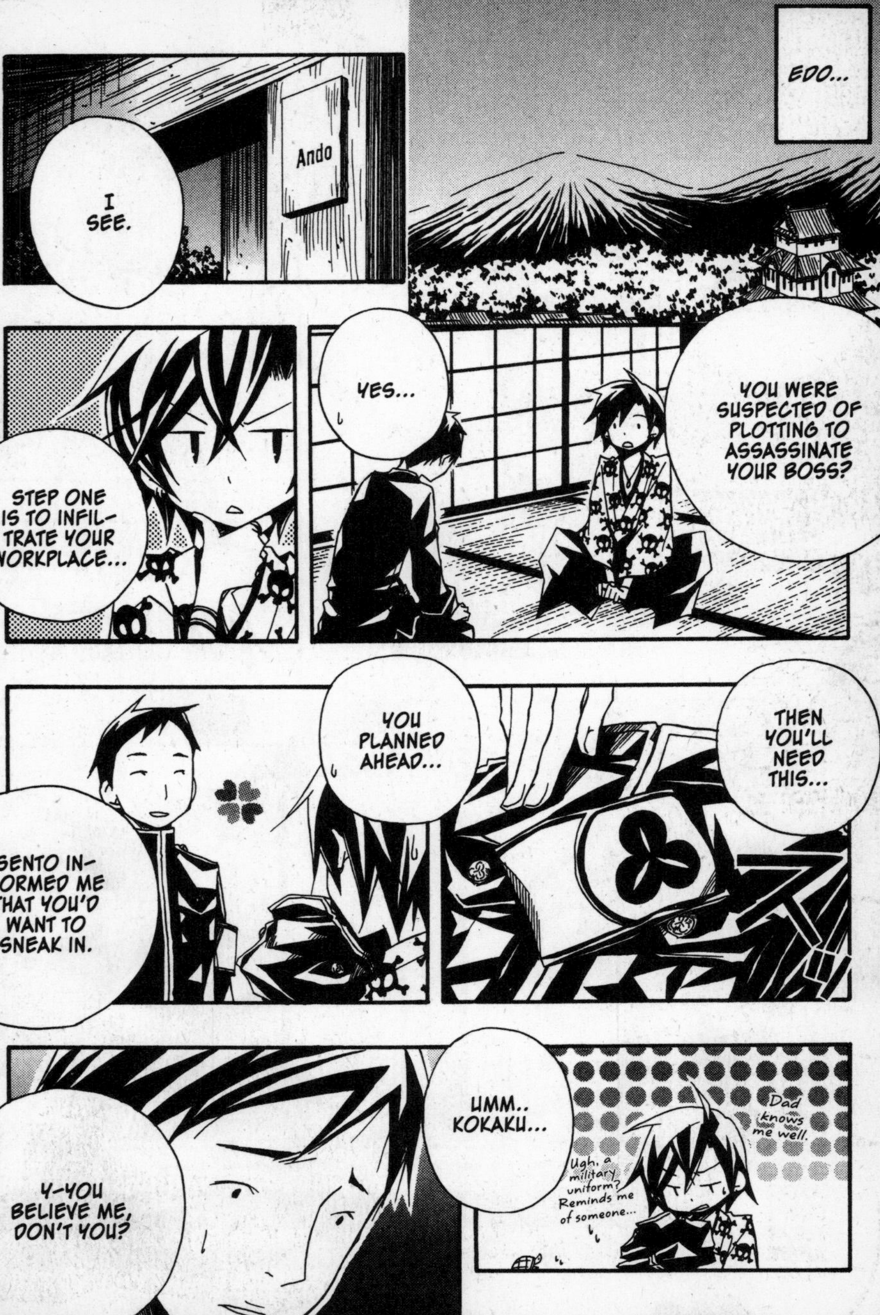
EDO...
Ando
I SEE.
YOU WERE SUSPECTED OF PLOTTING TO ASSASSINATE YOUR BOSS?
YES...
STEP ONE IS TO INFILTRATE YOUR WORKPLACE...
THEN YOU'LL NEED THIS...
YOU PLANNED AHEAD...
SENTO INFORMED ME THAT YOU'D WANT TO SNEAK IN.
Dad knows me well.
Ugh, a military uniform? Reminds me of someone...
UMM.. KOKAKU...
Y-YOU BELIEVE ME, DON'T YOU?

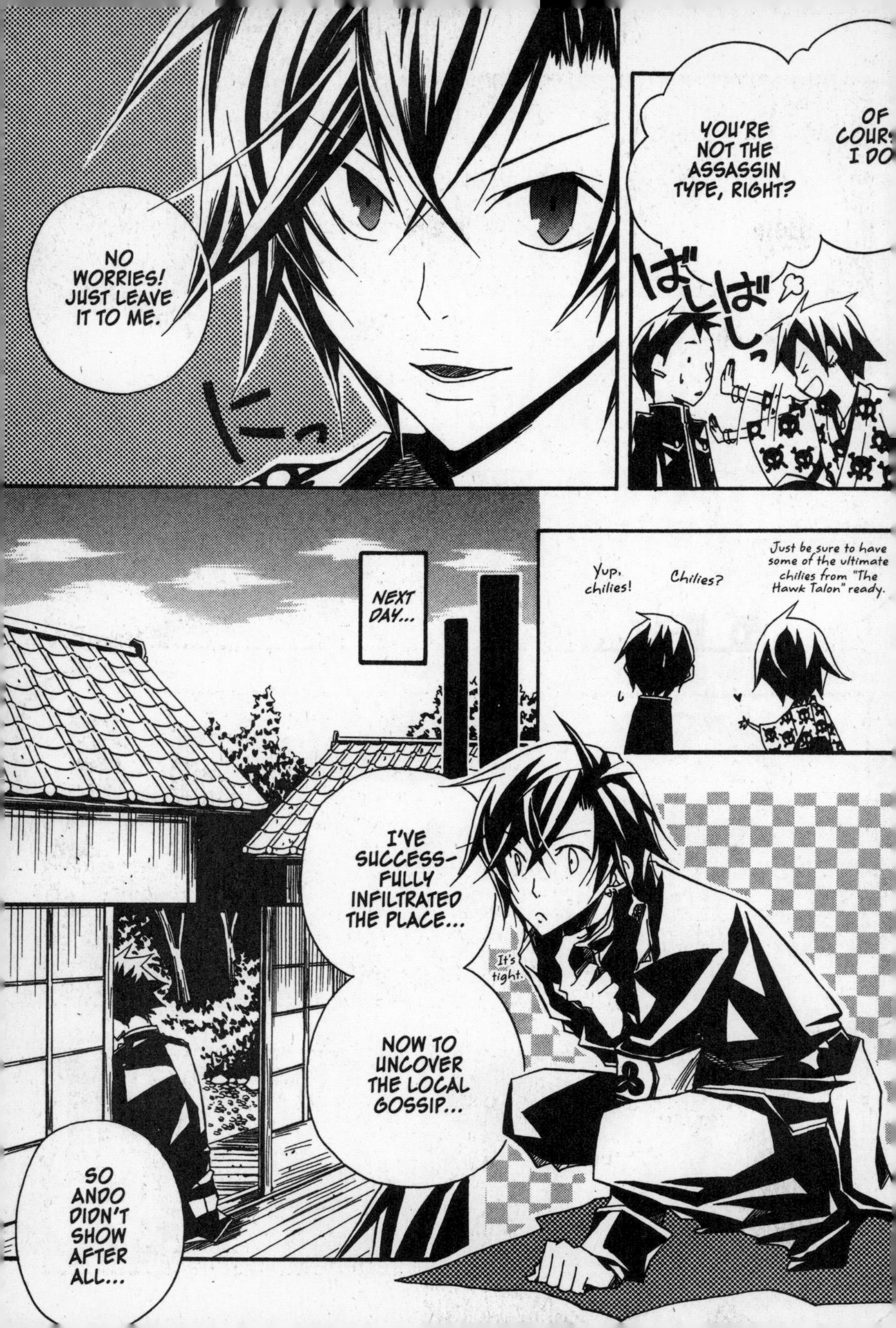
YOU'RE NOT THE ASSASSIN TYPE, RIGHT?
OF COURS I DO
ばしばしっ
NO WORRIES! JUST LEAVE IT TO ME.
Just be sure to have some of the ultimate chilies from "The Hawk Talon" ready.
Chilies?
Yup, chilies!
NEXT DAY...
I'VE SUCCESS-FULLY INFILTRATED THE PLACE...
NOW TO UNCOVER THE LOCAL GOSSIP...
It's tight.
SO ANDO DIDN'T SHOW AFTER ALL...

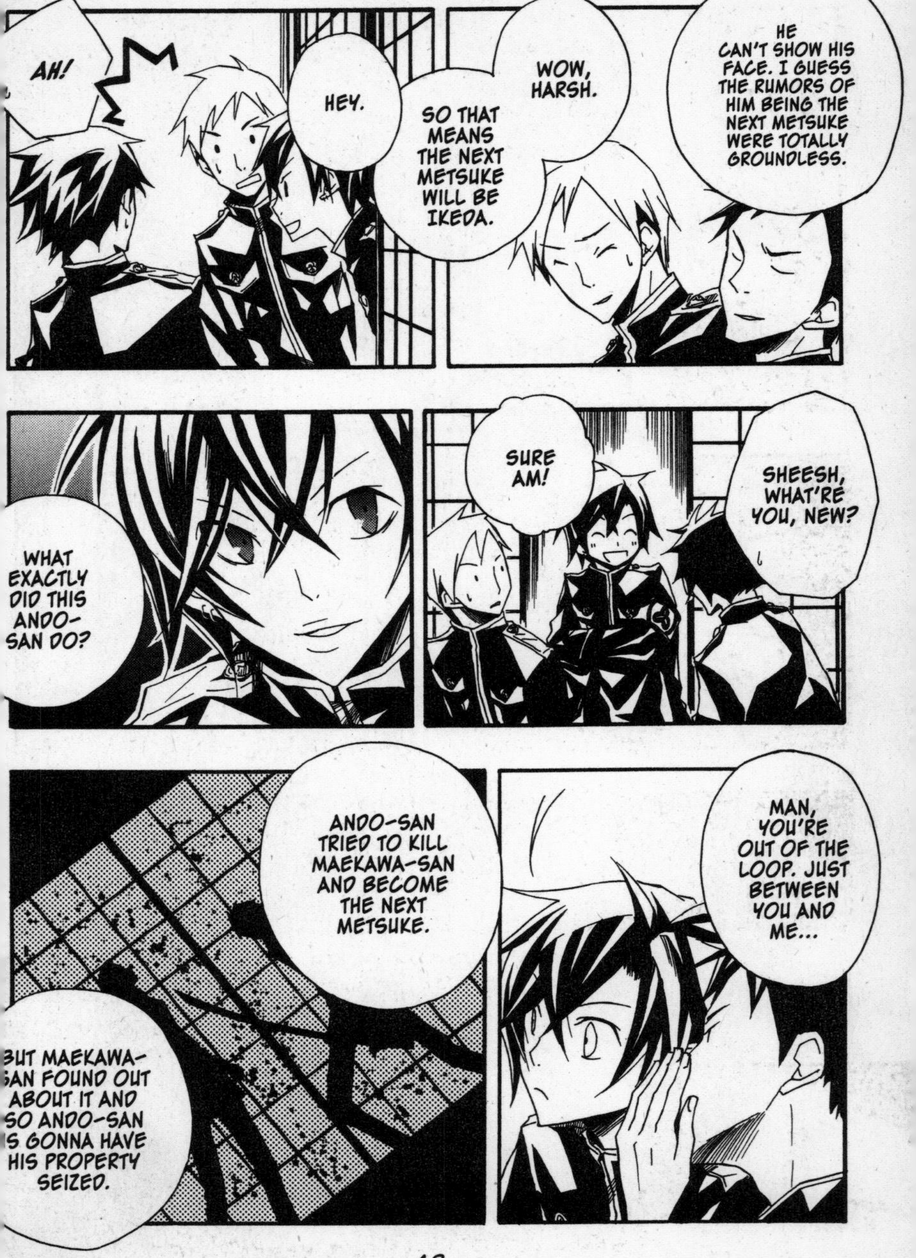
HE CAN'T SHOW HIS FACE. I GUESS THE RUMORS OF HIM BEING THE NEXT METSUKE WERE TOTALLY GROUNDLESS.
WOW, HARSH.
SO THAT MEANS THE NEXT METSUKE WILL BE IKEDA.
HEY.
AH!
SHEESH, WHAT'RE YOU, NEW?
SURE AM!
WHAT EXACTLY DID THIS ANDO-SAN DO?
MAN, YOU'RE OUT OF THE LOOP. JUST BETWEEN YOU AND ME...
ANDO-SAN TRIED TO KILL MAEKAWA-SAN AND BECOME THE NEXT METSUKE.
BUT MAEKAWA-SAN FOUND OUT ABOUT IT AND SO ANDO-SAN IS GONNA HAVE HIS PROPERTY SEIZED.

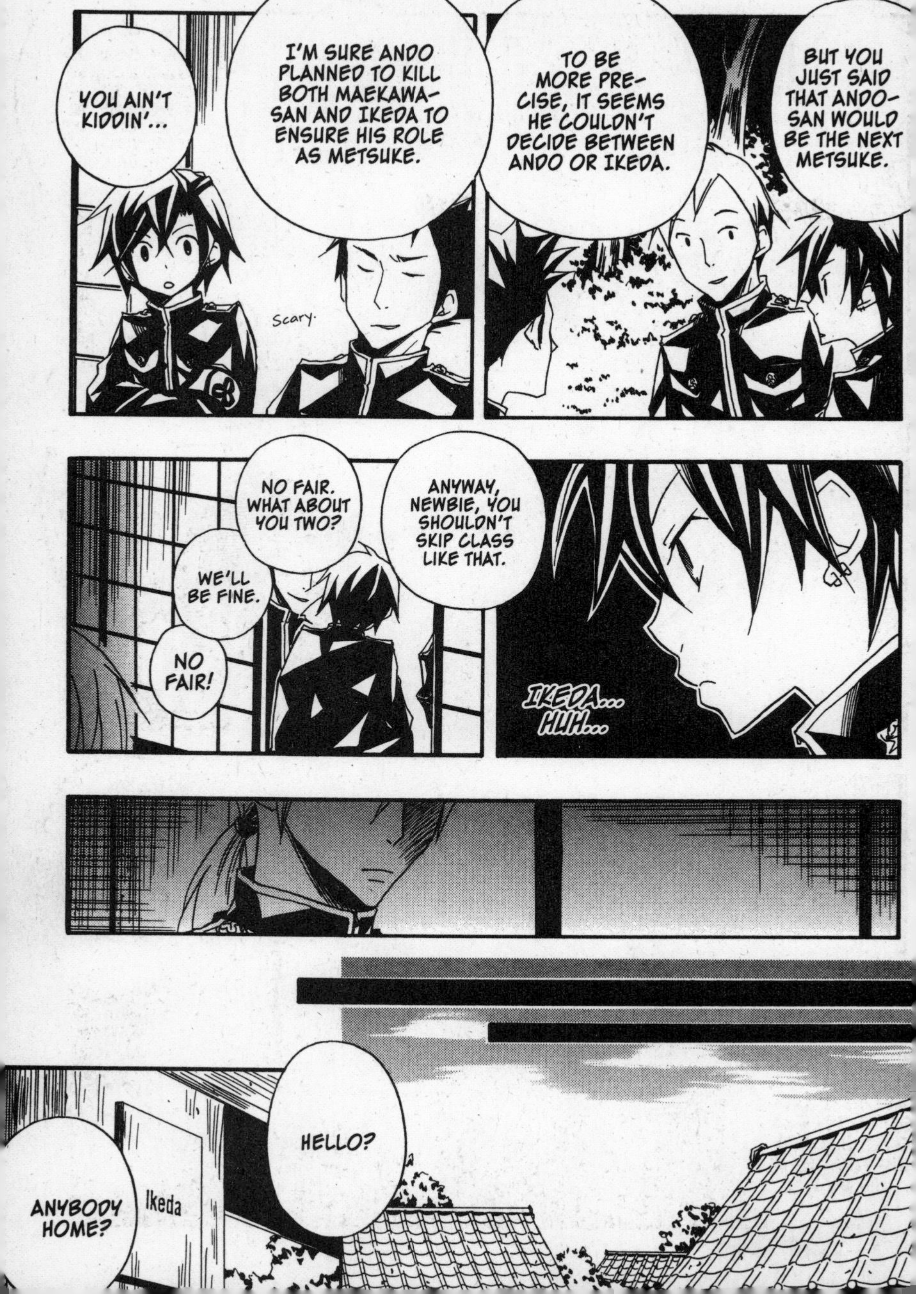
BUT YOU JUST SAID THAT ANDO-SAN WOULD BE THE NEXT METSUKE.
TO BE MORE PRE-CISE, IT SEEMS HE COULDN'T DECIDE BETWEEN ANDO OR IKEDA.
I'M SURE ANDO PLANNED TO KILL BOTH MAEKAWA-SAN AND IKEDA TO ENSURE HIS ROLE AS METSUKE.
YOU AIN'T KIDDIN'...
Scary.
IKEDA... HUH...
ANYWAY, NEWBIE, YOU SHOULDN'T SKIP CLASS LIKE THAT.
NO FAIR. WHAT ABOUT YOU TWO?
WE'LL BE FINE.
NO FAIR!
HELLO?
Ikeda
ANYBODY HOME?

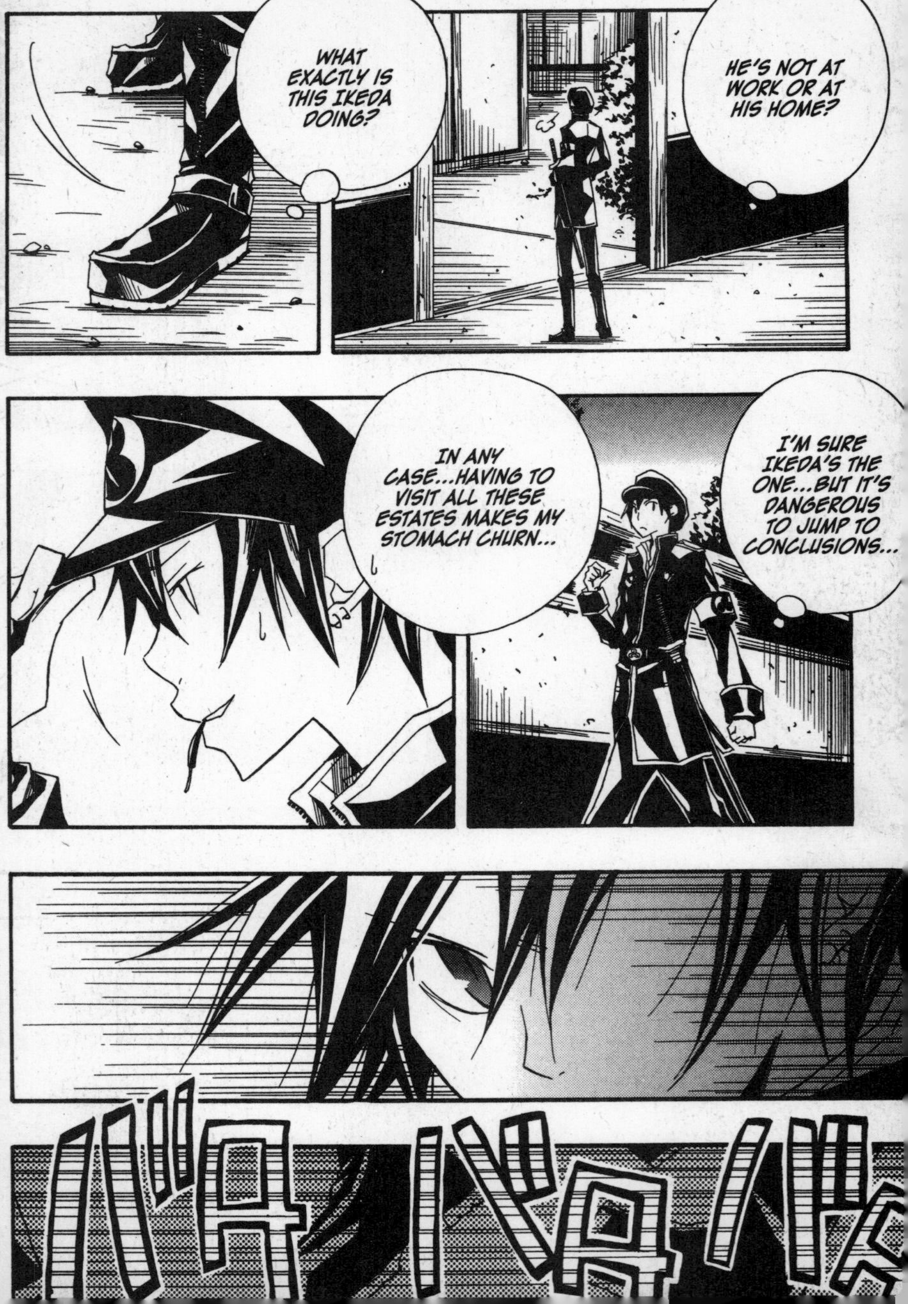
HE'S NOT AT WORK OR AT HIS HOME?
WHAT EXACTLY IS THIS IKEDA DOING?
I'M SURE IKEDA'S THE ONE...BUT IT'S DANGEROUS TO JUMP TO CONCLUSIONS...
IN ANY CASE...HAVING TO VISIT ALL THESE ESTATES MAKES MY STOMACH CHURN...

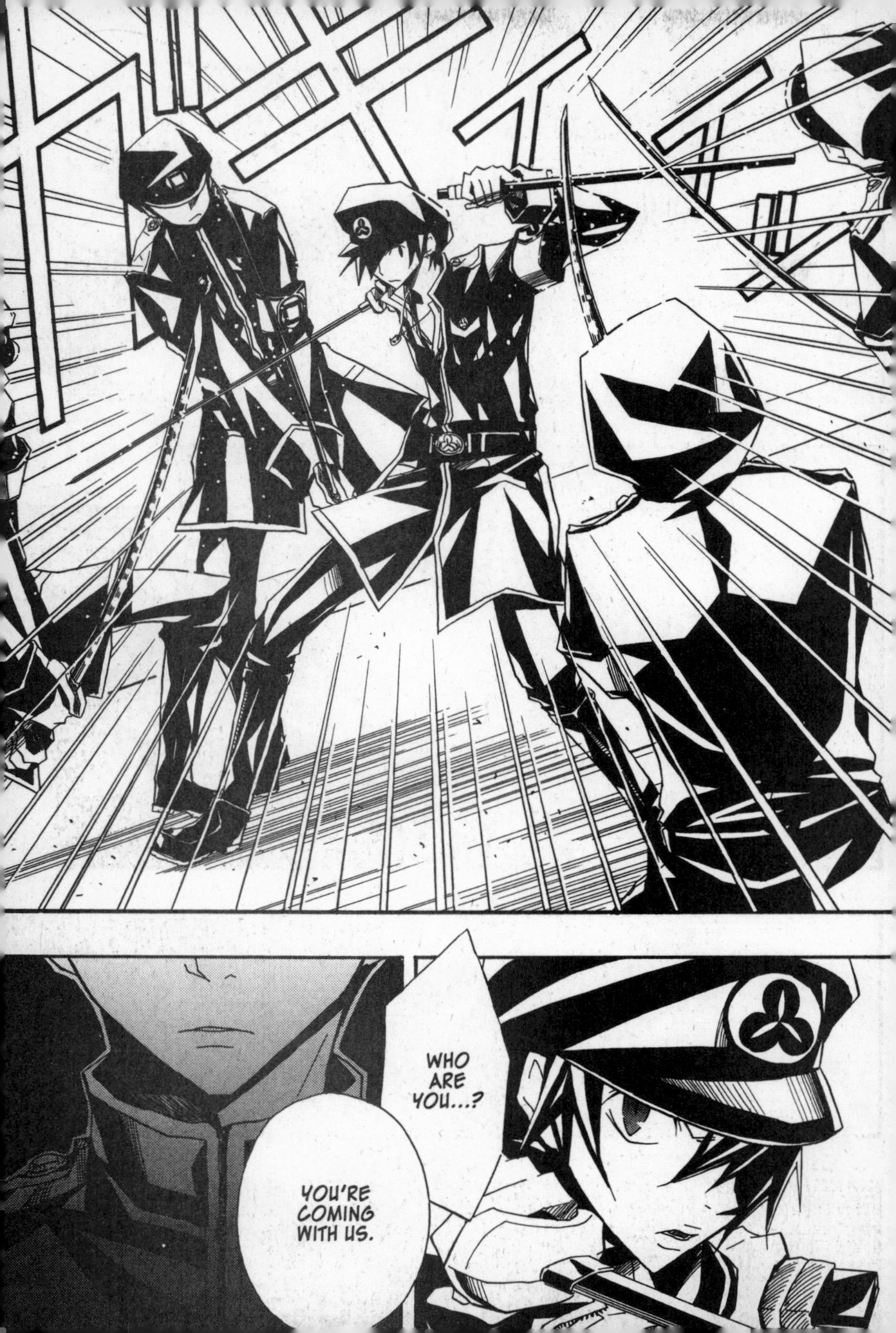
WHO ARE YOU...?
YOU'RE COMING WITH US.

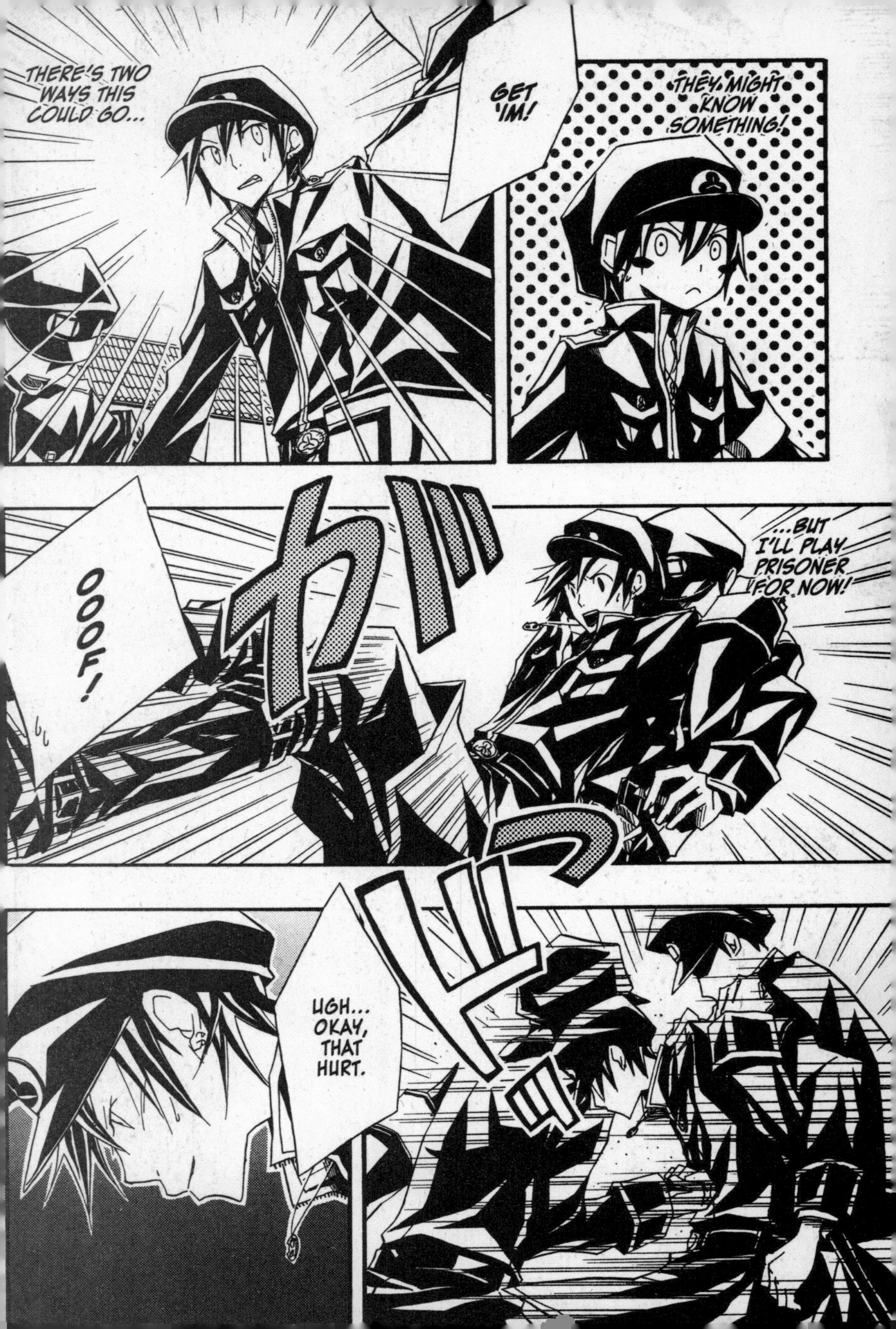
THEY MIGHT KNOW SOMETHING!
GET 'IM!
THERE'S TWO WAYS THIS COULD GO...
...BUT I'LL PLAY PRISONER FOR NOW!
OOOF!
UGH... OKAY, THAT HURT.

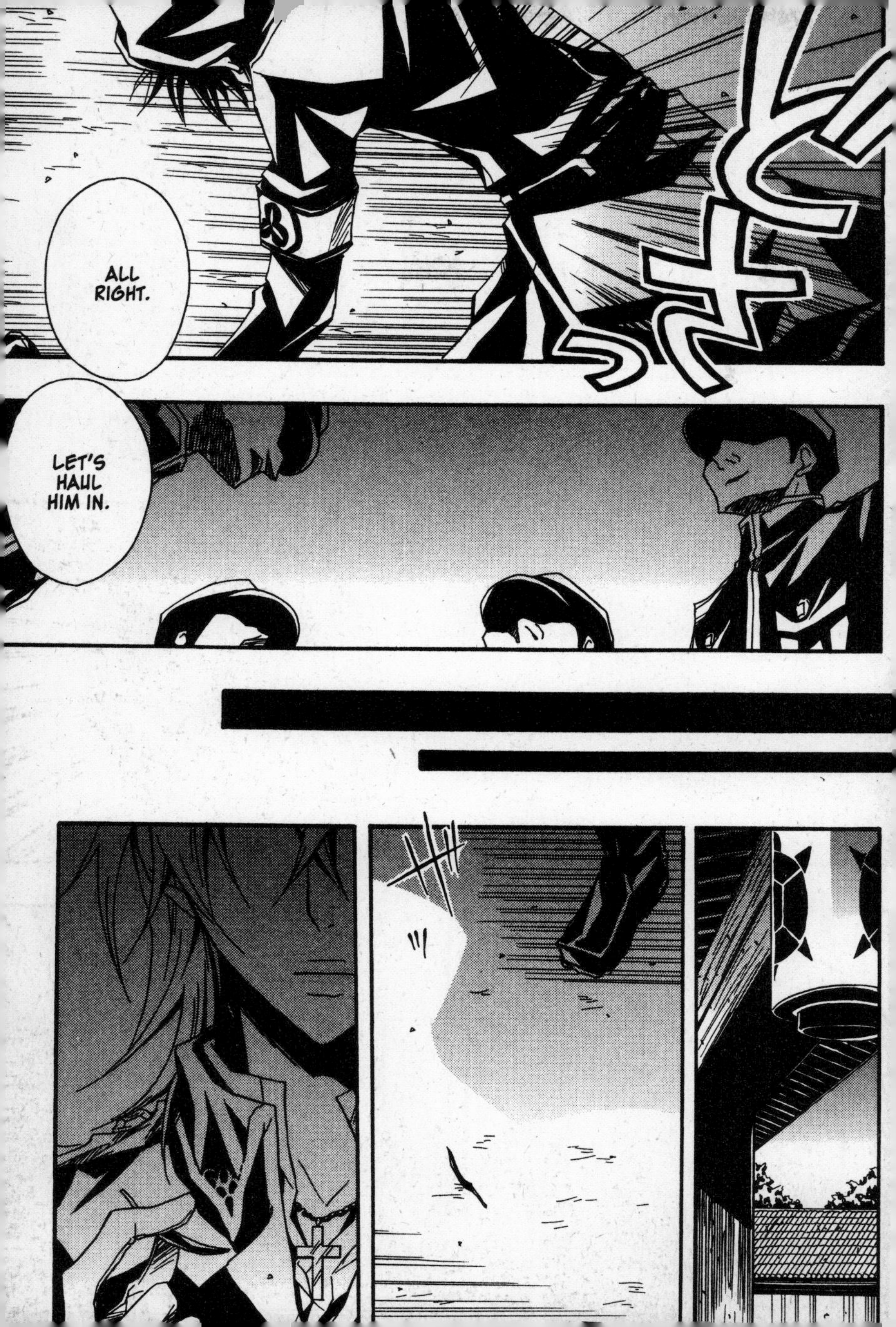
どさっ
ALL RIGHT.
LET'S HAUL HIM IN.

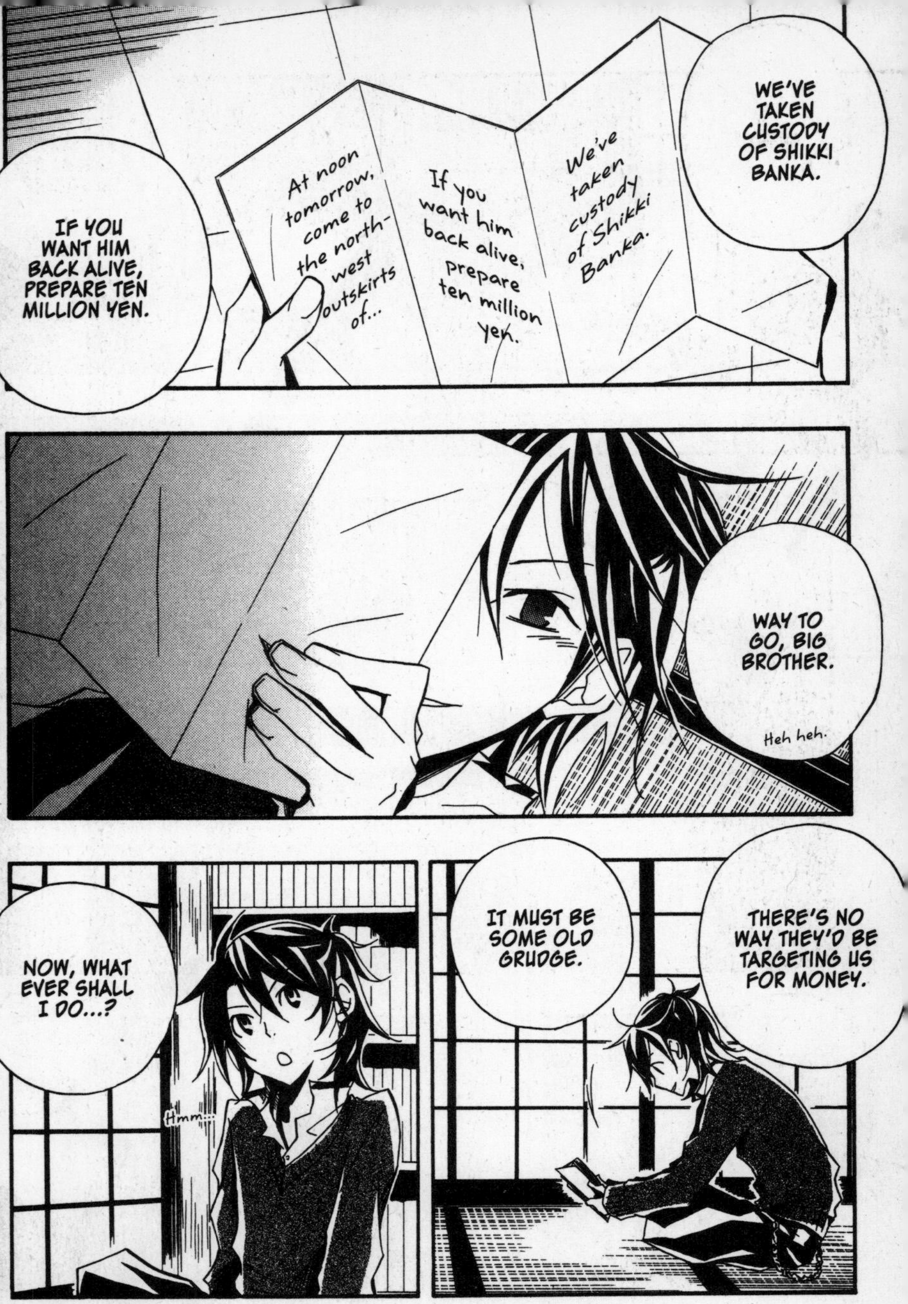
WE'VE TAKEN CUSTODY OF SHIKKI BANKA.
We've taken custody of Shikki Banka.
If you want him back alive, prepare ten million yen.
At noon tomorrow, come to the north-west outskirts of...
IF YOU WANT HIM BACK ALIVE, PREPARE TEN MILLION YEN.
WAY TO GO, BIG BROTHER.
Heh heh.
THERE'S NO WAY THEY'D BE TARGETING US FOR MONEY.
IT MUST BE SOME OLD GRUDGE.
NOW, WHAT EVER SHALL I DO...?
Hmm...

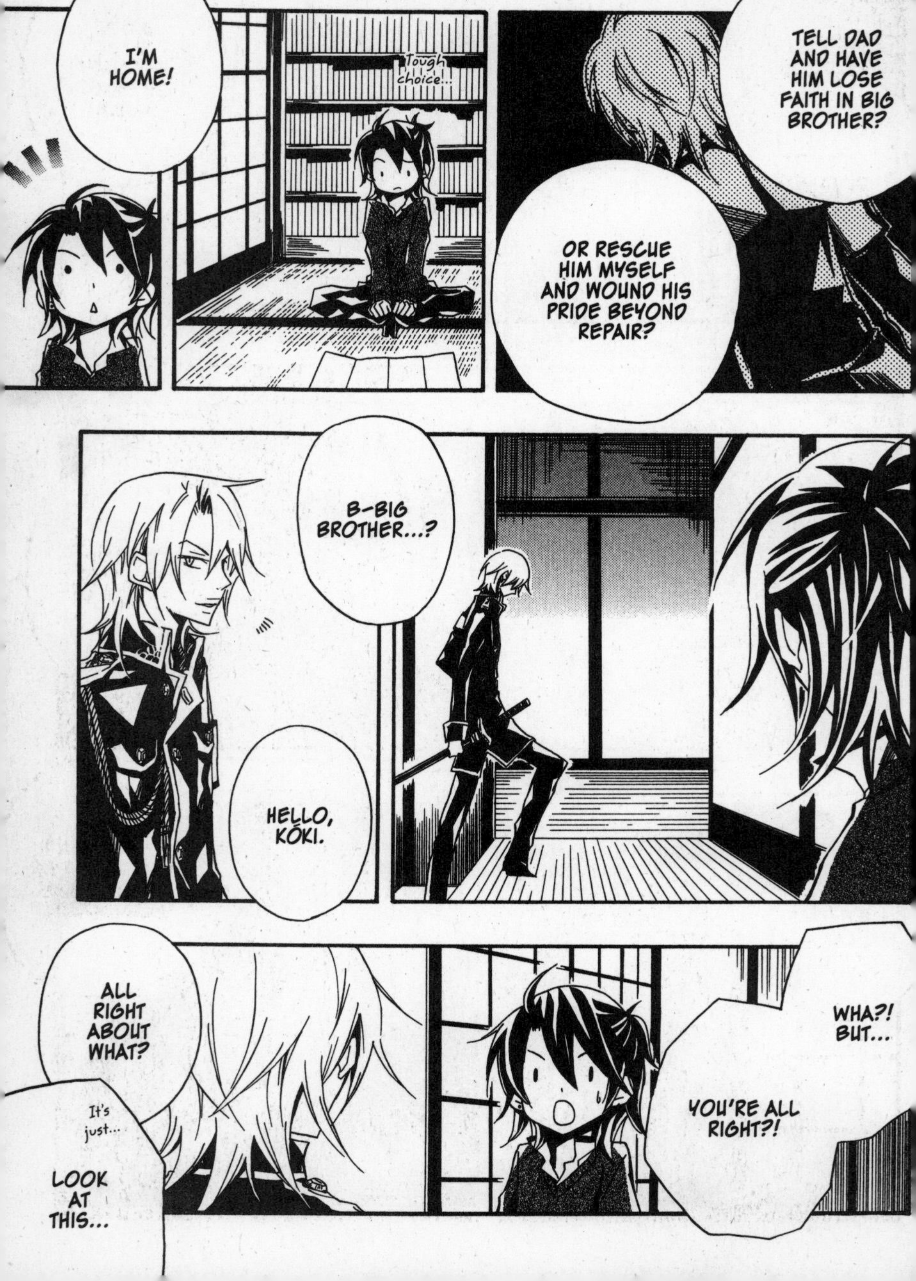
TELL DAD AND HAVE HIM LOSE FAITH IN BIG BROTHER?
OR RESCUE HIM MYSELF AND WOUND HIS PRIDE BEYOND REPAIR?
Tough choice...
I'M HOME!
B-BIG BROTHER...?
HELLO, KŌKI.
WHA?! BUT...
YOU'RE ALL RIGHT?!
ALL RIGHT ABOUT WHAT?
It's just...
LOOK AT THIS...

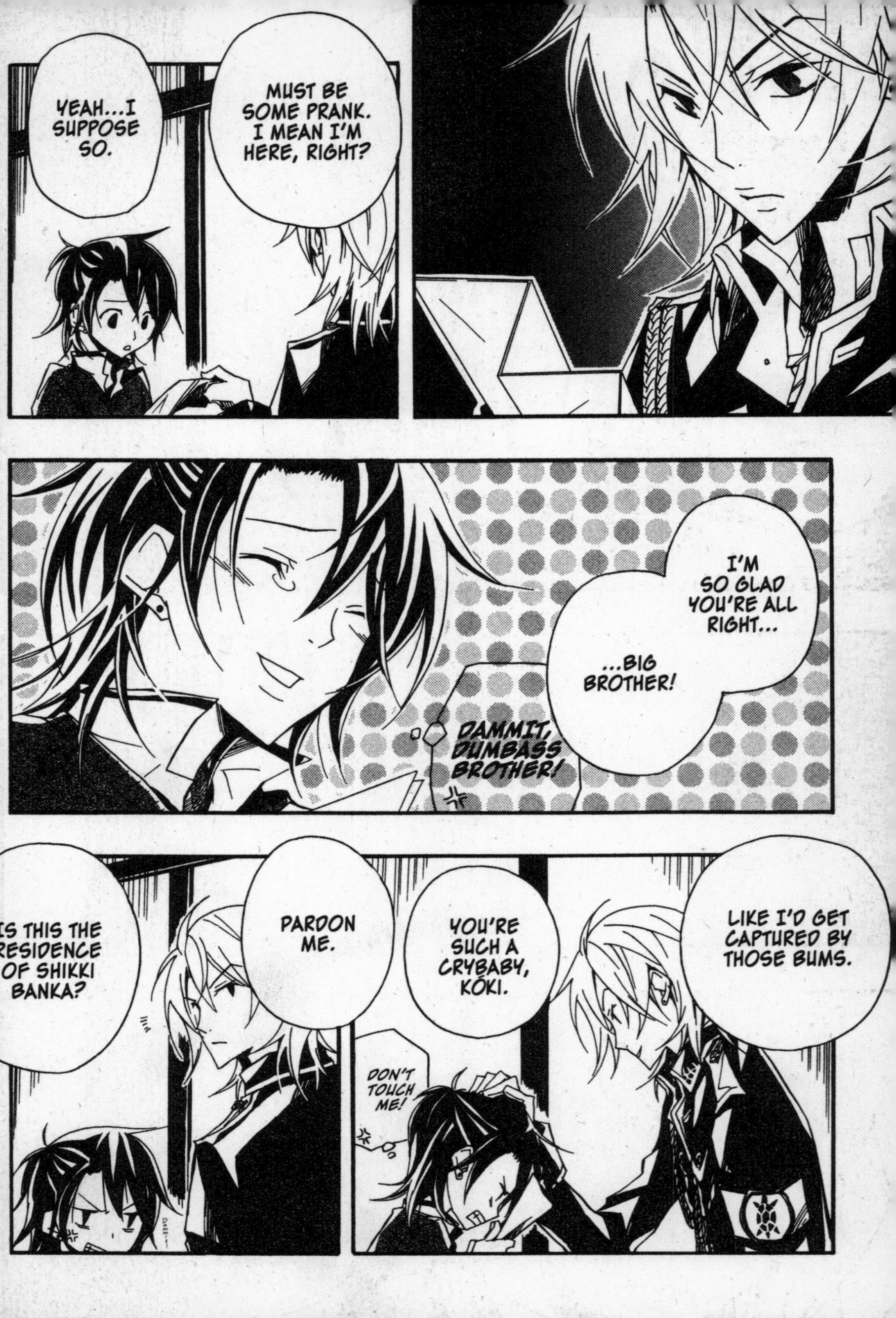
MUST BE SOME PRANK. I MEAN I'M HERE, RIGHT?
YEAH...I SUPPOSE SO.
I'M SO GLAD YOU'RE ALL RIGHT...
...BIG BROTHER!
DAMMIT, DUMBASS BROTHER!
LIKE I'D GET CAPTURED BY THOSE BUMS.
YOU'RE SUCH A CRYBABY, KŌKI.
DON'T TOUCH ME!
PARDON ME.
IS THIS THE RESIDENCE OF SHIKKI BANKA?

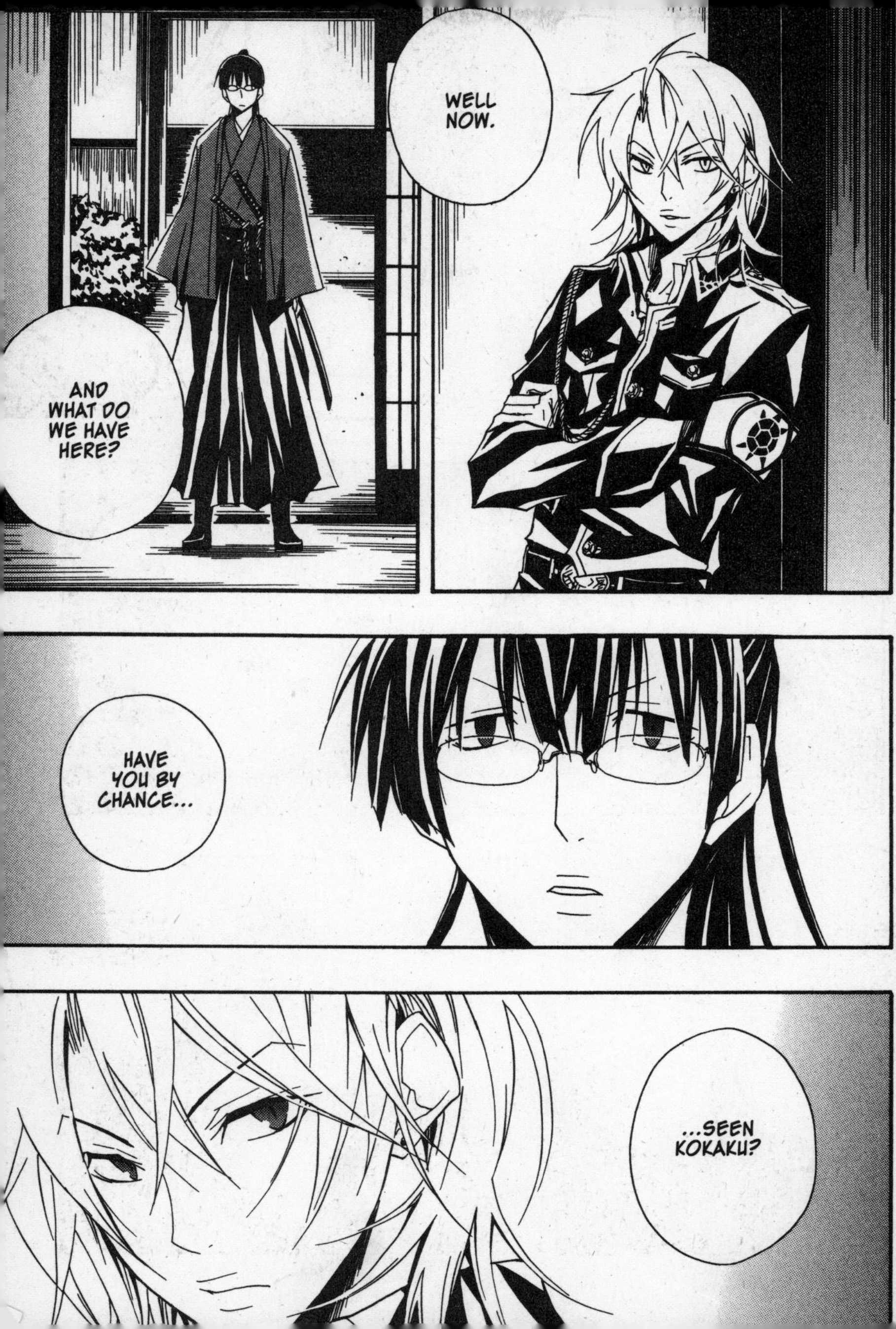
WELL NOW.
AND WHAT DO WE HAVE HERE?
HAVE YOU BY CHANCE...
...SEEN KOKAKU?

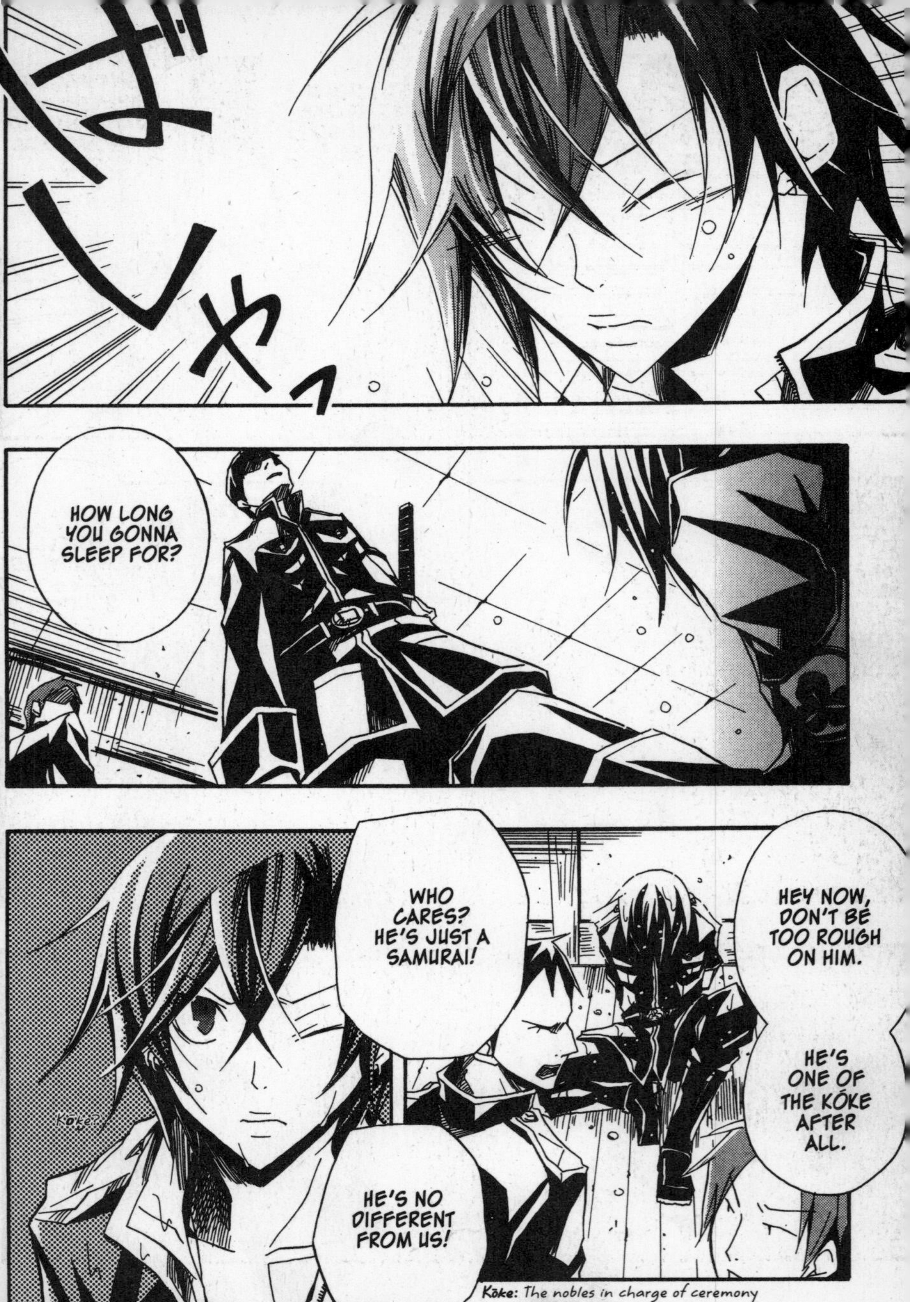
ばしゃっ
HOW LONG YOU GONNA SLEEP FOR?
HEY NOW, DON'T BE TOO ROUGH ON HIM.
HE'S ONE OF THE KŌKE AFTER ALL.
WHO CARES? HE'S JUST A SAMURAI!
Kōke?
HE'S NO DIFFERENT FROM US!

Kōke: The nobles in charge of ceremony and relaying imperial messages.

JUST BECAUSE THEY DELIVER MESSAGES TO THE IMPERIAL COURT...!
YOU LORD IT OVER US LIKE YOU'RE SO SPECIAL!
......
WELL, YOU'RE NOT SO HIGH AND MIGHTY NOW, ARE YOU?
WE'LL EVEN GET SOME RANSOM MONEY OUT OF IT. SERVES YOU RIGHT!
KIDNAPPING... I SEE.
SO THEY'VE MISTAKEN ME FOR ONE OF THE KŌKE.
WHAT IDIOTS!

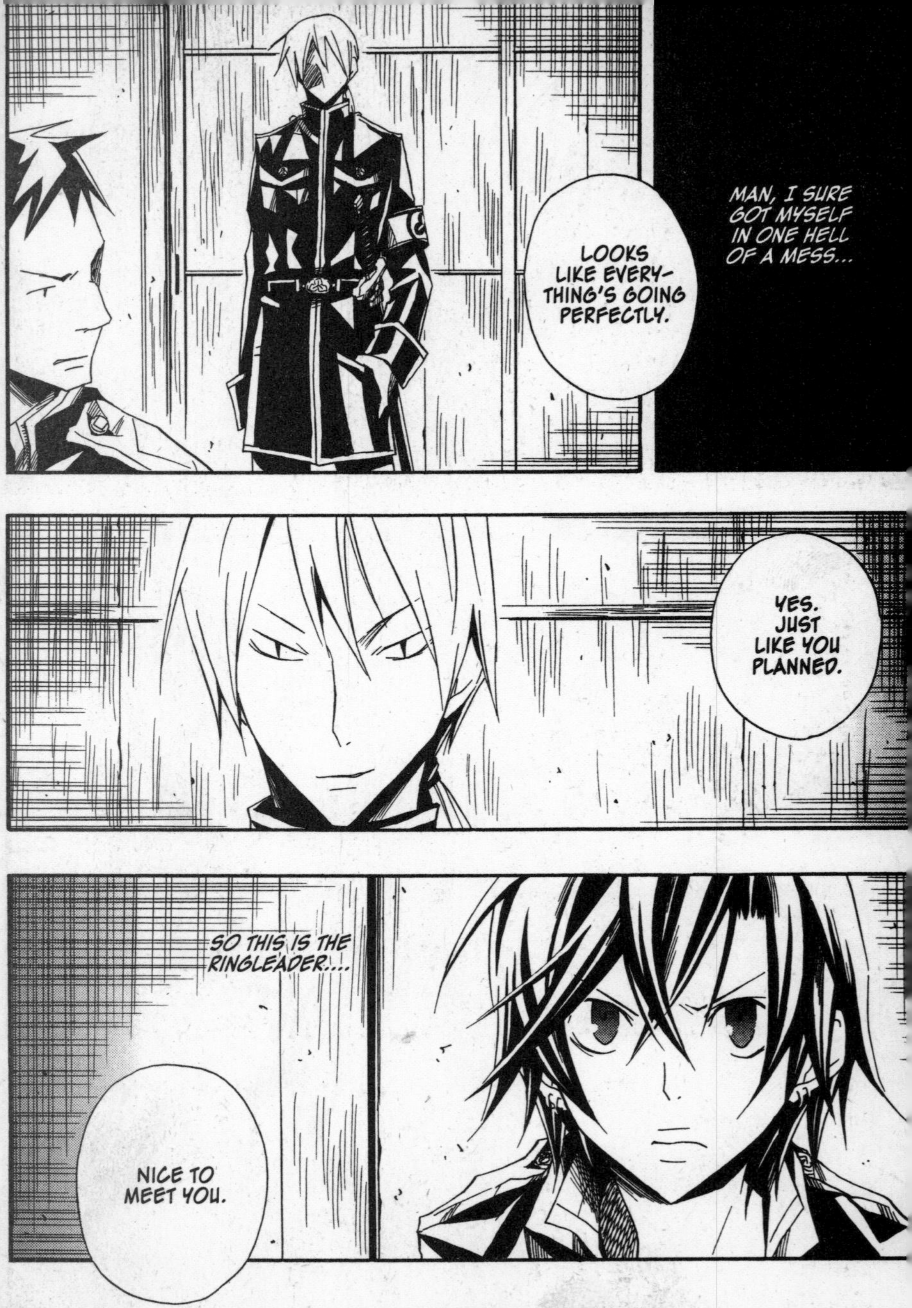
MAN, I SURE GOT MYSELF IN ONE HELL OF A MESS...
LOOKS LIKE EVERY-THING'S GOING PERFECTLY.
YES. JUST LIKE YOU PLANNED.
SO THIS IS THE RINGLEADER....
NICE TO MEET YOU.

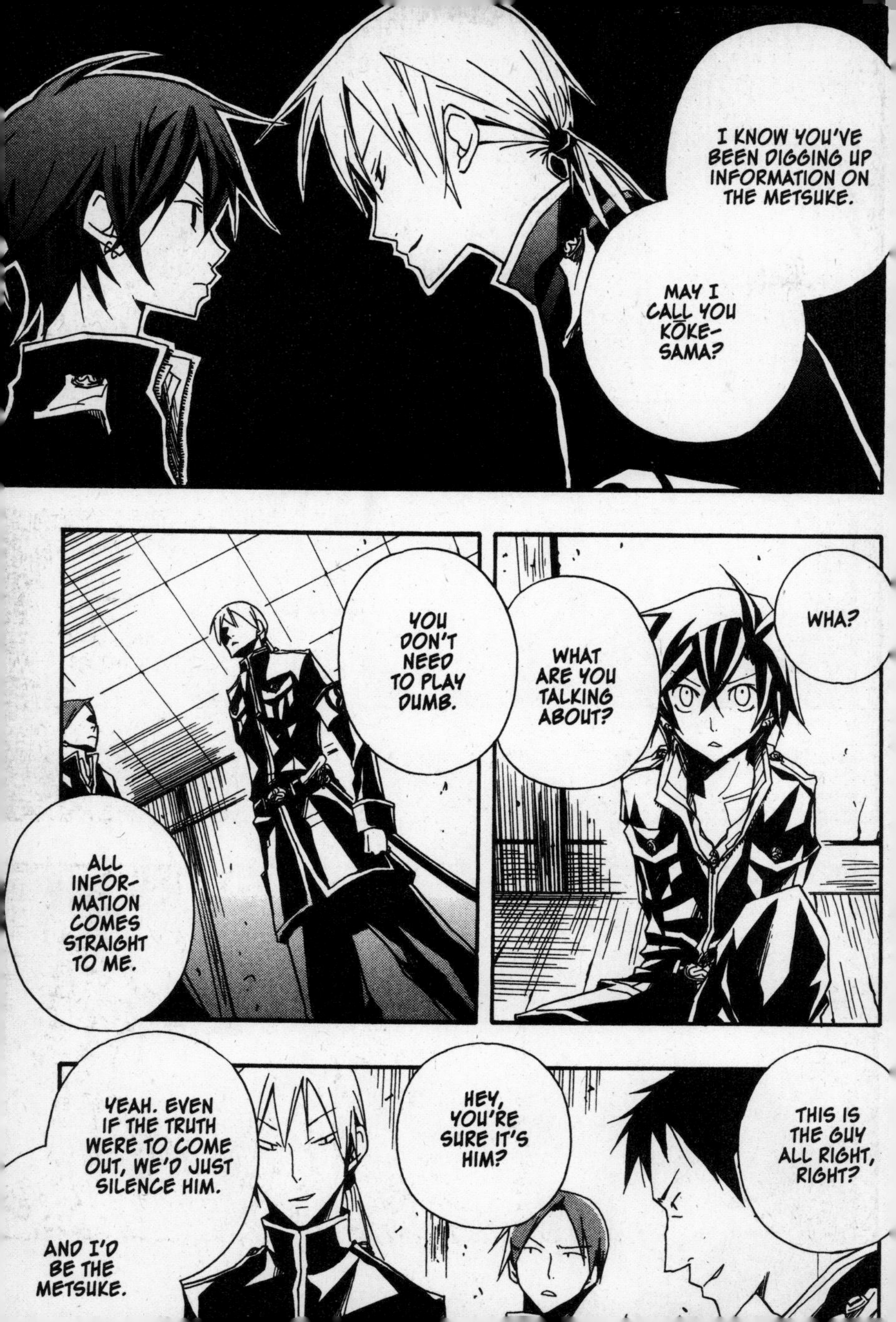
I KNOW YOU'VE BEEN DIGGING UP INFORMATION ON THE METSUKE.
MAY I CALL YOU KŌKE-SAMA?
WHA?
WHAT ARE YOU TALKING ABOUT?
YOU DON'T NEED TO PLAY DUMB.
ALL INFORMATION COMES STRAIGHT TO ME.
THIS IS THE GUY ALL RIGHT, RIGHT?
HEY, YOU'RE SURE IT'S HIM?
YEAH. EVEN IF THE TRUTH WERE TO COME OUT, WE'D JUST SILENCE HIM.
AND I'D BE THE METSUKE.

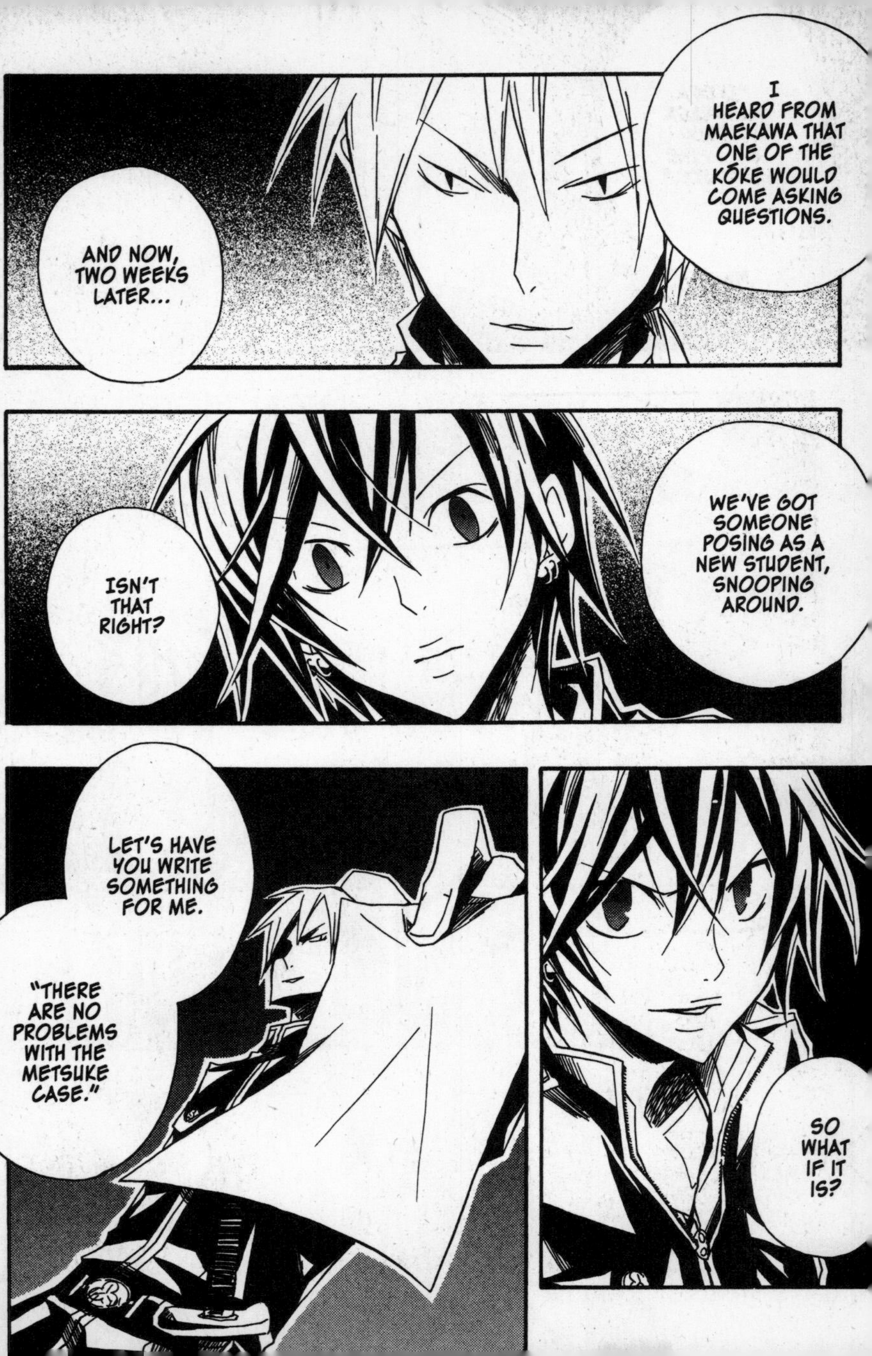
I HEARD FROM MAEKAWA THAT ONE OF THE KŌKE WOULD COME ASKING QUESTIONS.
AND NOW, TWO WEEKS LATER...
WE'VE GOT SOMEONE POSING AS A NEW STUDENT, SNOOPING AROUND.
ISN'T THAT RIGHT?
SO WHAT IF IT IS?
LET'S HAVE YOU WRITE SOMETHING FOR ME.
"THERE ARE NO PROBLEMS WITH THE METSUKE CASE."

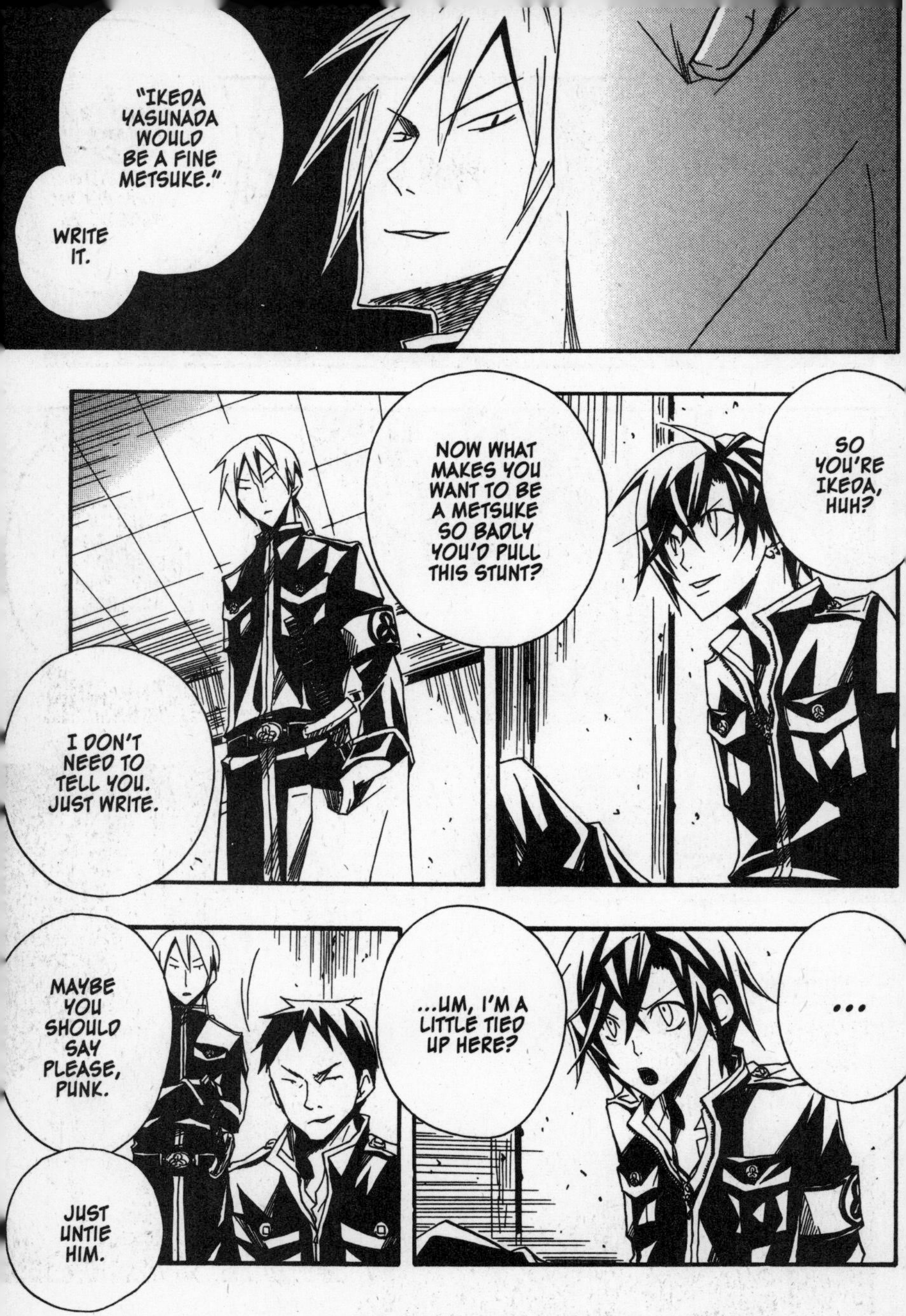
"IKEDA YASUNADA WOULD BE A FINE METSUKE."
WRITE IT.
SO YOU'RE IKEDA, HUH?
NOW WHAT MAKES YOU WANT TO BE A METSUKE SO BADLY YOU'D PULL THIS STUNT?
I DON'T NEED TO TELL YOU. JUST WRITE.
...
...UM, I'M A LITTLE TIED UP HERE?
MAYBE YOU SHOULD SAY PLEASE, PUNK.
JUST UNTIE HIM.

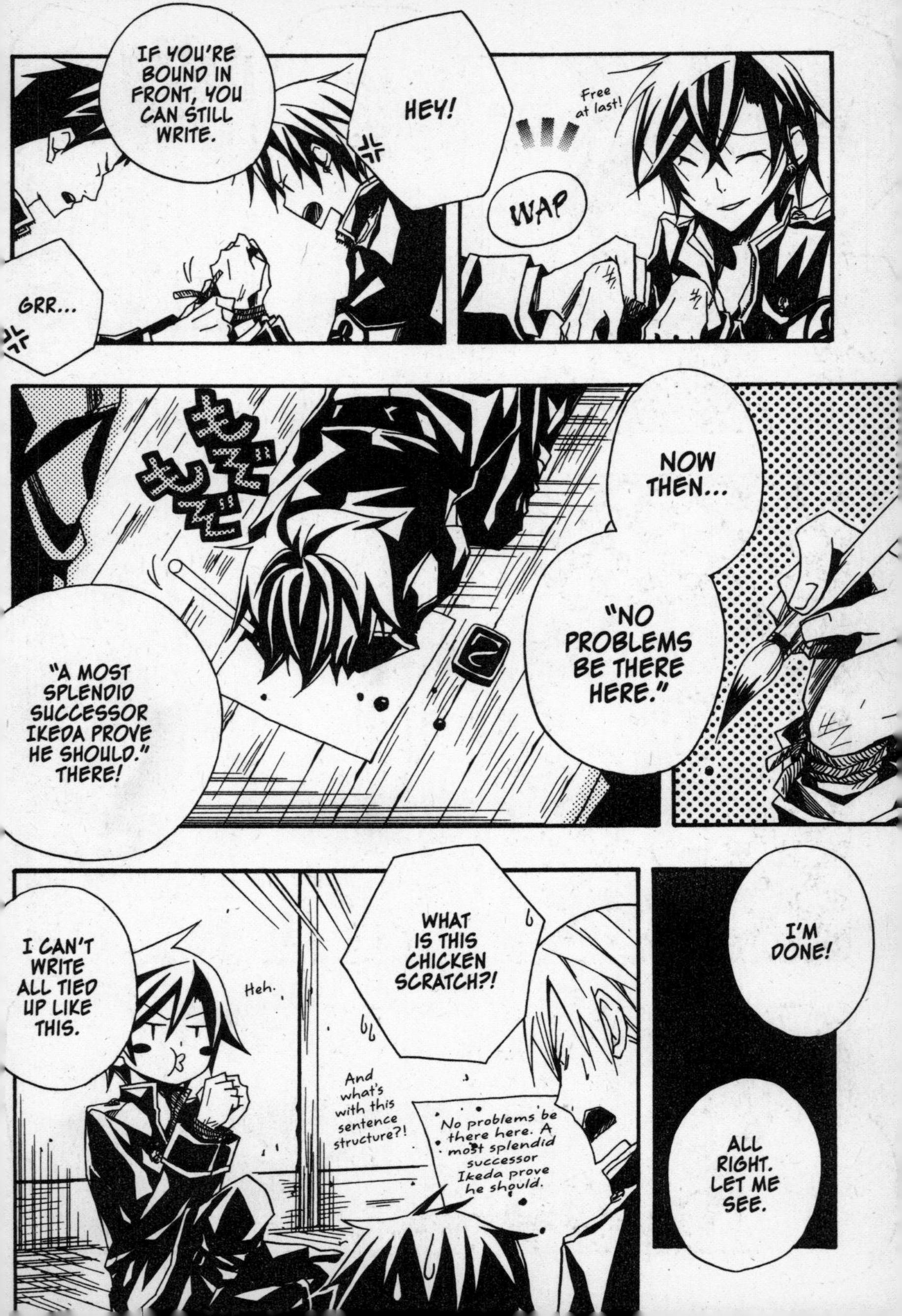
Free at last!
WAP
HEY!
IF YOU'RE BOUND IN FRONT, YOU CAN STILL WRITE.
GRR...
NOW THEN...
"NO PROBLEMS BE THERE HERE."
"A MOST SPLENDID SUCCESSOR IKEDA PROVE HE SHOULD." THERE!
I'M DONE!
ALL RIGHT. LET ME SEE.
WHAT IS THIS CHICKEN SCRATCH?!
And what's with this sentence structure?!
No problems be there here. A most splendid successor Ikeda prove he should.
I CAN'T WRITE ALL TIED UP LIKE THIS.
Heh.

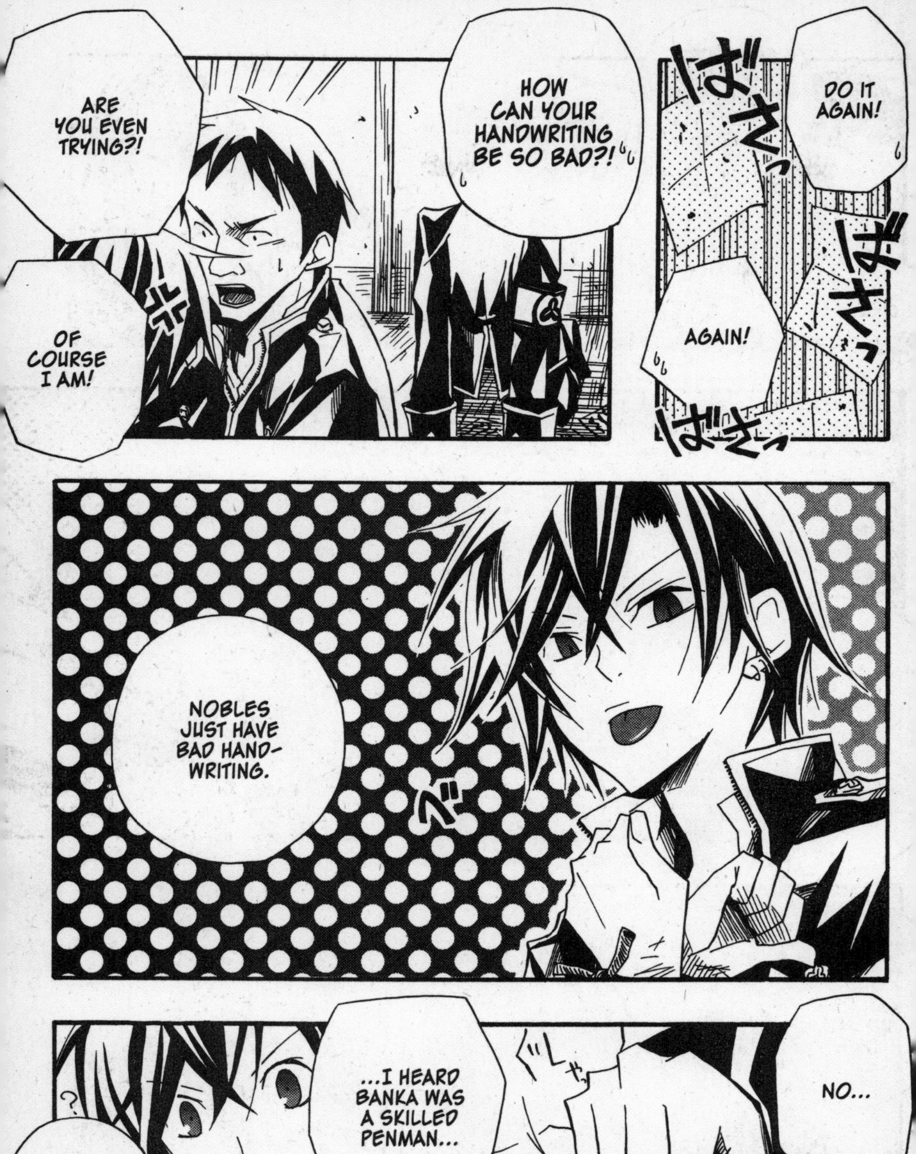
DO IT AGAIN!
ばさっ
ばさっ
AGAIN!
ばさっ
HOW CAN YOUR HANDWRITING BE SO BAD?!
ARE YOU EVEN TRYING?!
OF COURSE I AM!
NOBLES JUST HAVE BAD HAND-WRITING.
べ
NO...
...I HEARD BANKA WAS A SKILLED PENMAN...
BANKA?

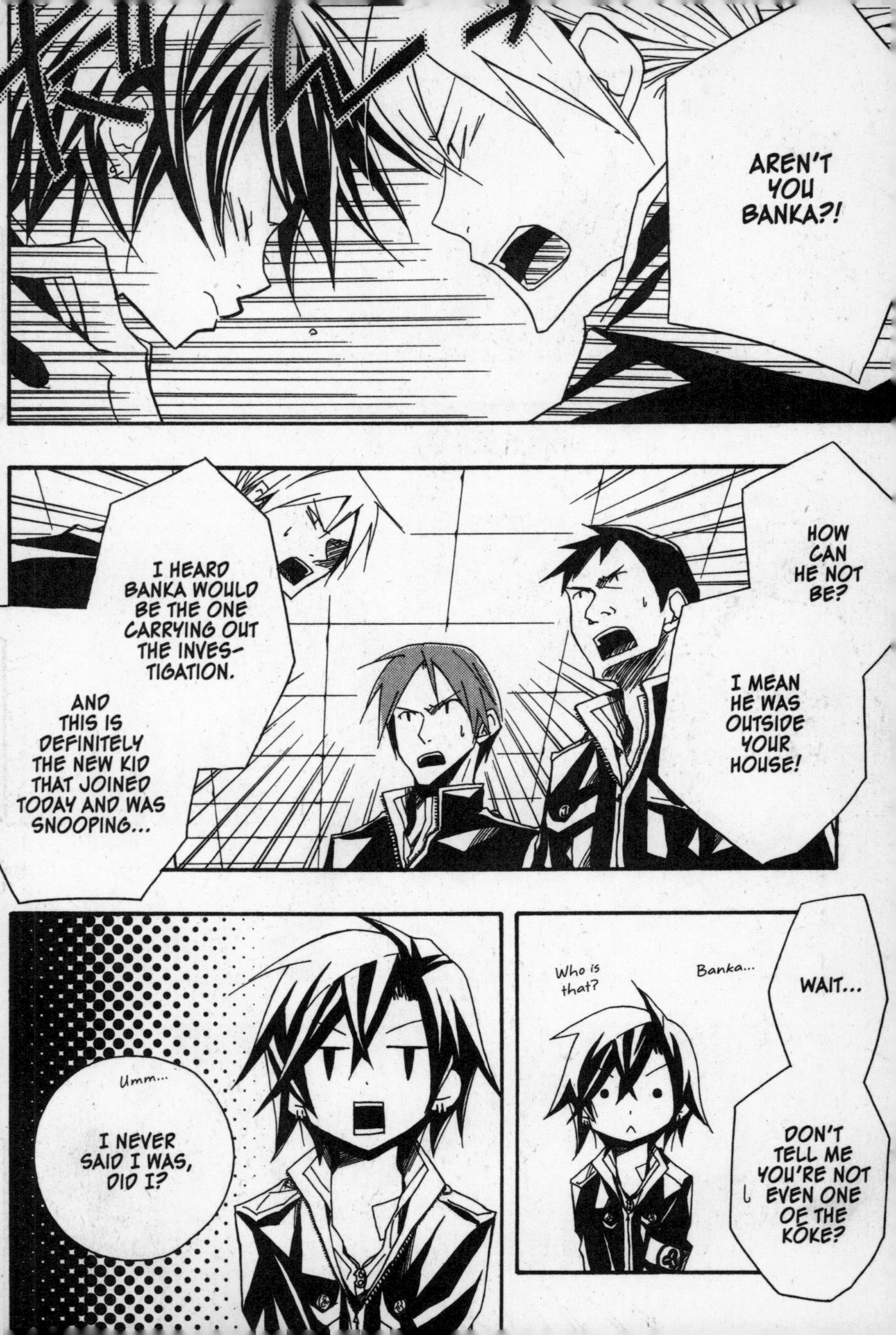
AREN'T YOU BANKA?!
HOW CAN HE NOT BE?
I MEAN HE WAS OUTSIDE YOUR HOUSE!
I HEARD BANKA WOULD BE THE ONE CARRYING OUT THE INVES-TIGATION.
AND THIS IS DEFINITELY THE NEW KID THAT JOINED TODAY AND WAS SNOOPING...
WAIT...
Banka...
Who is that?
DON'T TELL ME YOU'RE NOT EVEN ONE OF THE KŌKE?
Umm...
I NEVER SAID I WAS, DID I?

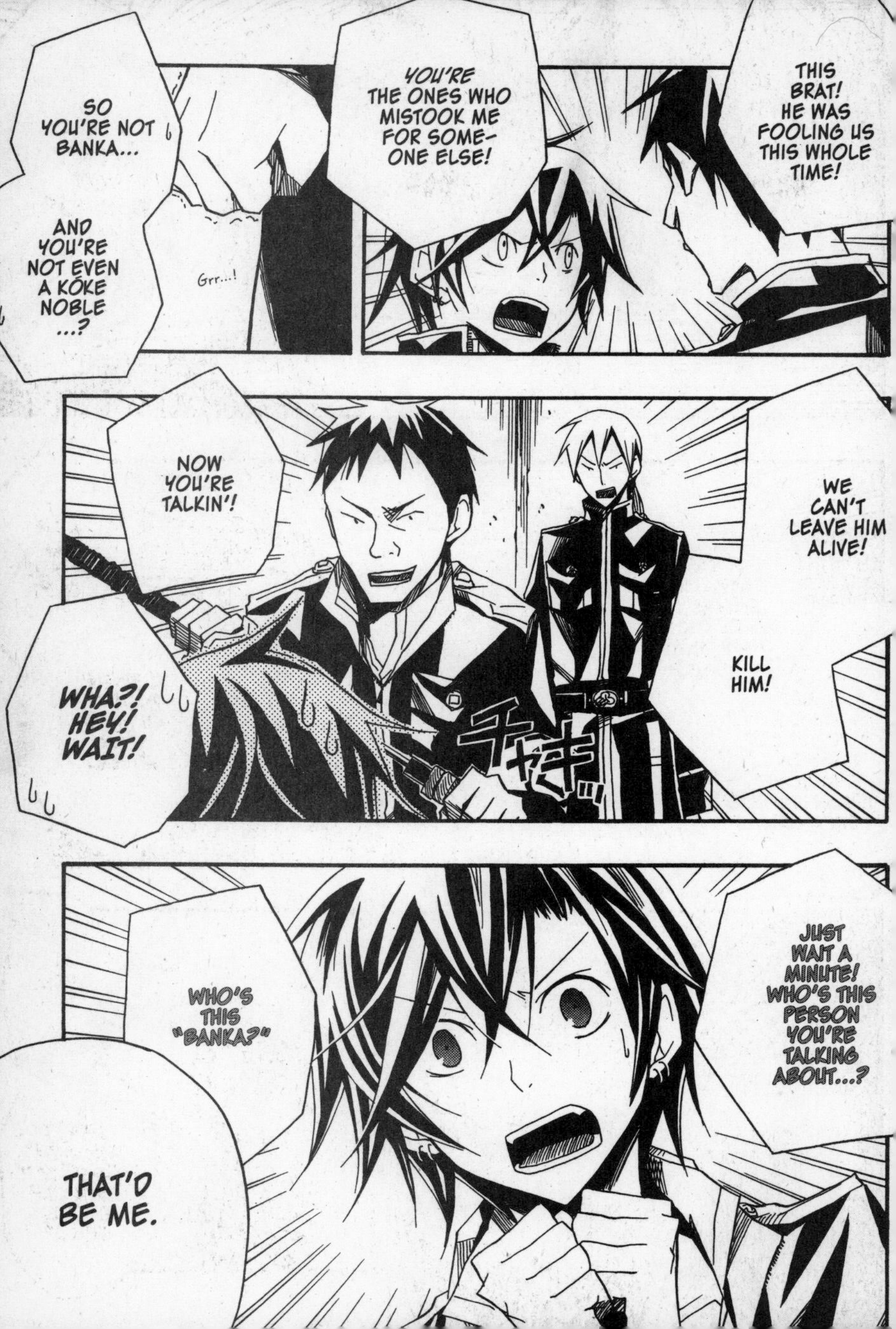
THIS BRAT! HE WAS FOOLING US THIS WHOLE TIME!
YOU'RE THE ONES WHO MISTOOK ME FOR SOME-ONE ELSE!
SO YOU'RE NOT BANKA...
AND YOU'RE NOT EVEN A KÓKE NOBLE ...?
Grr...!
WE CAN'T LEAVE HIM ALIVE!
KILL HIM!
NOW YOU'RE TALKIN'!
チャキッ
WHA?! HEY! WAIT!
JUST WAIT A MINUTE! WHO'S THIS PERSON YOU'RE TALKING ABOUT...?
WHO'S THIS "BANKA?"
THAT'D BE ME.

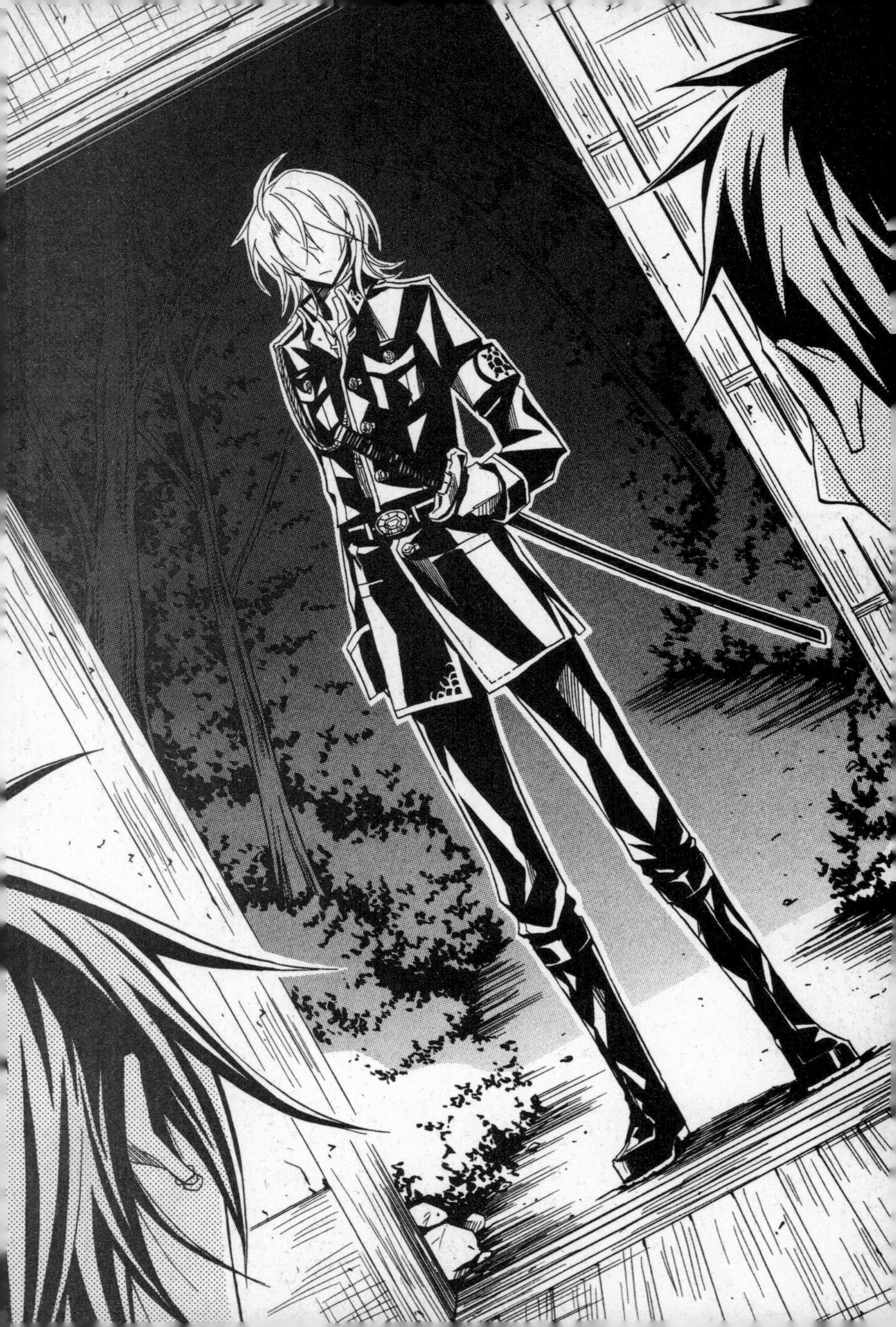

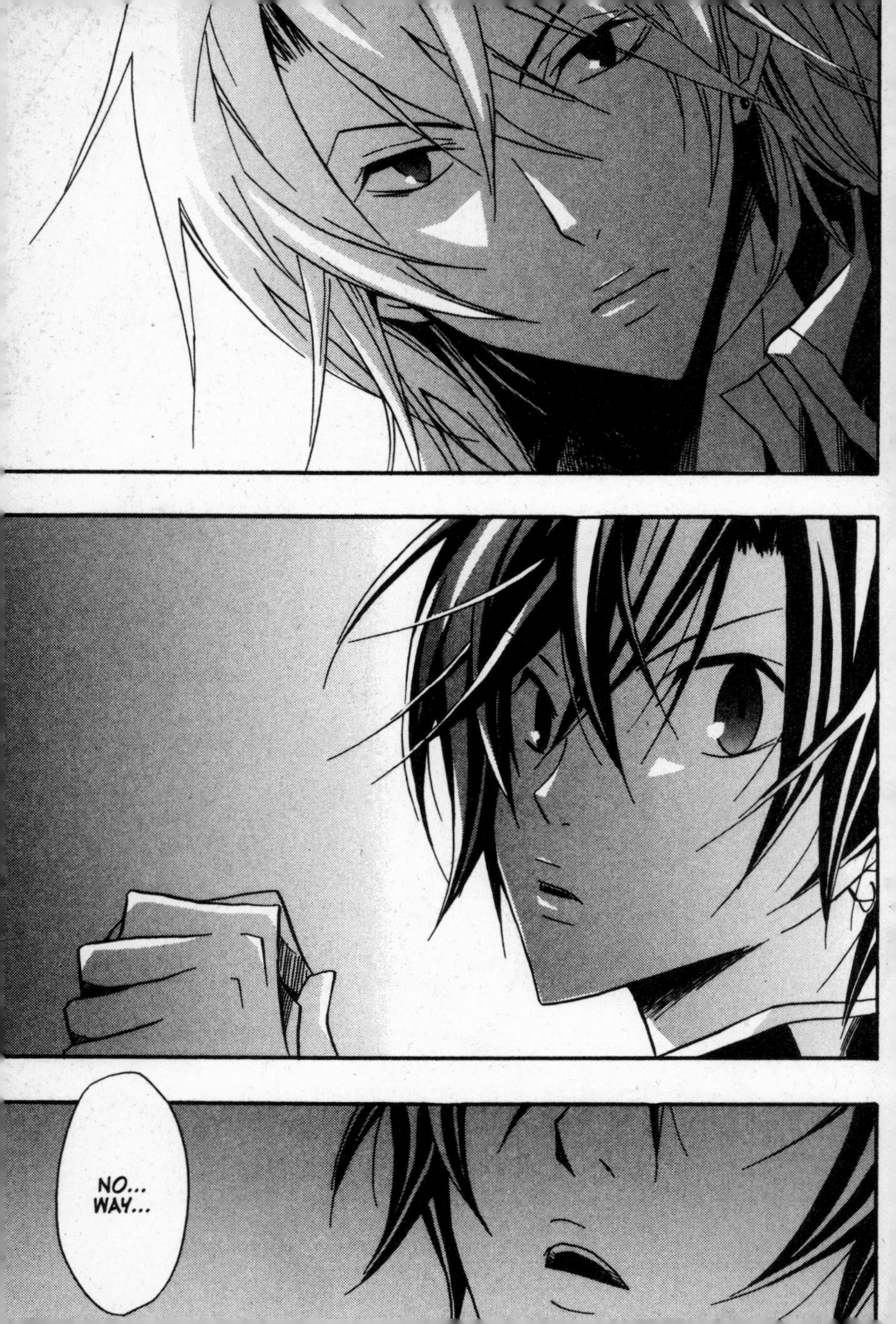
NO... WAY...

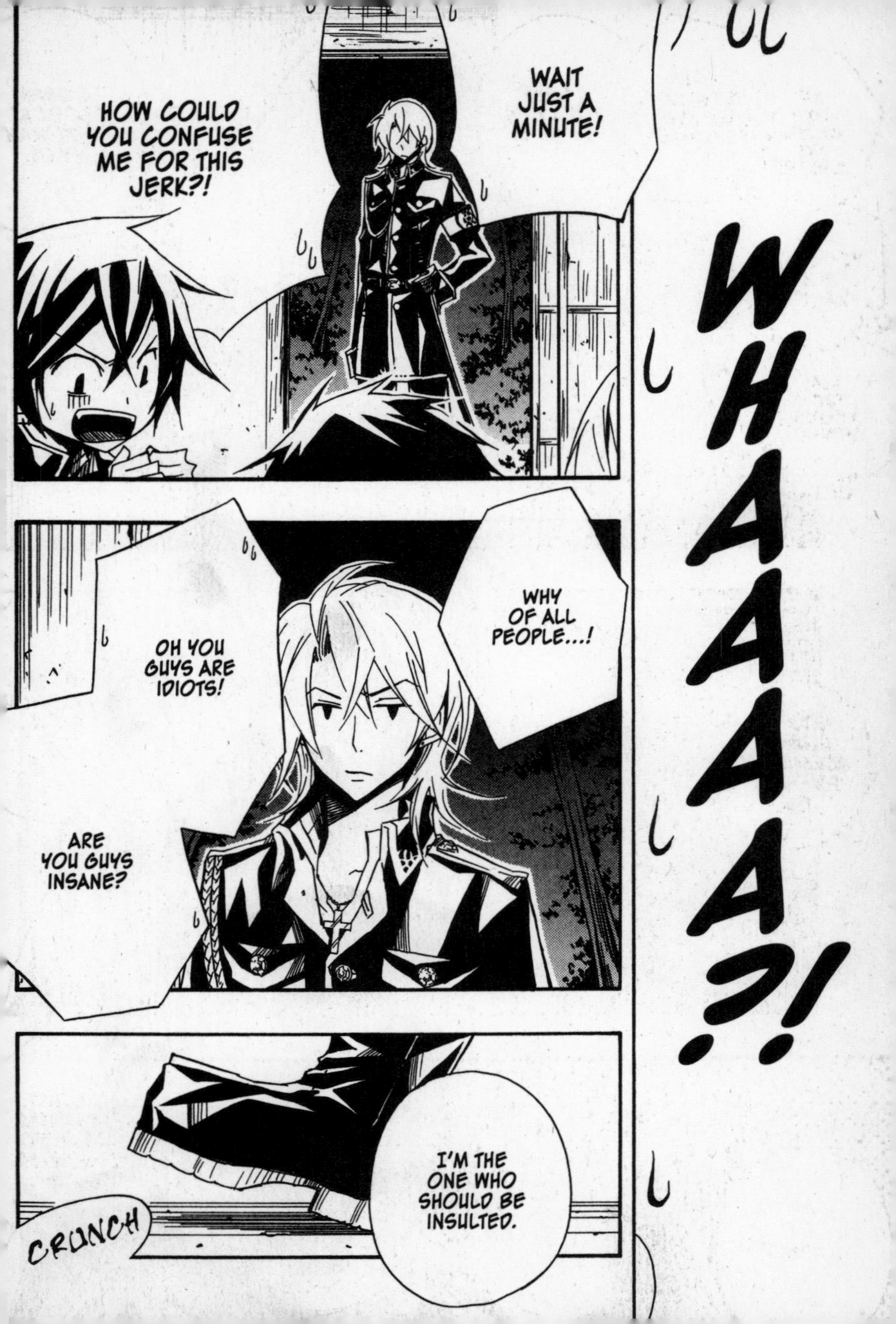
WHAAAA?!
WAIT JUST A MINUTE!
HOW COULD YOU CONFUSE ME FOR THIS JERK?!
WHY OF ALL PEOPLE...!
OH YOU GUYS ARE IDIOTS!
ARE YOU GUYS INSANE?
I'M THE ONE WHO SHOULD BE INSULTED.
CRUNCH

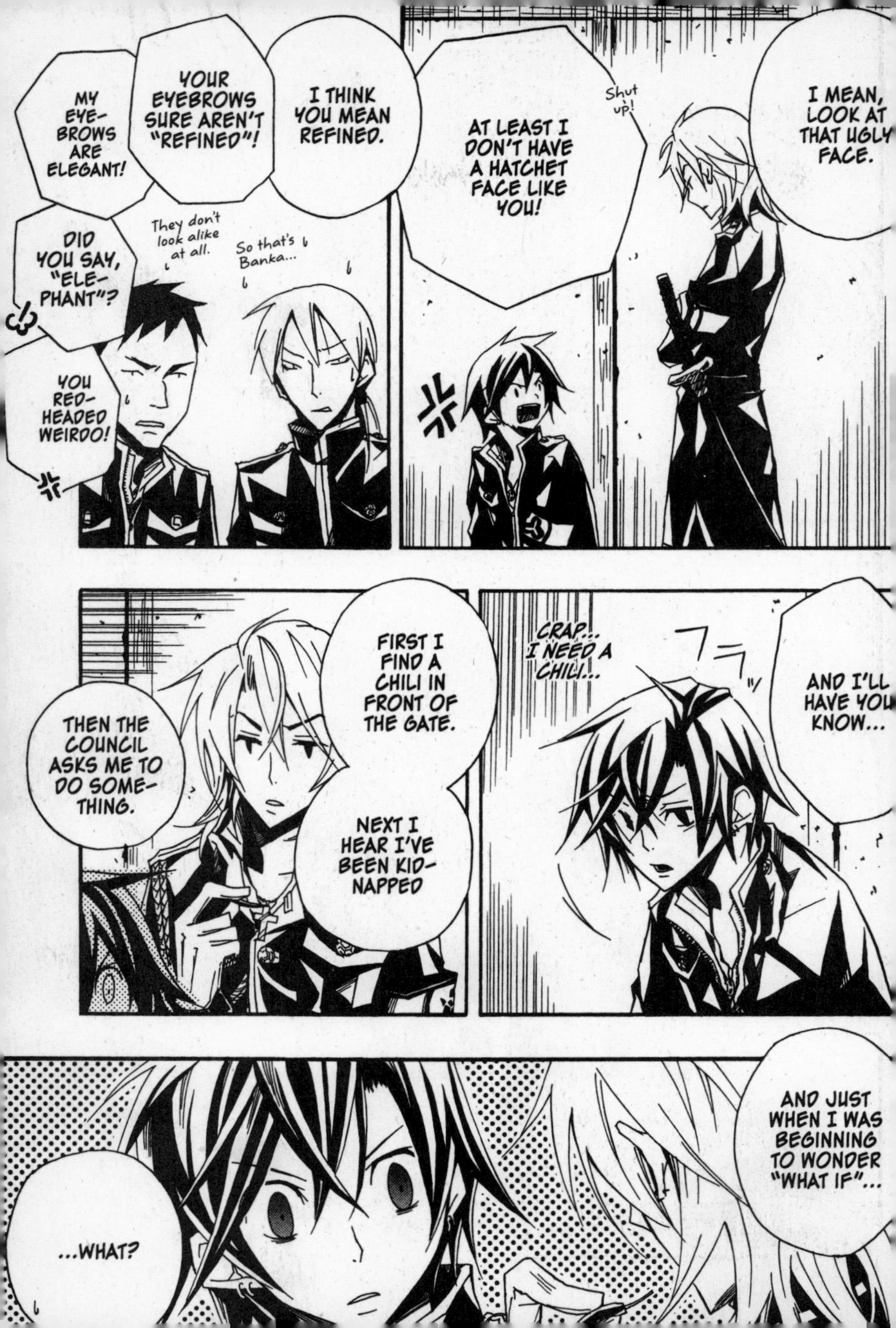
I MEAN, LOOK AT THAT UGLY FACE.
AT LEAST I DON'T HAVE A HATCHET FACE LIKE YOU!
Shut up!
I THINK YOU MEAN REFINED.
YOUR EYEBROWS SURE AREN'T "REFINED"!
MY EYE-BROWS ARE ELEGANT!
So that's Banka...
They don't look alike at all.
DID YOU SAY, "ELE-PHANT"?
YOU RED-HEADED WEIRDO!
AND I'LL HAVE YOU KNOW...
CRAP... I NEED A CHILI...
FIRST I FIND A CHILI IN FRONT OF THE GATE.
THEN THE COUNCIL ASKS ME TO DO SOME-THING.
NEXT I HEAR I'VE BEEN KID-NAPPED
AND JUST WHEN I WAS BEGINNING TO WONDER "WHAT IF"...
...WHAT?

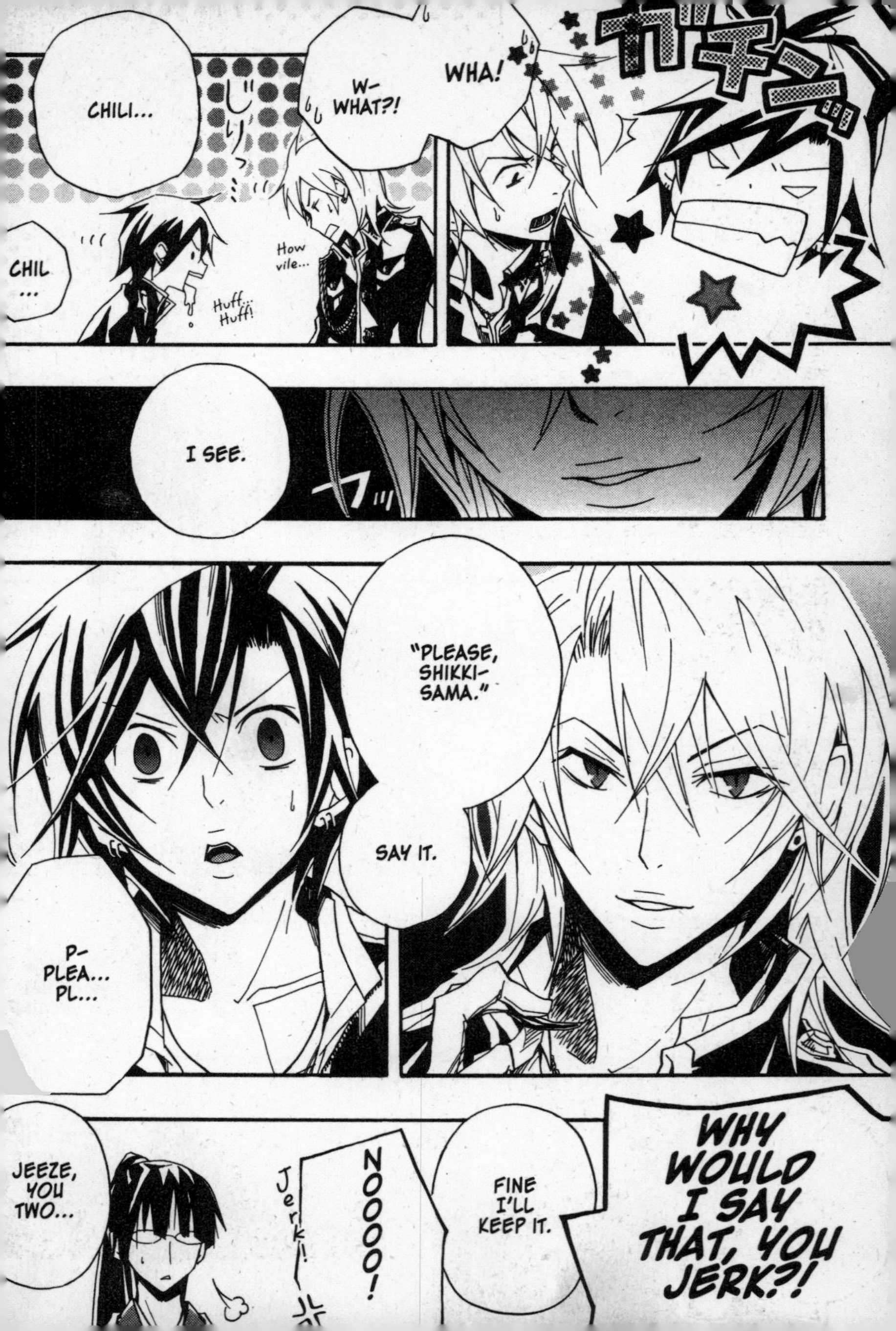
WHA!
W- WHAT?!
CHILI...
How vile...
CHIL ...
Huff... Huff!
I SEE.
"PLEASE, SHIKKI-SAMA."
SAY IT.
P- PLEA... PL...
WHY WOULD I SAY THAT, YOU JERK?!
FINE I'LL KEEP IT.
NOOOO!
Jerk!
JEEZE, YOU TWO...

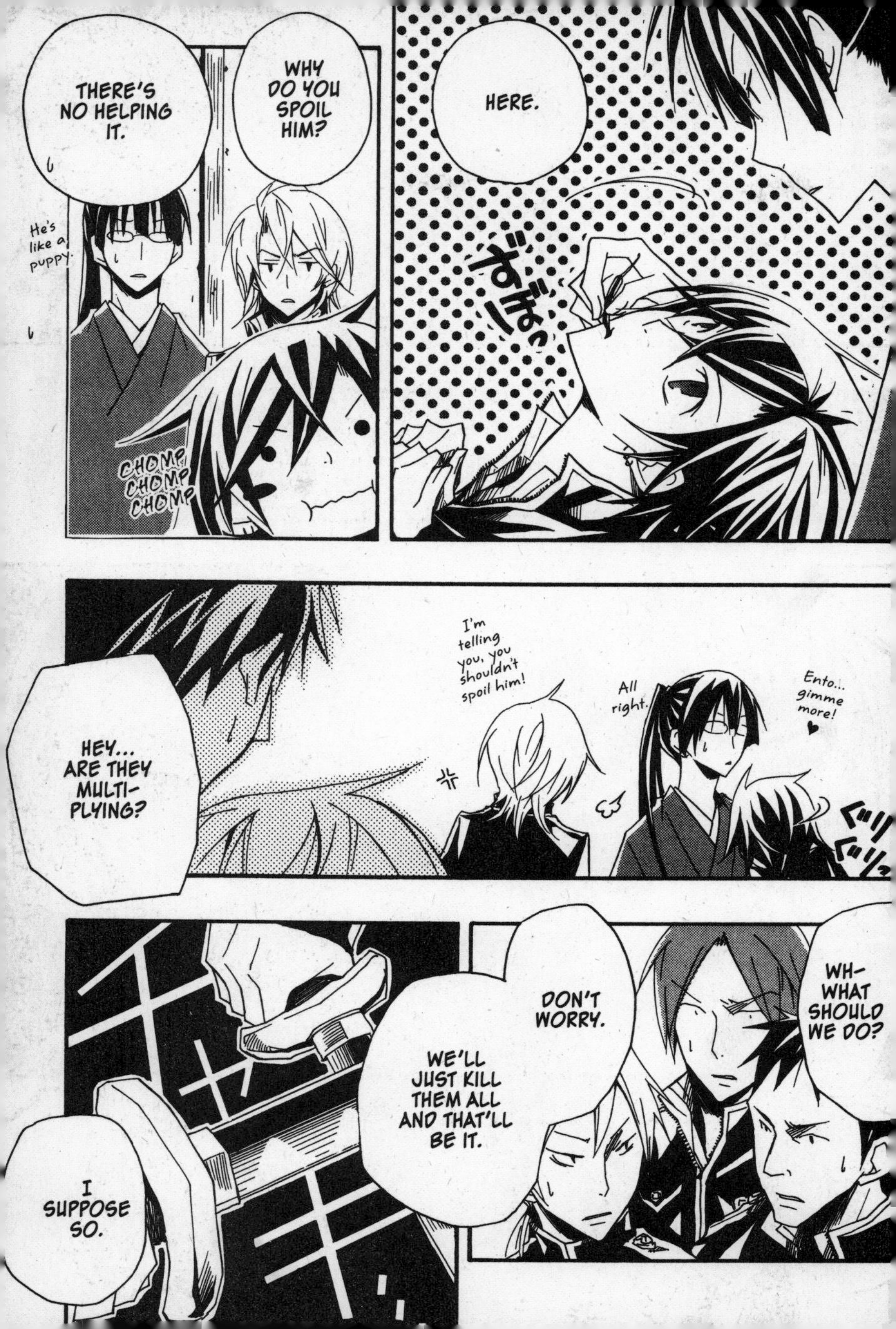
HERE.
ずぼっ
WHY DO YOU SPOIL HIM?
THERE'S NO HELPING IT.
He's like a puppy.
CHOMP CHOMP CHOMP
ぐりぐり
Ento... gimme more!
All right.
I'm telling you, you shouldn't spoil him!
HEY... ARE THEY MULTI-PLYING?
WH-WHAT SHOULD WE DO?
DON'T WORRY.
WE'LL JUST KILL THEM ALL AND THAT'LL BE IT.
I SUPPOSE SO.

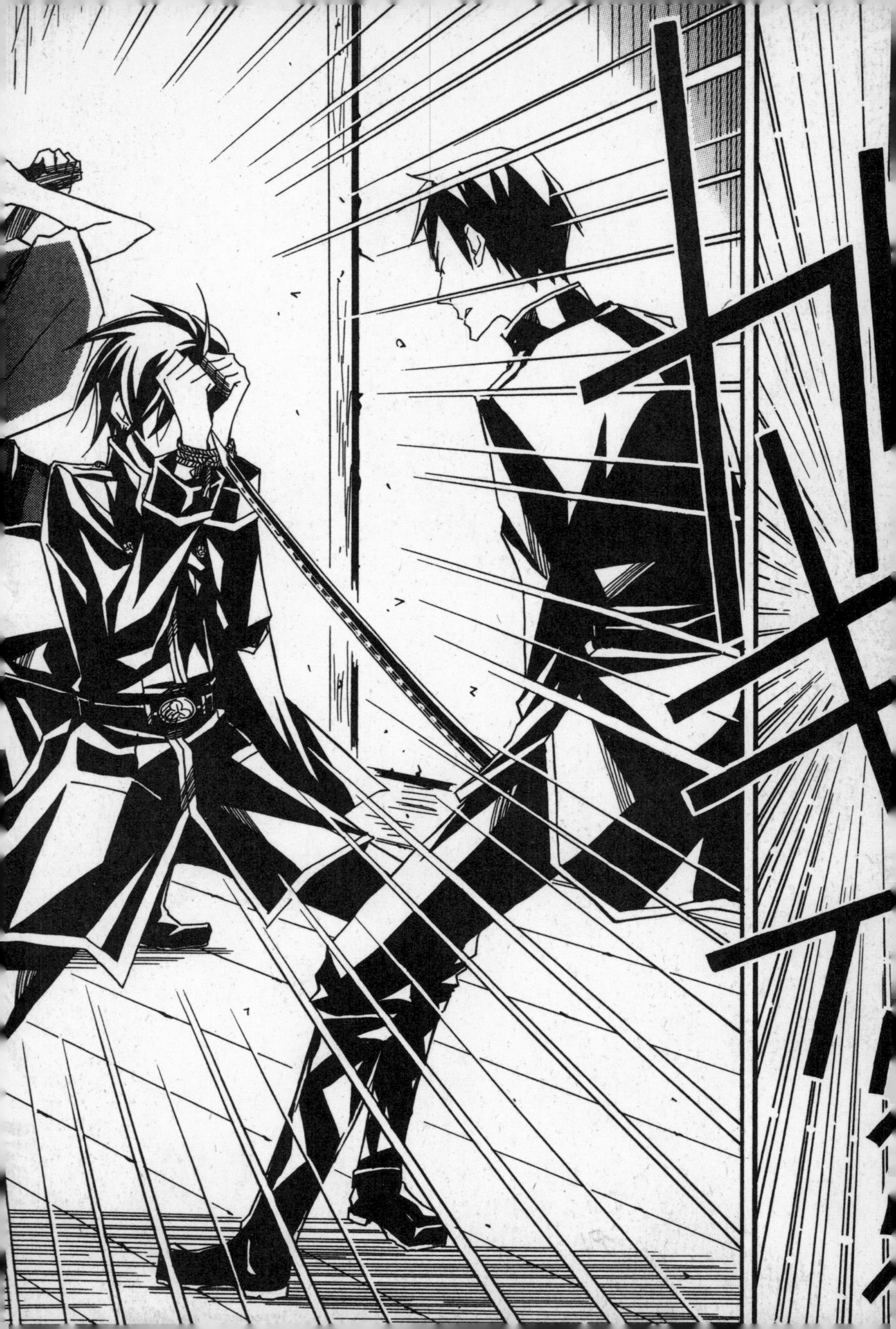

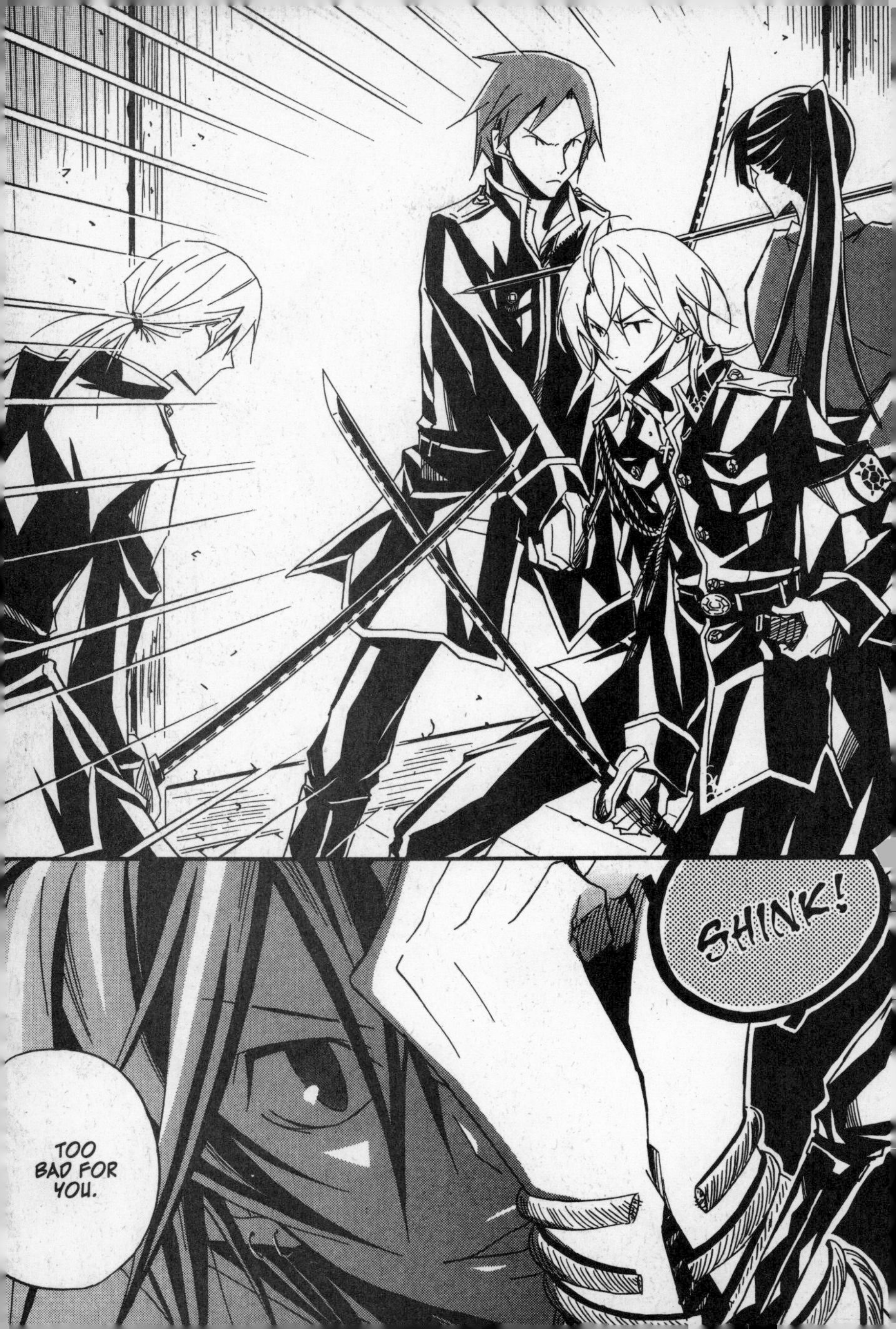
SHINK!
TOO BAD FOR YOU.

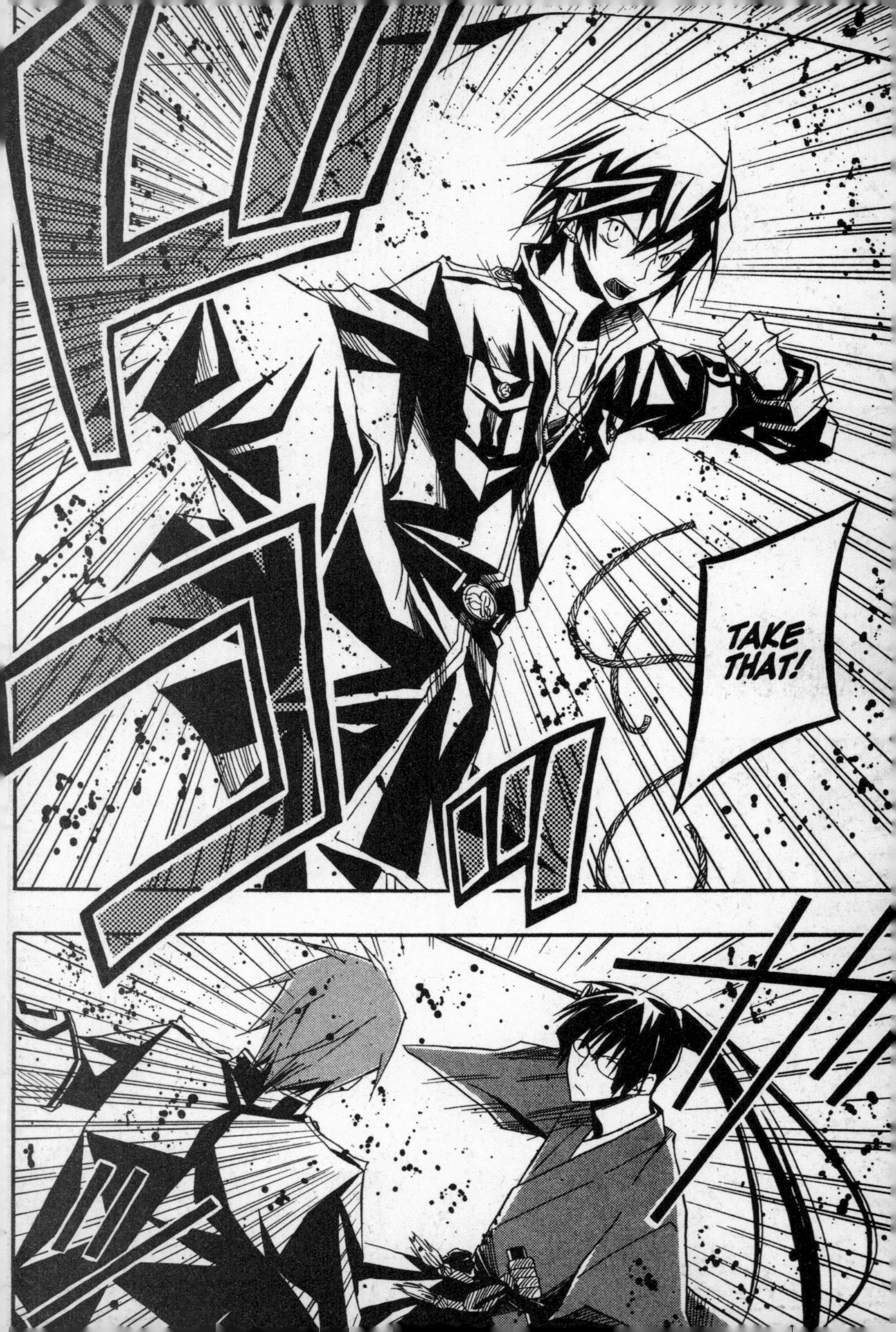
TAKE THAT!

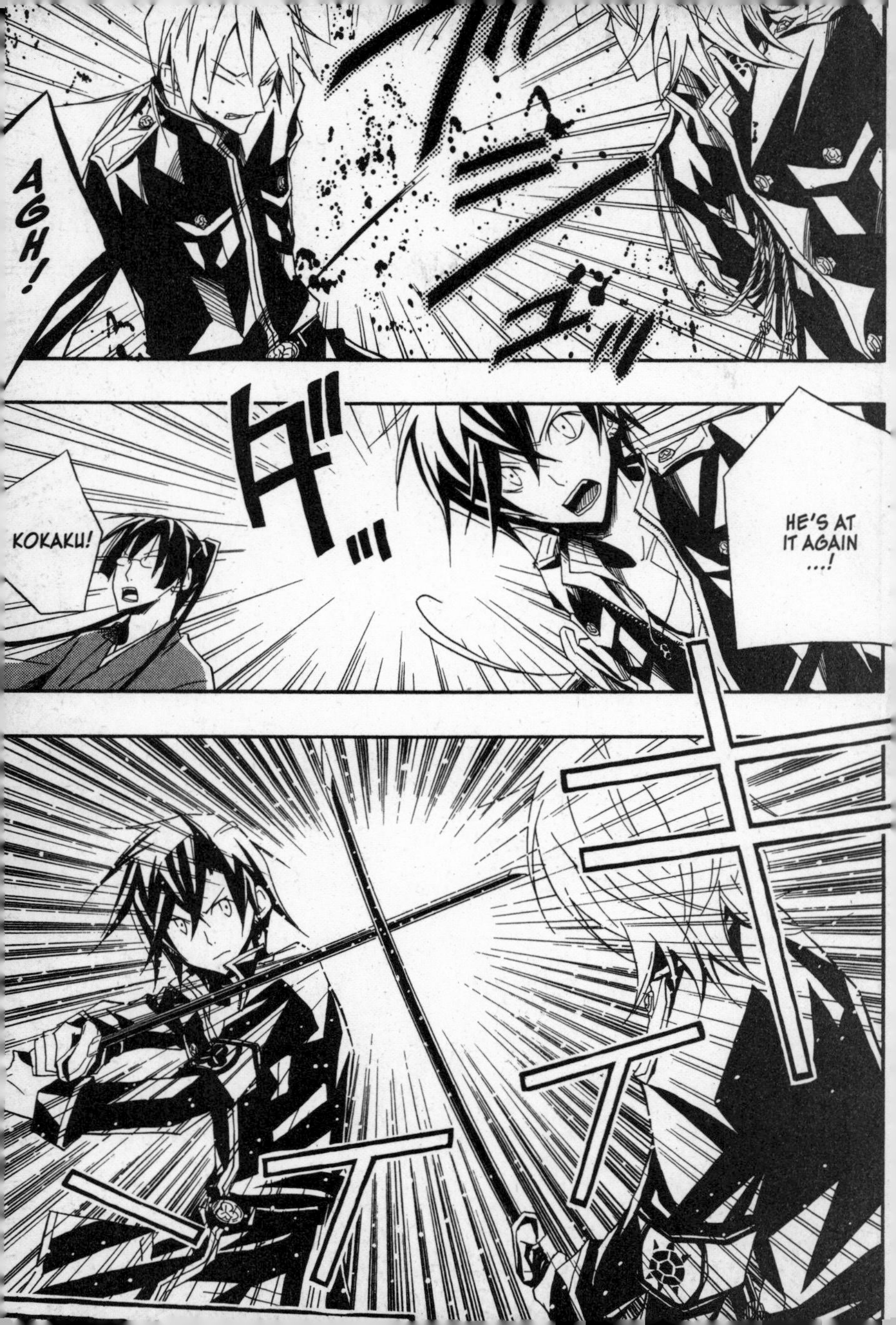
AGH!
HE'S AT IT AGAIN ...!
KOKAKU!

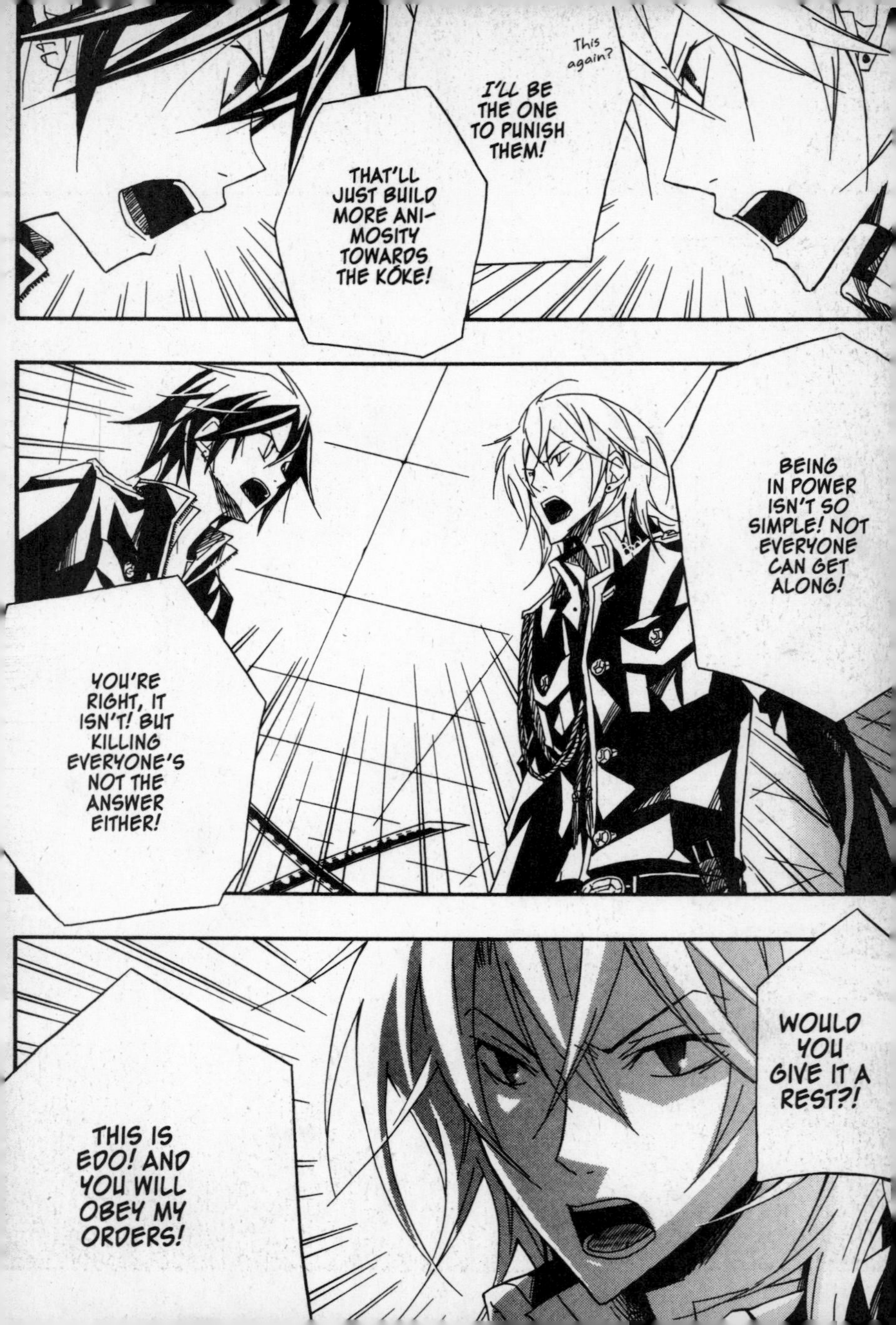
This again?
I'LL BE THE ONE TO PUNISH THEM!
THAT'LL JUST BUILD MORE ANI-MOSITY TOWARDS THE KŌKE!
BEING IN POWER ISN'T SO SIMPLE! NOT EVERYONE CAN GET ALONG!
YOU'RE RIGHT, IT ISN'T! BUT KILLING EVERYONE'S NOT THE ANSWER EITHER!
WOULD YOU GIVE IT A REST?!
THIS IS EDO! AND YOU WILL OBEY MY ORDERS!

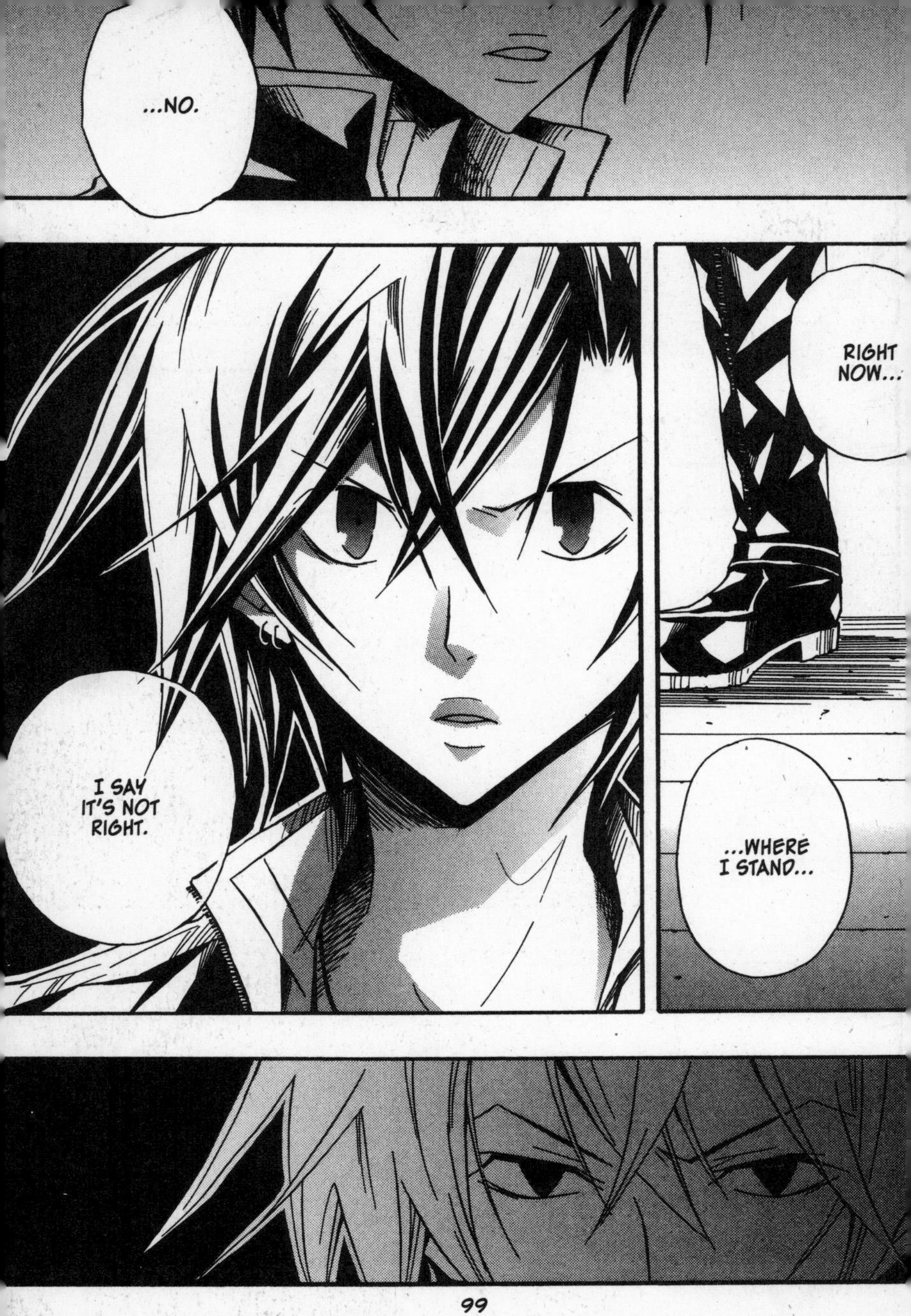
...NO.
RIGHT NOW...
...WHERE I STAND...
I SAY IT'S NOT RIGHT.

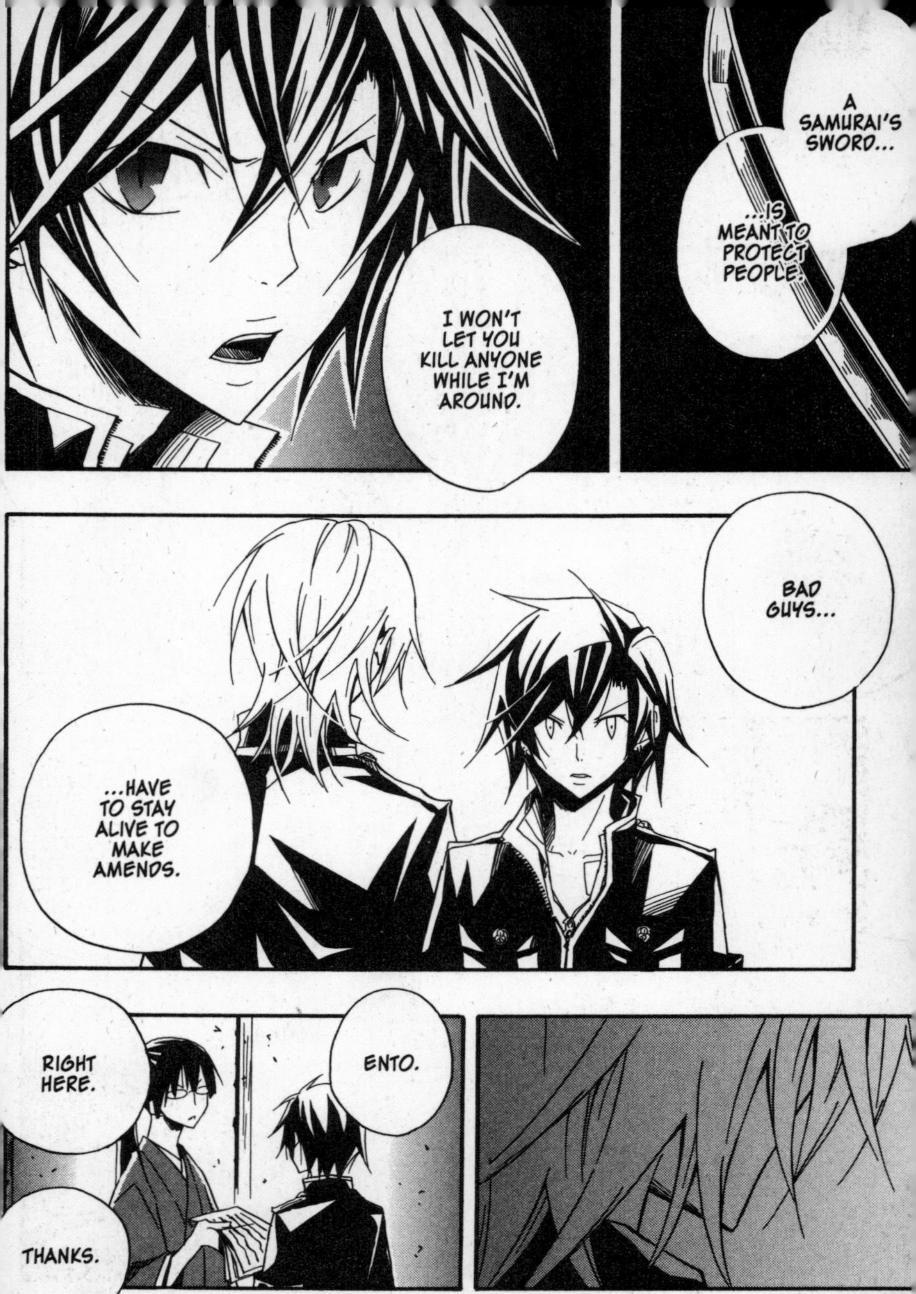
A SAMURAI'S SWORD...
...IS MEANT TO PROTECT PEOPLE.
I WON'T LET YOU KILL ANYONE WHILE I'M AROUND.
BAD GUYS...
...HAVE TO STAY ALIVE TO MAKE AMENDS.
ENTO.
RIGHT HERE.
THANKS.

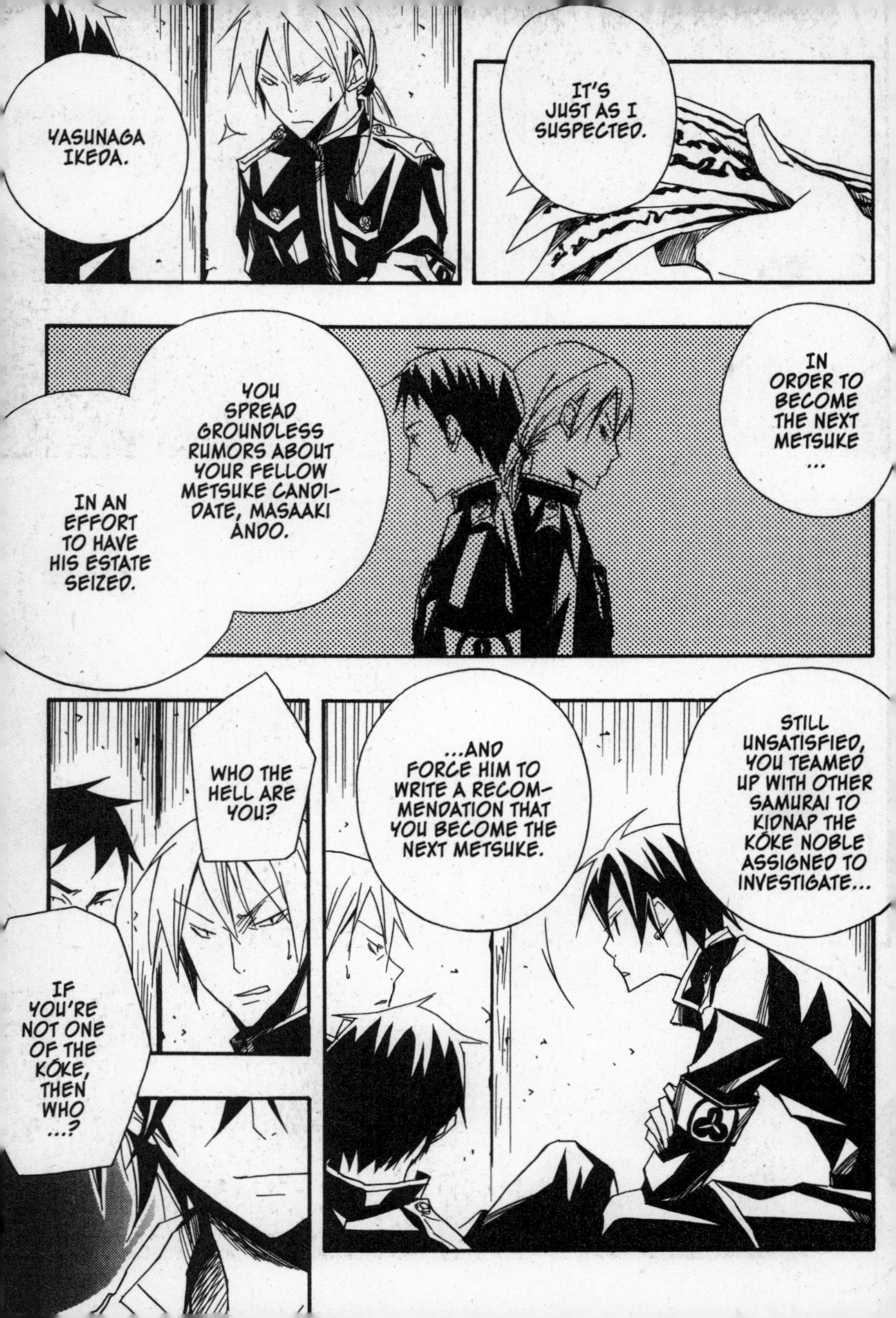
IT'S JUST AS I SUSPECTED.
YASUNAGA IKEDA.
IN ORDER TO BECOME THE NEXT METSUKE...
YOU SPREAD GROUNDLESS RUMORS ABOUT YOUR FELLOW METSUKE CANDIDATE, MASAAKI ANDO.
IN AN EFFORT TO HAVE HIS ESTATE SEIZED.
STILL UNSATISFIED, YOU TEAMED UP WITH OTHER SAMURAI TO KIDNAP THE KŌKE NOBLE ASSIGNED TO INVESTIGATE...
...AND FORCE HIM TO WRITE A RECOMMENDATION THAT YOU BECOME THE NEXT METSUKE.
WHO THE HELL ARE YOU?
IF YOU'RE NOT ONE OF THE KŌKE, THEN WHO...?

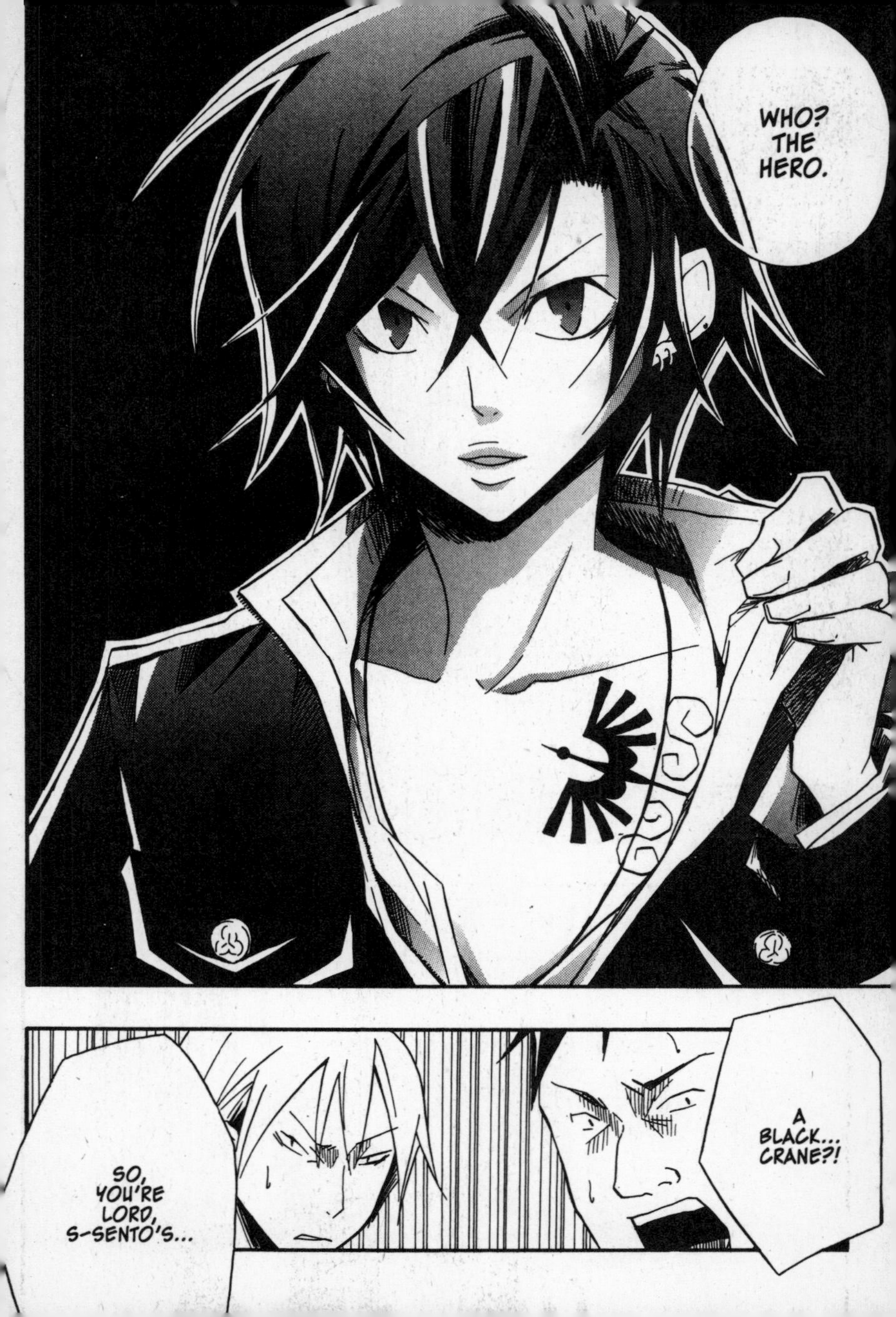
WHO? THE HERO.
A BLACK... CRANE?!
SO, YOU'RE LORD, S-SENTO'S...

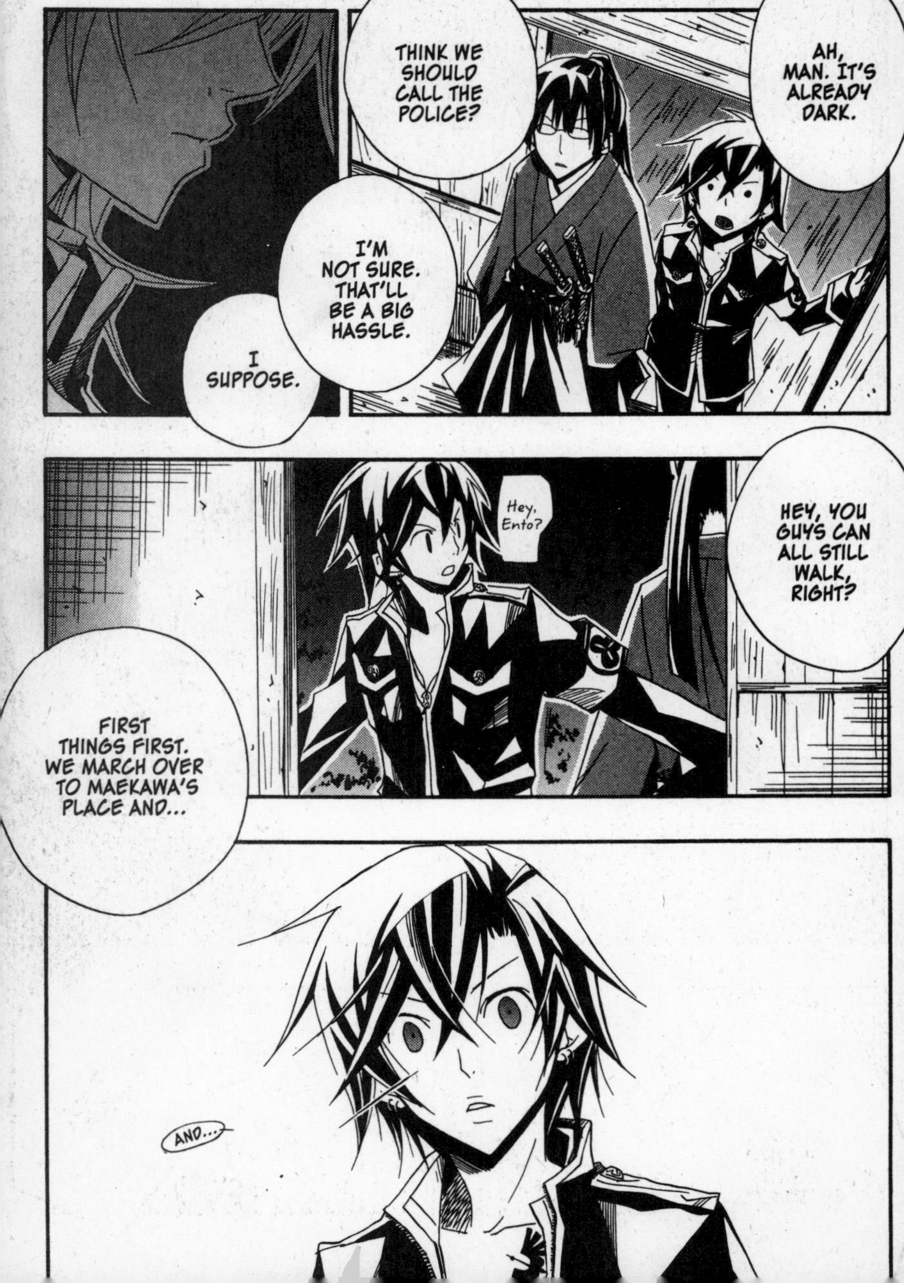
AH, MAN. IT'S ALREADY DARK.
THINK WE SHOULD CALL THE POLICE?
I'M NOT SURE. THAT'LL BE A BIG HASSLE.
I SUPPOSE.
HEY, YOU GUYS CAN ALL STILL WALK, RIGHT?
Hey, Ento?
FIRST THINGS FIRST. WE MARCH OVER TO MAEKAWA'S PLACE AND...
AND...

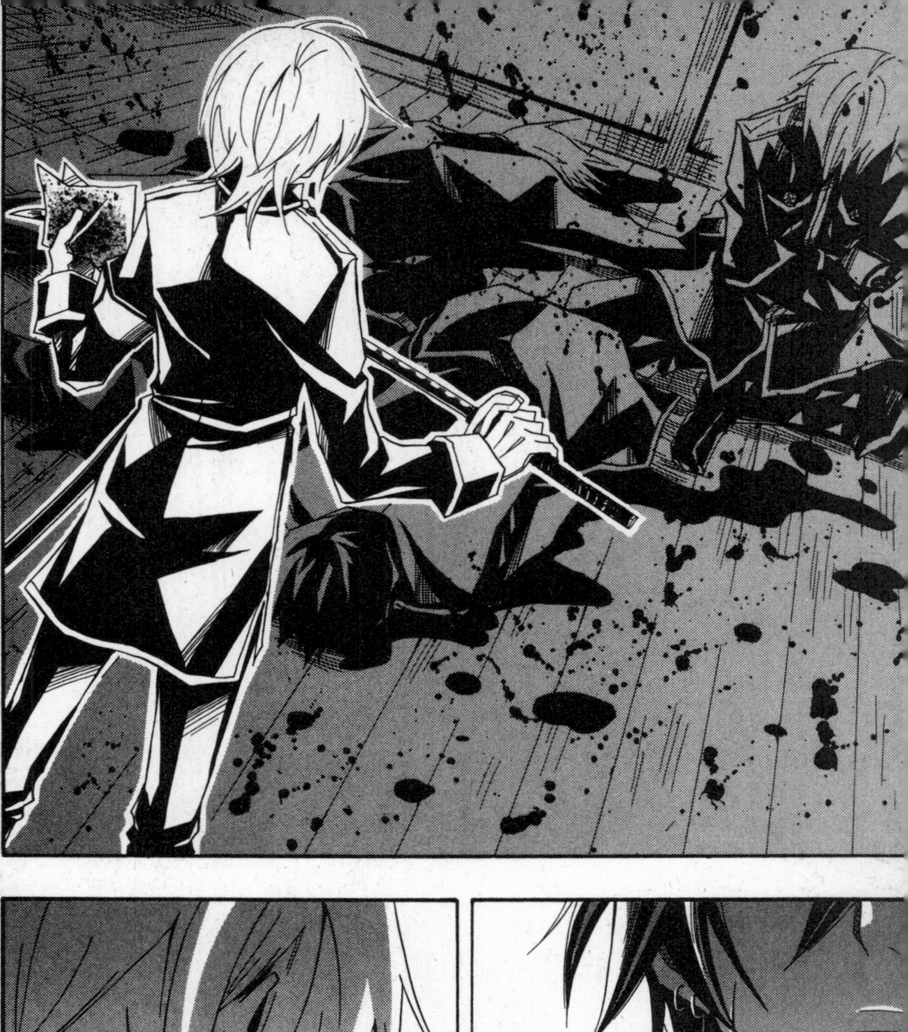
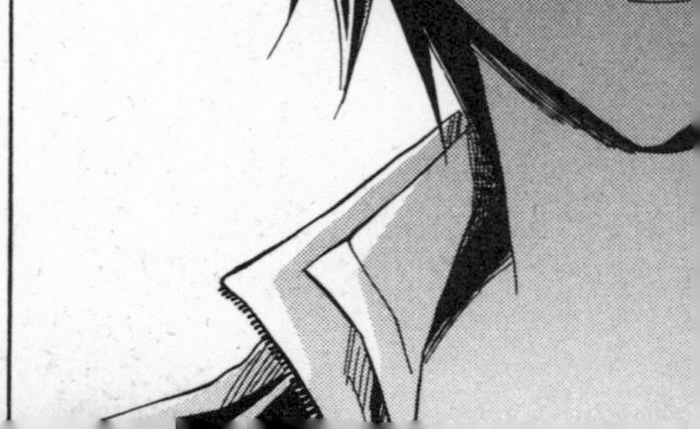
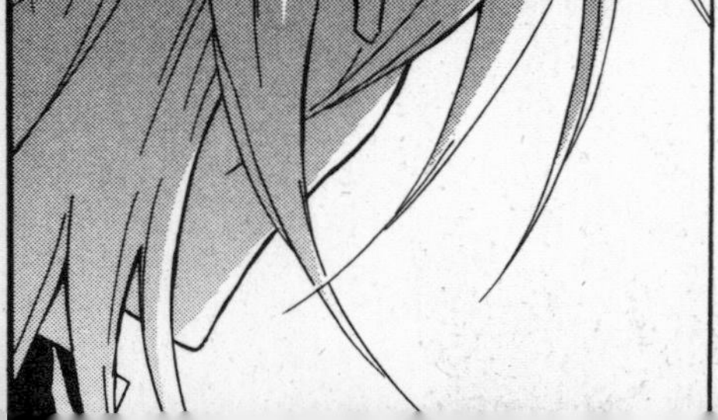

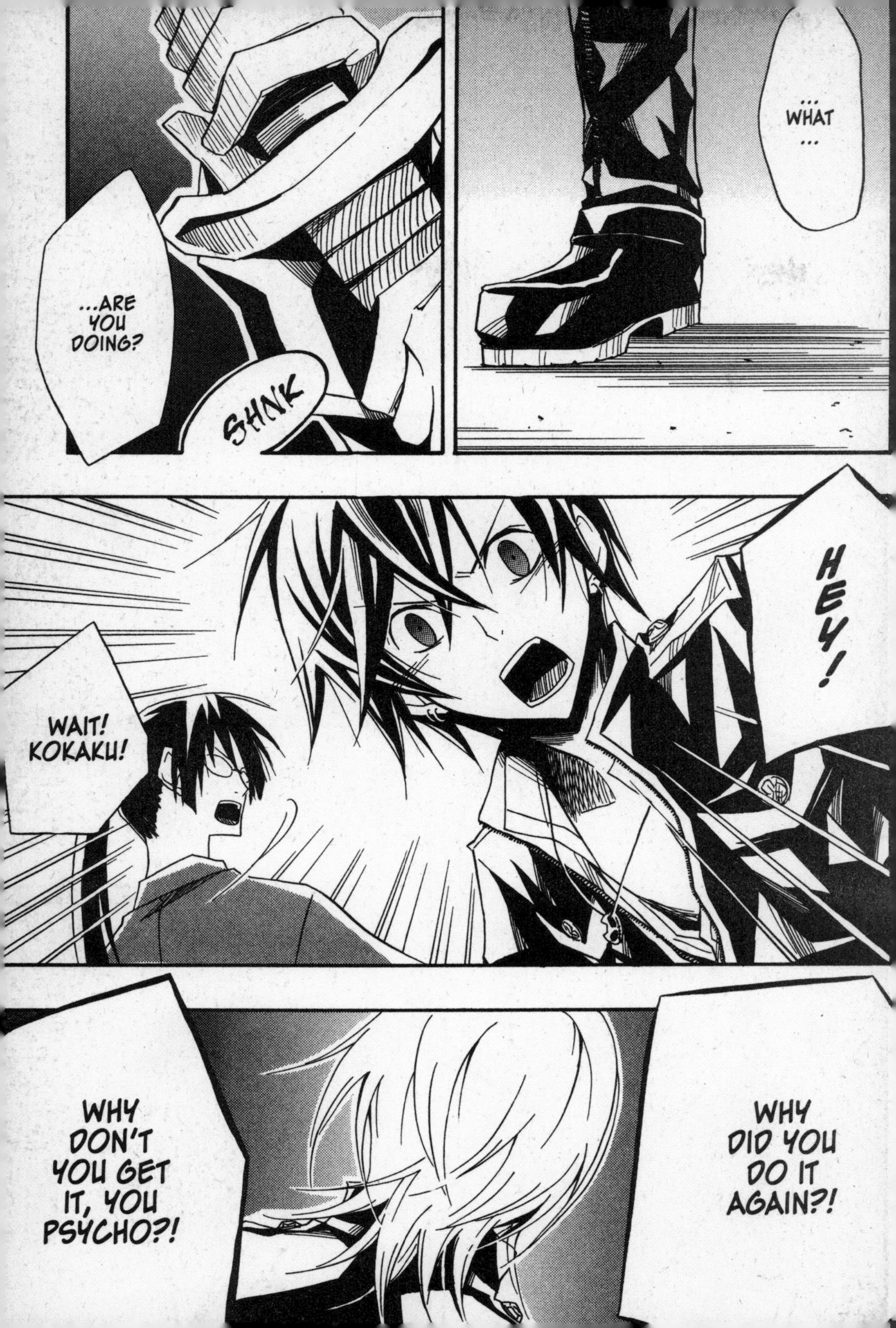
...WHAT...
...ARE YOU DOING?
SHNK
HEY!
WAIT! KOKAKU!
WHY DID YOU DO IT AGAIN?!
WHY DON'T YOU GET IT, YOU PSYCHO?!

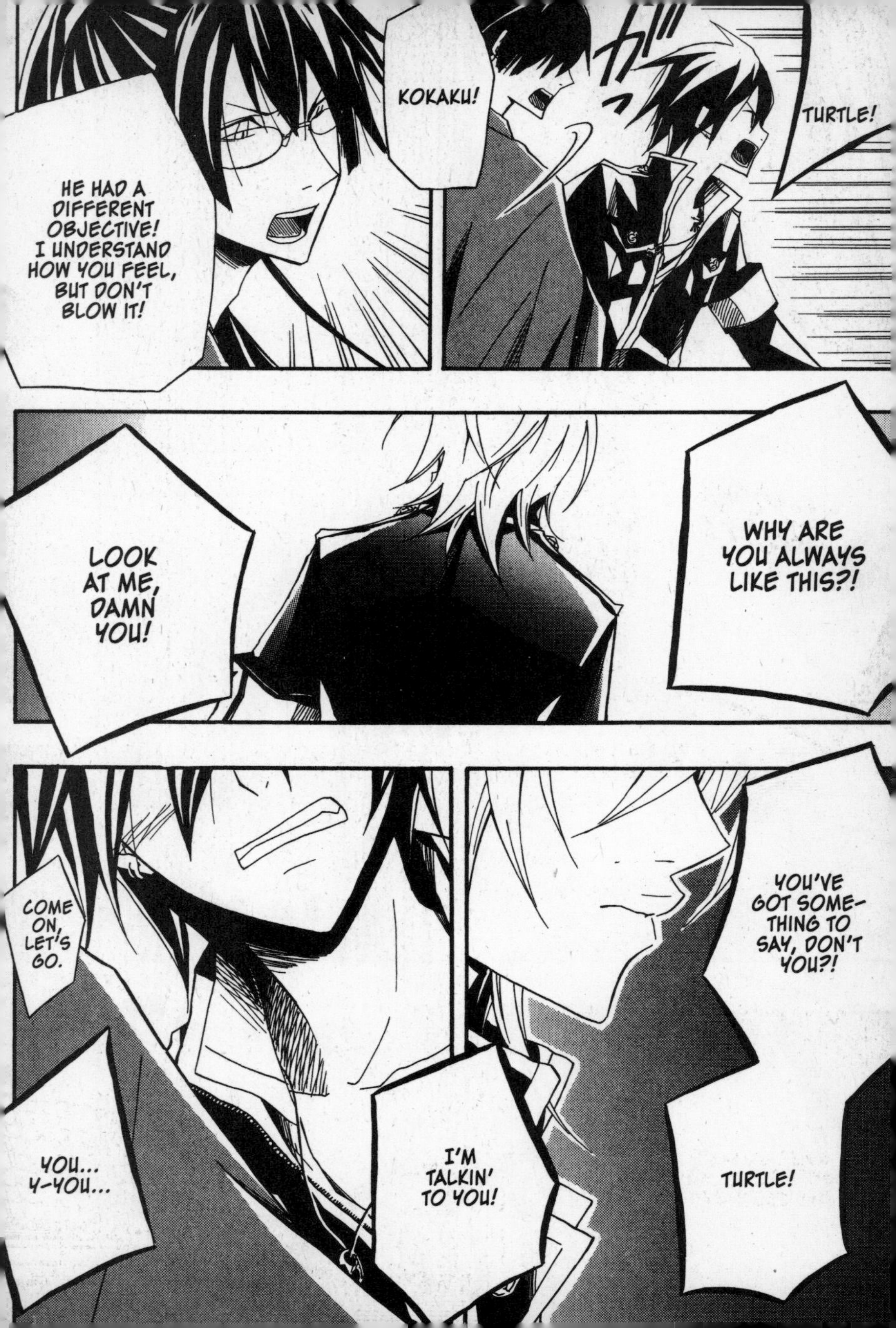
TURTLE!
KOKAKU!
HE HAD A DIFFERENT OBJECTIVE! I UNDERSTAND HOW YOU FEEL, BUT DON'T BLOW IT!
WHY ARE YOU ALWAYS LIKE THIS?!
LOOK AT ME, DAMN YOU!
YOU'VE GOT SOME-THING TO SAY, DON'T YOU?!
TURTLE!
I'M TALKIN' TO YOU!
COME ON, LET'S GO.
YOU... Y-YOU...

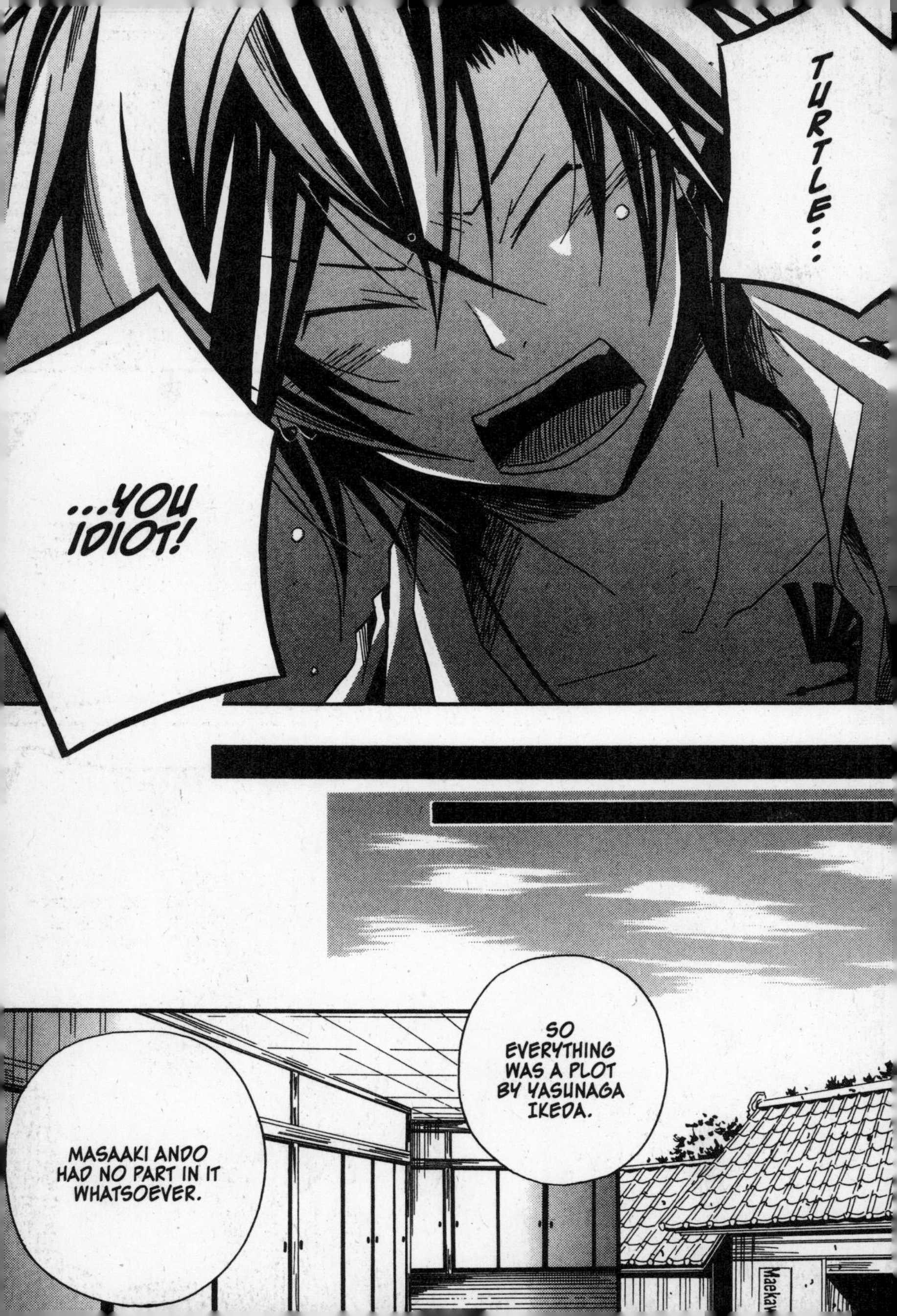
TURTLE...
...YOU IDIOT!
SO EVERYTHING WAS A PLOT BY YASUNAGA IKEDA.
MASAAKI ANDO HAD NO PART IN IT WHATSOEVER.

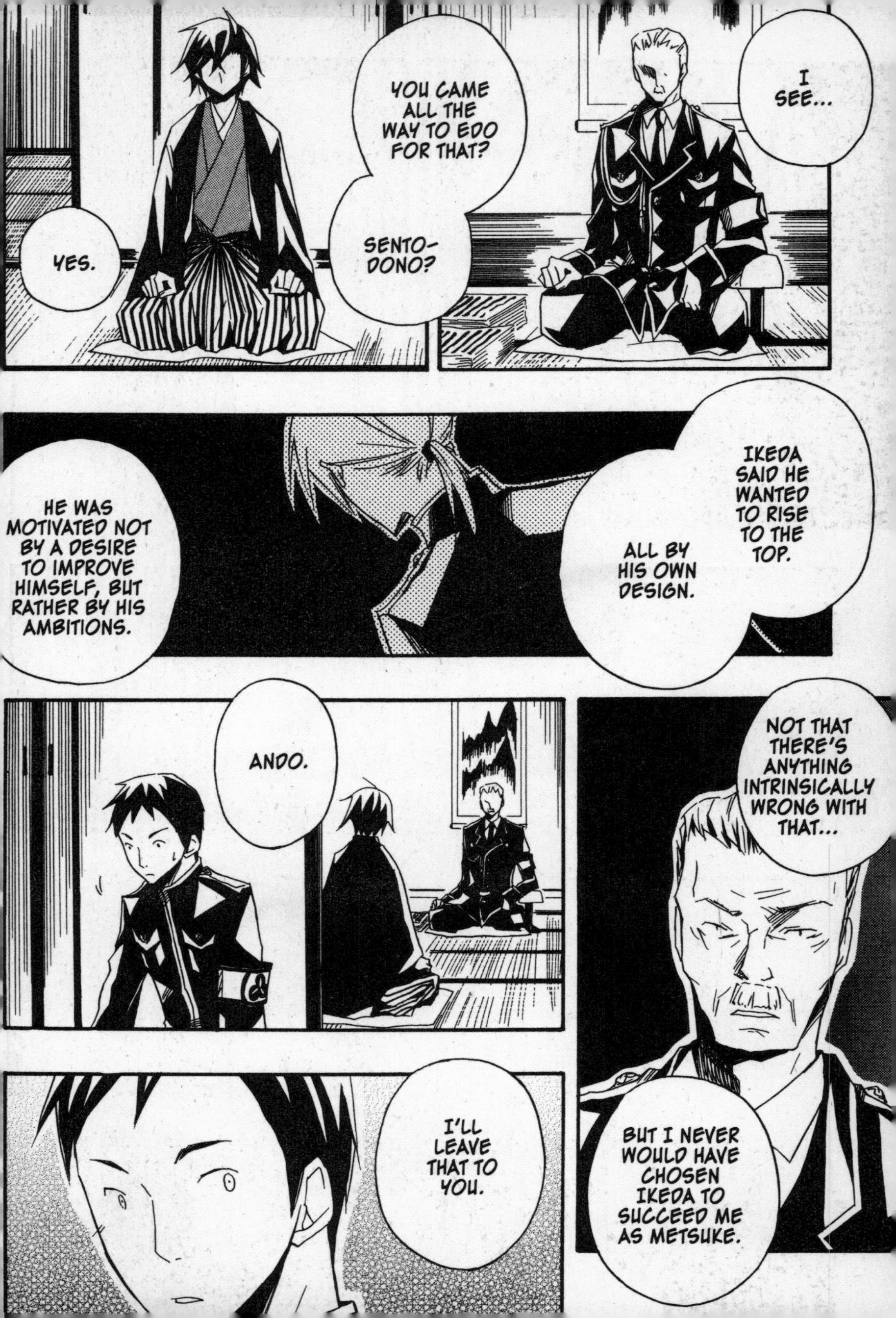
I SEE...
YOU CAME ALL THE WAY TO EDO FOR THAT?
SENTO-DONO?
YES.
IKEDA SAID HE WANTED TO RISE TO THE TOP.
ALL BY HIS OWN DESIGN.
HE WAS MOTIVATED NOT BY A DESIRE TO IMPROVE HIMSELF, BUT RATHER BY HIS AMBITIONS.
NOT THAT THERE'S ANYTHING INTRINSICALLY WRONG WITH THAT...
BUT I NEVER WOULD HAVE CHOSEN IKEDA TO SUCCEED ME AS METSUKE.
ANDO.
I'LL LEAVE THAT TO YOU.

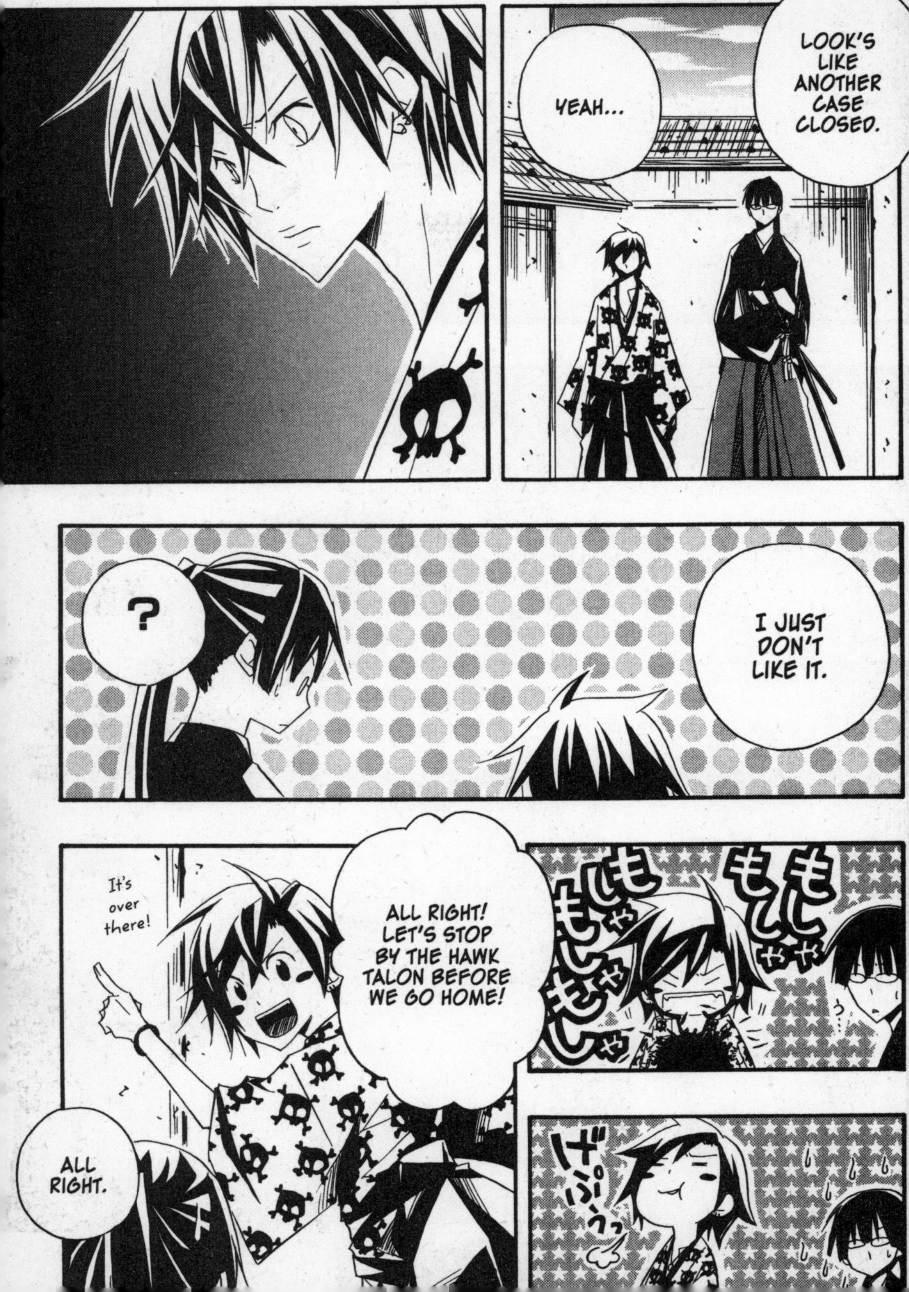
LOOK'S LIKE ANOTHER CASE CLOSED.
YEAH...
I JUST DON'T LIKE IT.
?
もしゃもしゃ
もしゃもしゃ
う…
げぷ〜っ
ALL RIGHT! LET'S STOP BY THE HAWK TALON BEFORE WE GO HOME!
It's over there!
ALL RIGHT.

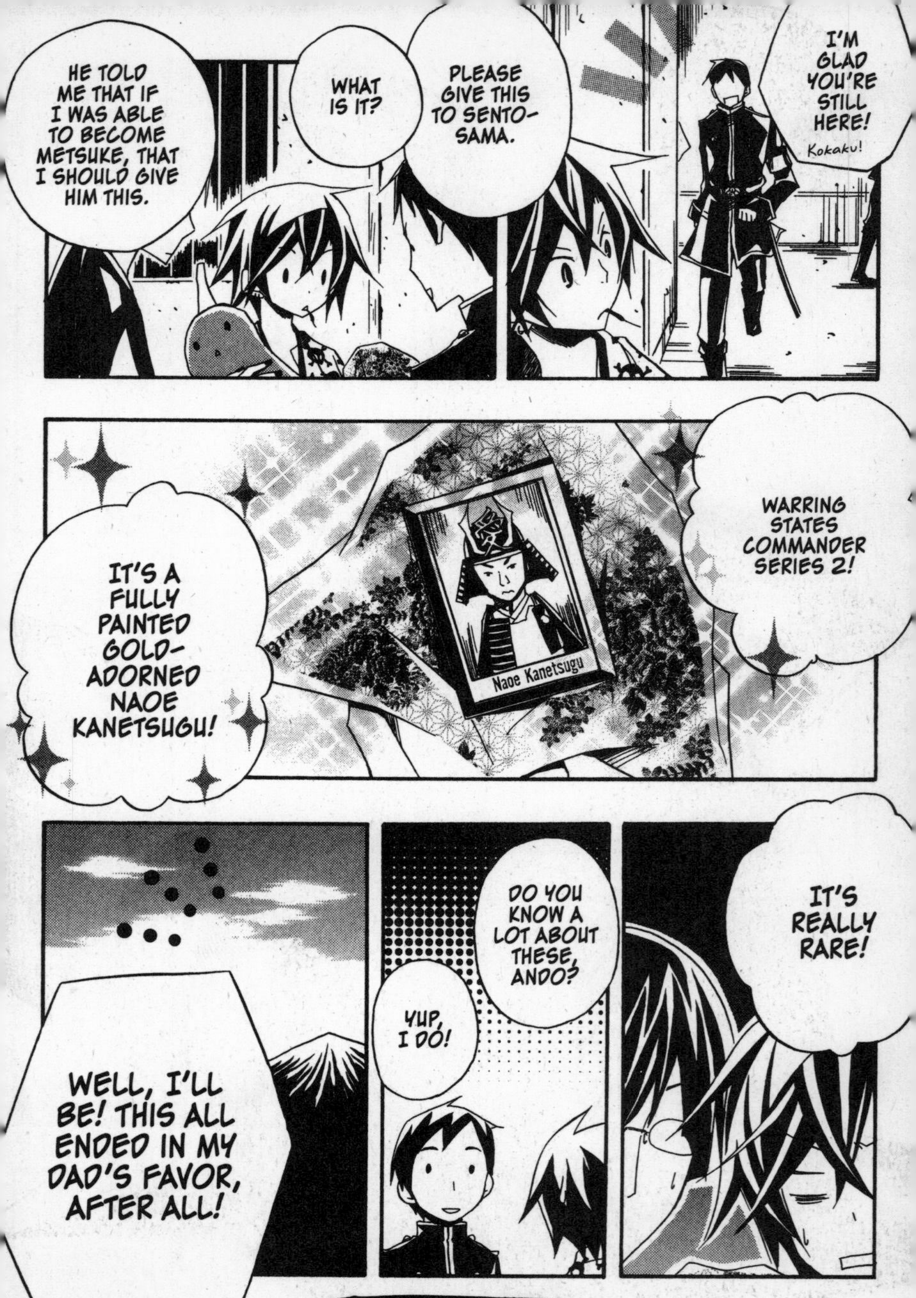
I'M GLAD YOU'RE STILL HERE!
Kokaku!
PLEASE GIVE THIS TO SENTO-SAMA.
WHAT IS IT?
HE TOLD ME THAT IF I WAS ABLE TO BECOME METSUKE, THAT I SHOULD GIVE HIM THIS.
WARRING STATES COMMANDER SERIES 2!
IT'S A FULLY PAINTED GOLD-ADORNED NAOE KANETSUGU!
Naoe Kanetsugu
IT'S REALLY RARE!
DO YOU KNOW A LOT ABOUT THESE, ANDO?
YUP, I DO!
WELL, I'LL BE! THIS ALL ENDED IN MY DAD'S FAVOR, AFTER ALL!

12TH SUBJECT: THE VOLUME OF TSURUMI/ THE END

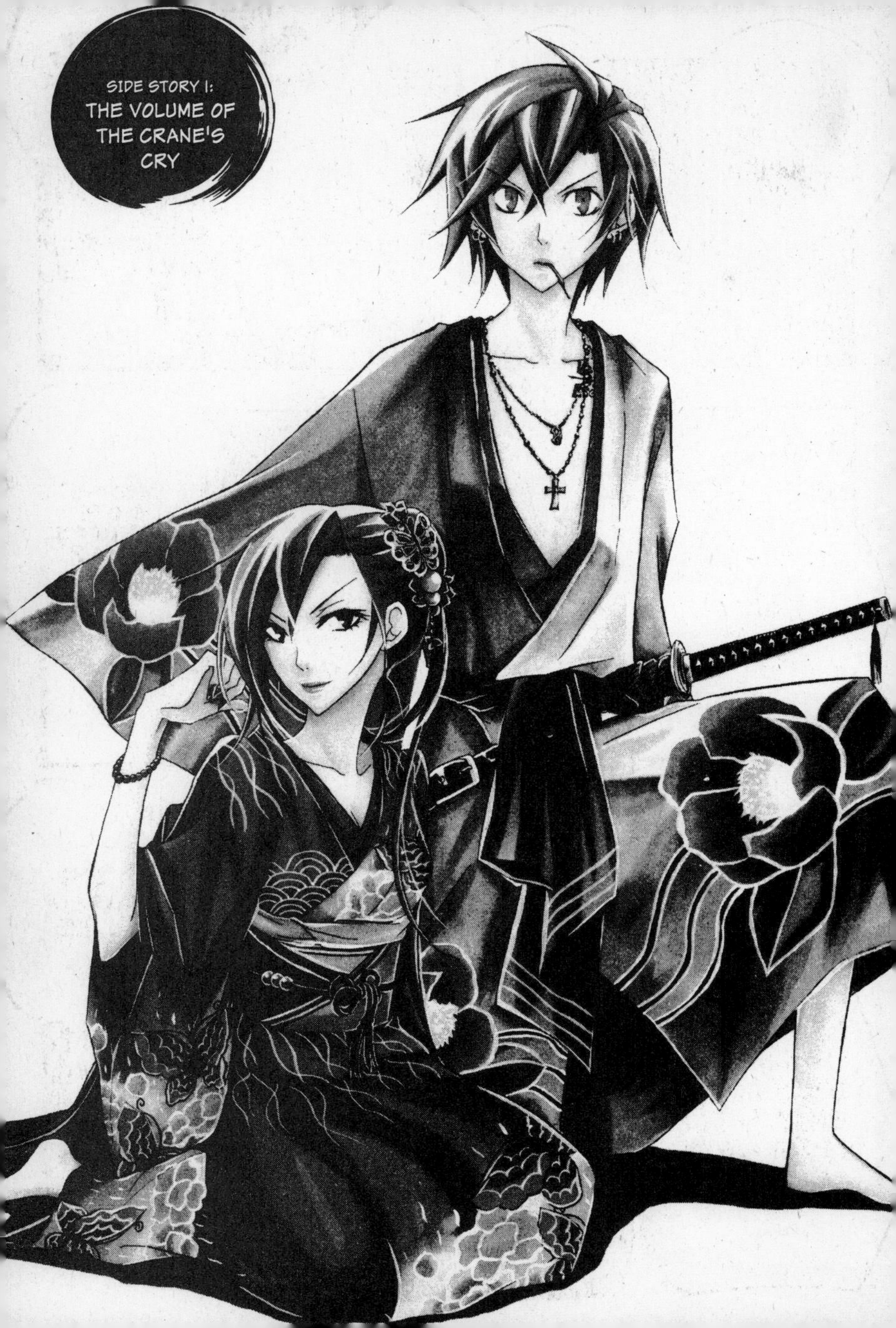
SIDE STORY 1:
THE VOLUME OF THE CRANE'S CRY

Father Figure

Tsurunoshin Sento

Born August 26th / 40 years old

Sign: Virgo / Blood Type: O

Favorite Food: Japanese-style confectionary and Sencha tea

Hobbies: Collecting figurines

Dislikes: Turtles among the Kōke nobility

Specialty: Getting the toys he wants

Has never forgotten how to have fun. Possibly based on one of my favorite adults. The way he speaks may also resemble said person. Quite skilled with the sword. Has a crane tattoo on his head. His image color is brown.

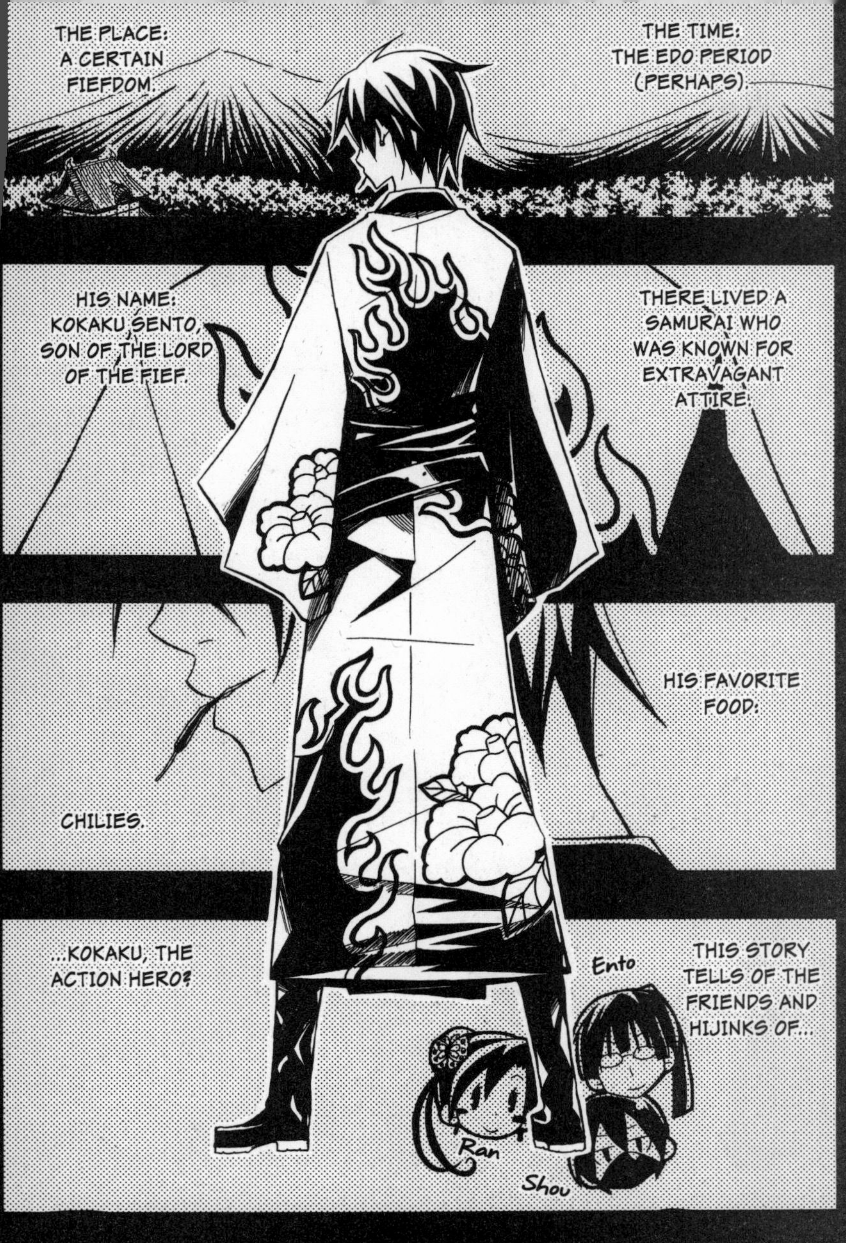
THE TIME: THE EDO PERIOD (PERHAPS).
THE PLACE: A CERTAIN FIEFDOM.
THERE LIVED A SAMURAI WHO WAS KNOWN FOR EXTRAVAGANT ATTIRE.
HIS NAME: KOKAKU SENTO, SON OF THE LORD OF THE FIEF.
HIS FAVORITE FOOD:
CHILIES.
THIS STORY TELLS OF THE FRIENDS AND HIJINKS OF...
Ento
Ran
Shou
...KOKAKU, THE ACTION HERO?

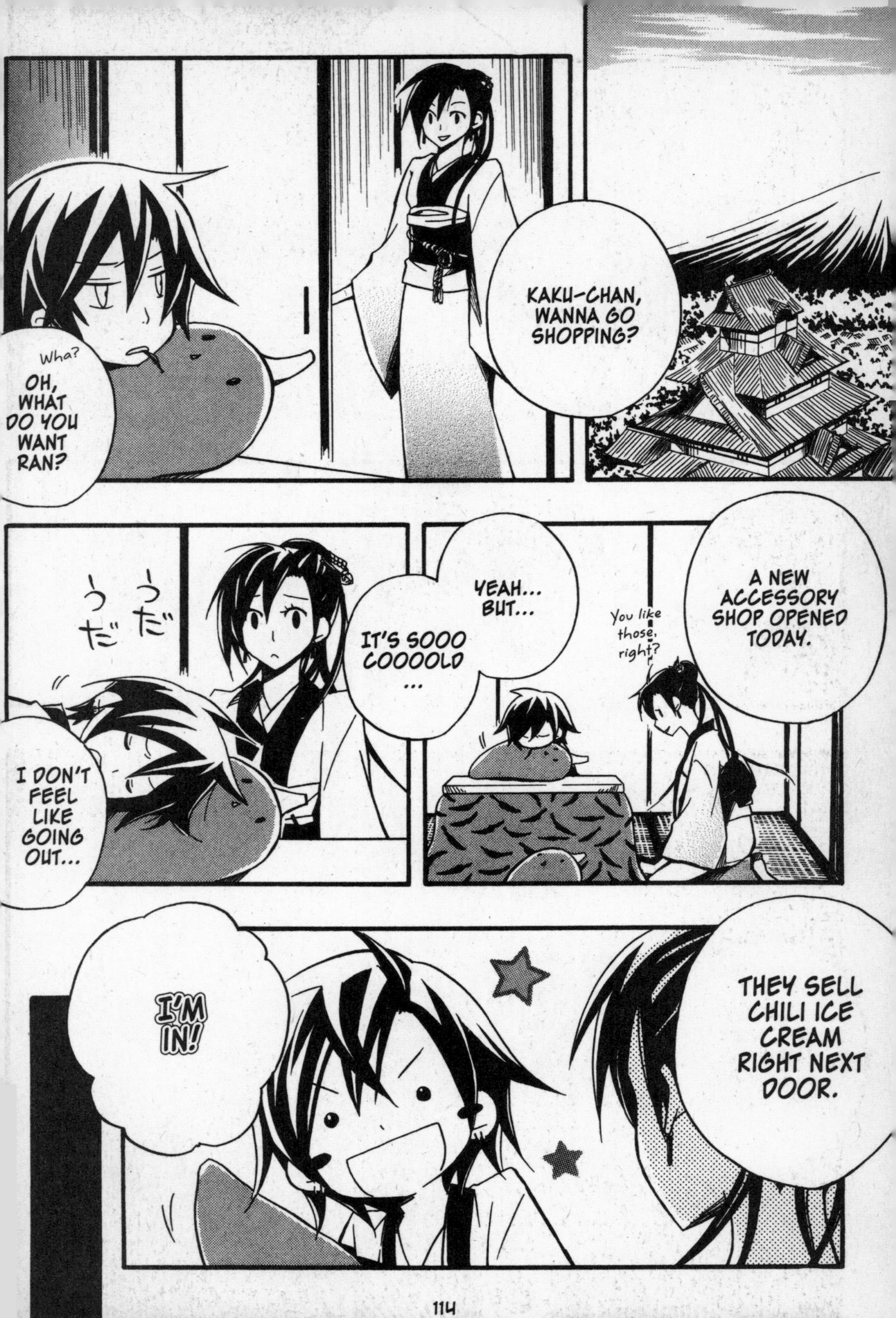
KAKU-CHAN, WANNA GO SHOPPING?
Wha?
OH, WHAT DO YOU WANT RAN?
A NEW ACCESSORY SHOP OPENED TODAY.
You like those, right?
YEAH... BUT...
IT'S SOOO COOOOLD ...
うだうだ
I DON'T FEEL LIKE GOING OUT...
THEY SELL CHILI ICE CREAM RIGHT NEXT DOOR.
I'M IN!

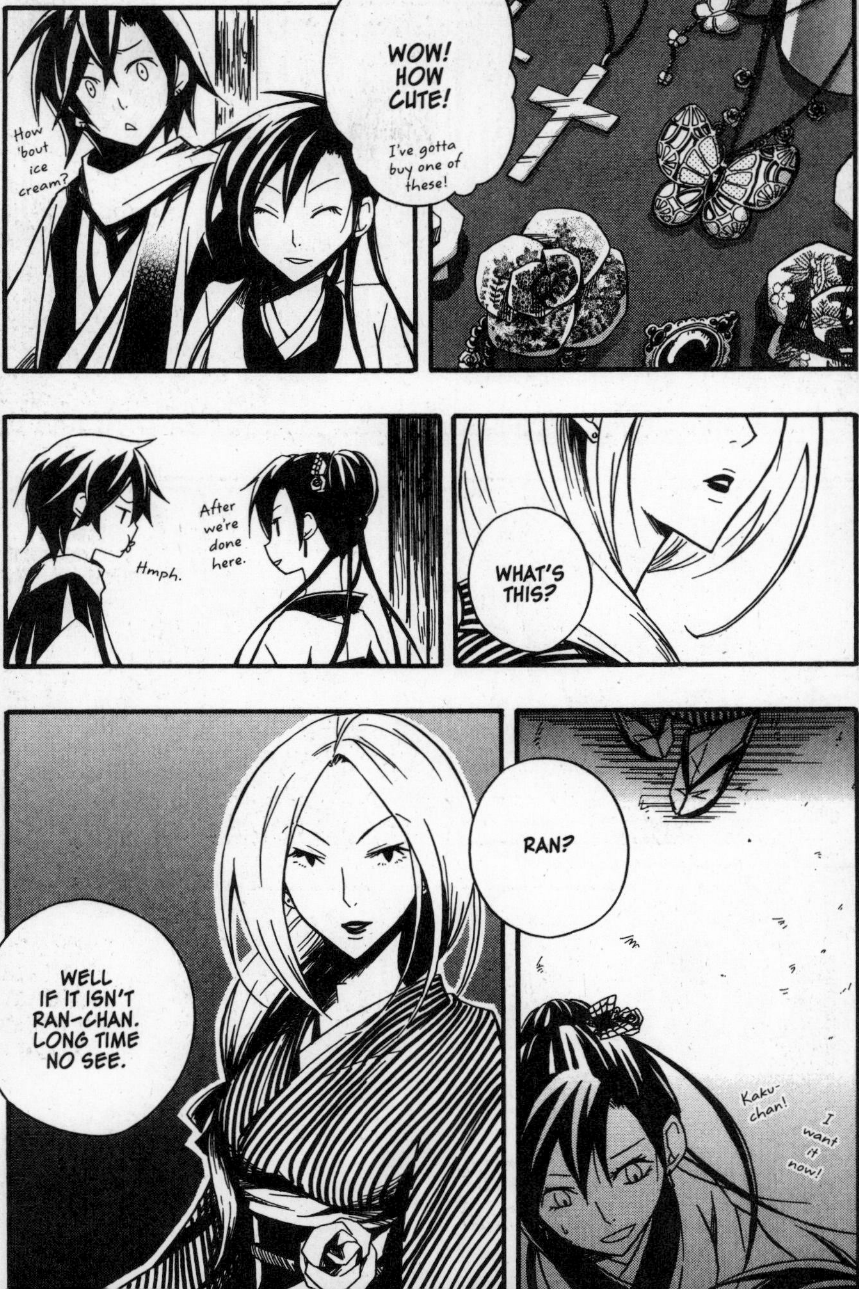
WOW! HOW CUTE!
I've gotta buy one of these!
How 'bout ice cream?
WHAT'S THIS?
After we're done here.
Hmph.
RAN?
Kaku-chan!
I want it now!
WELL IF IT ISN'T RAN-CHAN. LONG TIME NO SEE.

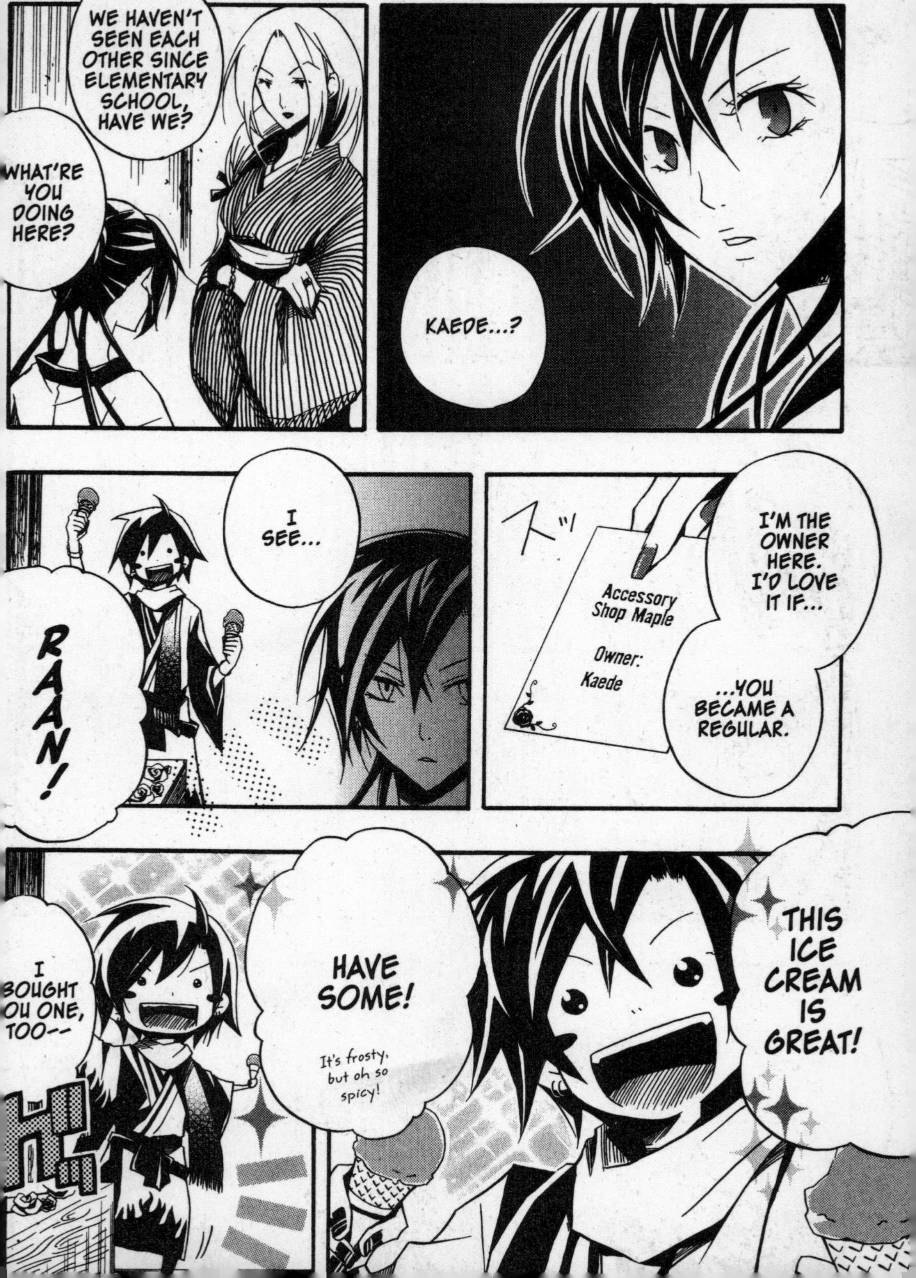
KAEDE...?
WE HAVEN'T SEEN EACH OTHER SINCE ELEMENTARY SCHOOL, HAVE WE?
WHAT'RE YOU DOING HERE?
スッ
I'M THE OWNER HERE. I'D LOVE IT IF...
Accessory Shop Maple
Owner:
Kaede
...YOU BECAME A REGULAR.
I SEE...
RAAN!
THIS ICE CREAM IS GREAT!
HAVE SOME!
It's frosty, but oh so spicy!
I BOUGHT OU ONE, TOO--

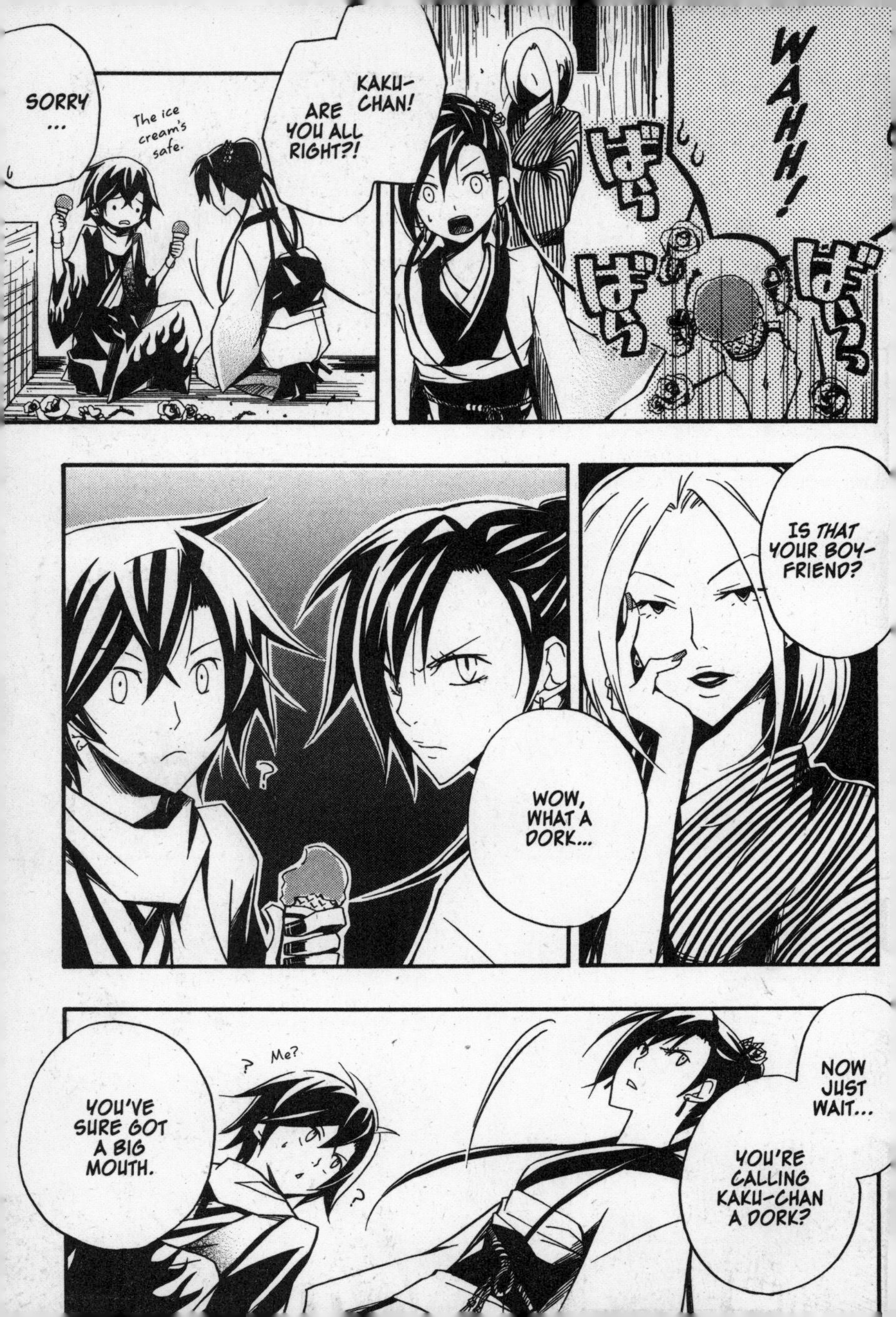
WAHH!
KAKU-CHAN! ARE YOU ALL RIGHT?!
SORRY ...
The ice cream's safe.
IS THAT YOUR BOY-FRIEND?
WOW, WHAT A DORK...
NOW JUST WAIT...
YOU'RE CALLING KAKU-CHAN A DORK?
Me?
YOU'VE SURE GOT A BIG MOUTH.

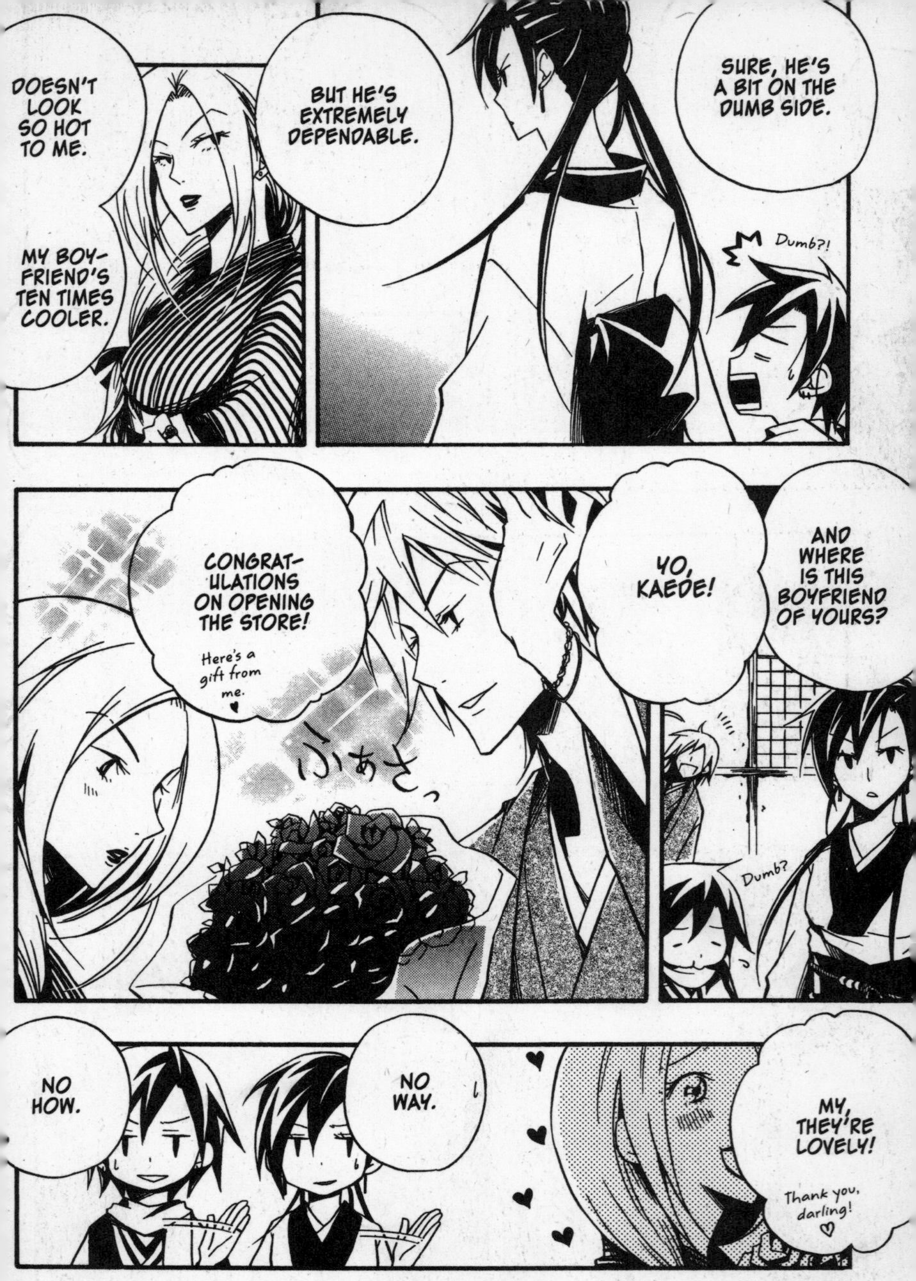
SURE, HE'S A BIT ON THE DUMB SIDE.
BUT HE'S EXTREMELY DEPENDABLE.
Dumb?!
DOESN'T LOOK SO HOT TO ME.
MY BOY-FRIEND'S TEN TIMES COOLER.
AND WHERE IS THIS BOYFRIEND OF YOURS?
Dumb?
YO, KAEDE!
CONGRAT-ULATIONS ON OPENING THE STORE!
Here's a gift from me. ♥
ふぁさっ
MY, THEY'RE LOVELY!
Thank you, darling! ♡
NO WAY.
NO HOW.

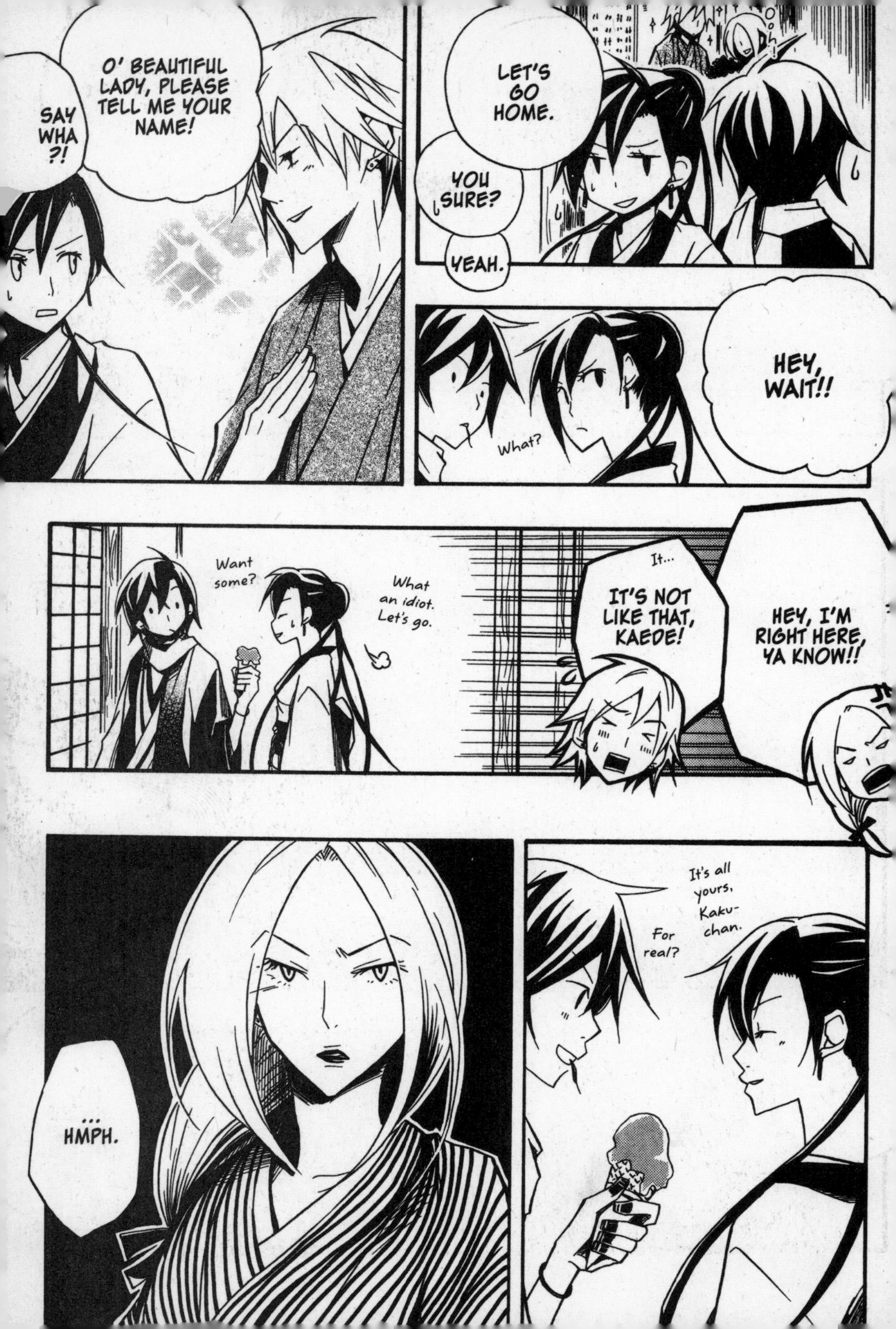

LET'S GO HOME.
YOU SURE?
YEAH.
HEY, WAIT!!
What?
O' BEAUTIFUL LADY, PLEASE TELL ME YOUR NAME!
SAY WHA ?!
HEY, I'M RIGHT HERE, YA KNOW!!
It...
IT'S NOT LIKE THAT, KAEDE!
What an idiot. Let's go.
Want some?
It's all yours, Kaku-chan.
For real?
...HMPH.

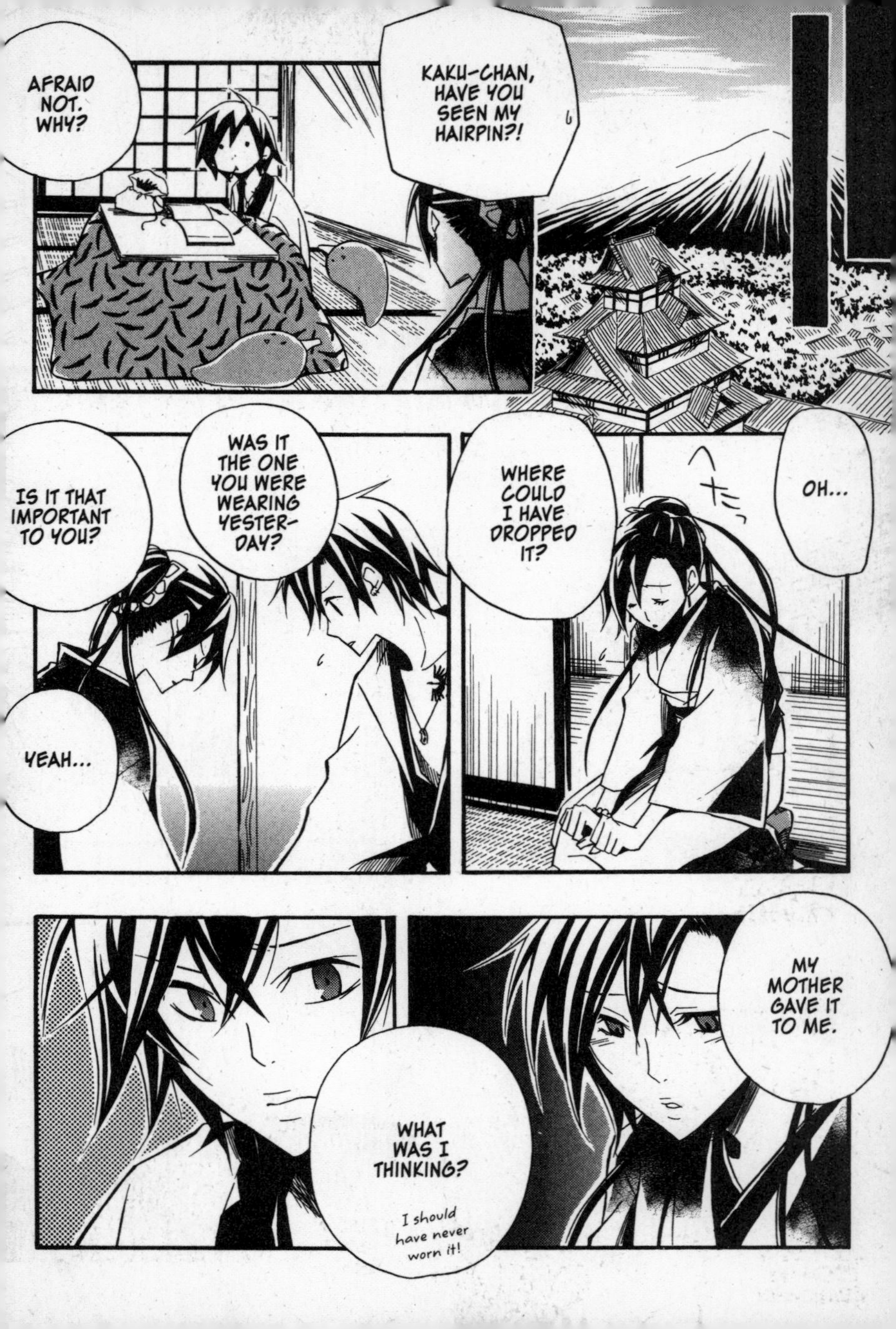
KAKU-CHAN, HAVE YOU SEEN MY HAIRPIN?!
AFRAID NOT. WHY?
OH...
へたっ
WHERE COULD I HAVE DROPPED IT?
WAS IT THE ONE YOU WERE WEARING YESTER-DAY?
IS IT THAT IMPORTANT TO YOU?
YEAH...
MY MOTHER GAVE IT TO ME.
WHAT WAS I THINKING?
I should have never worn it!

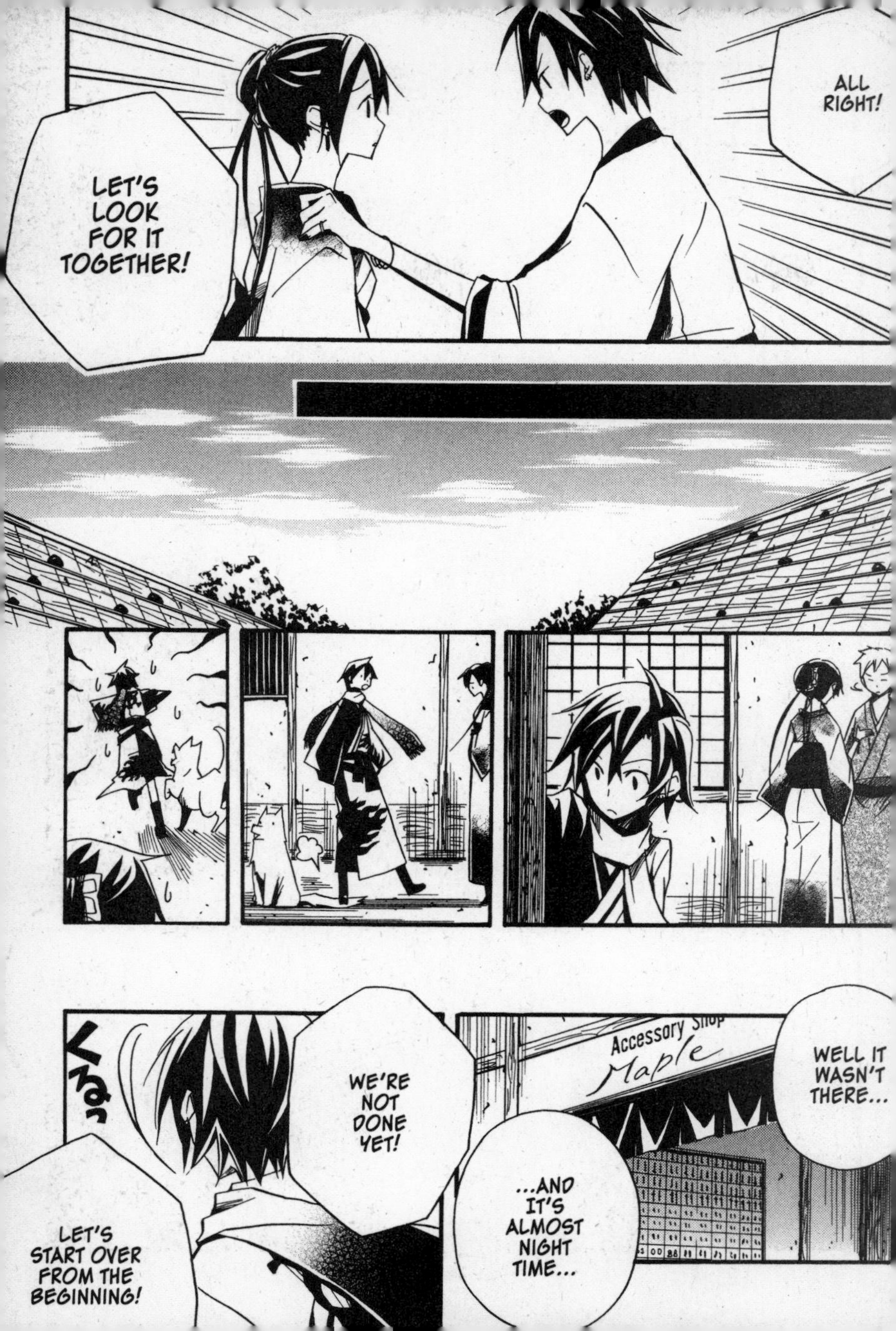
ALL RIGHT!
LET'S LOOK FOR IT TOGETHER!
Accessory Shop Maple
WELL IT WASN'T THERE...
...AND IT'S ALMOST NIGHT TIME...
WE'RE NOT DONE YET!
LET'S START OVER FROM THE BEGINNING!
くるっ

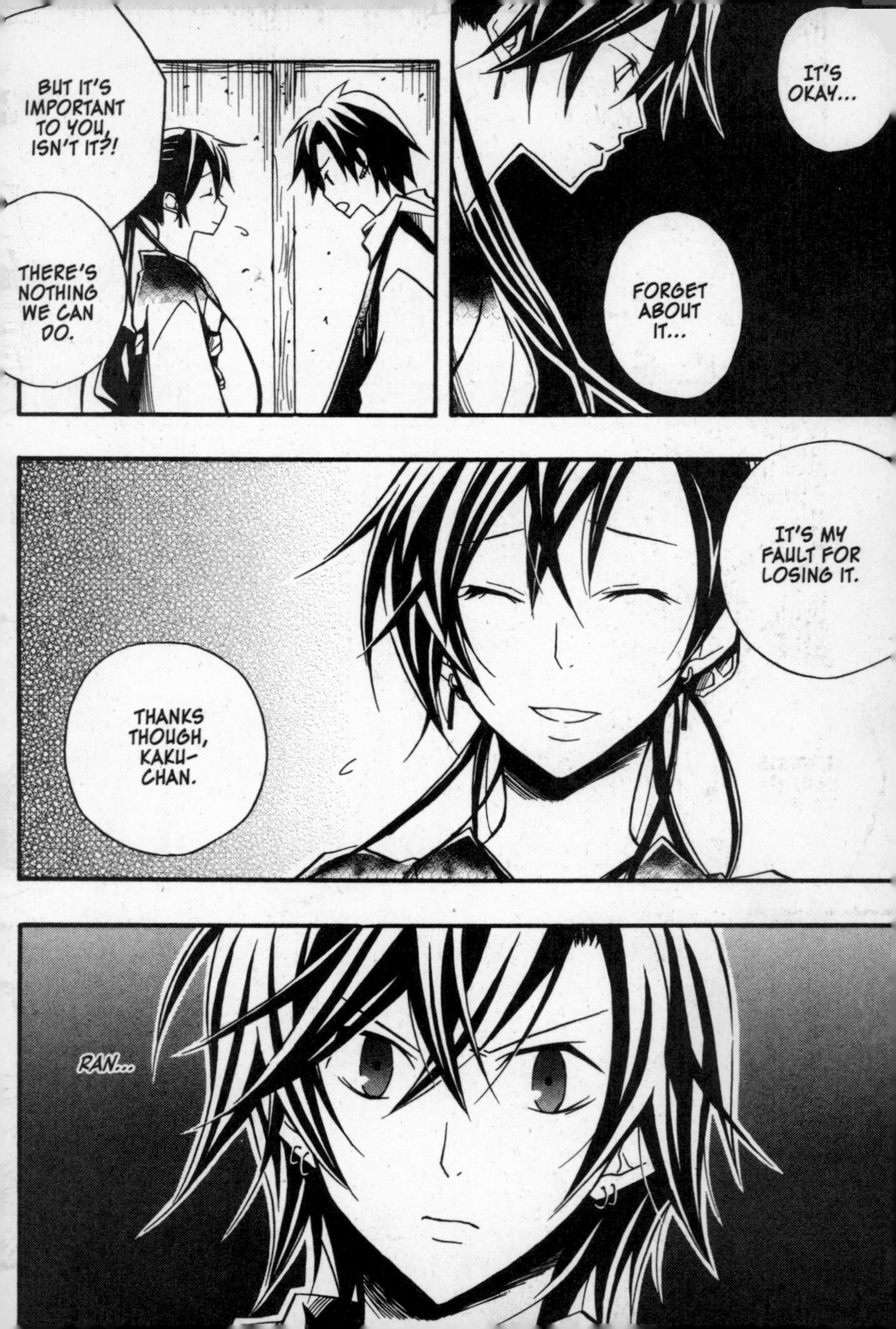
IT'S OKAY...
FORGET ABOUT IT...
BUT IT'S IMPORTANT TO YOU, ISN'T IT?!
THERE'S NOTHING WE CAN DO.
IT'S MY FAULT FOR LOSING IT.
THANKS THOUGH, KAKU-CHAN.
RAN...

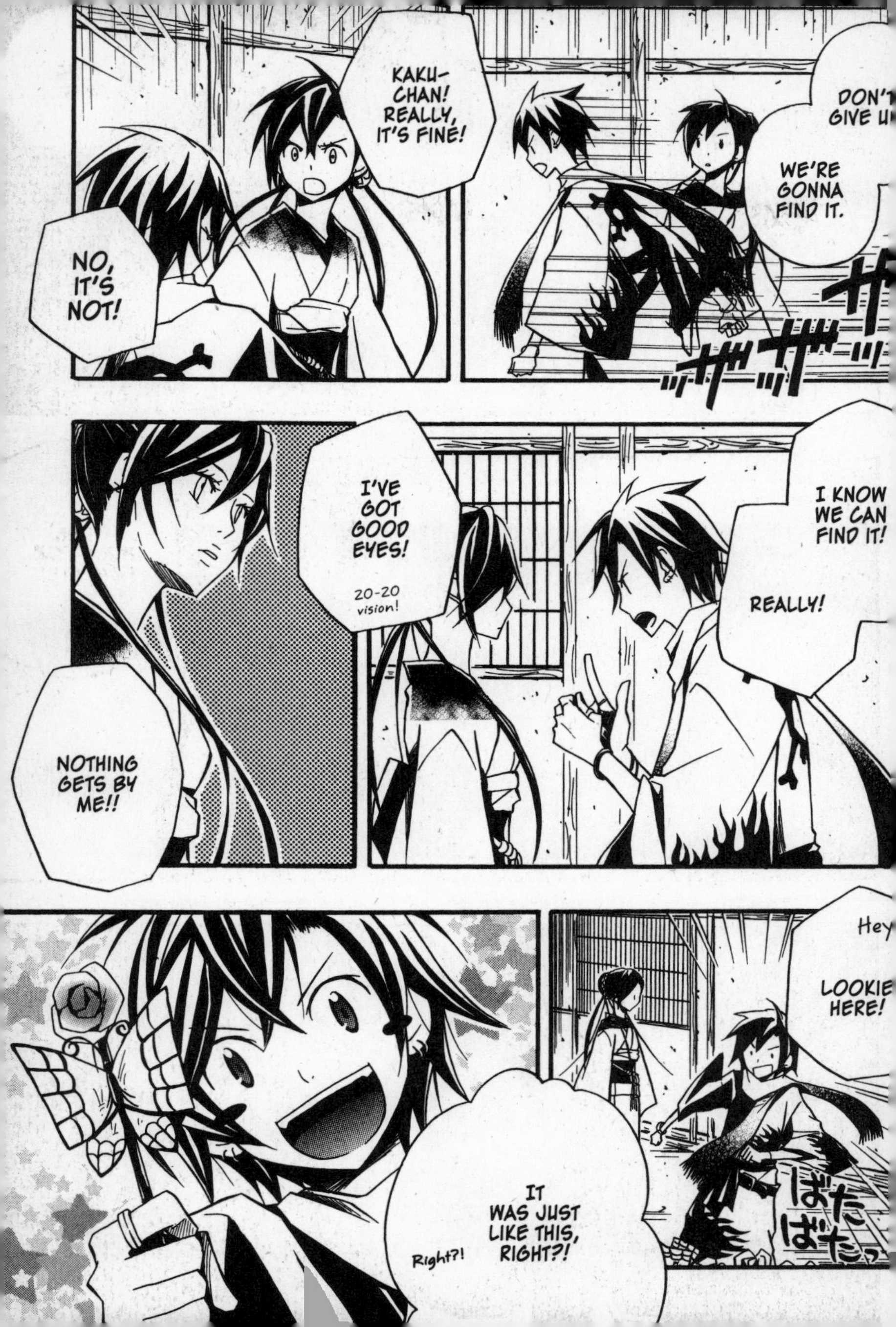
DON'T GIVE U
WE'RE GONNA FIND IT.
ザザッ ザザッ
KAKU-CHAN! REALLY, IT'S FINE!
NO, IT'S NOT!
I KNOW WE CAN FIND IT!
REALLY!
I'VE GOT GOOD EYES!
20-20 vision!
NOTHING GETS BY ME!!
Hey
LOOKIE HERE!
ばたばたっ
IT WAS JUST LIKE THIS, RIGHT?!
Right?!

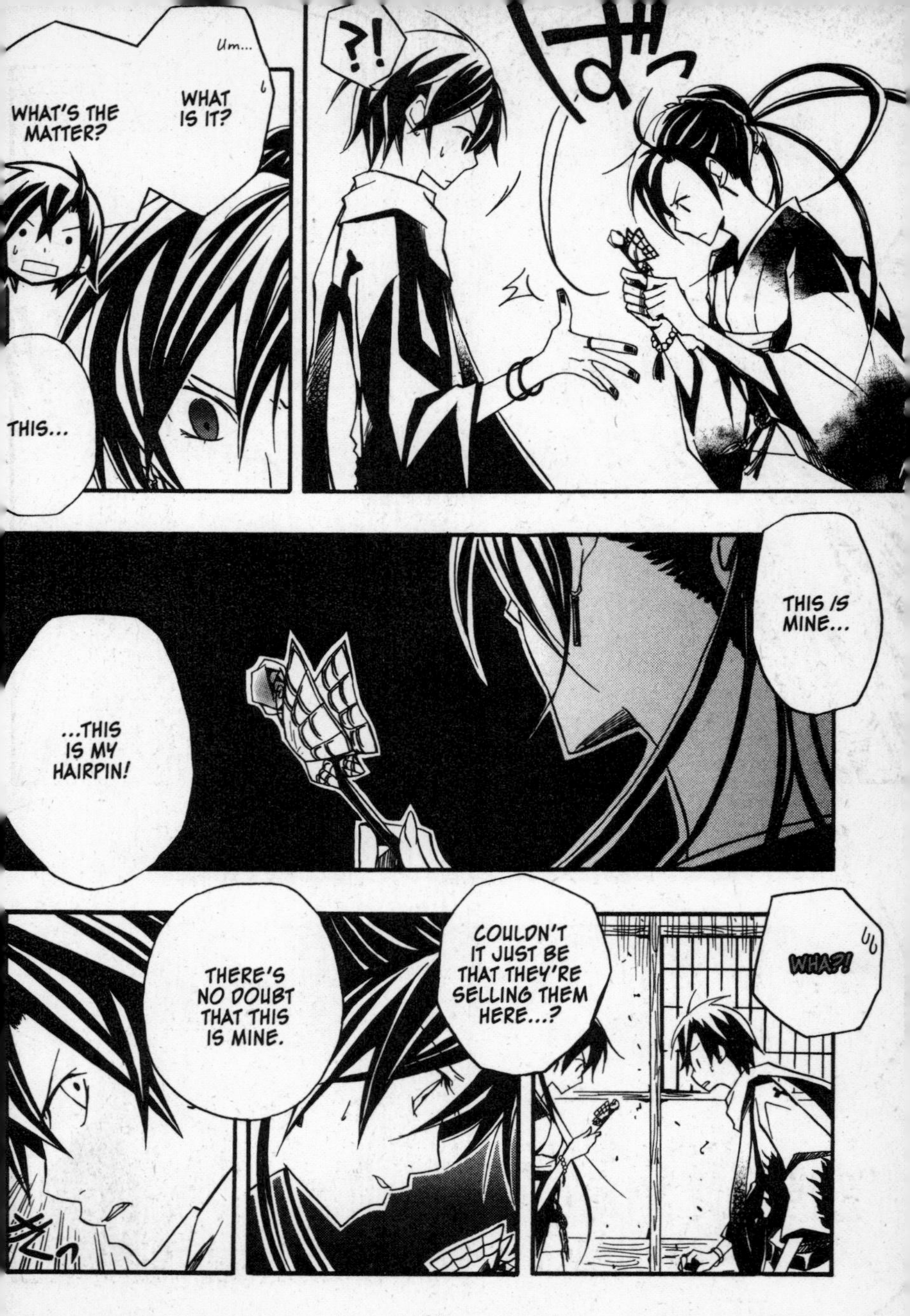
?!
Um...
WHAT IS IT?
WHAT'S THE MATTER?
THIS...
THIS IS MINE...
...THIS IS MY HAIRPIN!
WHA?!
COULDN'T IT JUST BE THAT THEY'RE SELLING THEM HERE...?
THERE'S NO DOUBT THAT THIS IS MINE.

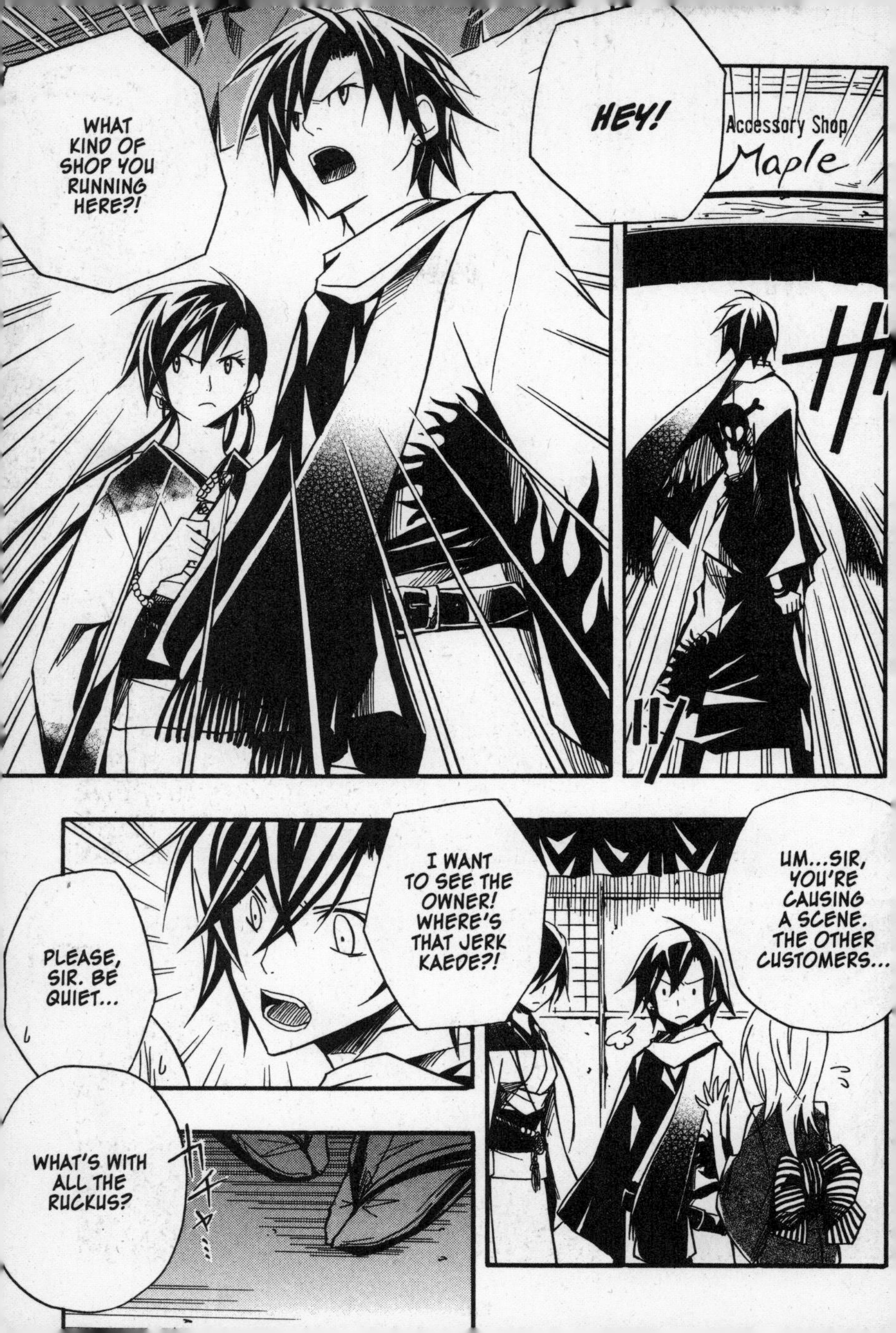

Accessory Shop
Maple
HEY!
WHAT KIND OF SHOP YOU RUNNING HERE?!
UM...SIR, YOU'RE CAUSING A SCENE. THE OTHER CUSTOMERS...
I WANT TO SEE THE OWNER! WHERE'S THAT JERK KAEDE?!
PLEASE, SIR. BE QUIET...
WHAT'S WITH ALL THE RUCKUS?

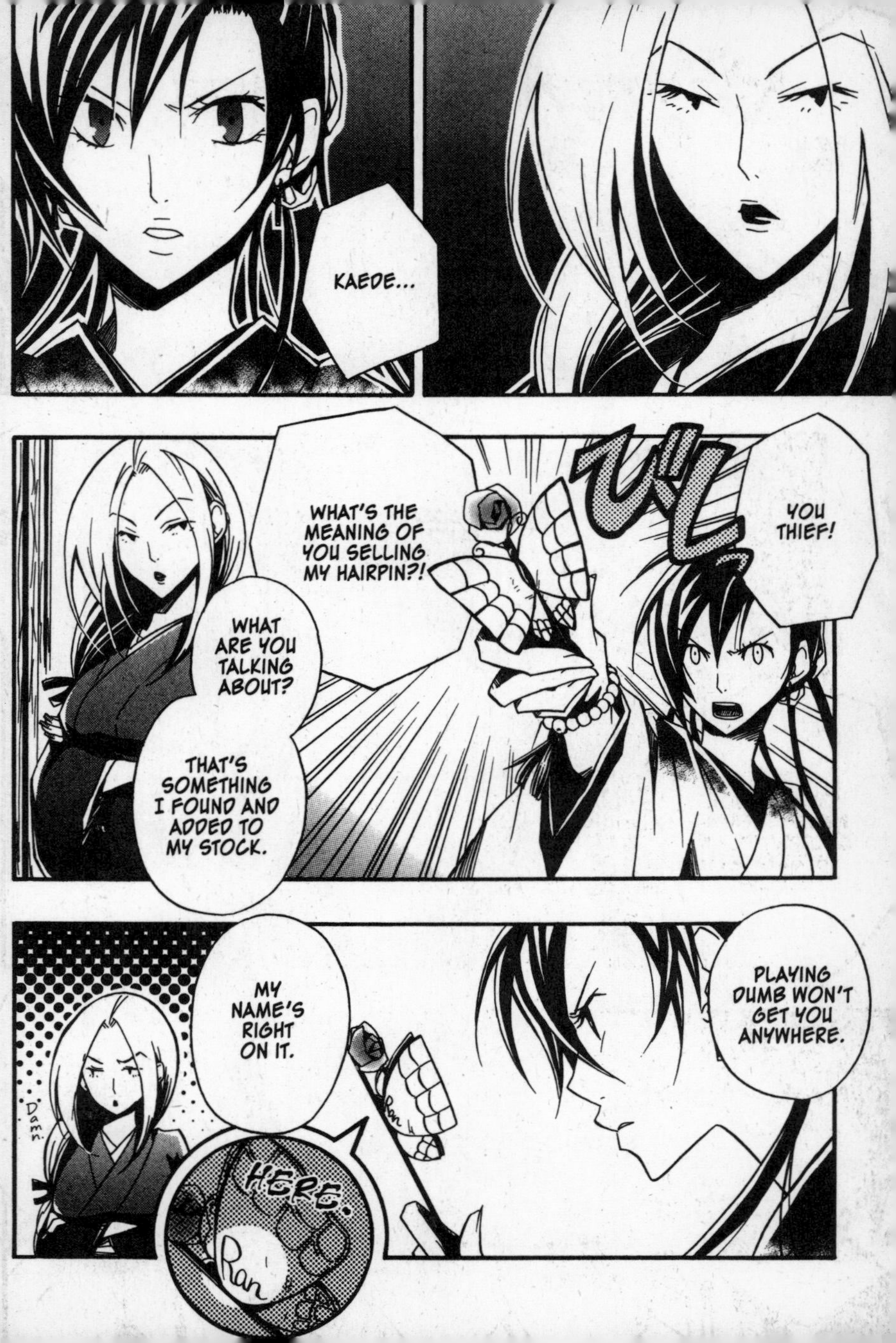
KAEDE...
YOU THIEF!
WHAT'S THE MEANING OF YOU SELLING MY HAIRPIN?!
WHAT ARE YOU TALKING ABOUT?
THAT'S SOMETHING I FOUND AND ADDED TO MY STOCK.
PLAYING DUMB WON'T GET YOU ANYWHERE.
MY NAME'S RIGHT ON IT.
Ran
HERE.
Ran
Damn.

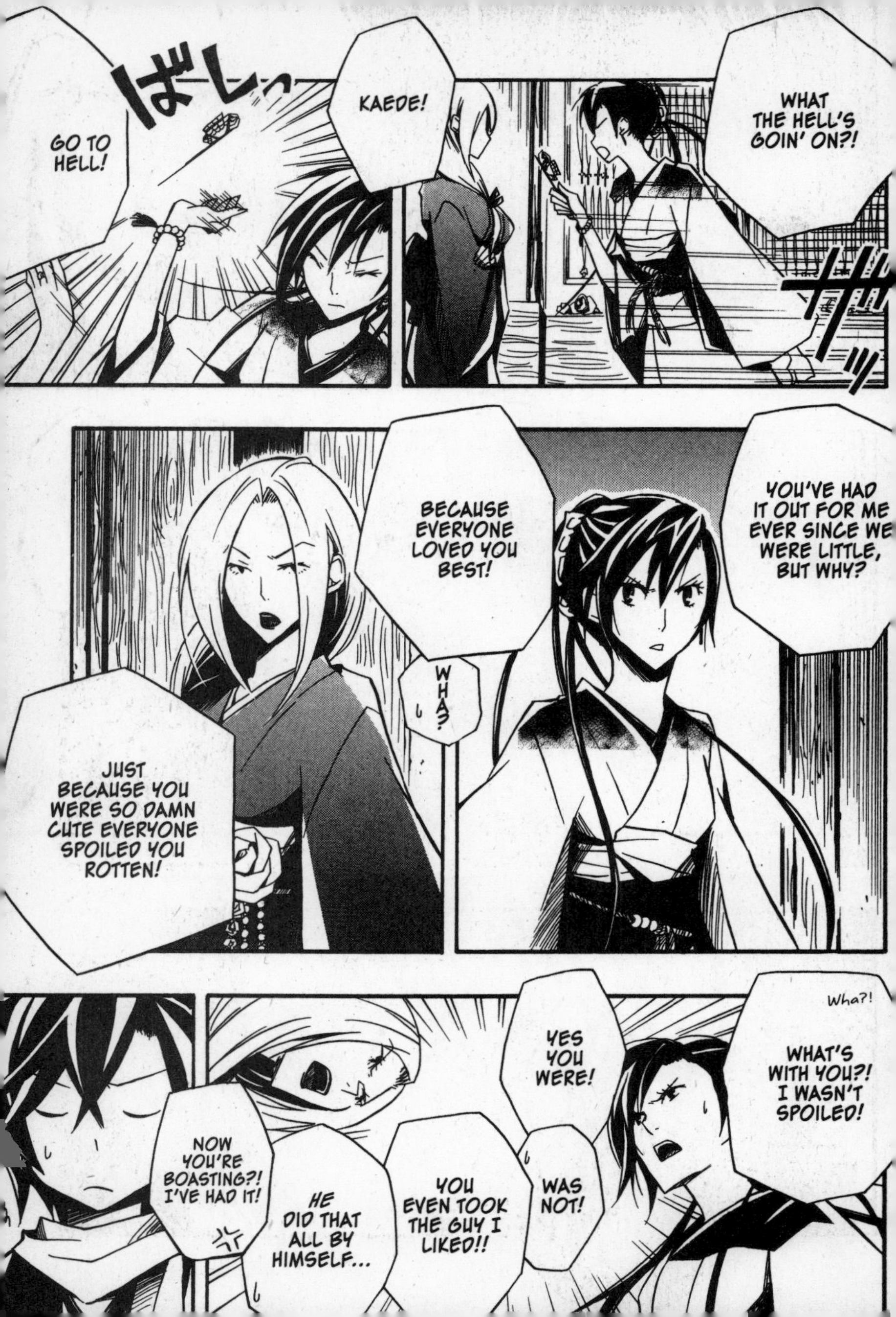
WHAT THE HELL'S GOIN' ON?!
ザッ
KAEDE!
ばしっ
GO TO HELL!
YOU'VE HAD IT OUT FOR ME EVER SINCE WE WERE LITTLE, BUT WHY?
BECAUSE EVERYONE LOVED YOU BEST!
WHA?
JUST BECAUSE YOU WERE SO DAMN CUTE EVERYONE SPOILED YOU ROTTEN!
Wha?!
WHAT'S WITH YOU?! I WASN'T SPOILED!
YES YOU WERE!
WAS NOT!
YOU EVEN TOOK THE GUY I LIKED!!
NOW YOU'RE BOASTING?! I'VE HAD IT!
HE DID THAT ALL BY HIMSELF...

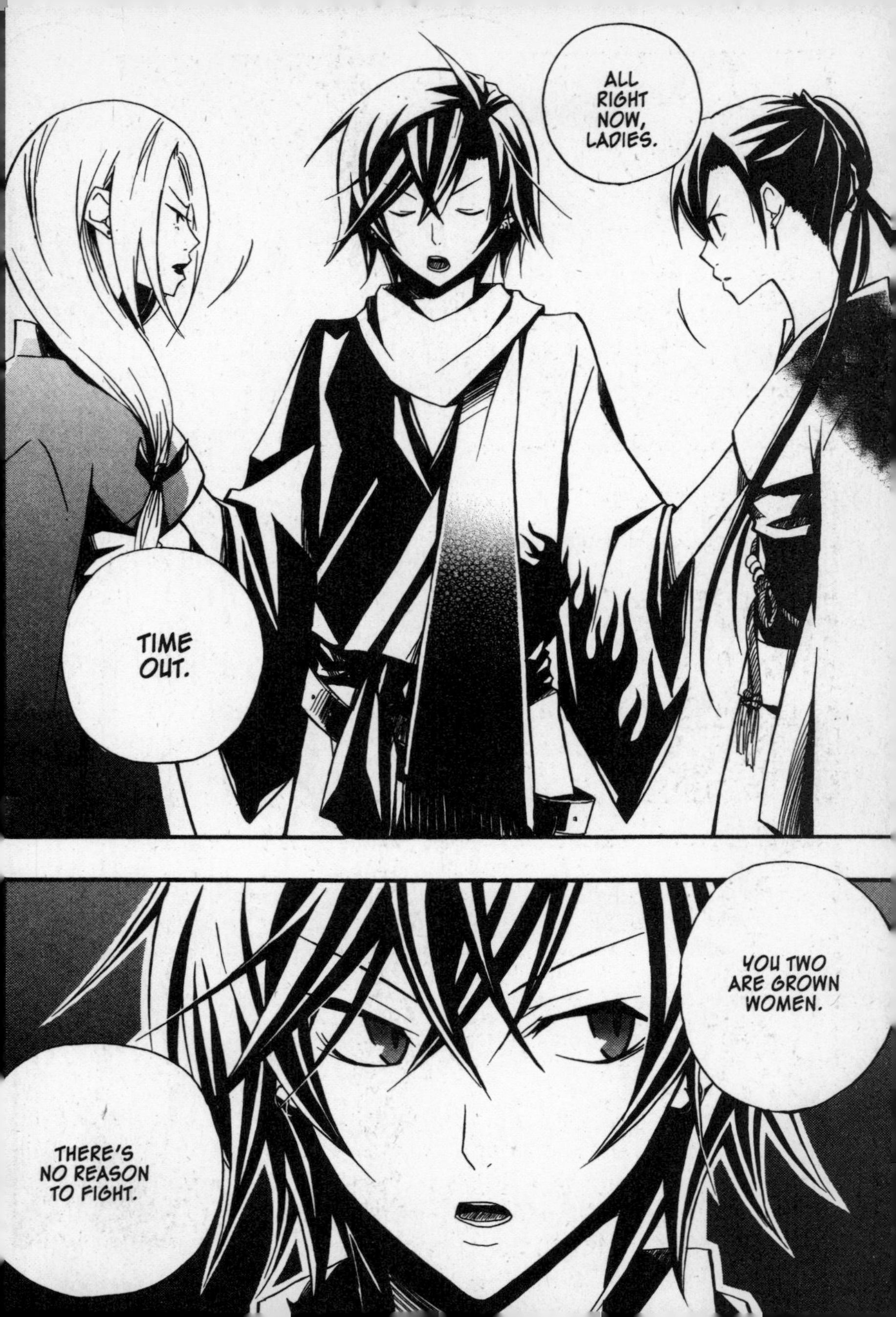
ALL RIGHT NOW, LADIES.
TIME OUT.
YOU TWO ARE GROWN WOMEN.
THERE'S NO REASON TO FIGHT.

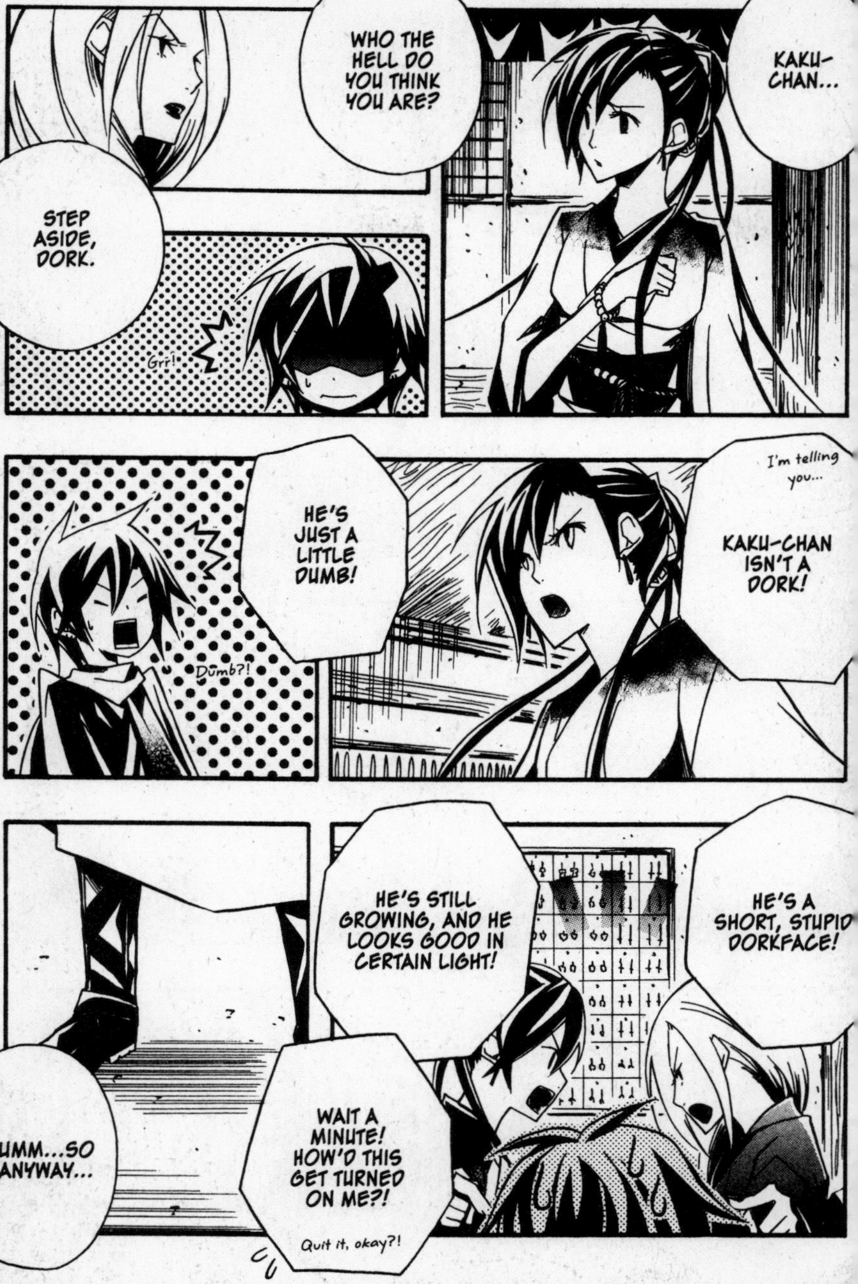
KAKU-CHAN...
WHO THE HELL DO YOU THINK YOU ARE?
STEP ASIDE, DORK.
Grr!
I'm telling you...
KAKU-CHAN ISN'T A DORK!
HE'S JUST A LITTLE DUMB!
Dumb?!
HE'S A SHORT, STUPID DORKFACE!
HE'S STILL GROWING, AND HE LOOKS GOOD IN CERTAIN LIGHT!
WAIT A MINUTE! HOW'D THIS GET TURNED ON ME?!
Quit it, okay?!
UMM...SO ANYWAY...

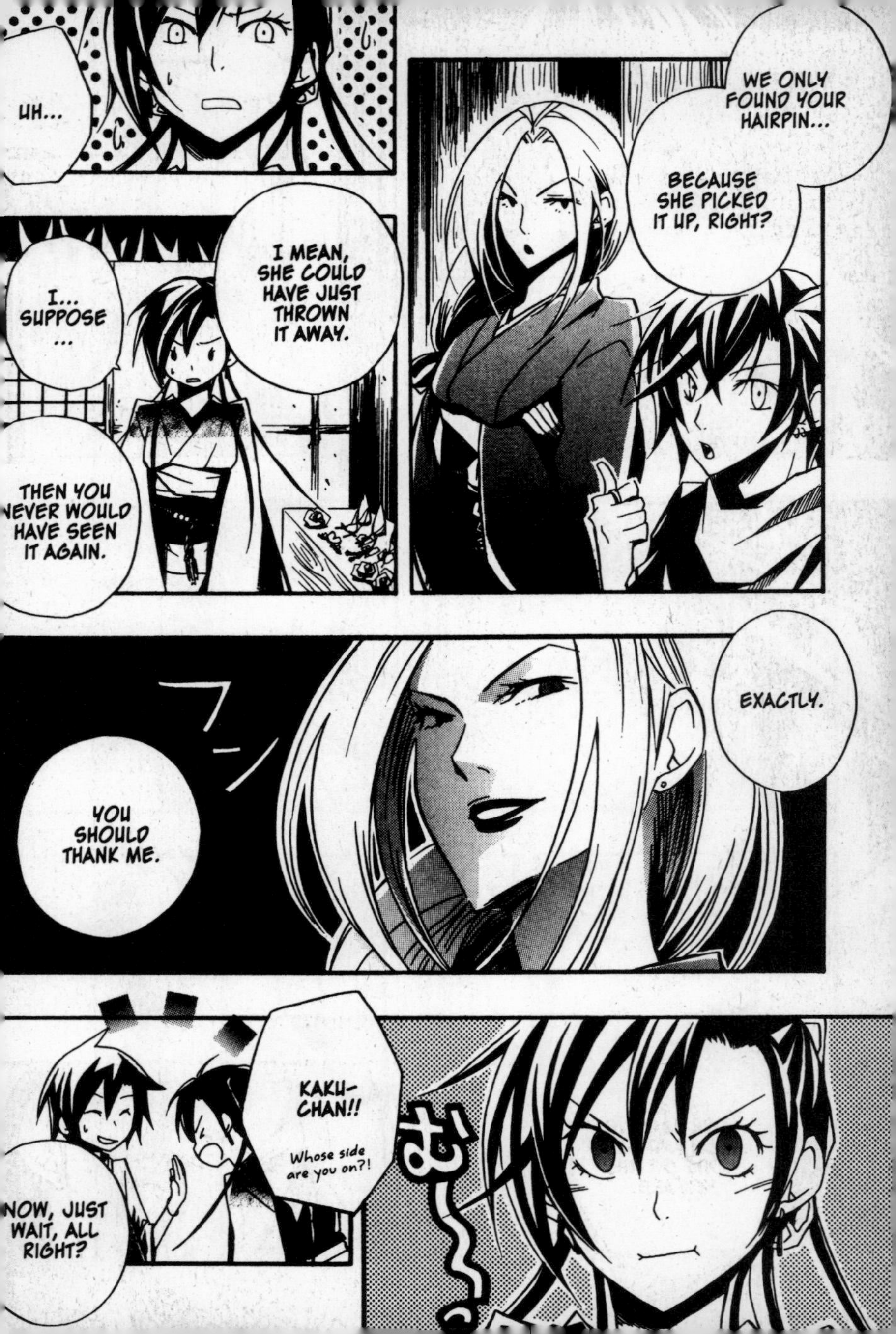
WE ONLY FOUND YOUR HAIRPIN...
BECAUSE SHE PICKED IT UP, RIGHT?
UH...
I MEAN, SHE COULD HAVE JUST THROWN IT AWAY.
I... SUPPOSE ...
THEN YOU NEVER WOULD HAVE SEEN IT AGAIN.
EXACTLY.
YOU SHOULD THANK ME.
む
KAKU-CHAN!!
Whose side are you on?!
NOW, JUST WAIT, ALL RIGHT?

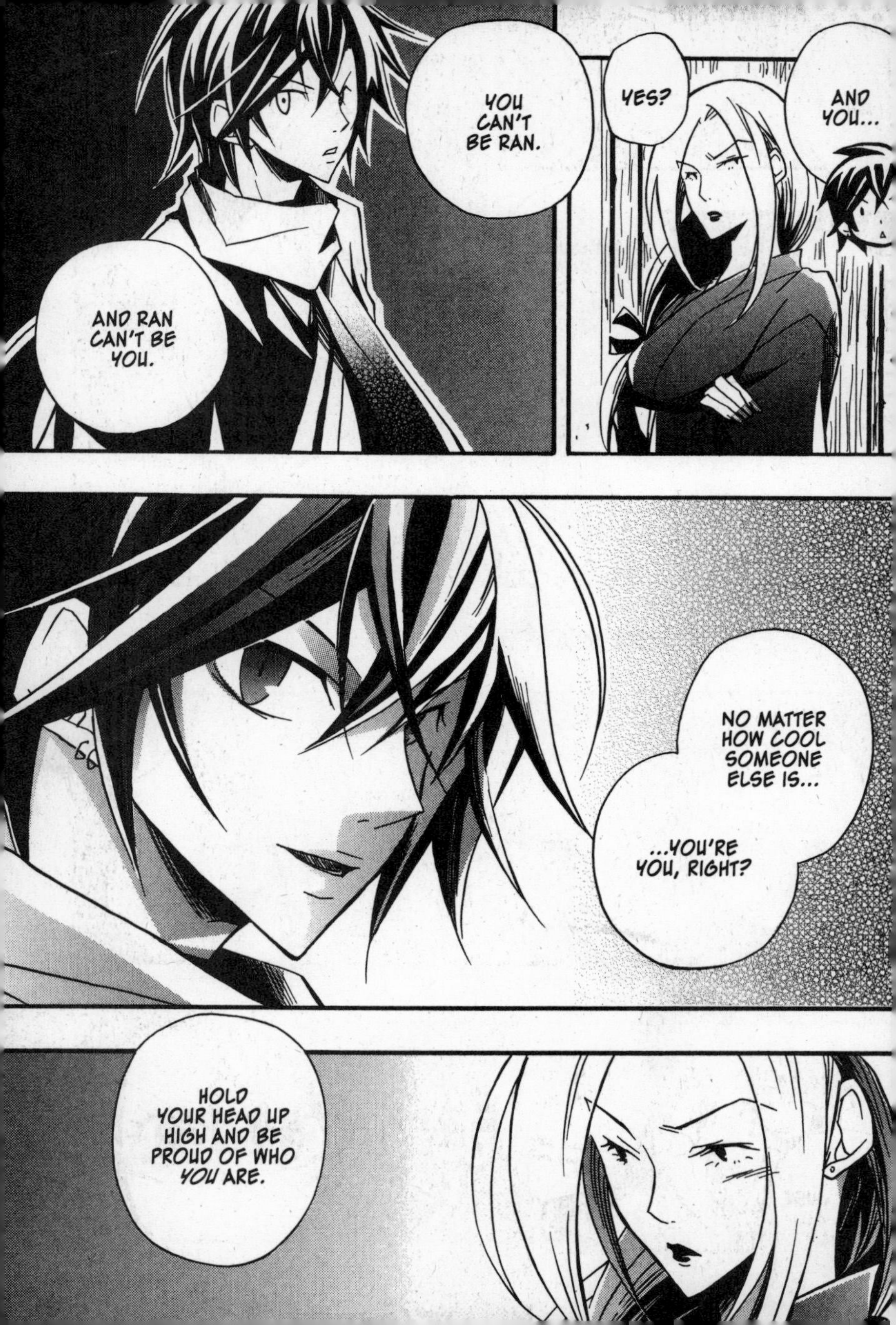
AND YOU...
YES?
YOU CAN'T BE RAN.
AND RAN CAN'T BE YOU.
NO MATTER HOW COOL SOMEONE ELSE IS...
...YOU'RE YOU, RIGHT?
HOLD YOUR HEAD UP HIGH AND BE PROUD OF WHO *YOU* ARE.

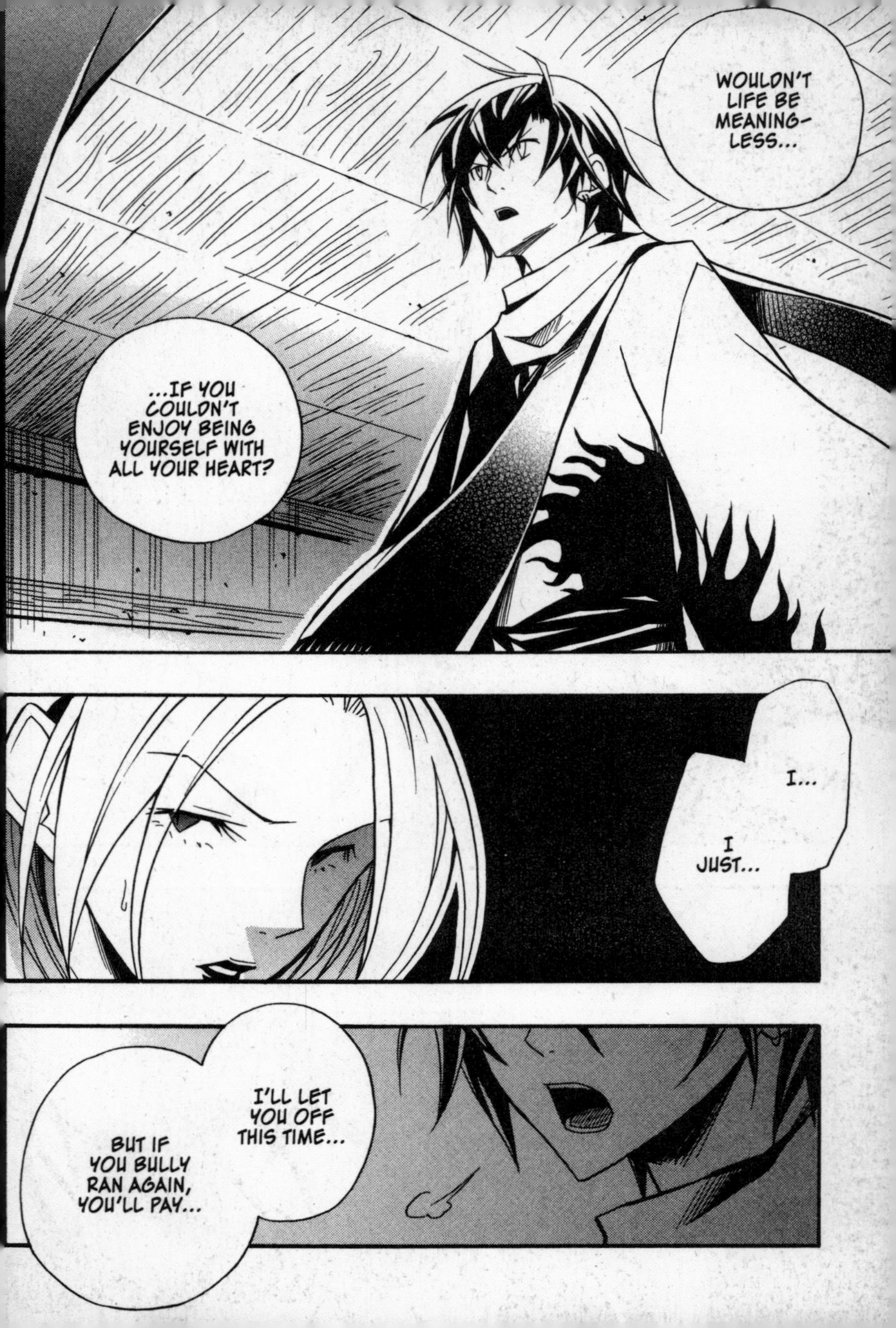
WOULDN'T LIFE BE MEANINGLESS...
...IF YOU COULDN'T ENJOY BEING YOURSELF WITH ALL YOUR HEART?
I...
I JUST...
I'LL LET YOU OFF THIS TIME...
BUT IF YOU BULLY RAN AGAIN, YOU'LL PAY...

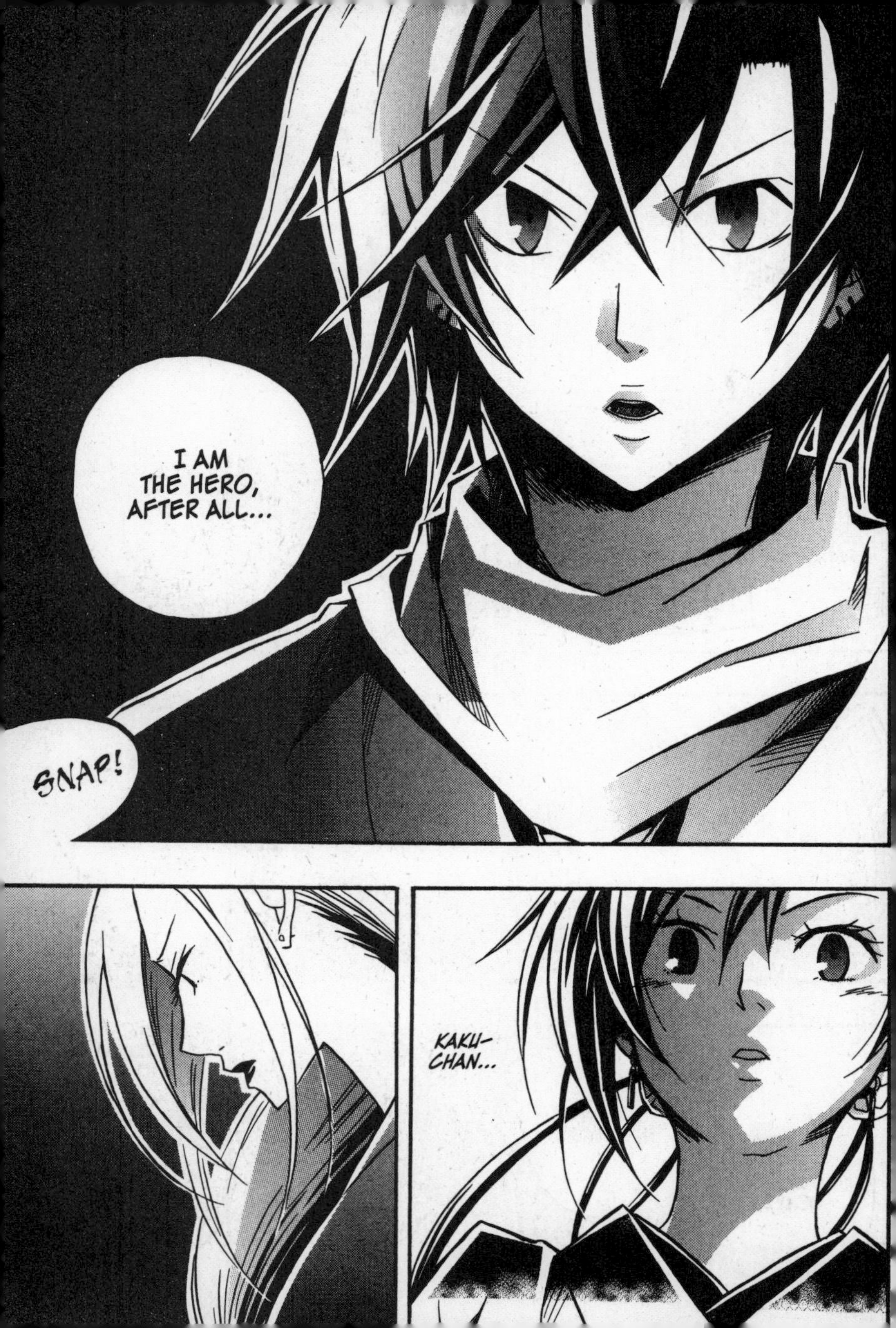
I AM THE HERO, AFTER ALL...
SNAP!
KAKU-CHAN...

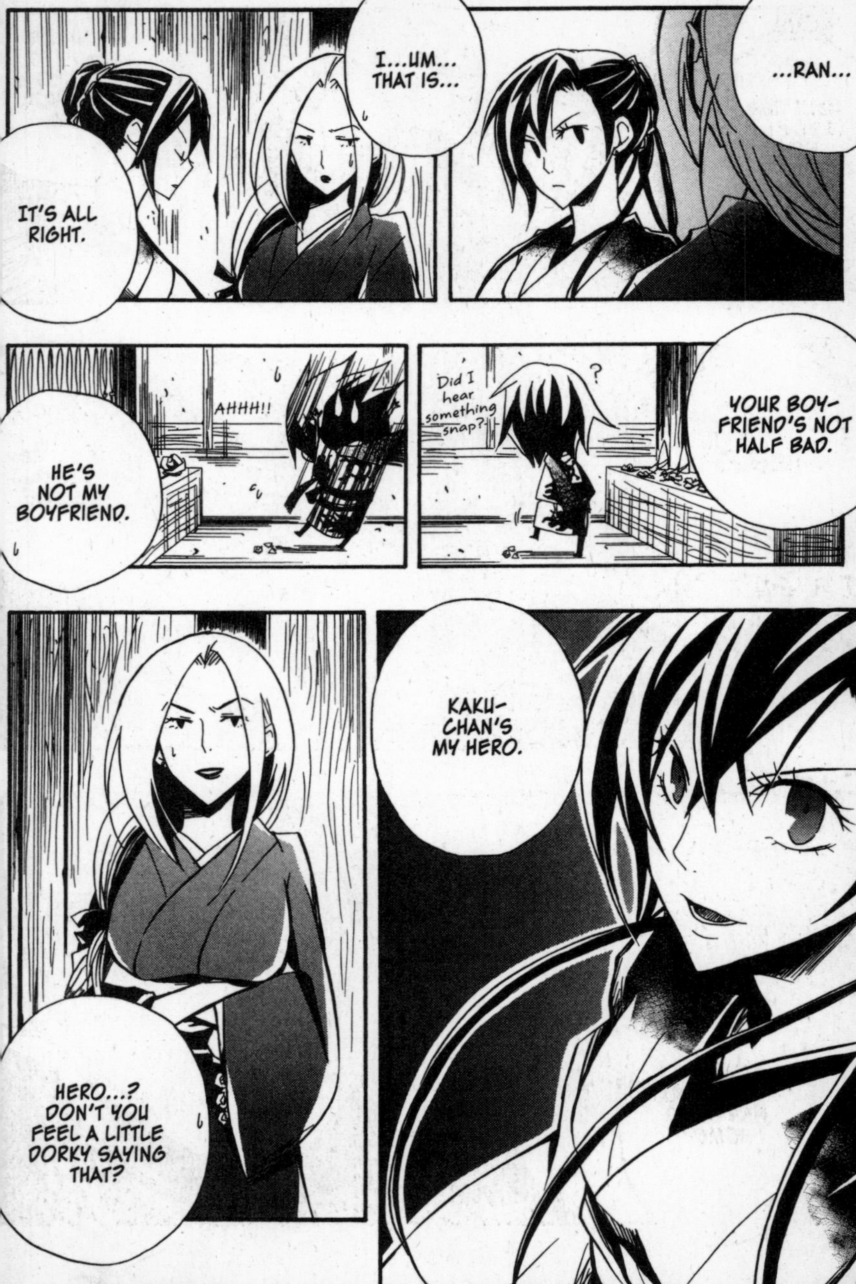
...RAN...
I...UM... THAT IS...
IT'S ALL RIGHT.
YOUR BOY-FRIEND'S NOT HALF BAD.
Did I hear something snap?
AHHH!!
HE'S NOT MY BOYFRIEND.
KAKU-CHAN'S MY HERO.
HERO...? DON'T YOU FEEL A LITTLE DORKY SAYING THAT?

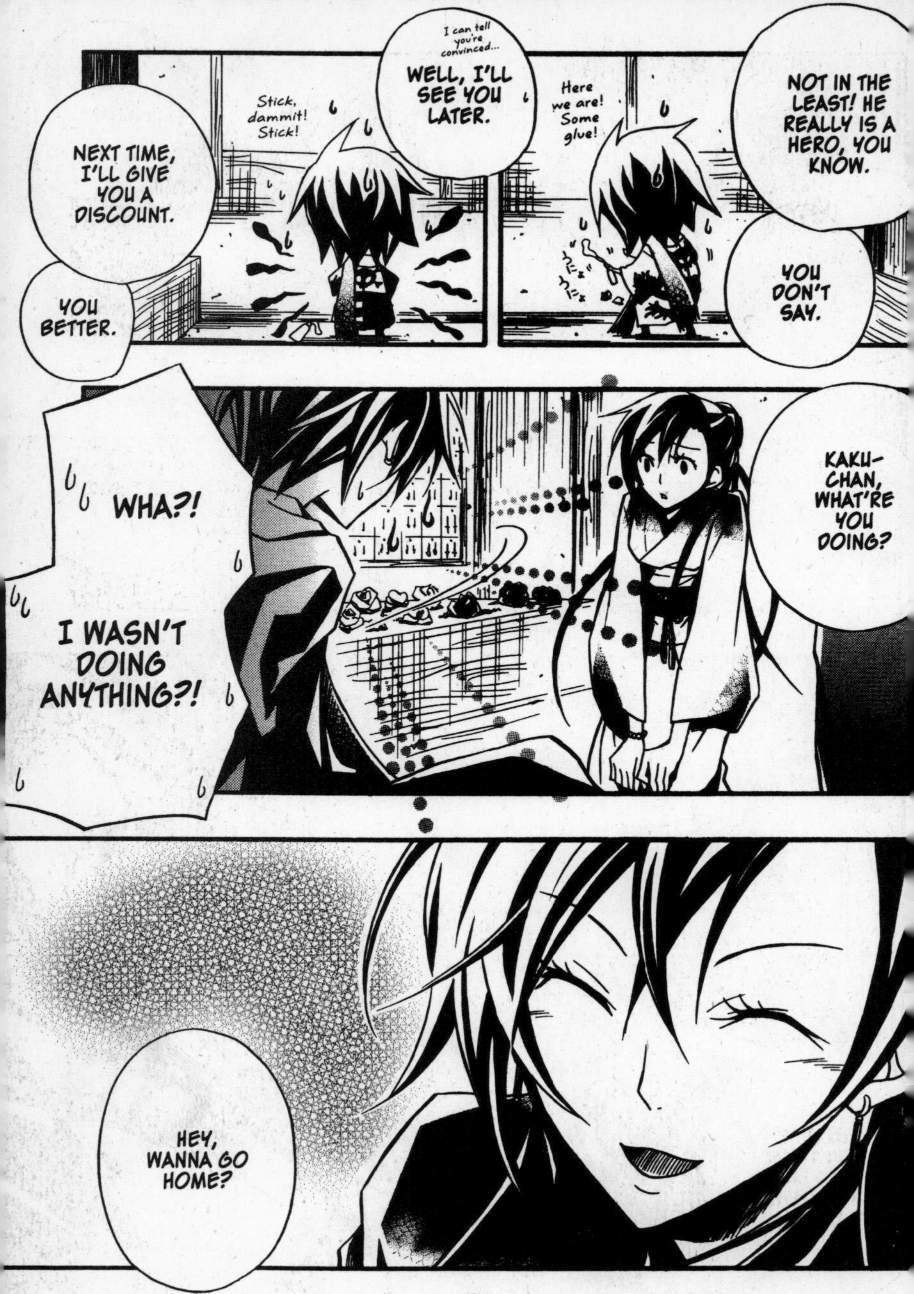
NOT IN THE LEAST! HE REALLY IS A HERO, YOU KNOW.
Here we are! Some glue!
YOU DON'T SAY.
I can tell you're convinced...
WELL, I'LL SEE YOU LATER.
Stick, dammit! Stick!
NEXT TIME, I'LL GIVE YOU A DISCOUNT.
YOU BETTER.
KAKU-CHAN, WHAT'RE YOU DOING?
WHA?!
I WASN'T DOING ANYTHING?!
HEY, WANNA GO HOME?

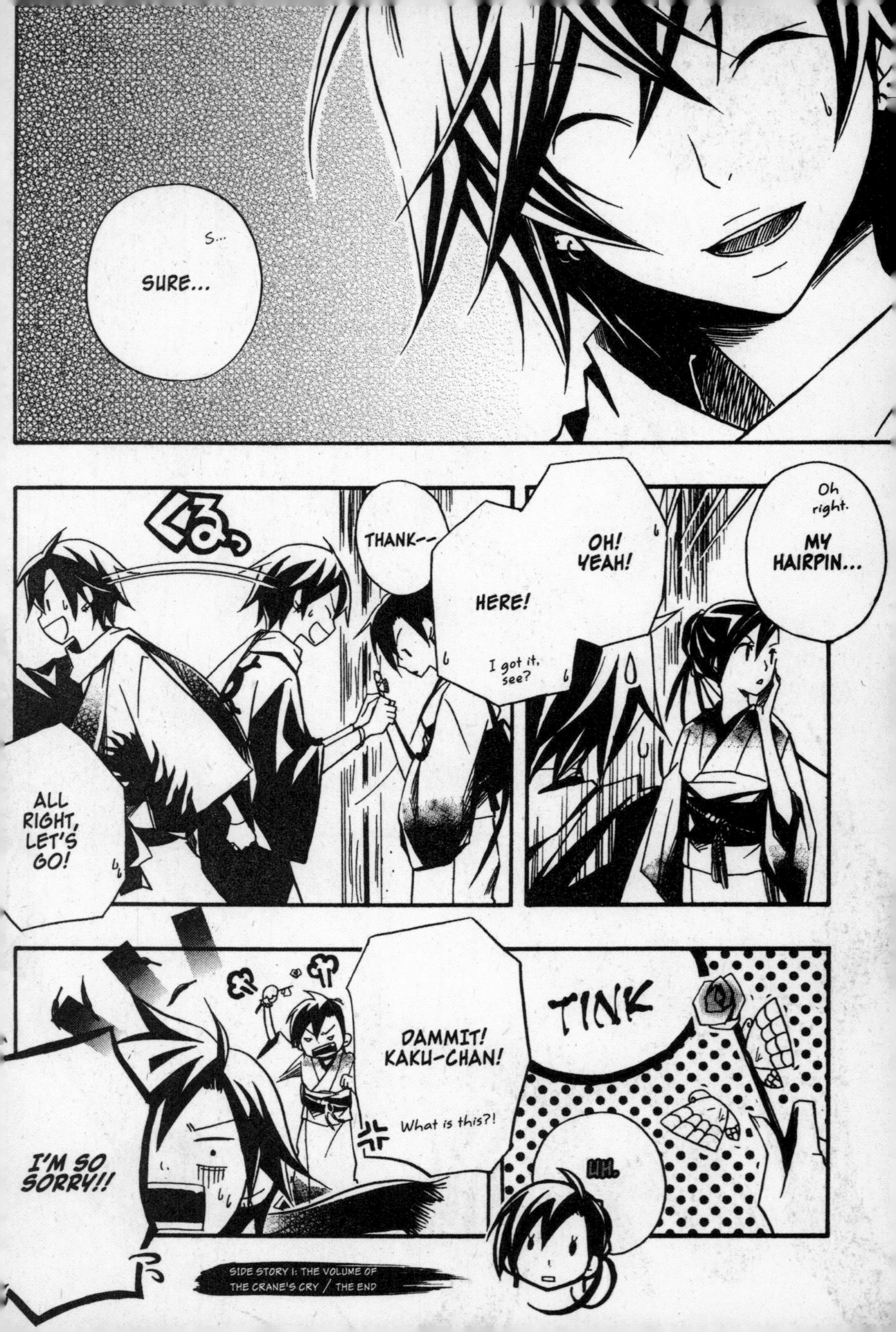
S...
SURE...
Oh right.
MY HAIRPIN...
OH! YEAH!
HERE!
I got it, see?
THANK--
くるっ
ALL RIGHT, LET'S GO!
TINK
UH.
DAMMIT! KAKU-CHAN!
What is this?!
I'M SO SORRY!!
SIDE STORY 1: THE VOLUME OF THE CRANE'S CRY / THE END

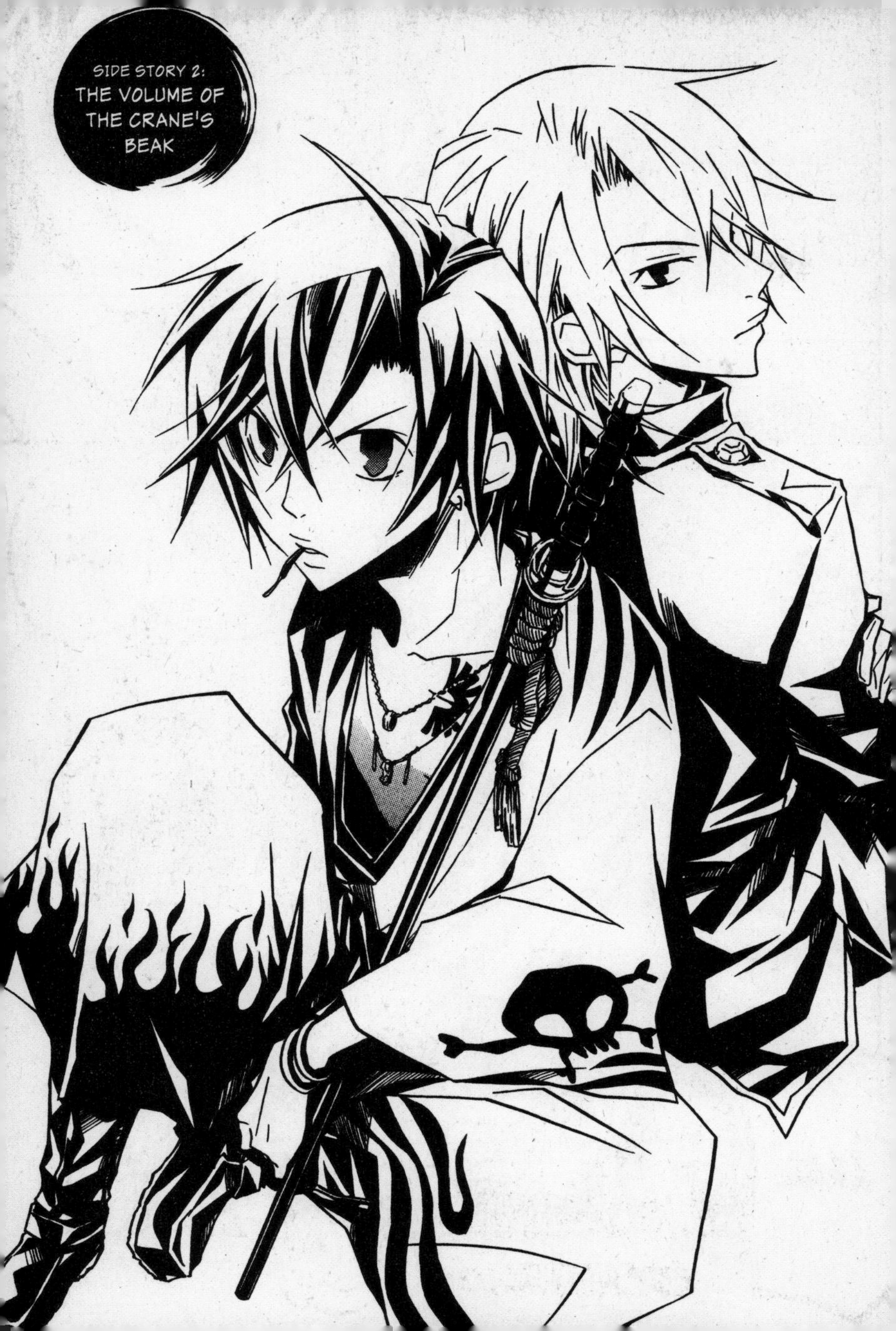
SIDE STORY 2:
THE VOLUME OF
THE CRANE'S
BEAK

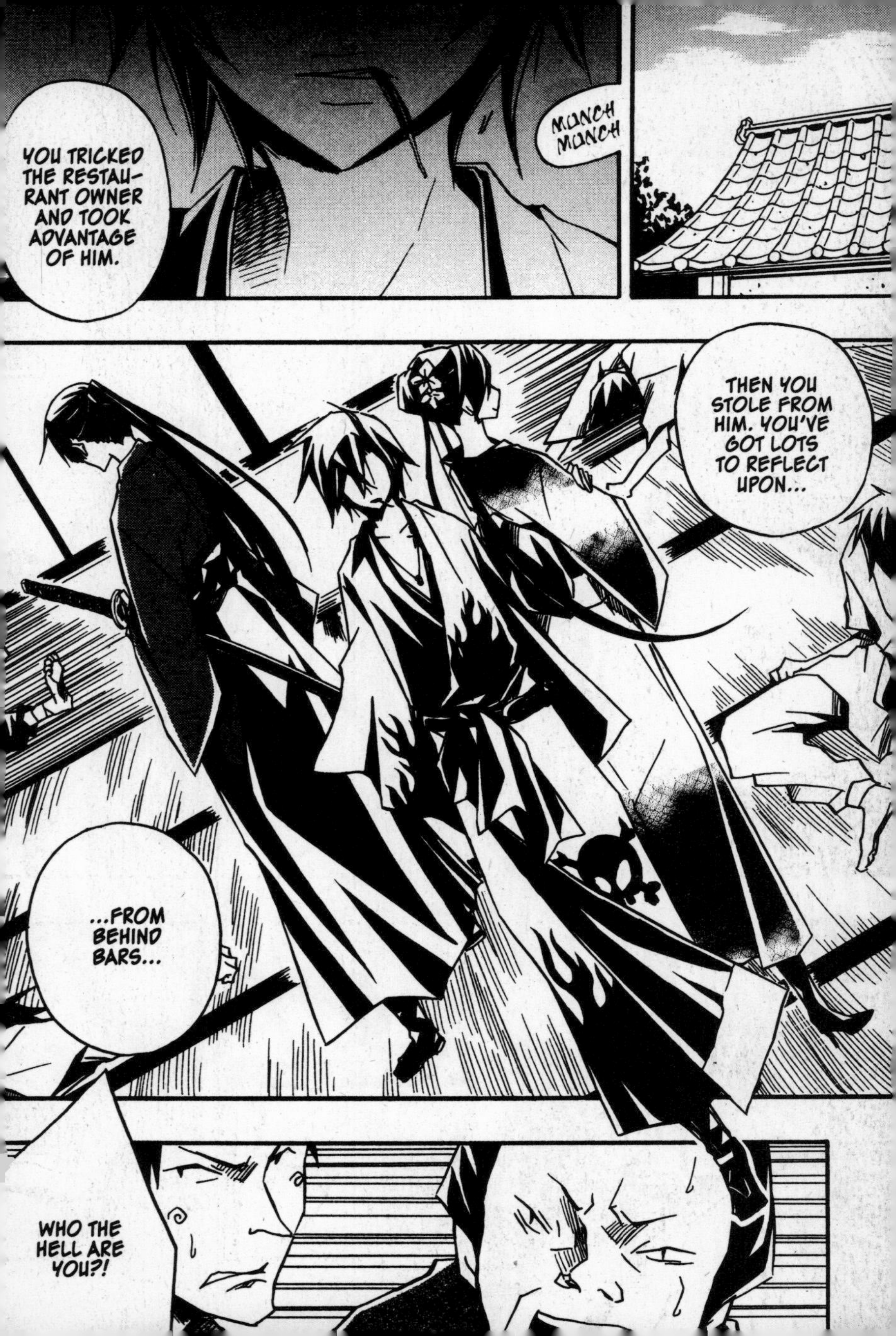
MONCH MONCH
YOU TRICKED THE RESTAU-RANT OWNER AND TOOK ADVANTAGE OF HIM.
THEN YOU STOLE FROM HIM. YOU'VE GOT LOTS TO REFLECT UPON...
...FROM BEHIND BARS...
WHO THE HELL ARE YOU?!

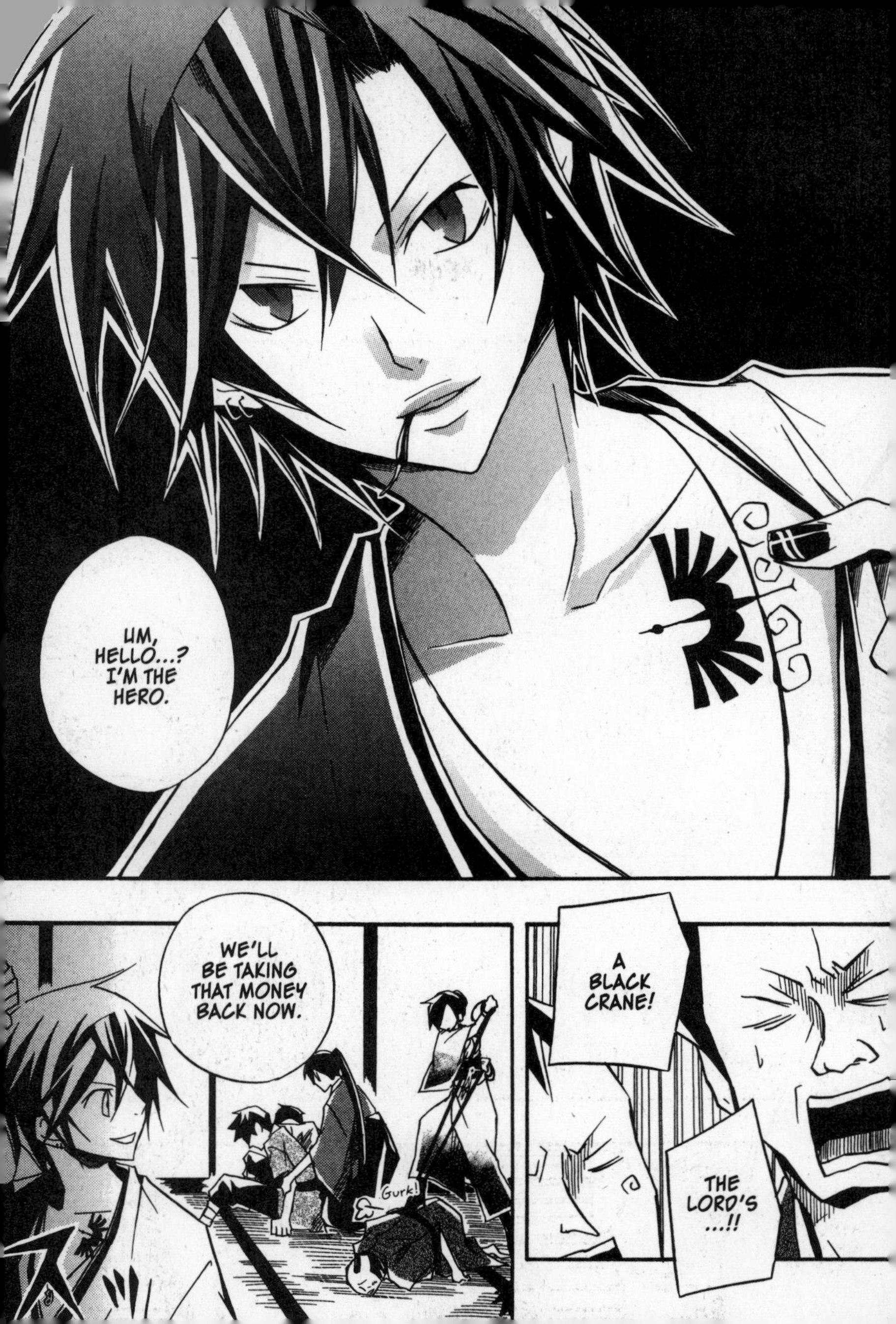
UM, HELLO...? I'M THE HERO.
A BLACK CRANE!
THE LORD'S ...!!
WE'LL BE TAKING THAT MONEY BACK NOW.
Gurk!

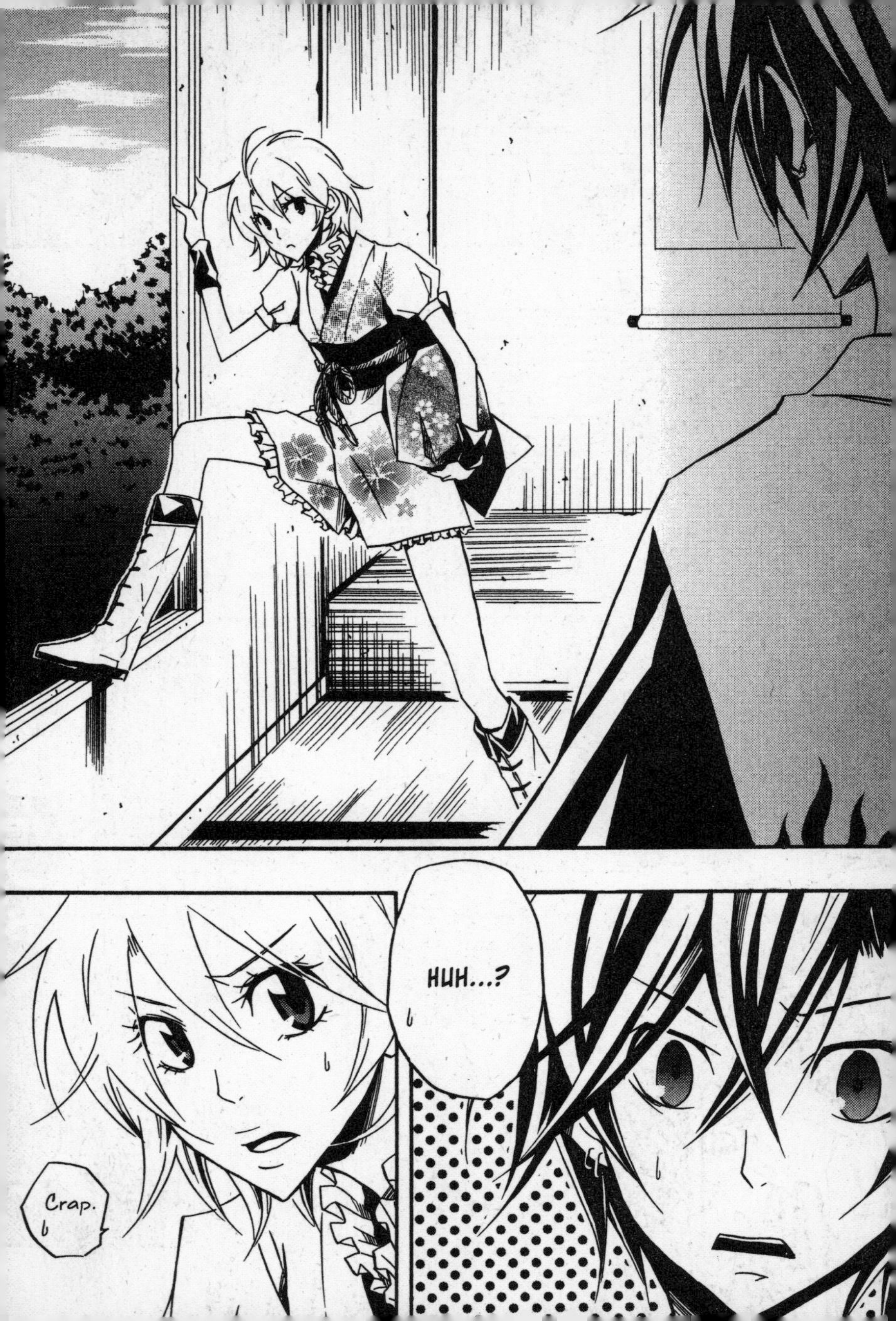
HUH...?
Crap.

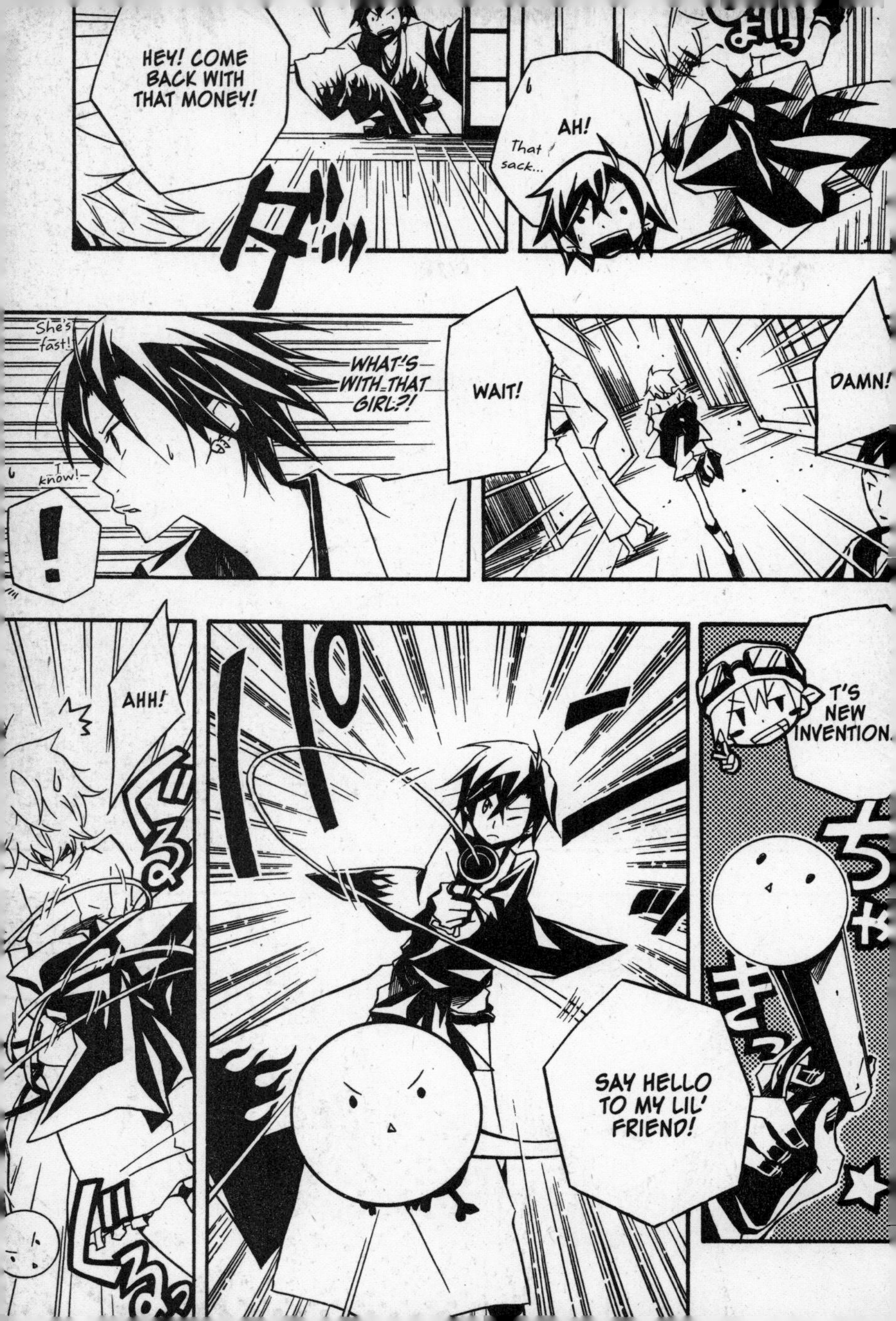
AH!
That sack...
HEY! COME BACK WITH THAT MONEY!
DAMN!
WAIT!
WHAT'S WITH THAT GIRL?!
She's fast!
I know!
!
T'S NEW INVENTION.
SAY HELLO TO MY LIL' FRIEND!
AHH!

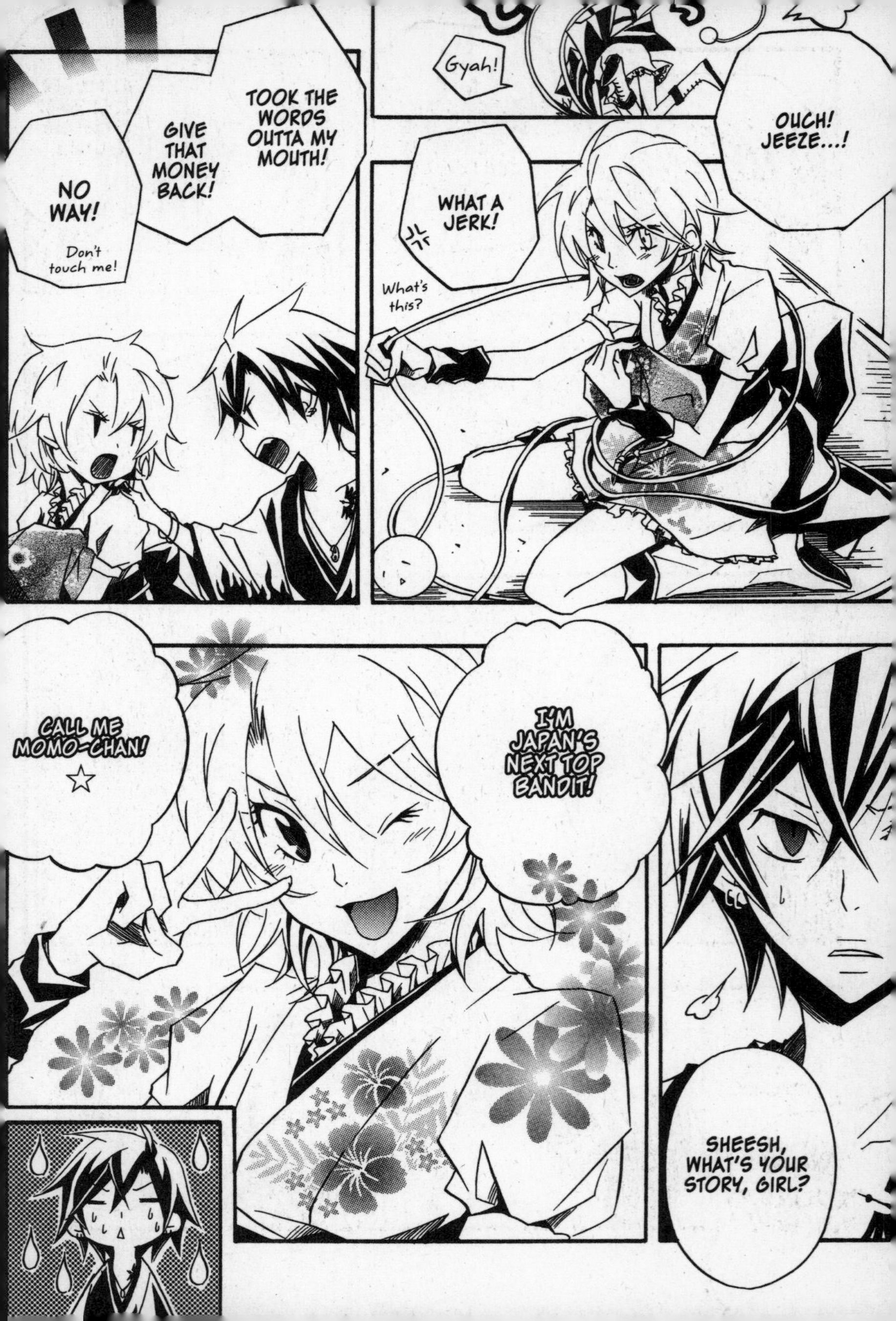
OUCH! JEEZE...!
Gyah!
WHAT A JERK!
What's this?
TOOK THE WORDS OUTTA MY MOUTH!
GIVE THAT MONEY BACK!
NO WAY!
Don't touch me!
SHEESH, WHAT'S YOUR STORY, GIRL?
I'M JAPAN'S NEXT TOP BANDIT!
CALL ME MOMO-CHAN! ☆

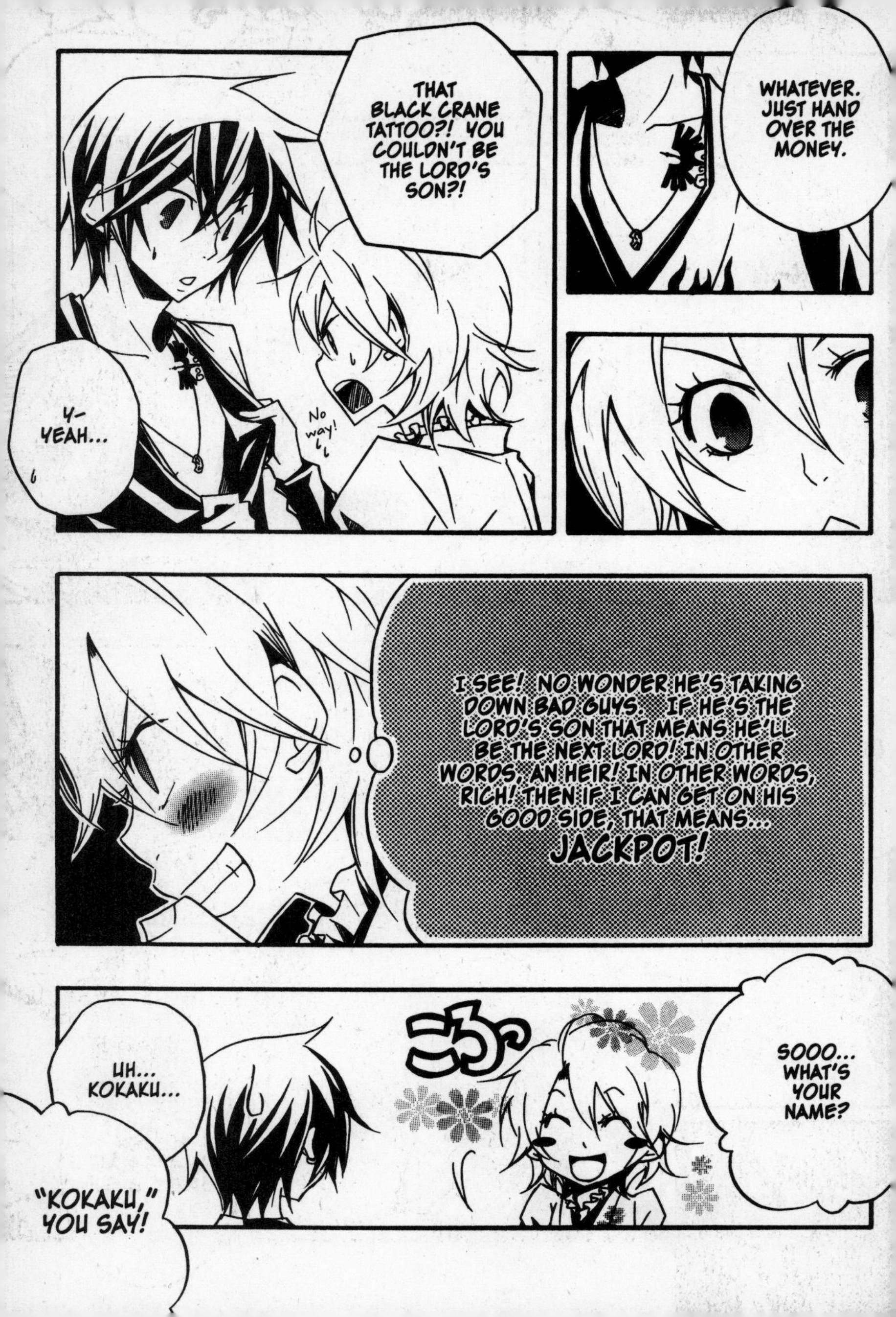
WHATEVER. JUST HAND OVER THE MONEY.
THAT BLACK CRANE TATTOO?! YOU COULDN'T BE THE LORD'S SON?!
No way!
Y-YEAH...
I SEE! NO WONDER HE'S TAKING DOWN BAD GUYS. IF HE'S THE LORD'S SON THAT MEANS HE'LL BE THE NEXT LORD! IN OTHER WORDS, AN HEIR! IN OTHER WORDS, RICH! THEN IF I CAN GET ON HIS GOOD SIDE, THAT MEANS...
JACKPOT!
SOOO... WHAT'S YOUR NAME?
ころっ
UH... KOKAKU...
"KOKAKU," YOU SAY!

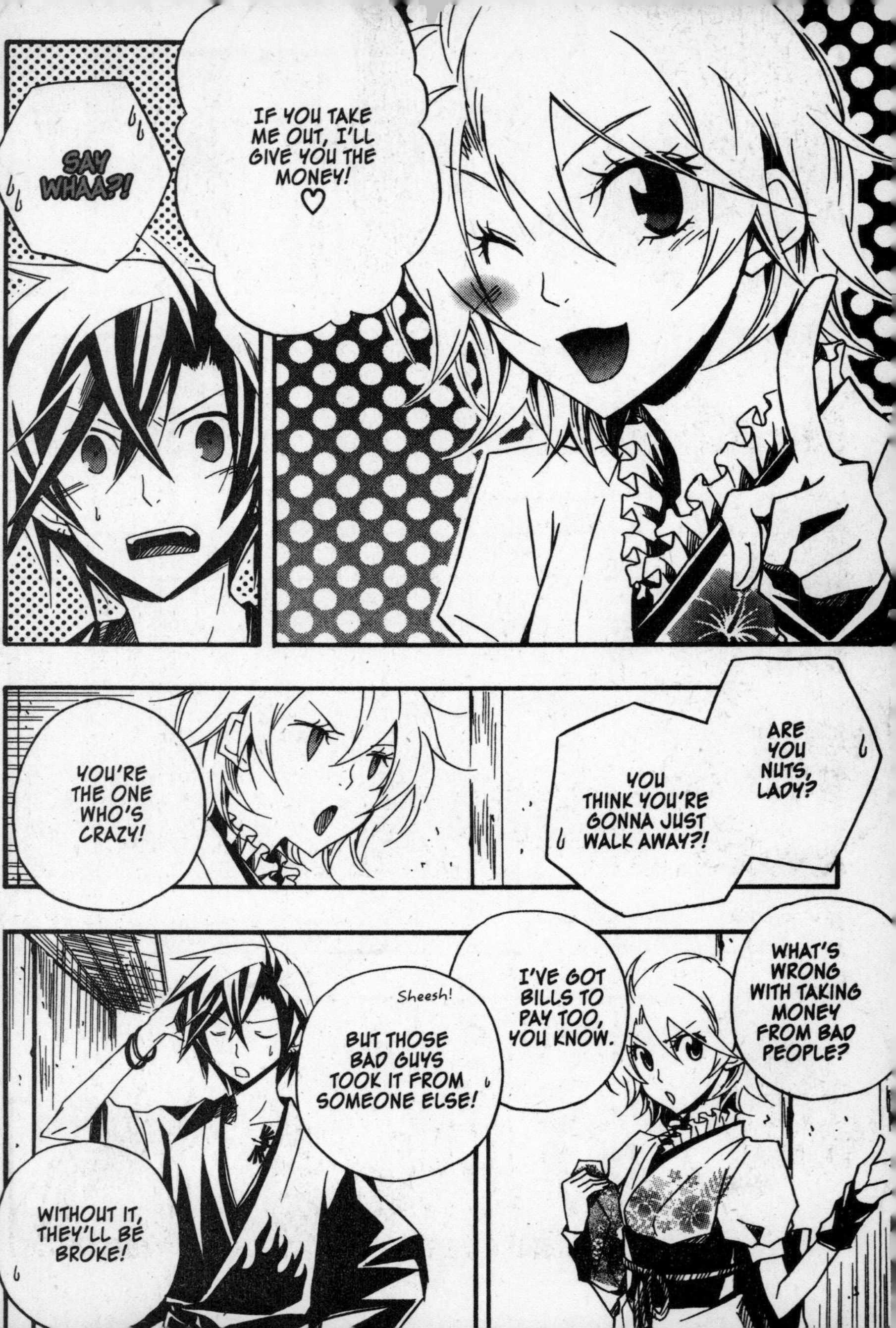
IF YOU TAKE ME OUT, I'LL GIVE YOU THE MONEY! ♡
SAY WHAA?!
ARE YOU NUTS, LADY?
YOU THINK YOU'RE GONNA JUST WALK AWAY?!
YOU'RE THE ONE WHO'S CRAZY!
WHAT'S WRONG WITH TAKING MONEY FROM BAD PEOPLE?
I'VE GOT BILLS TO PAY TOO, YOU KNOW.
Sheesh!
BUT THOSE BAD GUYS TOOK IT FROM SOMEONE ELSE!
WITHOUT IT, THEY'LL BE BROKE!

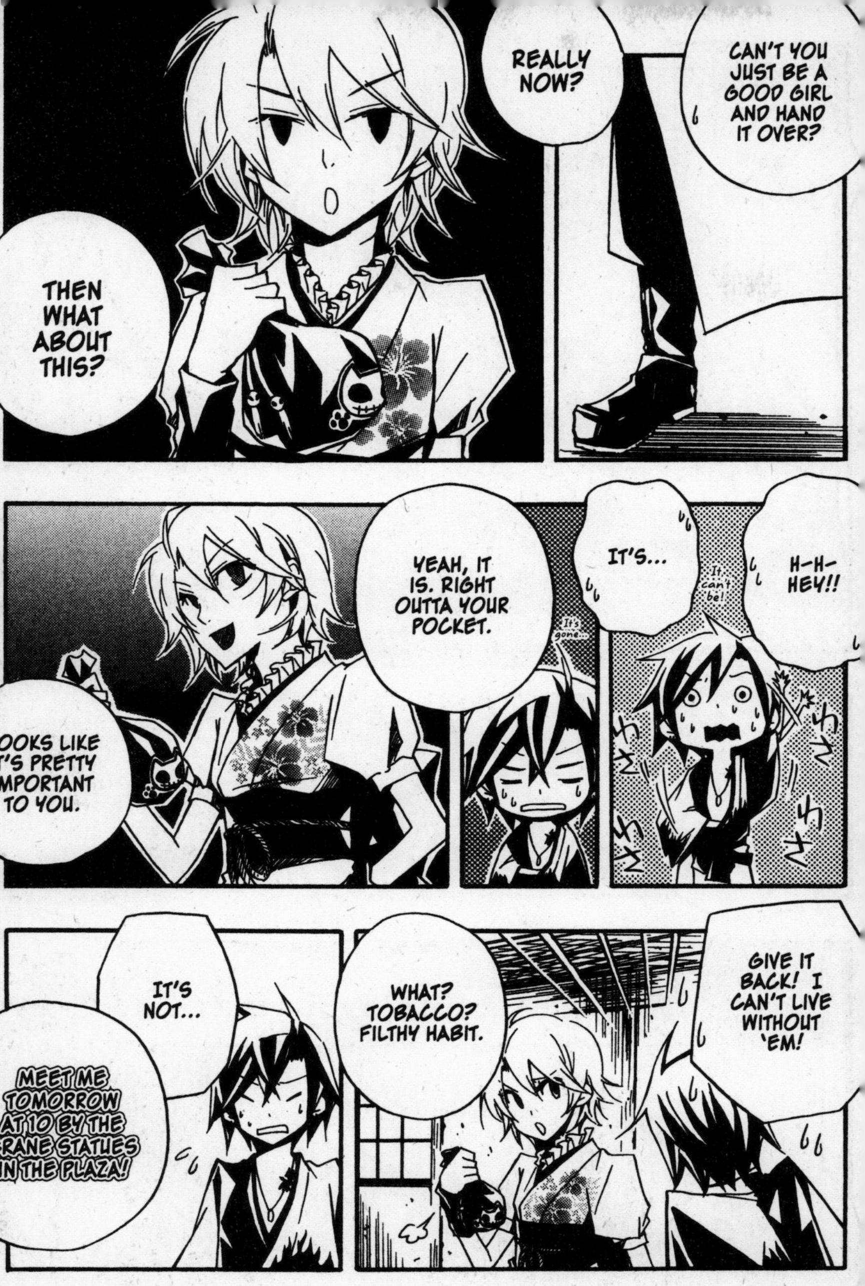
CAN'T YOU JUST BE A GOOD GIRL AND HAND IT OVER?
REALLY NOW?
THEN WHAT ABOUT THIS?
H-H-HEY!!
It can't be!
IT'S...
It's gone...
YEAH, IT IS. RIGHT OUTTA YOUR POCKET.
LOOKS LIKE IT'S PRETTY IMPORTANT TO YOU.
GIVE IT BACK! I CAN'T LIVE WITHOUT 'EM!
WHAT? TOBACCO? FILTHY HABIT.
IT'S NOT...
MEET ME TOMORROW AT 10 BY THE CRANE STATUES IN THE PLAZA!

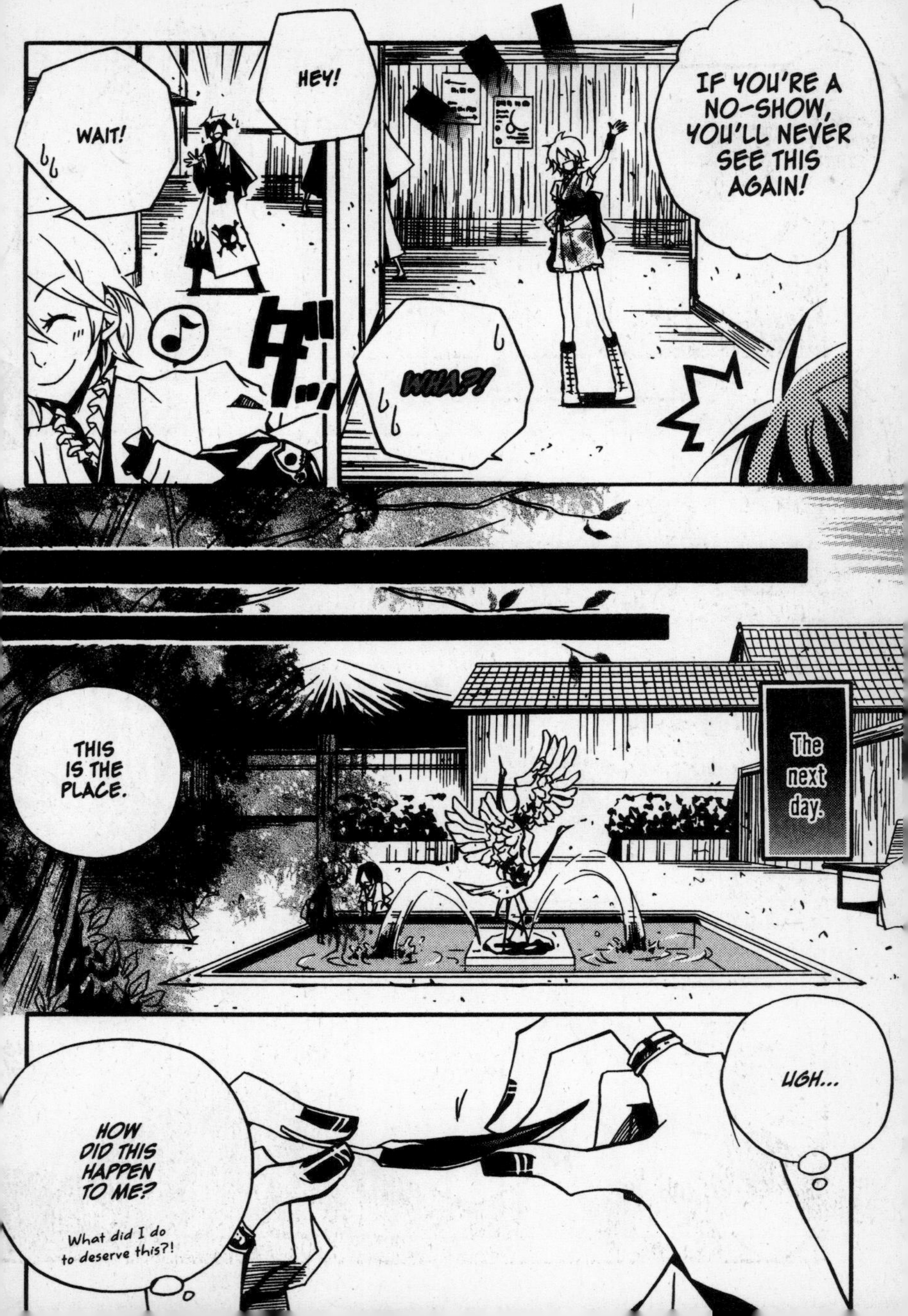
IF YOU'RE A NO-SHOW, YOU'LL NEVER SEE THIS AGAIN!
WHA?!
HEY!
WAIT!
ダッ
The next day.
THIS IS THE PLACE.
UGH...
HOW DID THIS HAPPEN TO ME?
What did I do to deserve this?!

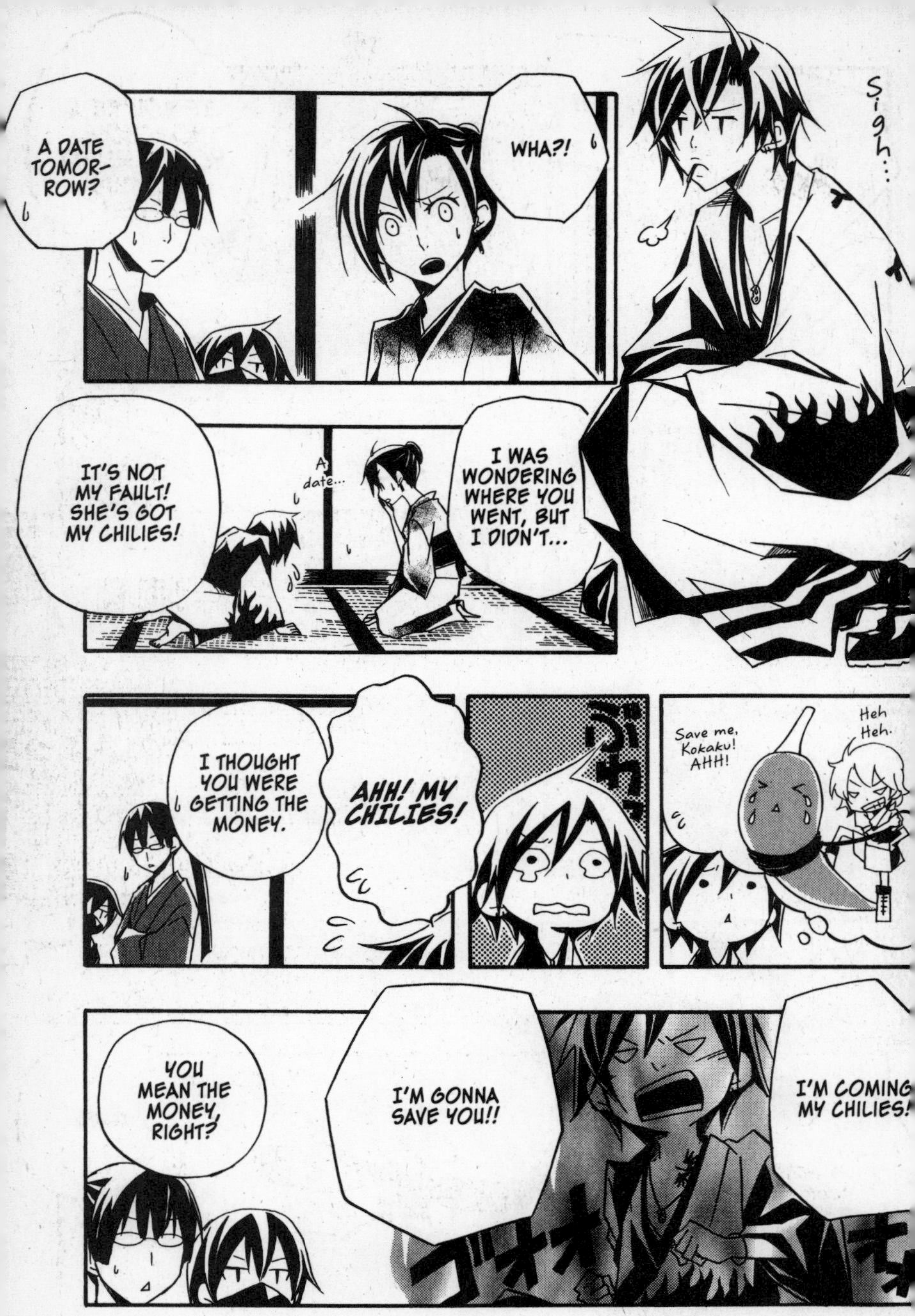
Sigh...
WHA?!
A DATE TOMORROW?
I WAS WONDERING WHERE YOU WENT, BUT I DIDN'T...
A date...
IT'S NOT MY FAULT! SHE'S GOT MY CHILIES!
Heh Heh.
Save me, Kokaku! AHH!
AHH! MY CHILIES!
I THOUGHT YOU WERE GETTING THE MONEY.
I'M COMING MY CHILIES!
I'M GONNA SAVE YOU!!
YOU MEAN THE MONEY, RIGHT?

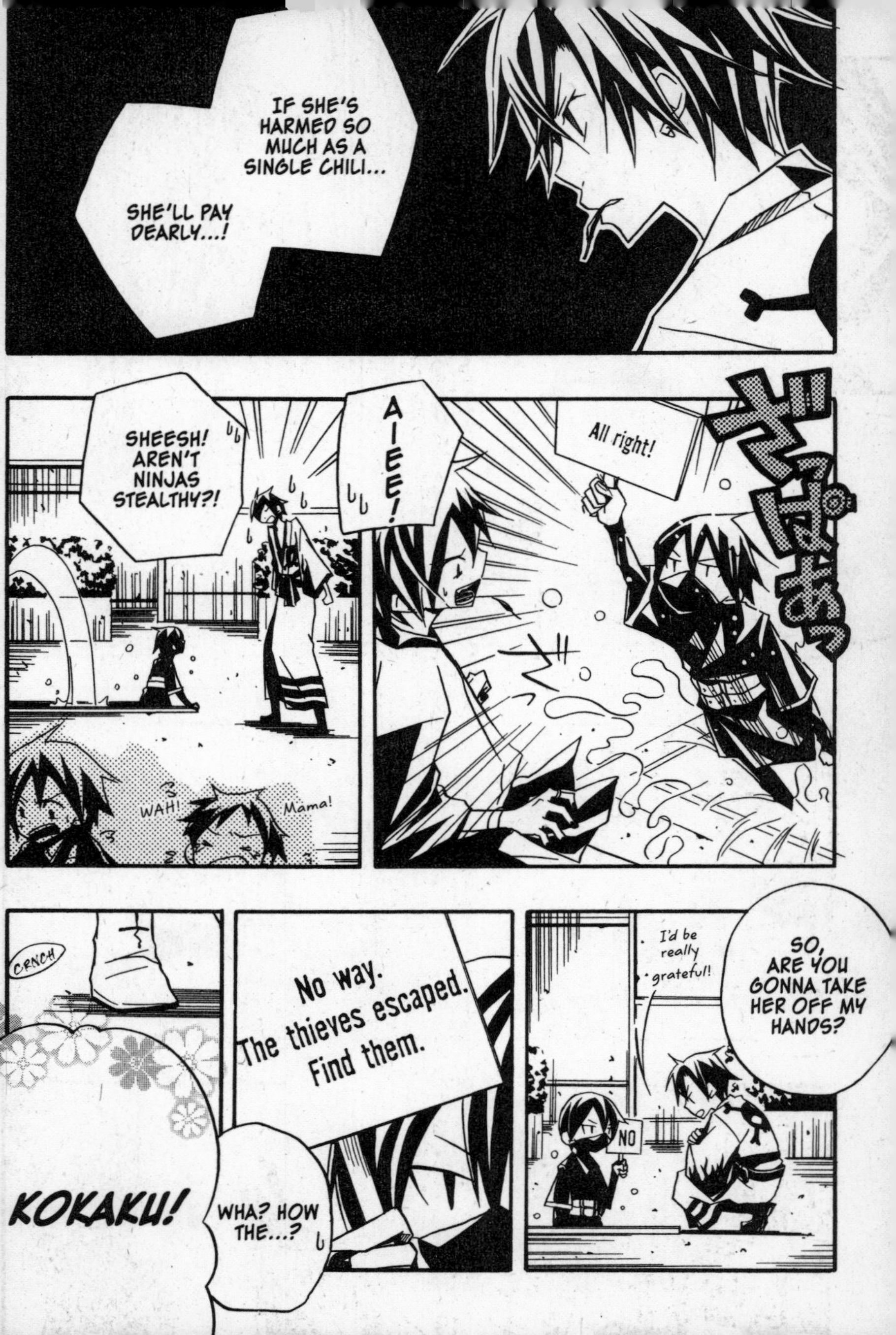
IF SHE'S HARMED SO MUCH AS A SINGLE CHILI...
SHE'LL PAY DEARLY...!
ざぱぁっ
All right!
AIEE!
SHEESH! AREN'T NINJAS STEALTHY?!
Mama!
WAH!
SO, ARE YOU GONNA TAKE HER OFF MY HANDS?
I'd be really grateful!
NO
No way. The thieves escaped. Find them.
WHA? HOW THE...?
CRNCH
KOKAKU!

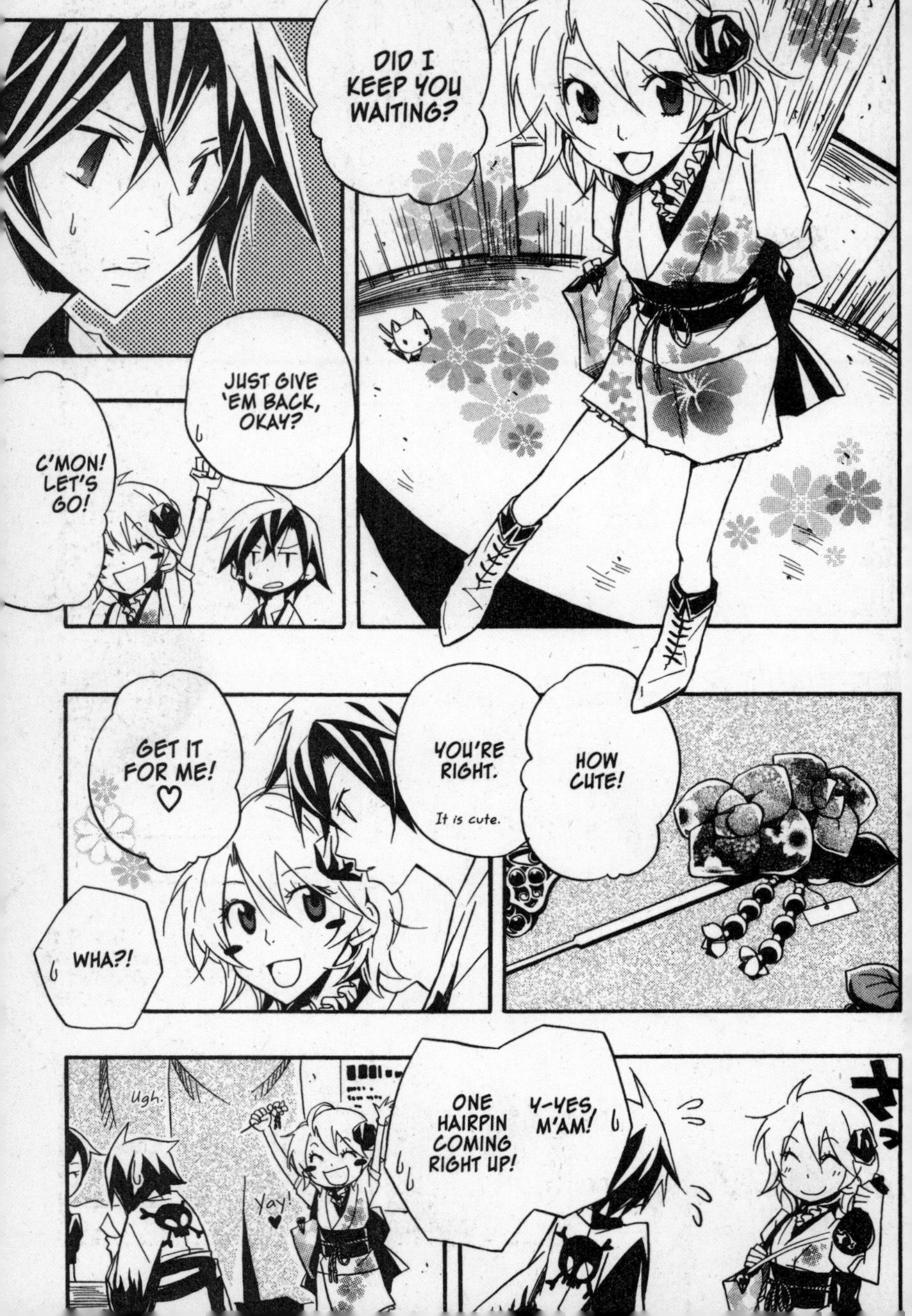
DID I KEEP YOU WAITING?
JUST GIVE 'EM BACK, OKAY?
C'MON! LET'S GO!
HOW CUTE!
YOU'RE RIGHT.
It is cute.
GET IT FOR ME! ♡
WHA?!
Y-YES, M'AM!
ONE HAIRPIN COMING RIGHT UP!
Yay! ♡
Ugh.

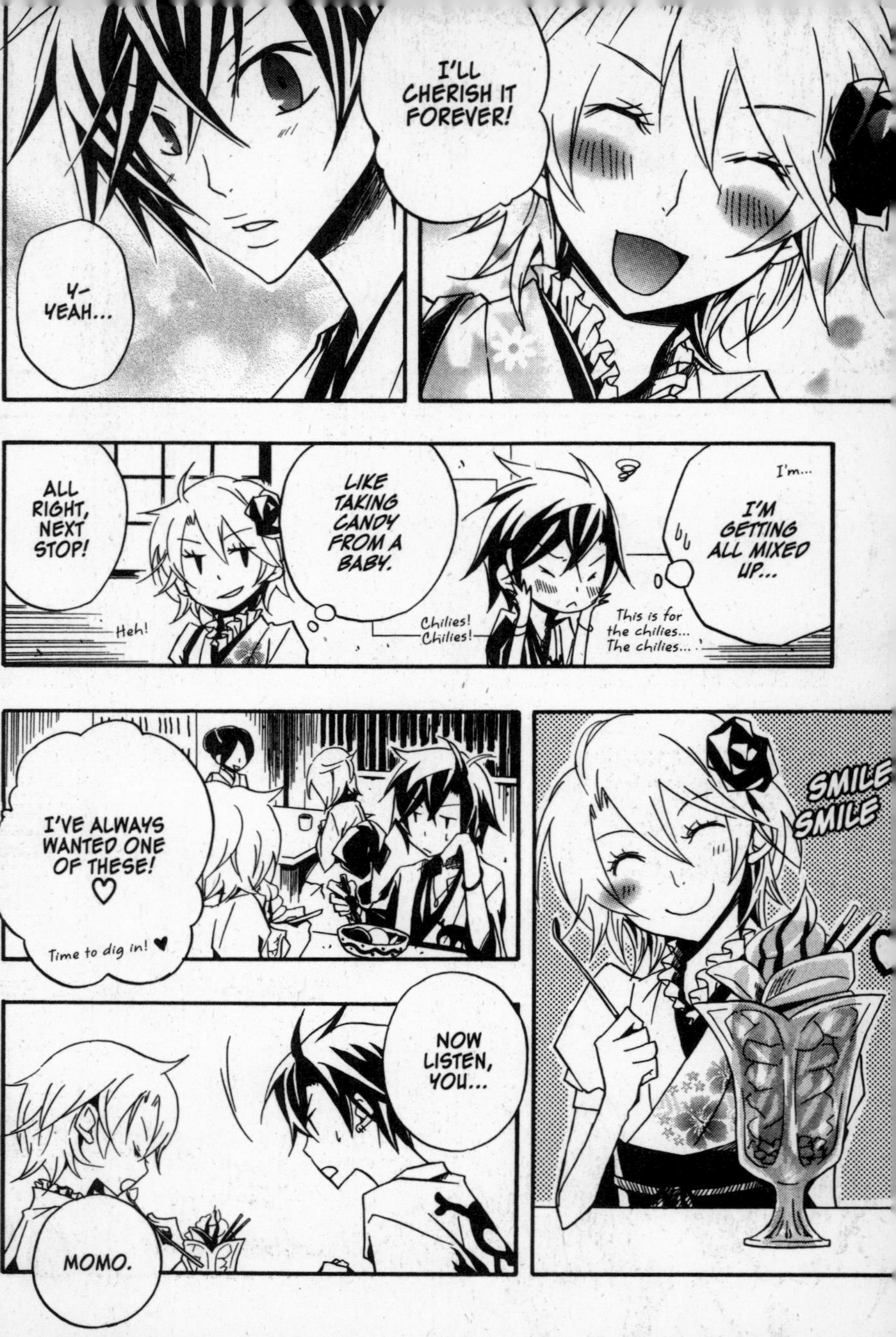
I'LL CHERISH IT FOREVER!
Y-YEAH...
I'm...
I'M GETTING ALL MIXED UP...
This is for the chilies... The chilies...
Chilies! Chilies!
LIKE TAKING CANDY FROM A BABY.
ALL RIGHT, NEXT STOP!
Heh!
SMILE SMILE
I'VE ALWAYS WANTED ONE OF THESE! ♡
Time to dig in! ♥
NOW LISTEN, YOU...
MOMO.

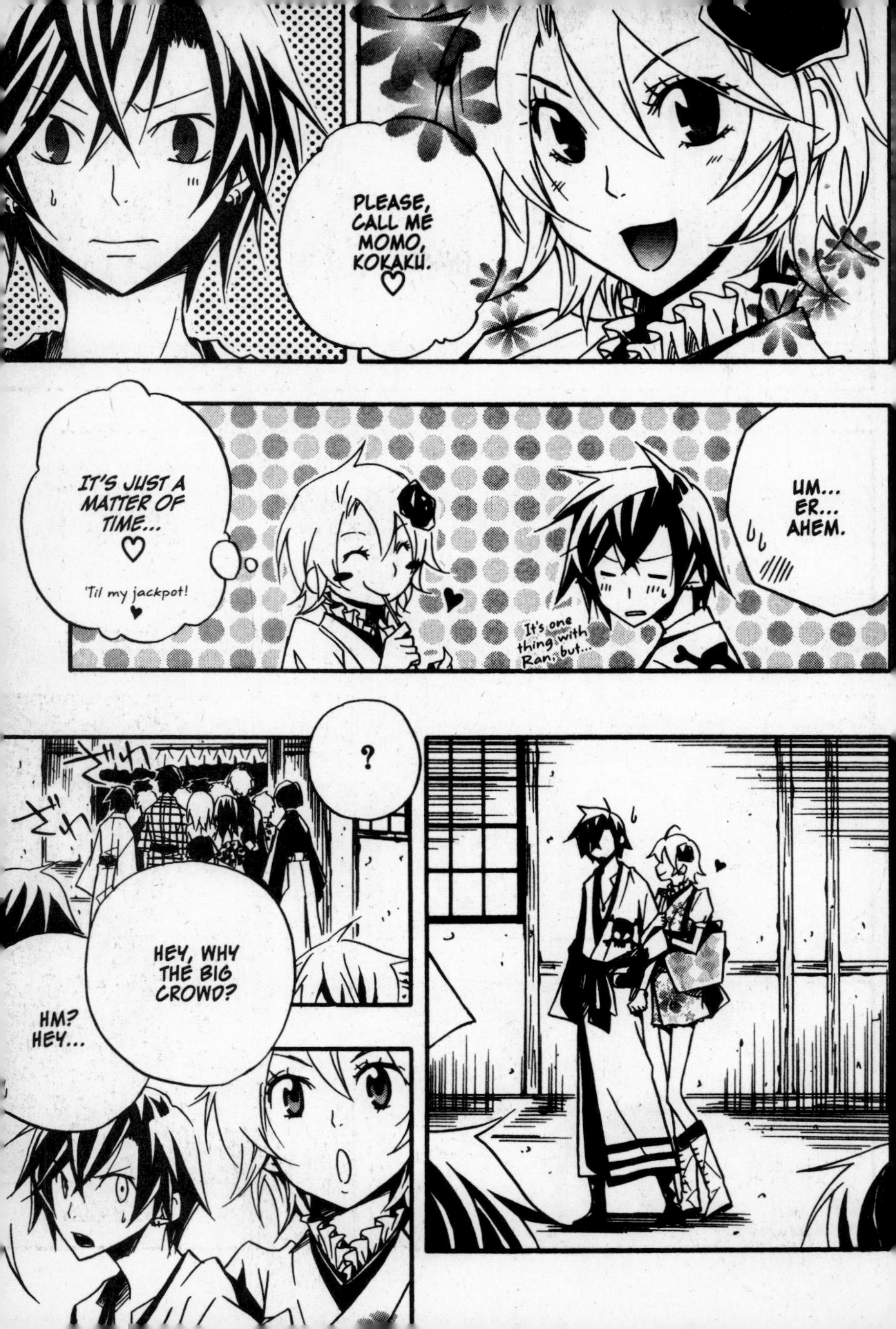
PLEASE, CALL ME MOMO, KOKAKU. ♡
UM... ER... AHEM.
It's one thing with Ran, but...
IT'S JUST A MATTER OF TIME... ♡
'Til my jackpot! ♥
?
HEY, WHY THE BIG CROWD?
HM? HEY...

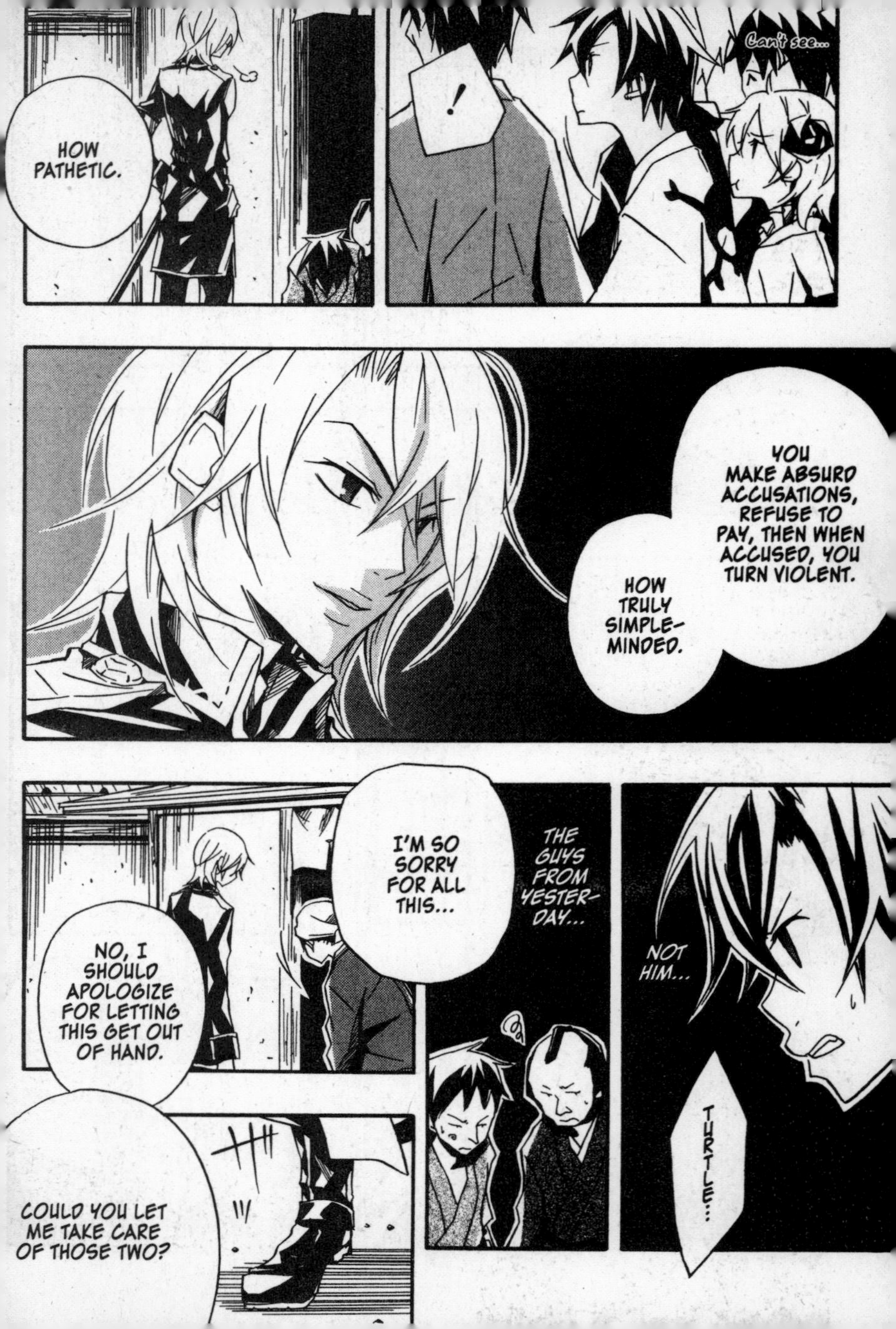
Can't see...
!
HOW PATHETIC.
YOU MAKE ABSURD ACCUSATIONS, REFUSE TO PAY, THEN WHEN ACCUSED, YOU TURN VIOLENT.
HOW TRULY SIMPLE-MINDED.
NOT HIM...
TURTLE...
THE GUYS FROM YESTER-DAY...
I'M SO SORRY FOR ALL THIS...
NO, I SHOULD APOLOGIZE FOR LETTING THIS GET OUT OF HAND.
COULD YOU LET ME TAKE CARE OF THOSE TWO?

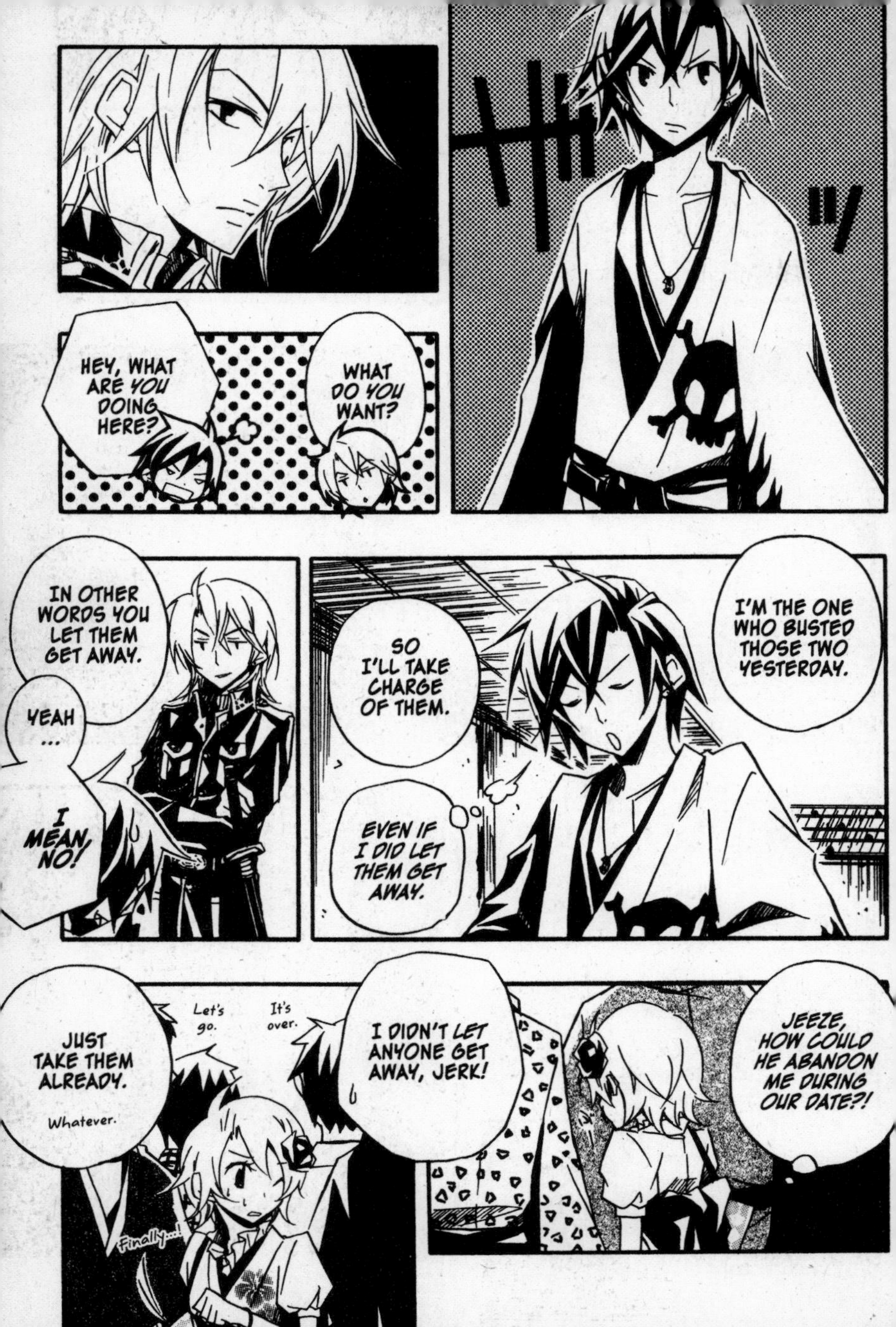
WHAT DO YOU WANT?
HEY, WHAT ARE YOU DOING HERE?
I'M THE ONE WHO BUSTED THOSE TWO YESTERDAY.
SO I'LL TAKE CHARGE OF THEM.
EVEN IF I DID LET THEM GET AWAY.
IN OTHER WORDS YOU LET THEM GET AWAY.
YEAH ...
I MEAN, NO!
JEEZE, HOW COULD HE ABANDON ME DURING OUR DATE?!
I DIDN'T LET ANYONE GET AWAY, JERK!
It's over.
Let's go.
JUST TAKE THEM ALREADY.
Whatever.
Finally...!

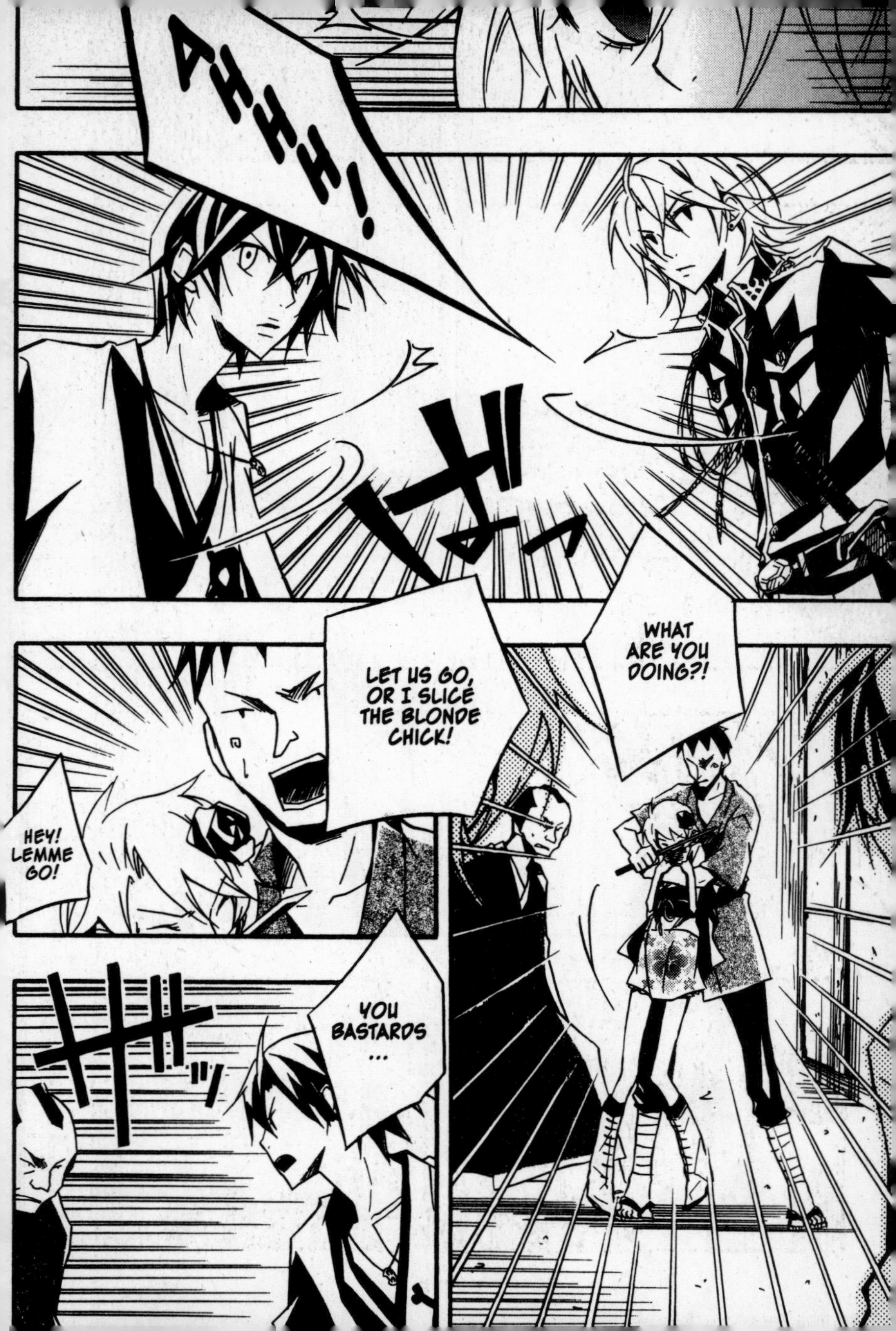
AHHH!
WHAT ARE YOU DOING?!
LET US GO, OR I SLICE THE BLONDE CHICK!
HEY! LEMME GO!
YOU BASTARDS ...

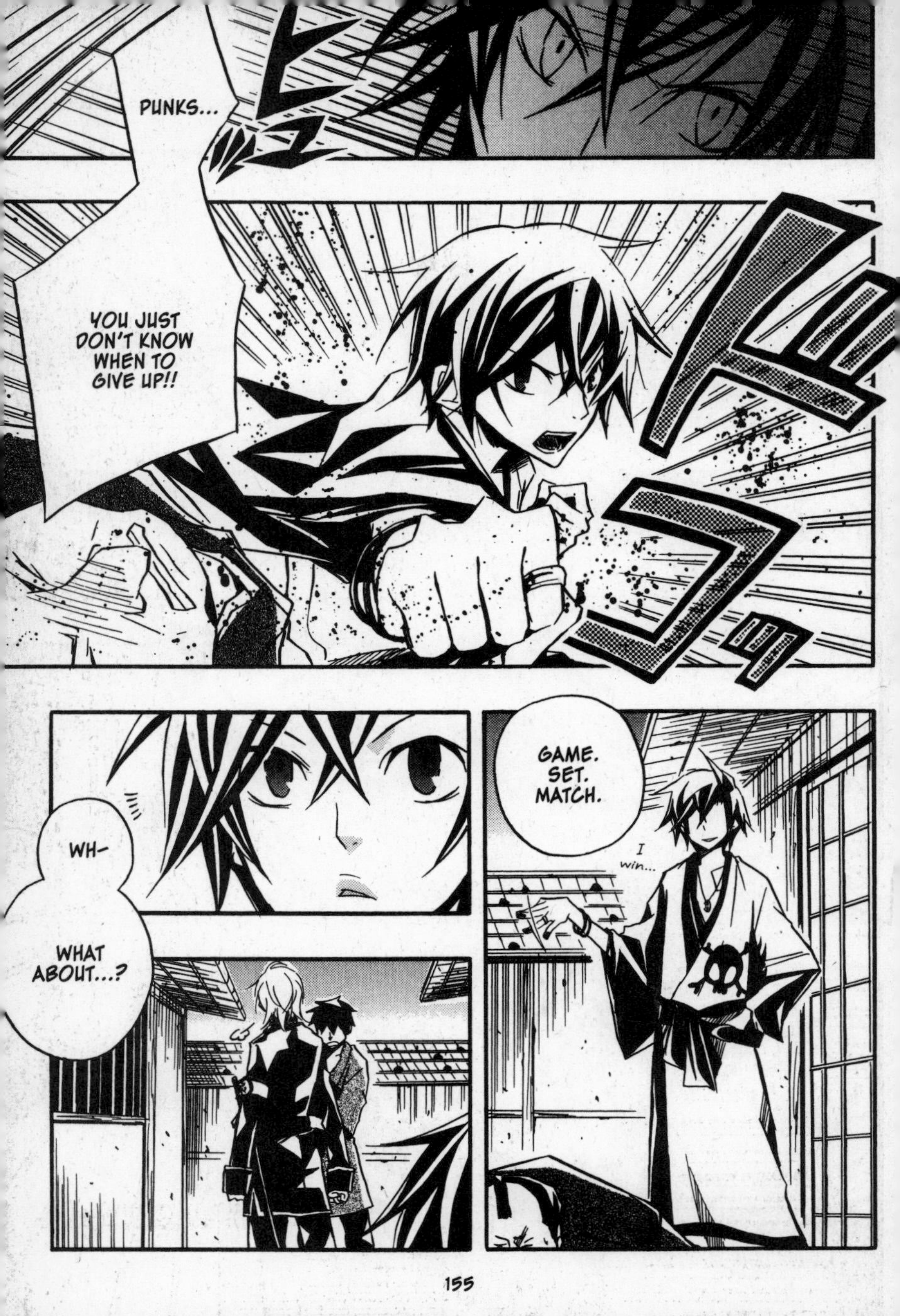
PUNKS...
YOU JUST DON'T KNOW WHEN TO GIVE UP!!
GAME. SET. MATCH.
I win...
WH-
WHAT ABOUT...?

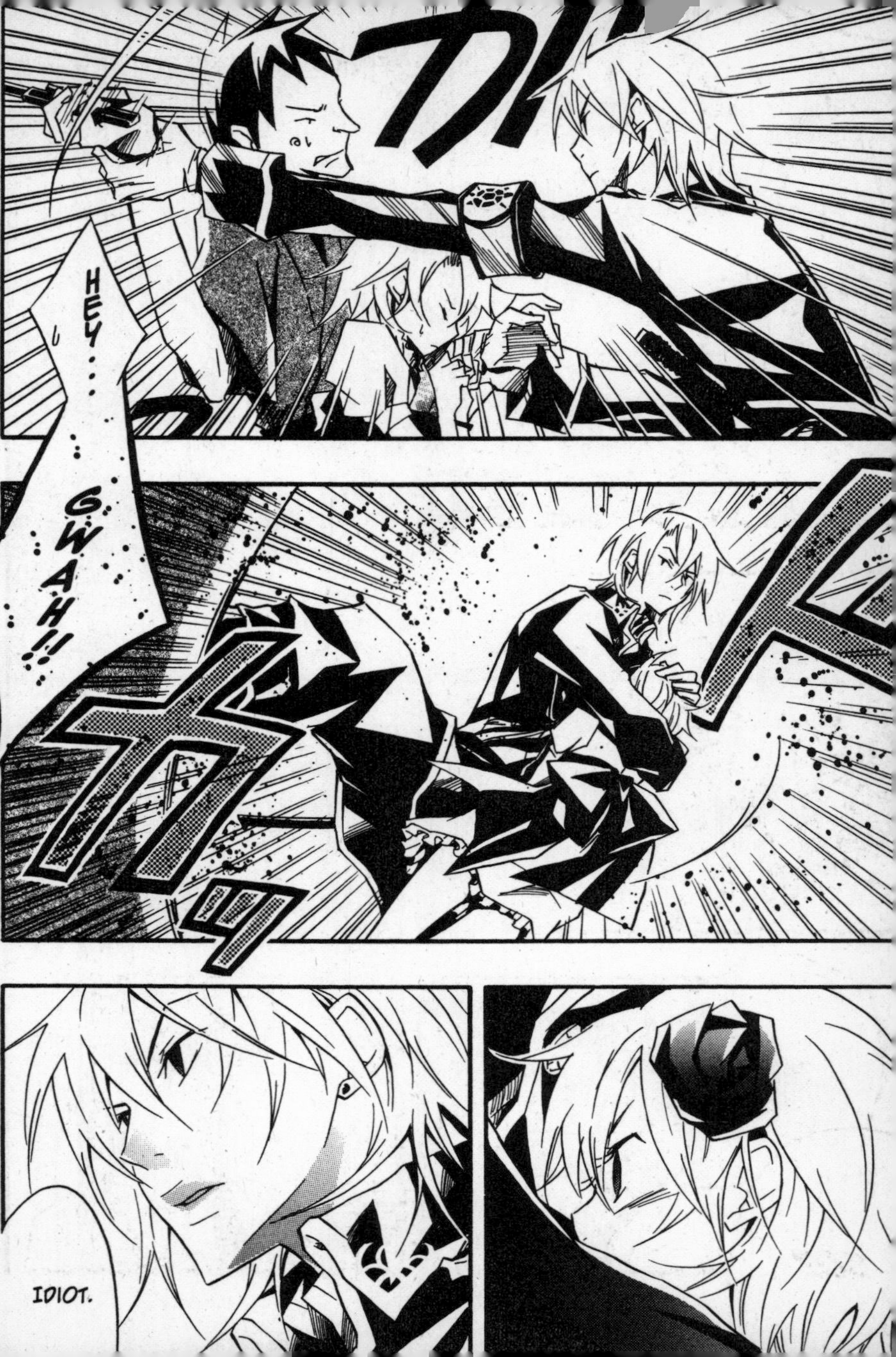
HEY... GWAH!!!
IDIOT.

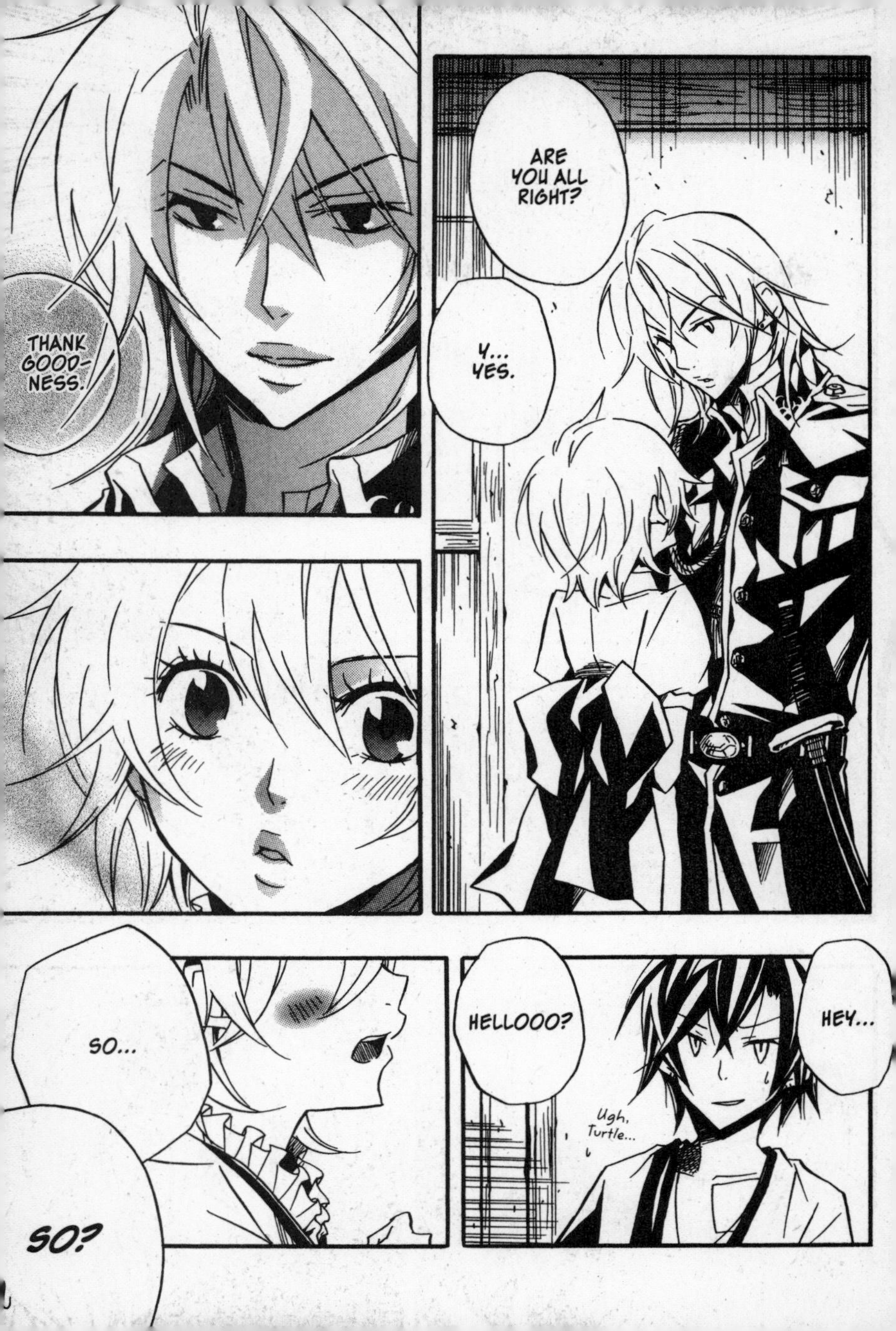
ARE YOU ALL RIGHT?
Y... YES.
THANK GOOD-NESS.
HEY...
HELLOOO?
Ugh, Turtle...
SO...
SO?

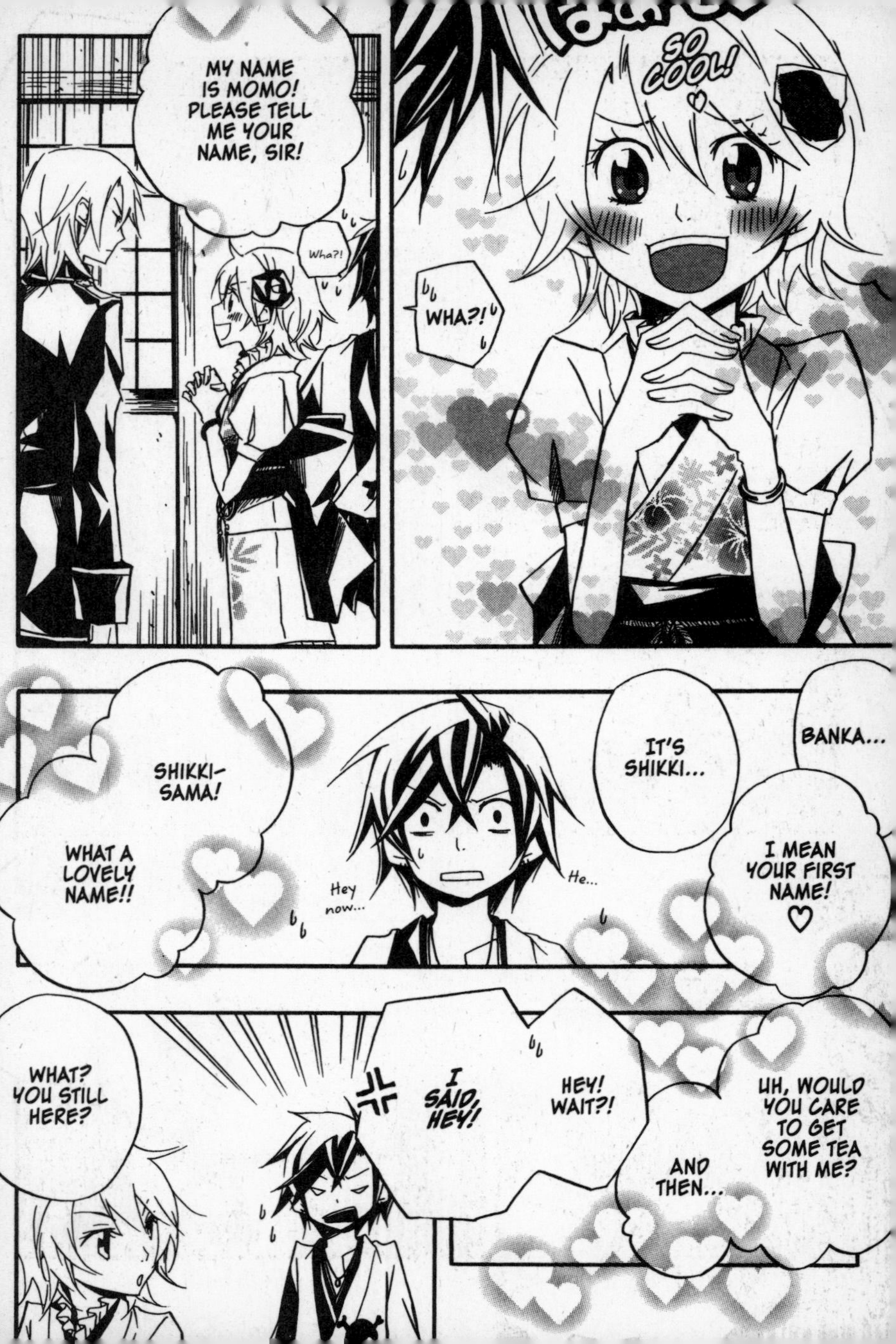
SO COOL! ♡
WHA?!
MY NAME IS MOMO! PLEASE TELL ME YOUR NAME, SIR!
Wha?!
BANKA...
IT'S SHIKKI...
I MEAN YOUR FIRST NAME! ♡
He...
SHIKKI-SAMA!
WHAT A LOVELY NAME!!
Hey now...
UH, WOULD YOU CARE TO GET SOME TEA WITH ME?
AND THEN...
HEY! WAIT?!
I SAID, HEY!
WHAT? YOU STILL HERE?

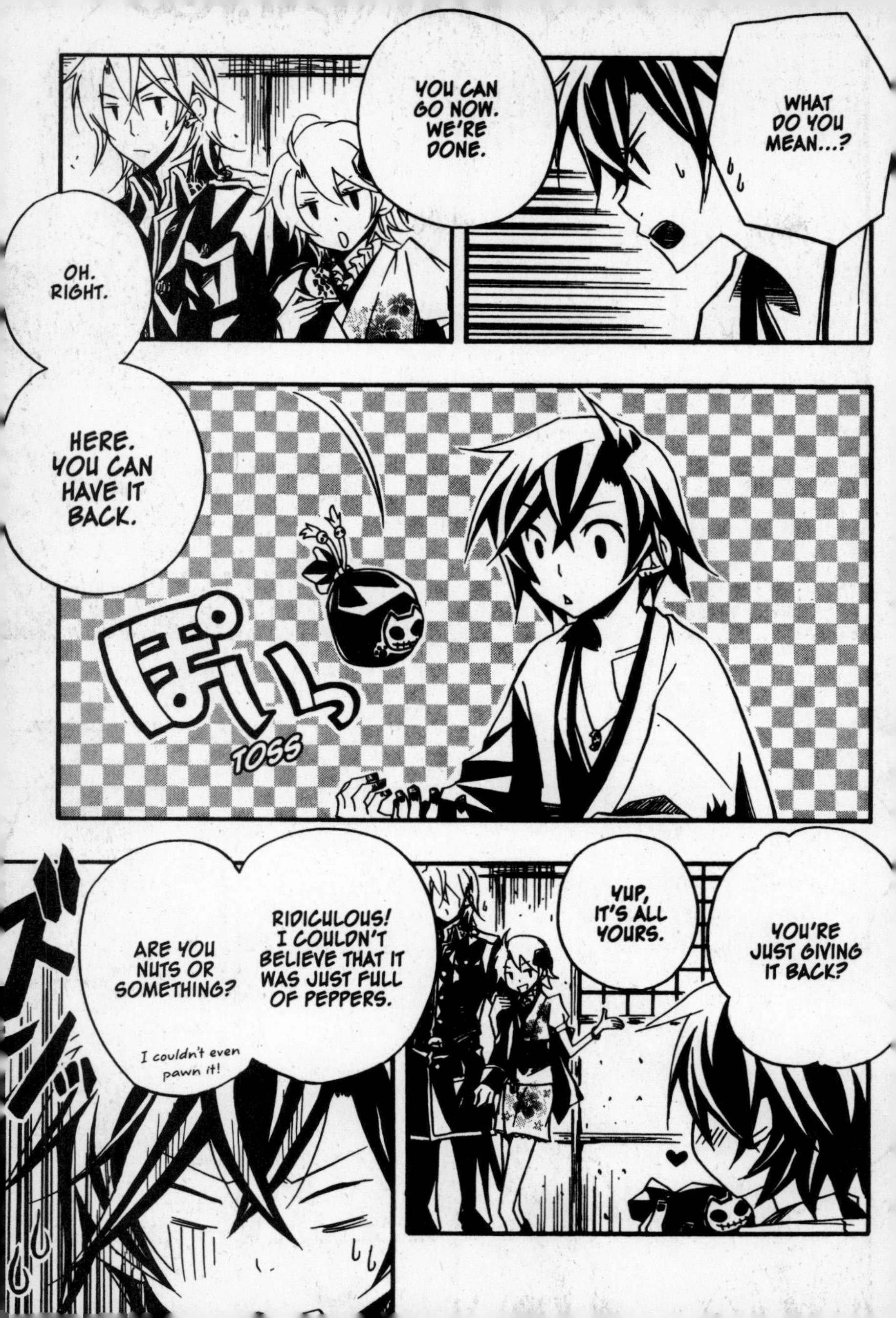
WHAT DO YOU MEAN...?
YOU CAN GO NOW. WE'RE DONE.
OH. RIGHT.
HERE. YOU CAN HAVE IT BACK.
ぽいっ
TOSS
YOU'RE JUST GIVING IT BACK?
YUP, IT'S ALL YOURS.
RIDICULOUS! I COULDN'T BELIEVE THAT IT WAS JUST FULL OF PEPPERS.
ARE YOU NUTS OR SOMETHING?
I couldn't even pawn it!

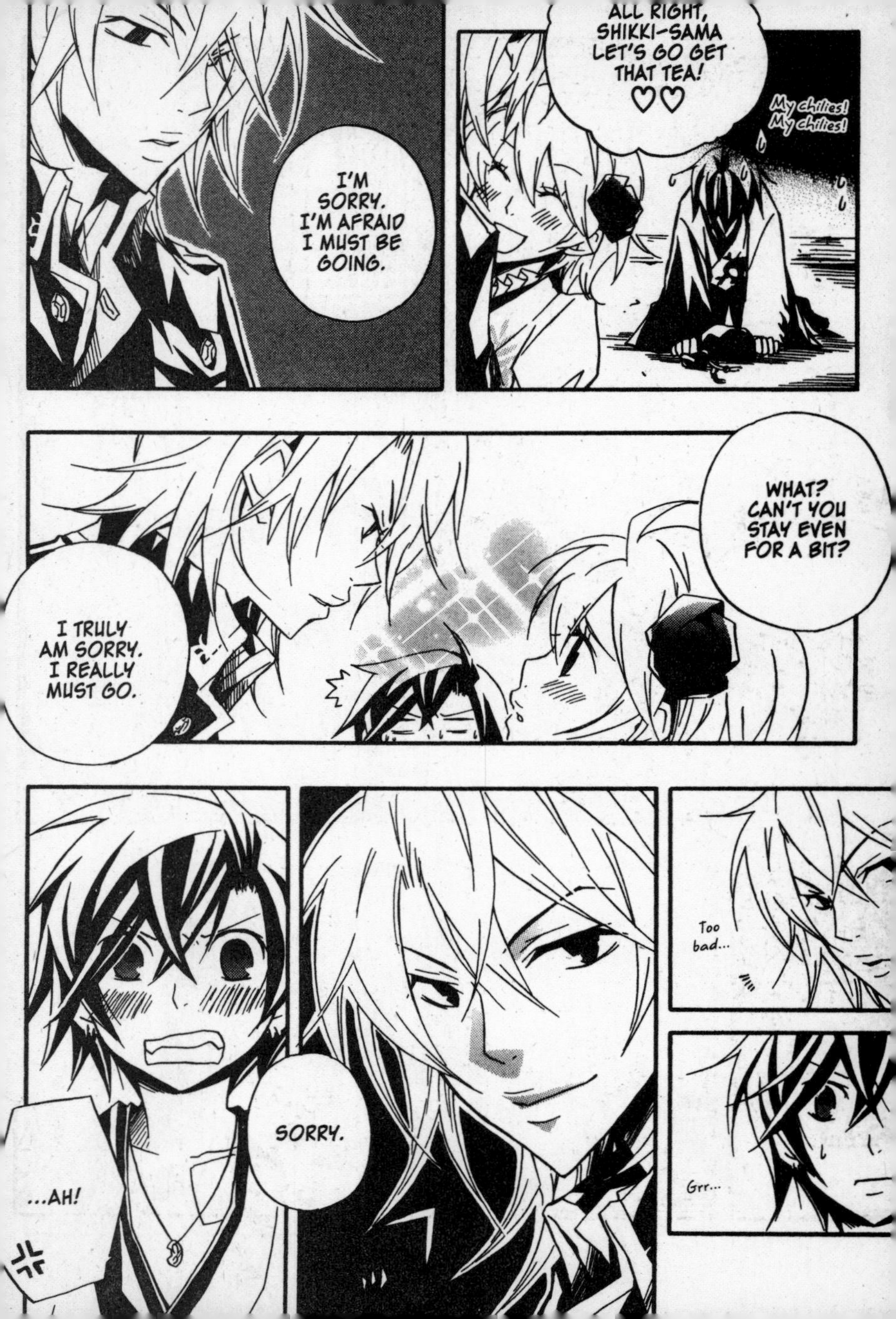
ALL RIGHT, SHIKKI-SAMA LET'S GO GET THAT TEA! ♡♡
My chilies! My chilies!
I'M SORRY. I'M AFRAID I MUST BE GOING.
WHAT? CAN'T YOU STAY EVEN FOR A BIT?
I TRULY AM SORRY. I REALLY MUST GO.
Too bad...
Grr...
SORRY.
...AH!

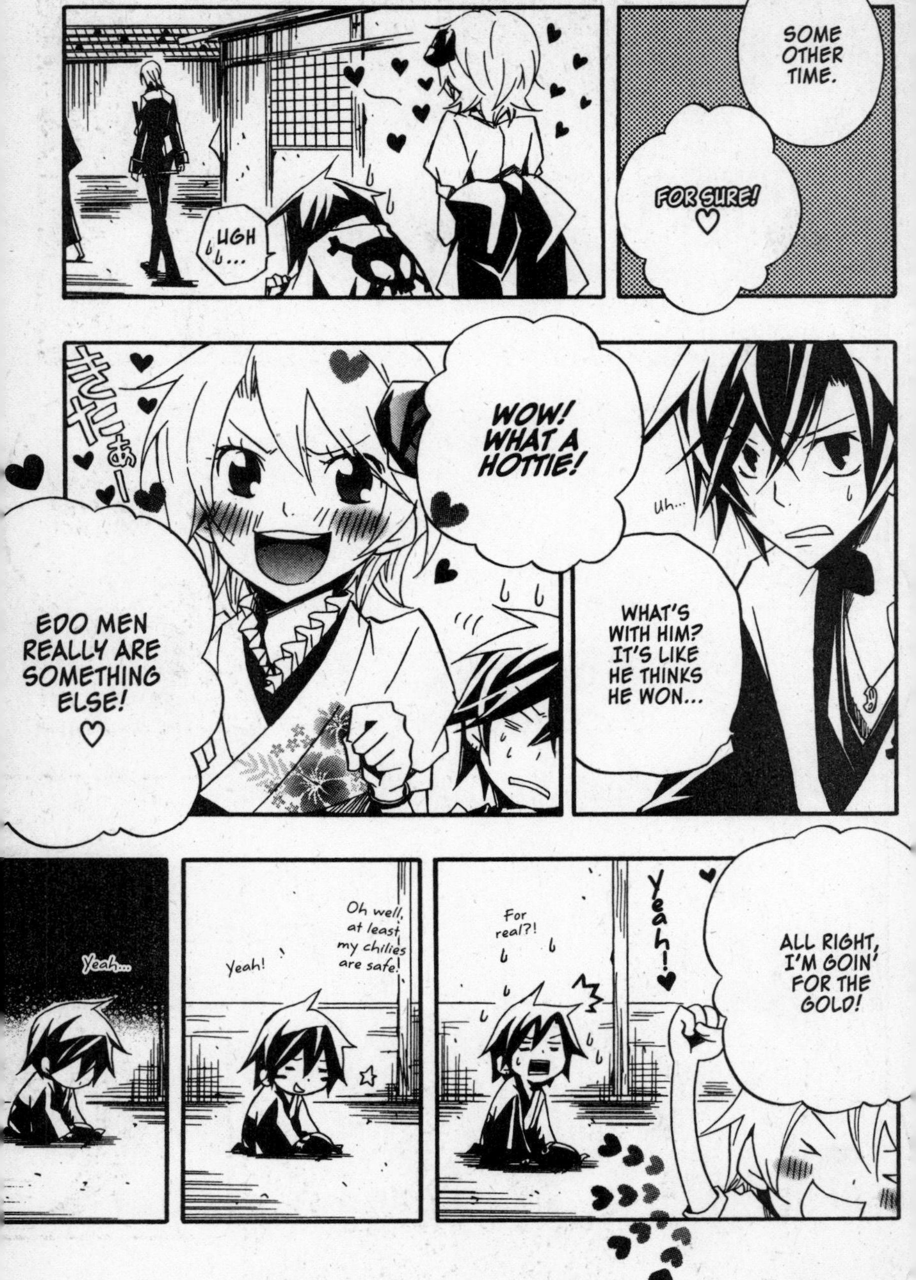

SOME OTHER TIME.
FOR SURE! ♡
UGH...
Uh...
WHAT'S WITH HIM? IT'S LIKE HE THINKS HE WON...
WOW! WHAT A HOTTIE!
EDO MEN REALLY ARE SOMETHING ELSE! ♡
ALL RIGHT, I'M GOIN' FOR THE GOLD!
Yeah! ♥
For real?!
Oh well, at least my chilies are safe!
Yeah!
Yeah...

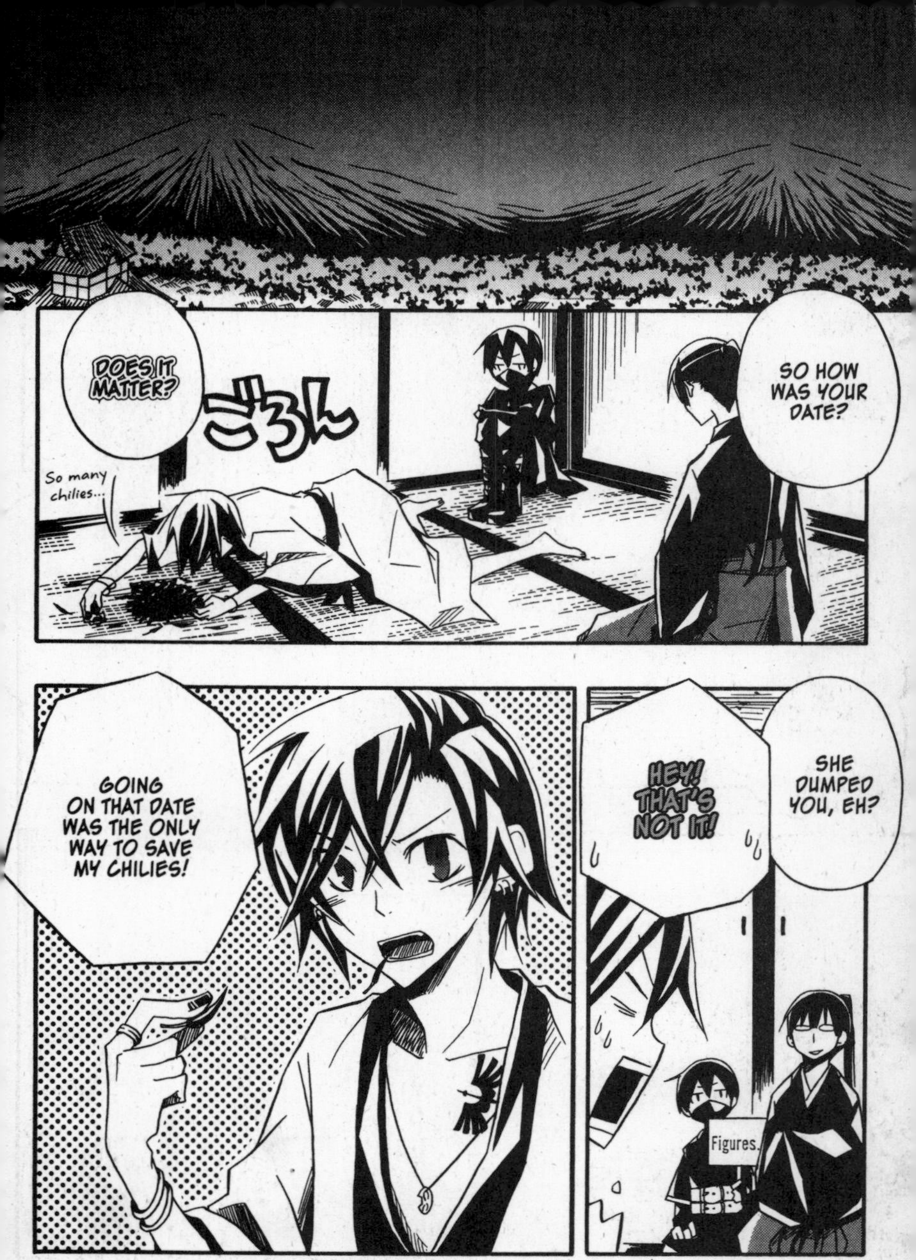
SO HOW WAS YOUR DATE?
DOES IT MATTER?
ごろん
So many chilies...
SHE DUMPED YOU, EH?
HEY! THAT'S NOT IT!
Figures.
GOING ON THAT DATE WAS THE ONLY WAY TO SAVE MY CHILIES!

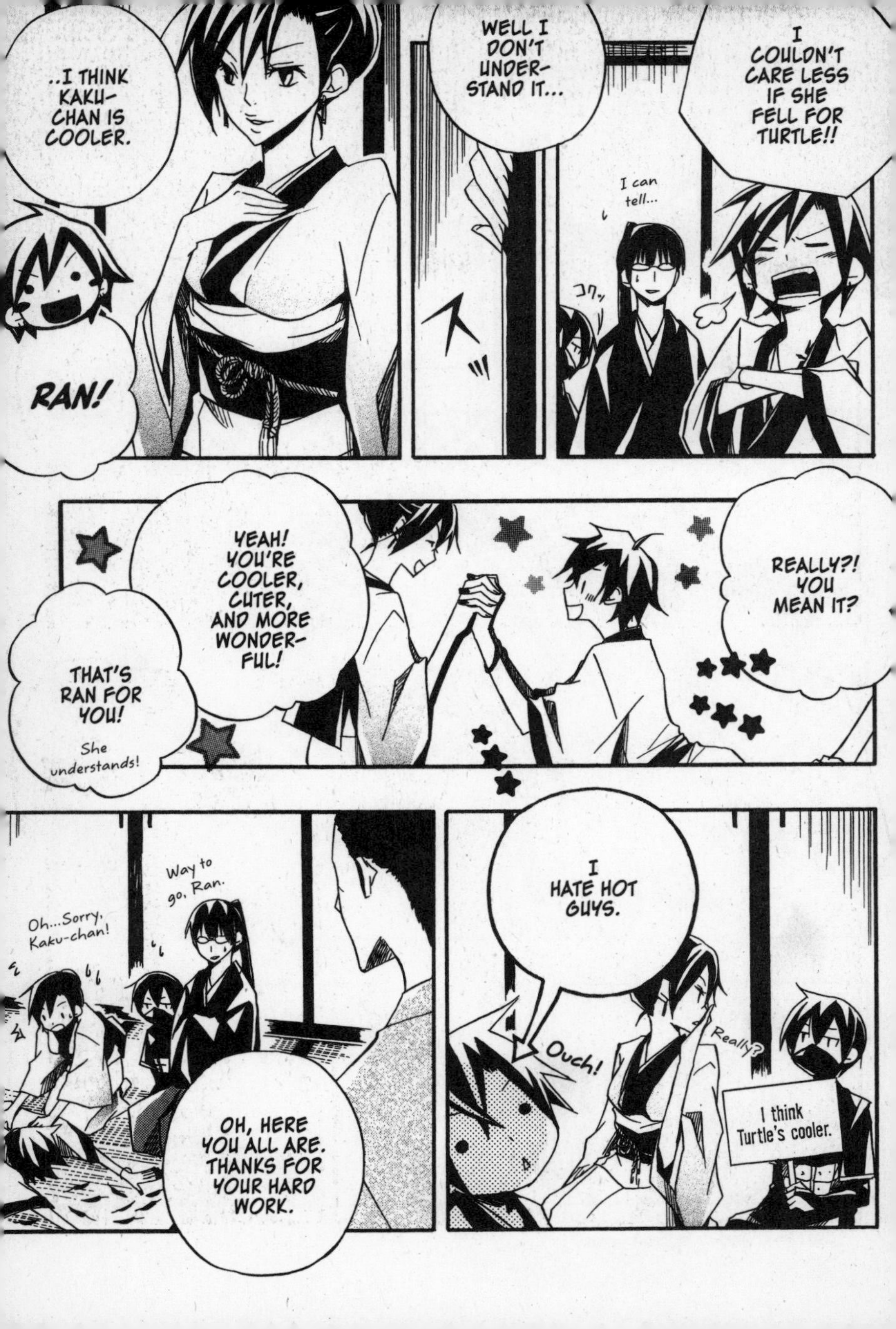

I COULDN'T CARE LESS IF SHE FELL FOR TURTLE!!
I can tell...
コクッ
WELL I DON'T UNDERSTAND IT...
..I THINK KAKU-CHAN IS COOLER.
RAN!
REALLY?! YOU MEAN IT?
YEAH! YOU'RE COOLER, CUTER, AND MORE WONDERFUL!
THAT'S RAN FOR YOU!
She understands!
I HATE HOT GUYS.
Ouch!
Really?
I think Turtle's cooler.
Way to go, Ran.
Oh...Sorry, Kaku-chan!
OH, HERE YOU ALL ARE. THANKS FOR YOUR HARD WORK.

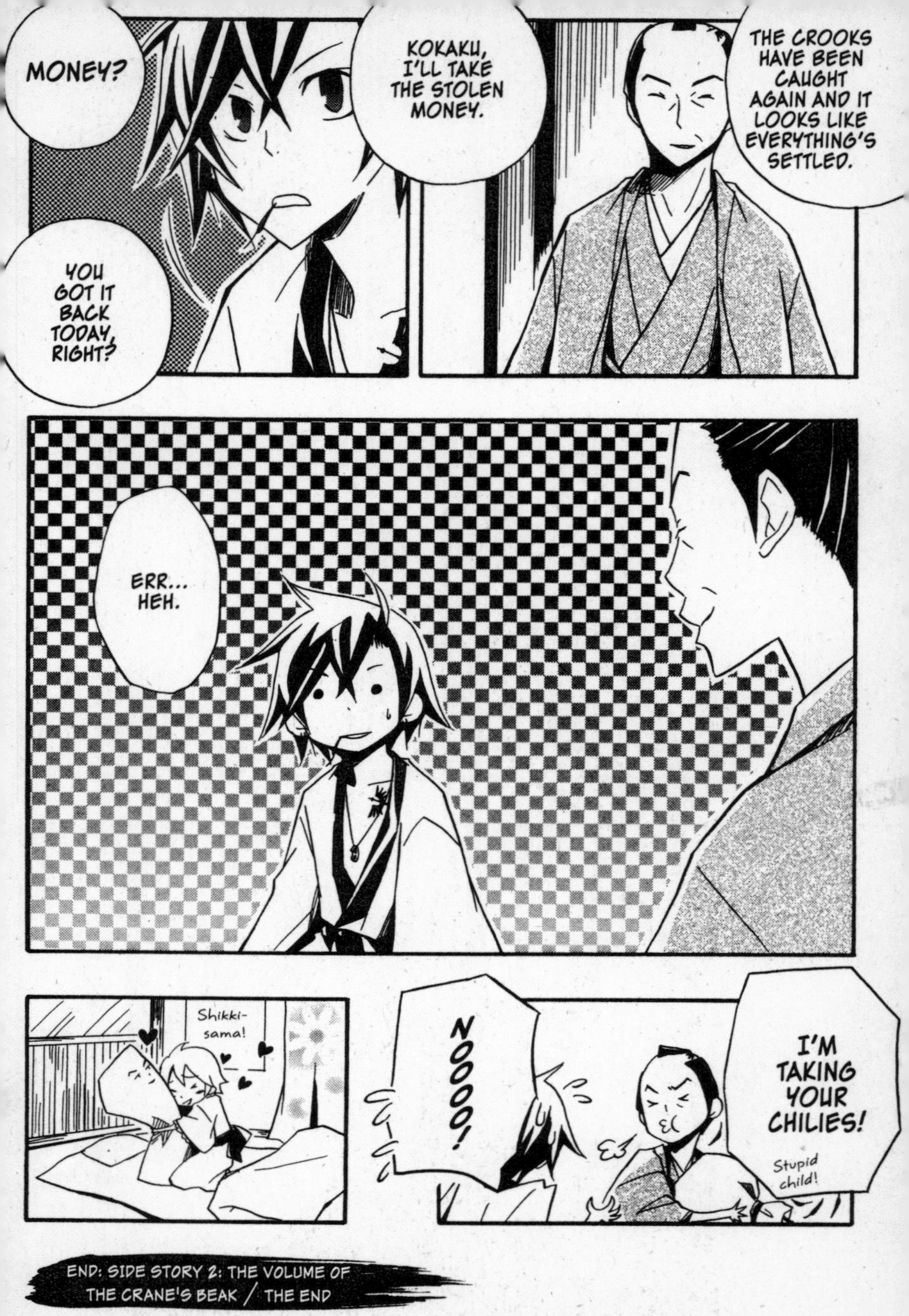
THE CROOKS HAVE BEEN CAUGHT AGAIN AND IT LOOKS LIKE EVERYTHING'S SETTLED.
KOKAKU, I'LL TAKE THE STOLEN MONEY.
MONEY?
YOU GOT IT BACK TODAY, RIGHT?
ERR... HEH.
I'M TAKING YOUR CHILIES!
NOOOO!
Stupid child!
Shikki-sama!

END: SIDE STORY 2: THE VOLUME OF THE CRANE'S BEAK / THE END

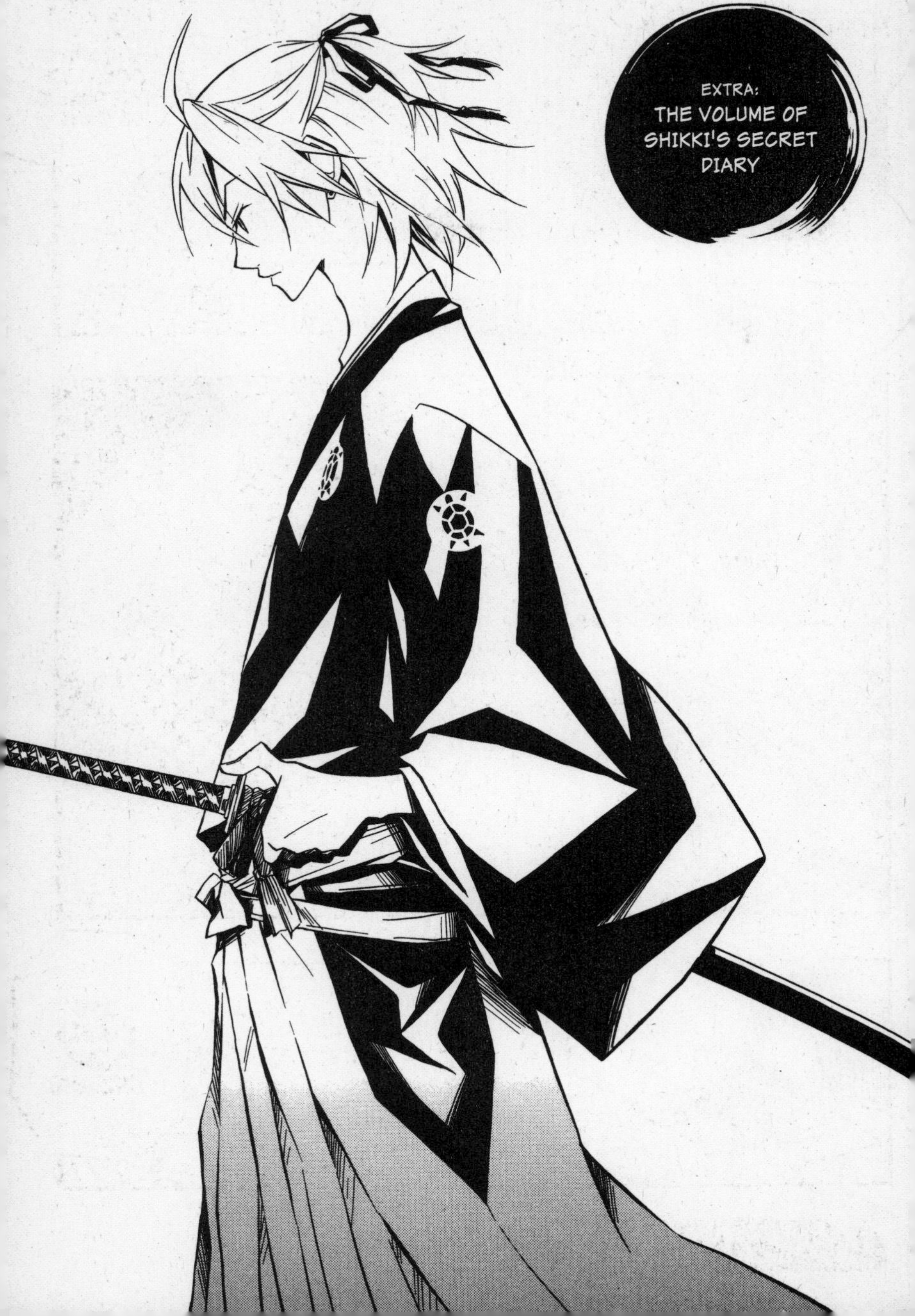
EXTRA:
THE VOLUME OF
SHIKKI'S SECRET
DIARY

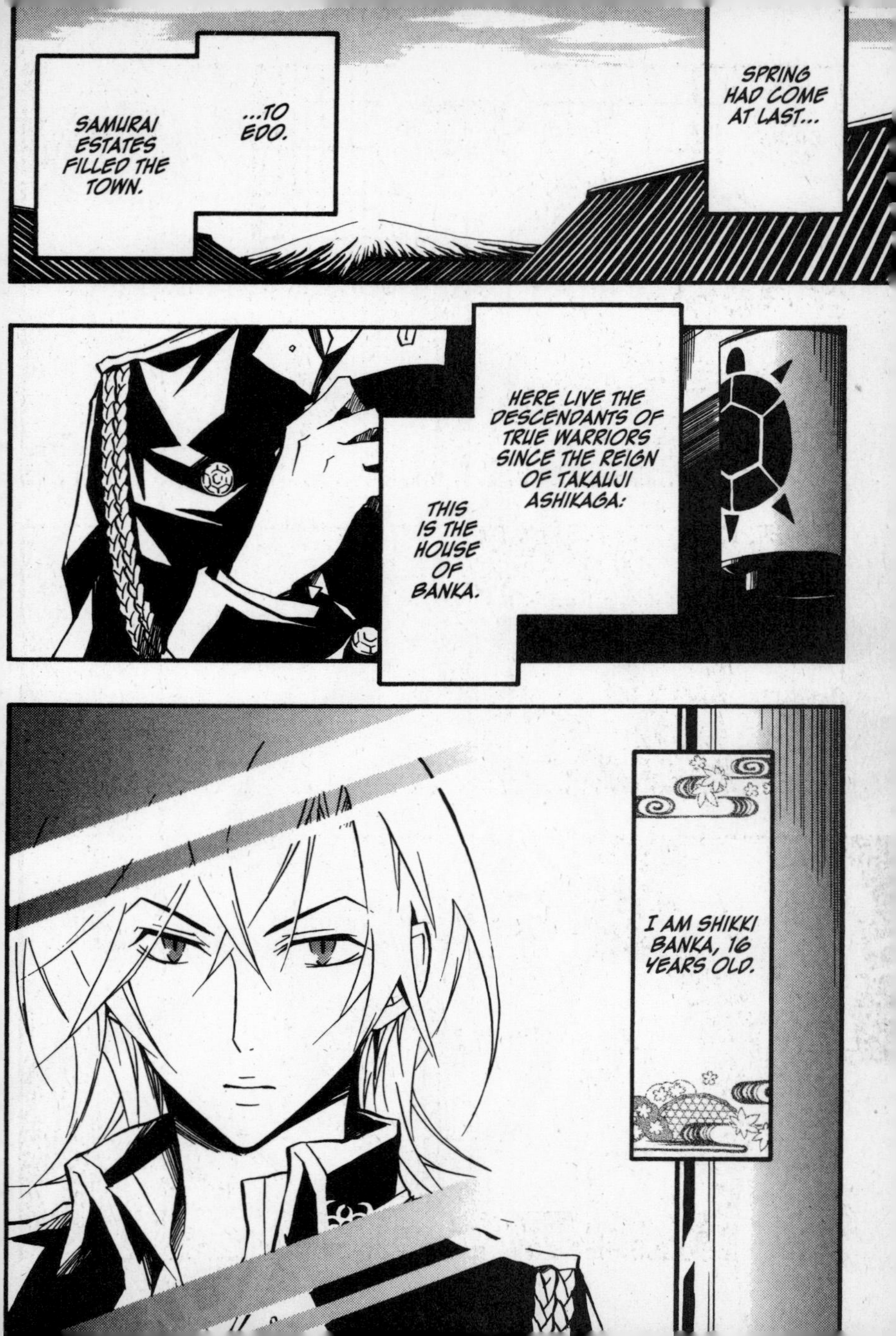
SPRING HAD COME AT LAST...
...TO EDO.
SAMURAI ESTATES FILLED THE TOWN.
HERE LIVE THE DESCENDANTS OF TRUE WARRIORS SINCE THE REIGN OF TAKAUJI ASHIKAGA:
THIS IS THE HOUSE OF BANKA.
I AM SHIKKI BANKA, 16 YEARS OLD.

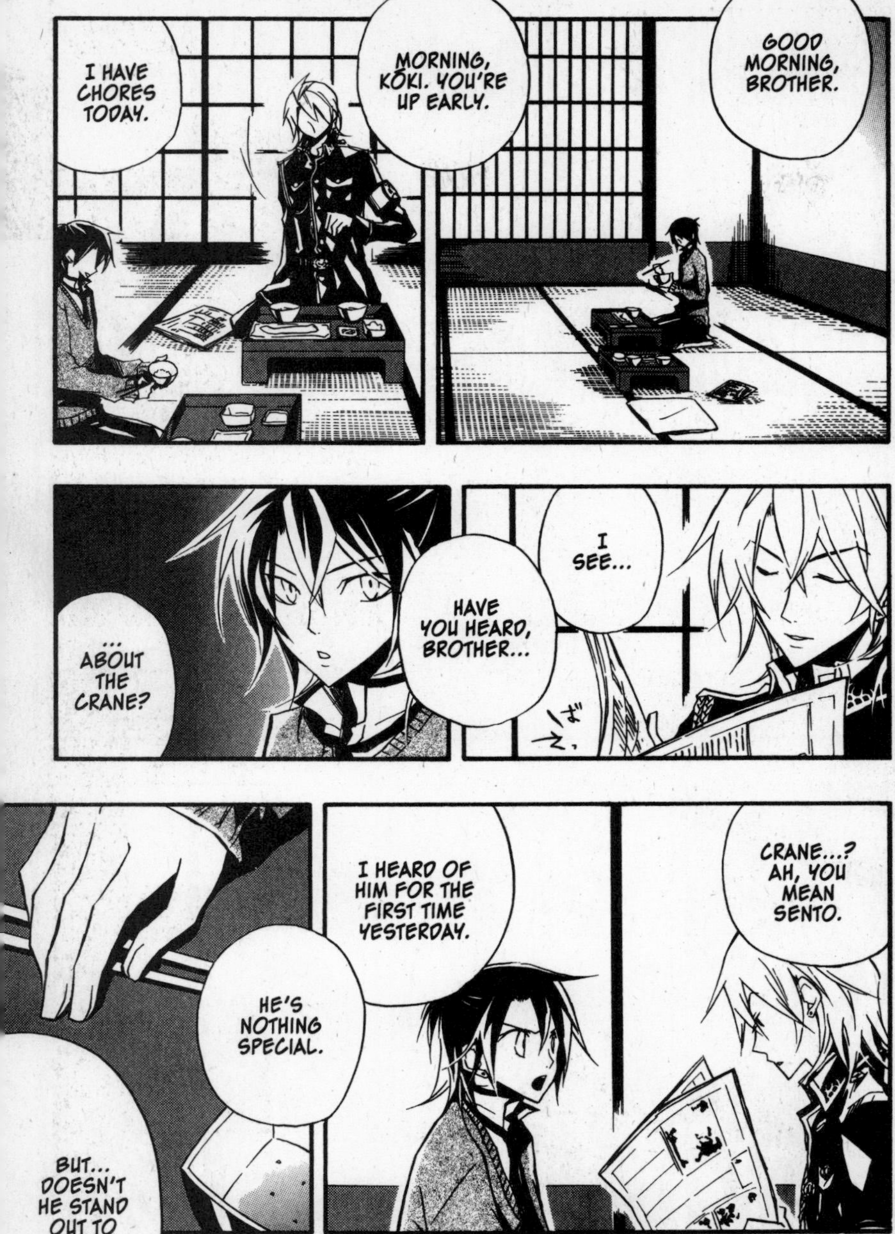
GOOD MORNING, BROTHER.
MORNING, KŌKI. YOU'RE UP EARLY.
I HAVE CHORES TODAY.
I SEE...
HAVE YOU HEARD, BROTHER...
...ABOUT THE CRANE?
CRANE...? AH, YOU MEAN SENTO.
I HEARD OF HIM FOR THE FIRST TIME YESTERDAY.
HE'S NOTHING SPECIAL.
BUT... DOESN'T HE STAND OUT TO YOU?

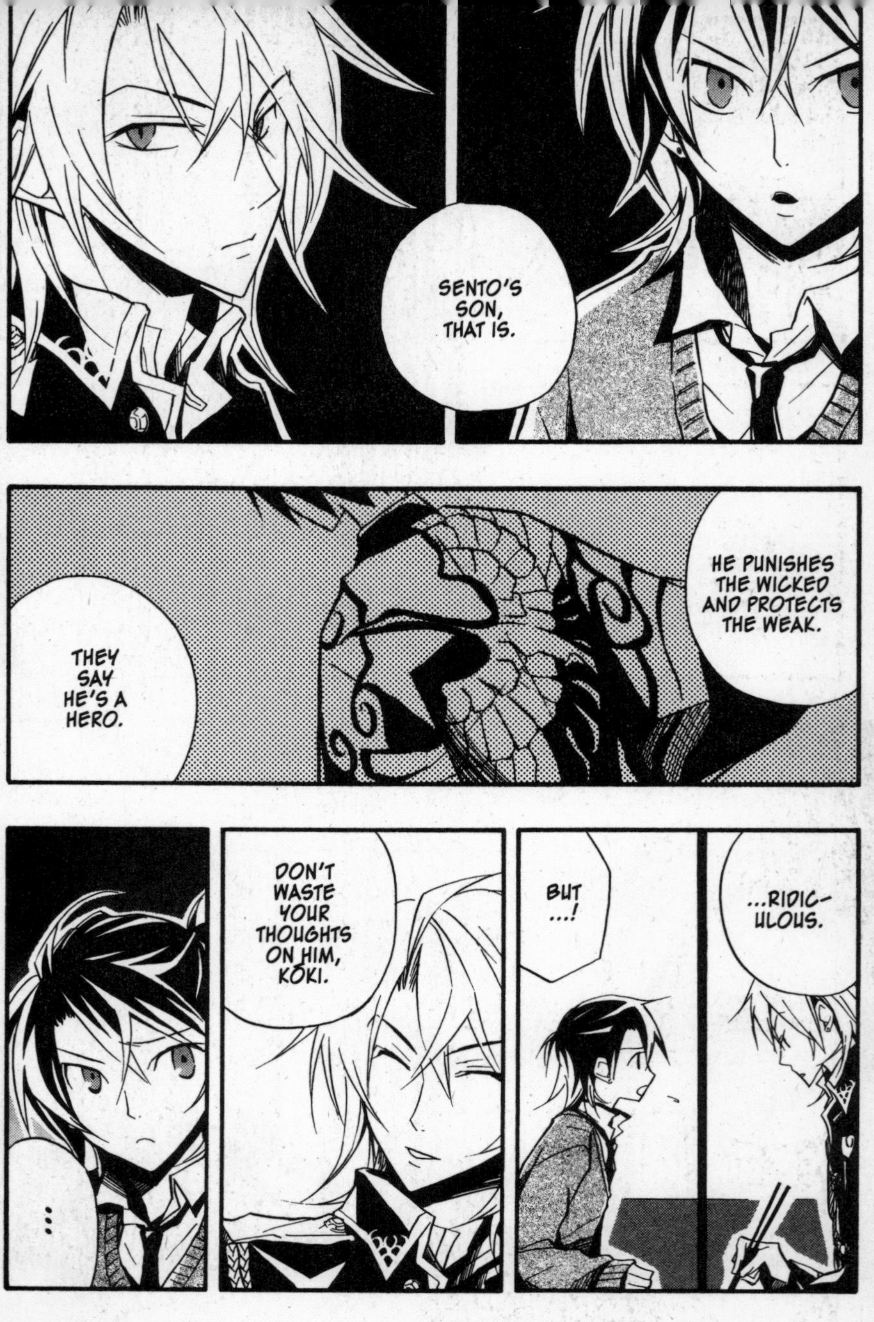
SENTO'S SON, THAT IS.
HE PUNISHES THE WICKED AND PROTECTS THE WEAK.
THEY SAY HE'S A HERO.
...RIDIC-ULOUS.
BUT ...!
DON'T WASTE YOUR THOUGHTS ON HIM, KŌKI.
...

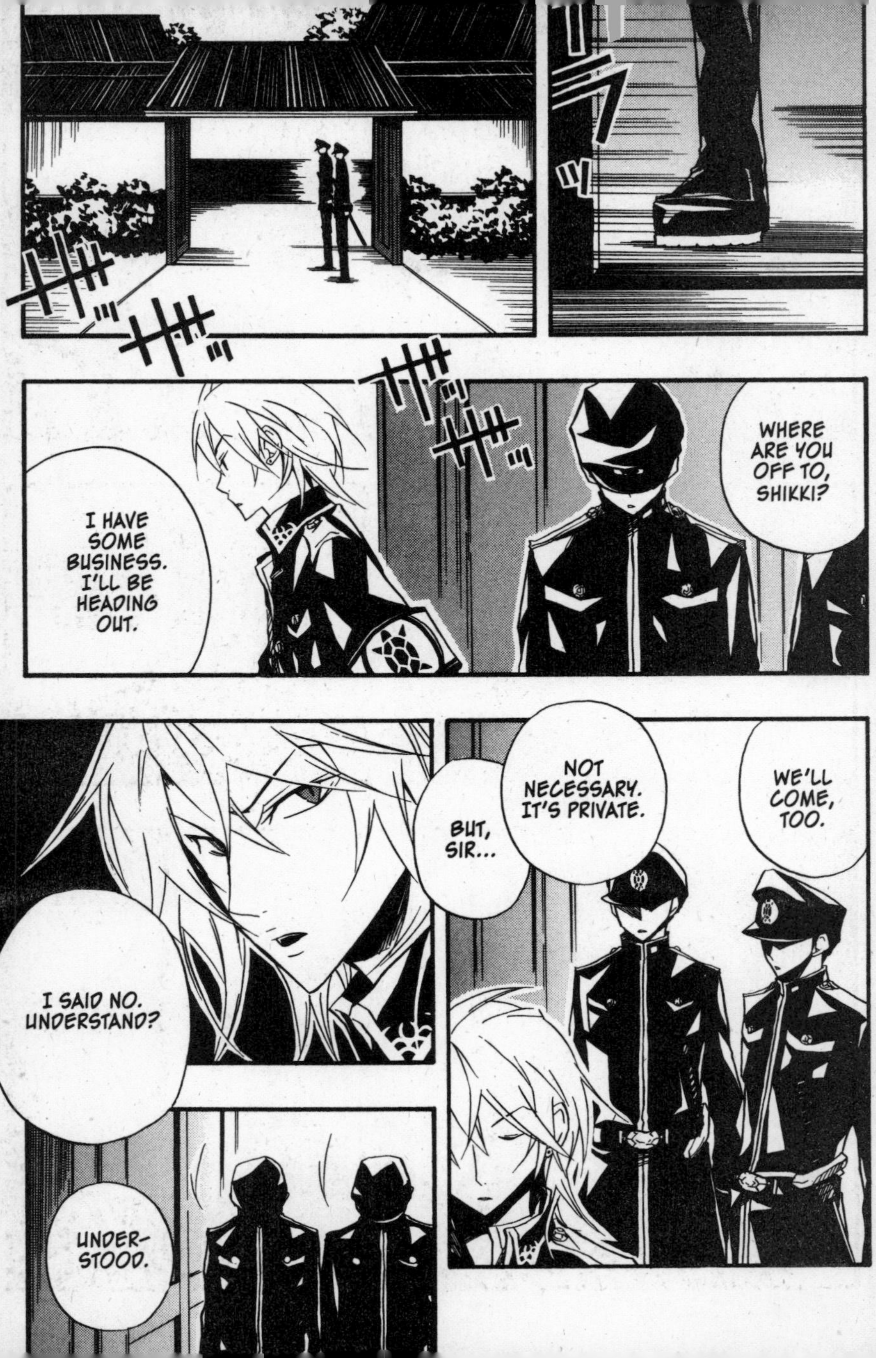
WHERE ARE YOU OFF TO, SHIKKI?
I HAVE SOME BUSINESS. I'LL BE HEADING OUT.
WE'LL COME, TOO.
NOT NECESSARY. IT'S PRIVATE.
BUT, SIR...
I SAID NO. UNDERSTAND?
UNDER-STOOD.

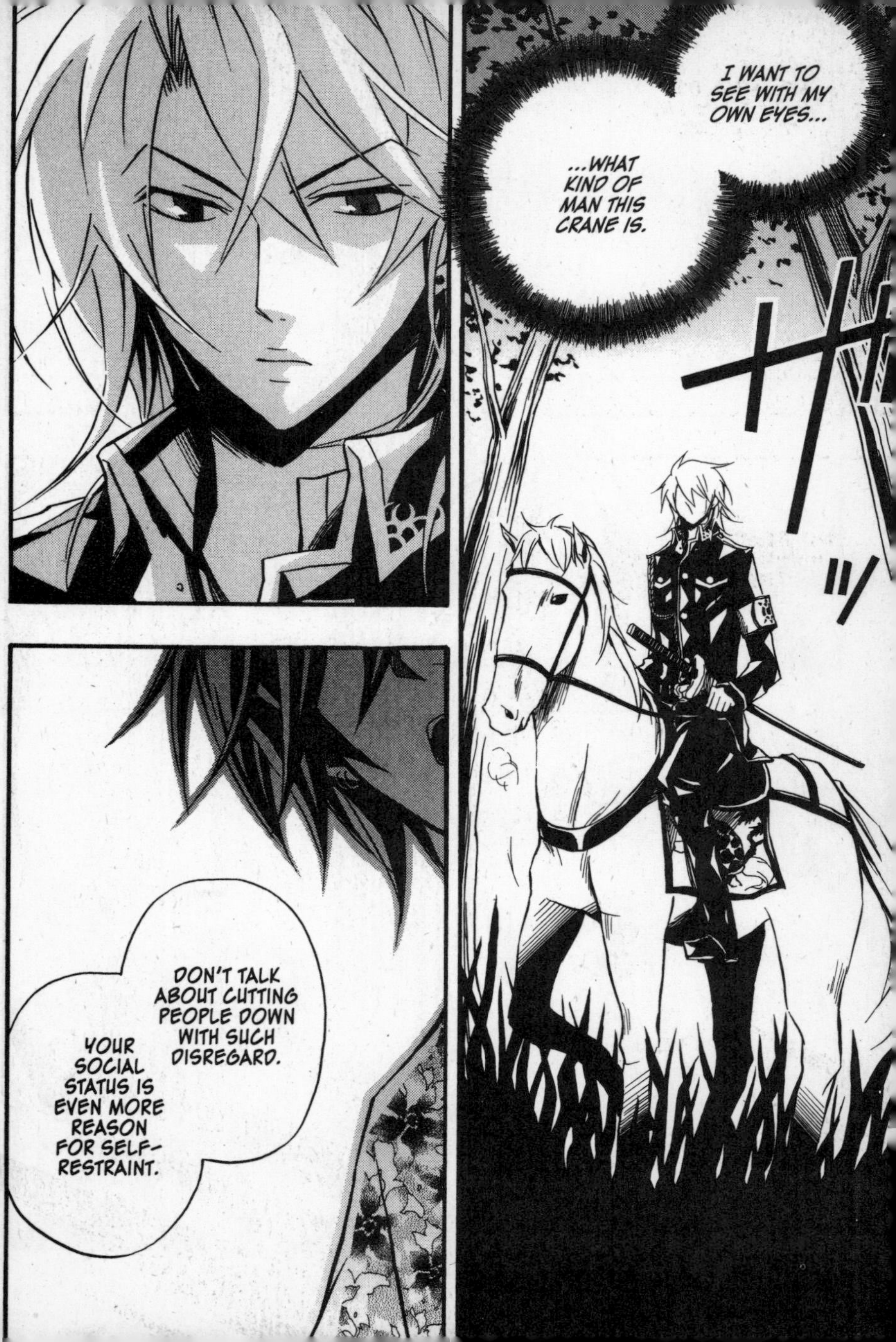
I WANT TO SEE WITH MY OWN EYES...
...WHAT KIND OF MAN THIS CRANE IS.
DON'T TALK ABOUT CUTTING PEOPLE DOWN WITH SUCH DISREGARD.
YOUR SOCIAL STATUS IS EVEN MORE REASON FOR SELF-RESTRAINT.

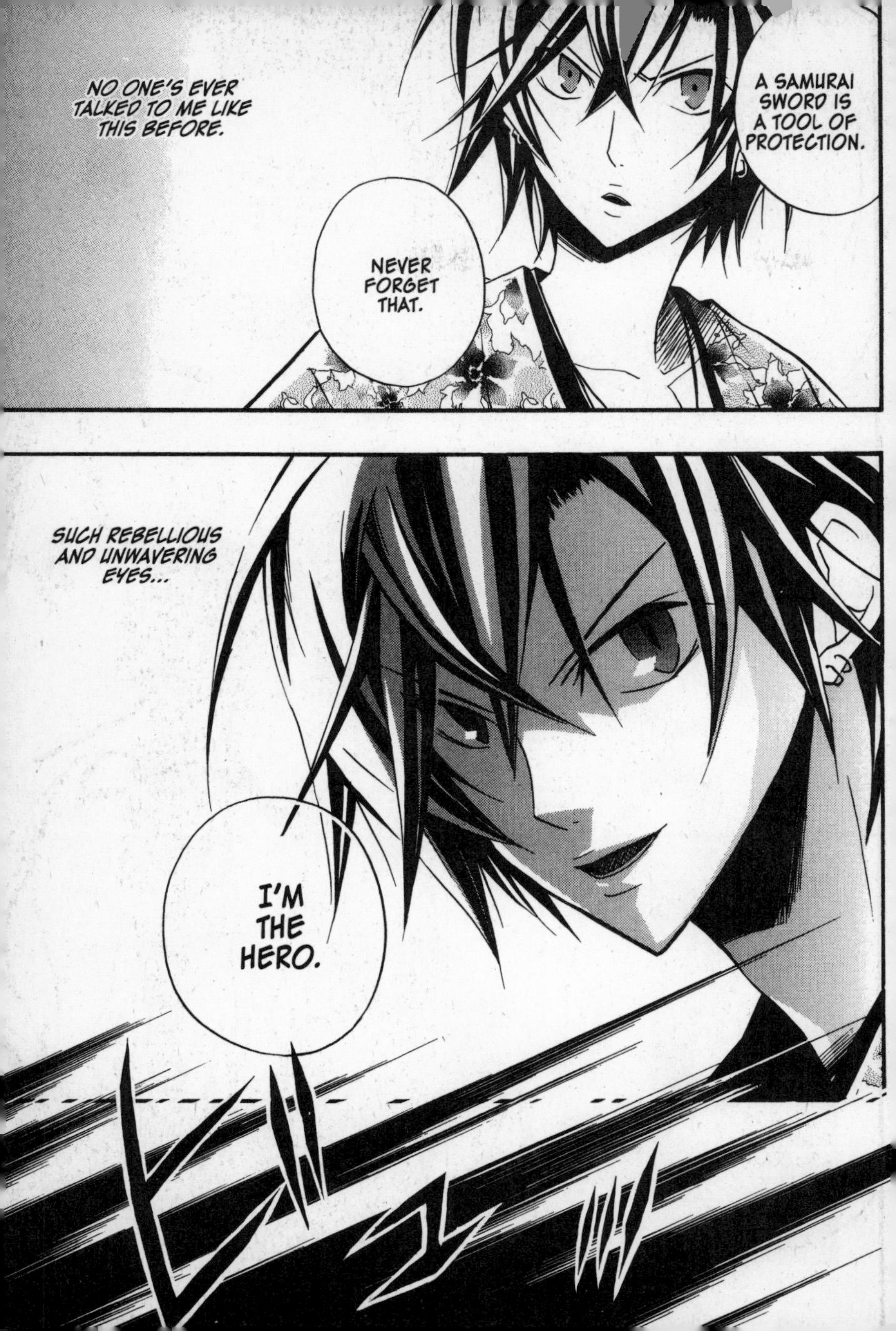
A SAMURAI SWORD IS A TOOL OF PROTECTION.
NEVER FORGET THAT.
NO ONE'S EVER TALKED TO ME LIKE THIS BEFORE.
SUCH REBELLIOUS AND UNWAVERING EYES...
I'M THE HERO.

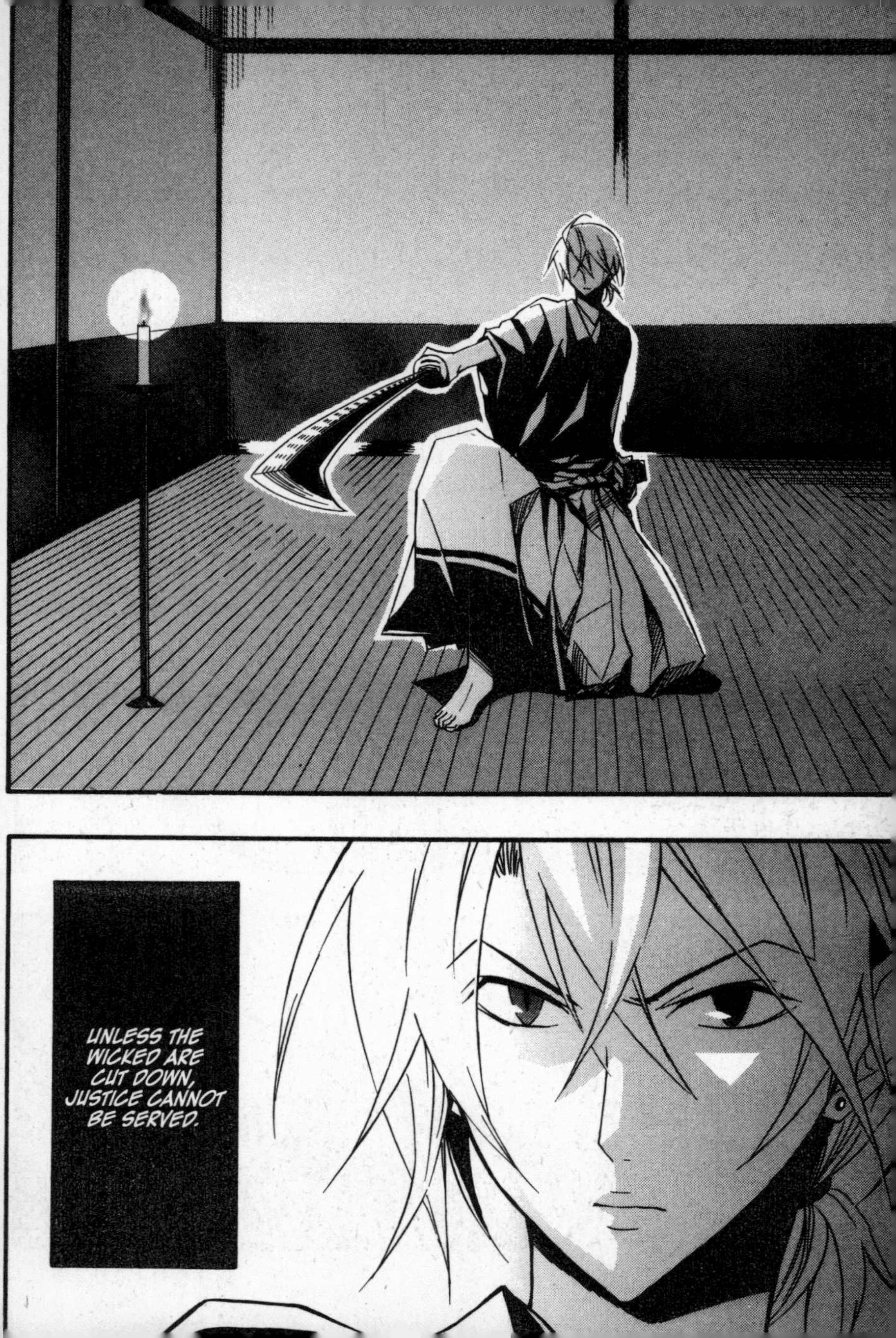
UNLESS THE WICKED ARE CUT DOWN, JUSTICE CANNOT BE SERVED.

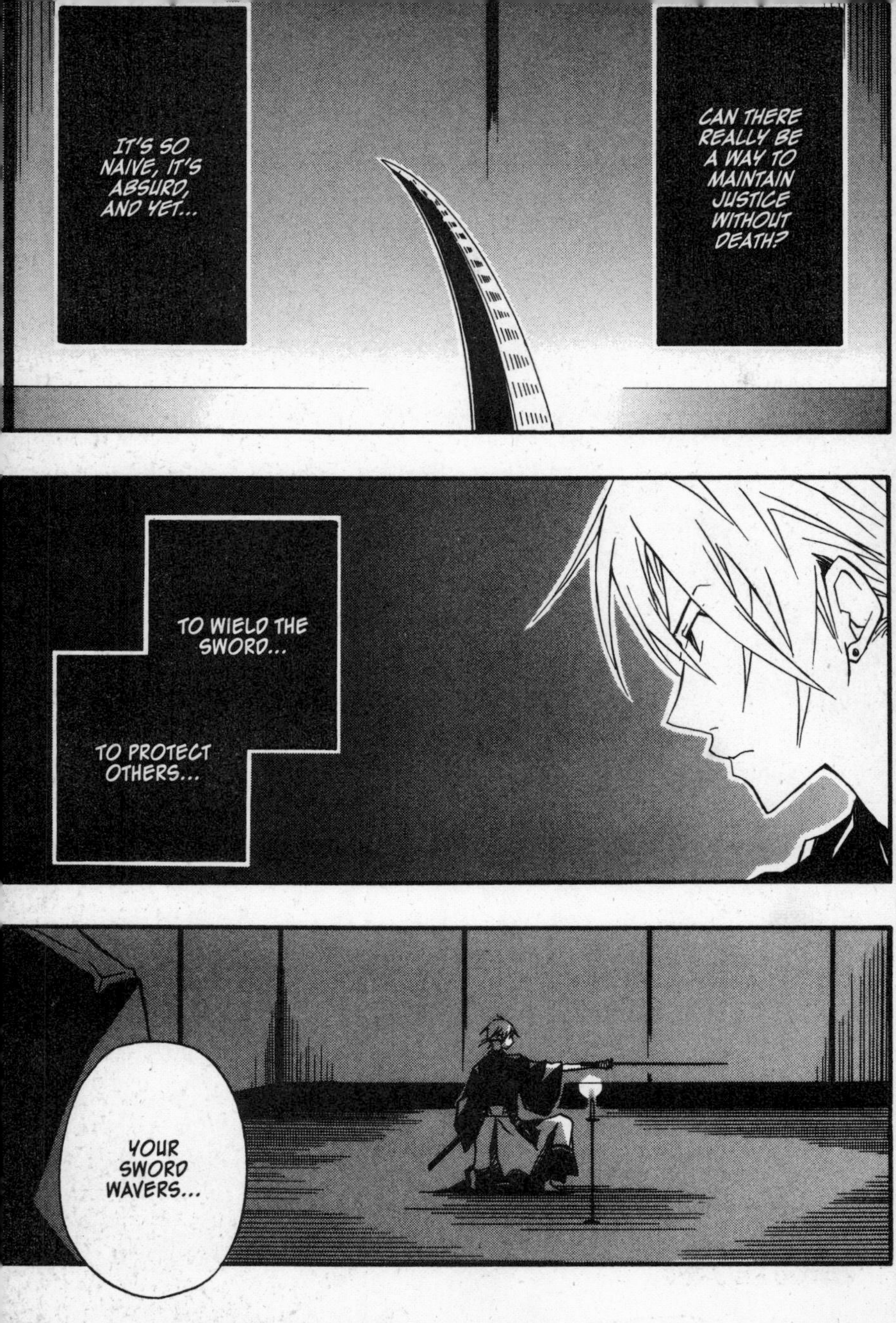
CAN THERE REALLY BE A WAY TO MAINTAIN JUSTICE WITHOUT DEATH?
IT'S SO NAIVE, IT'S ABSURD, AND YET...
TO WIELD THE SWORD...
TO PROTECT OTHERS...
YOUR SWORD WAVERS...

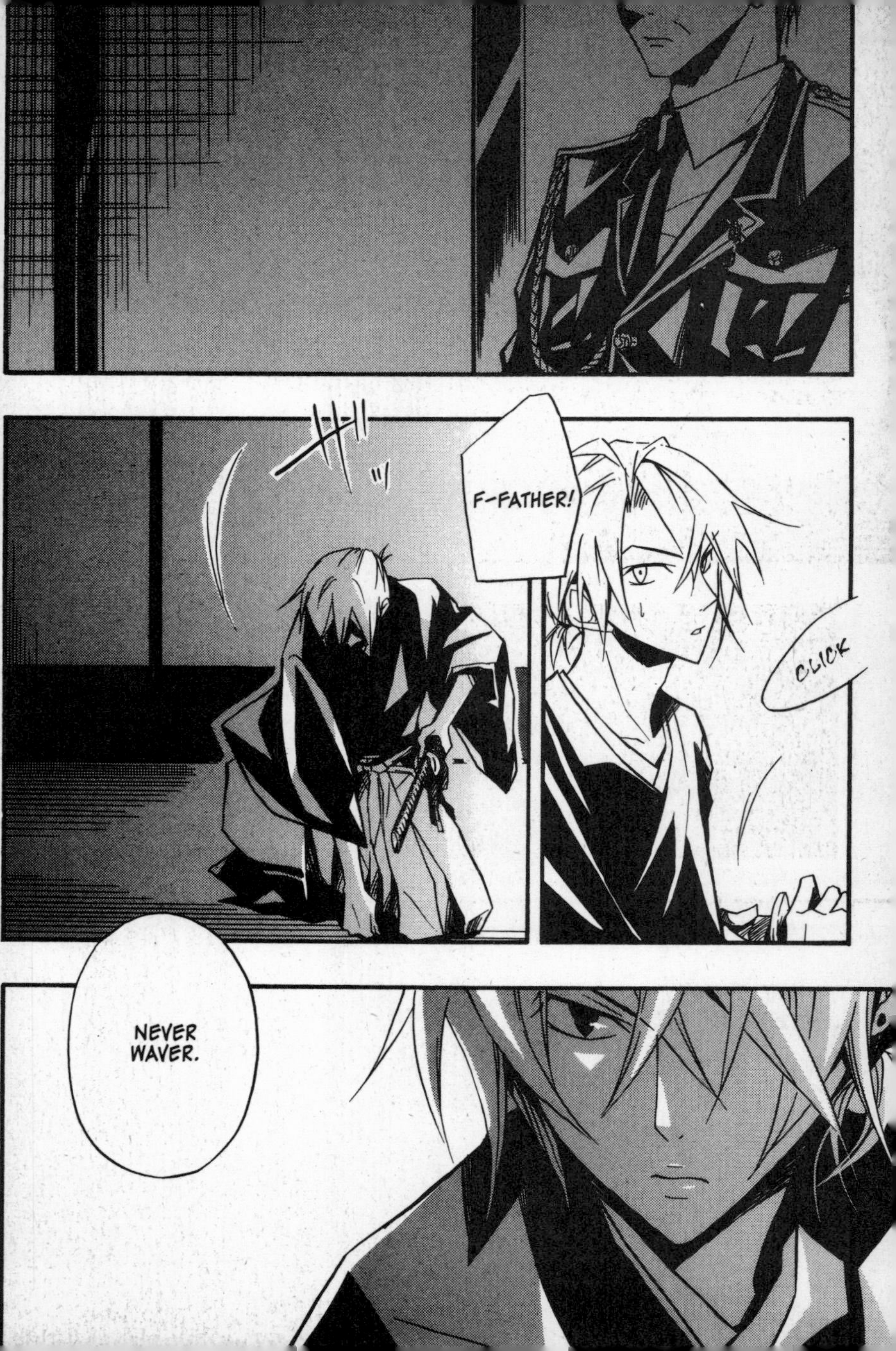
F-FATHER!
CLICK
NEVER WAVER.

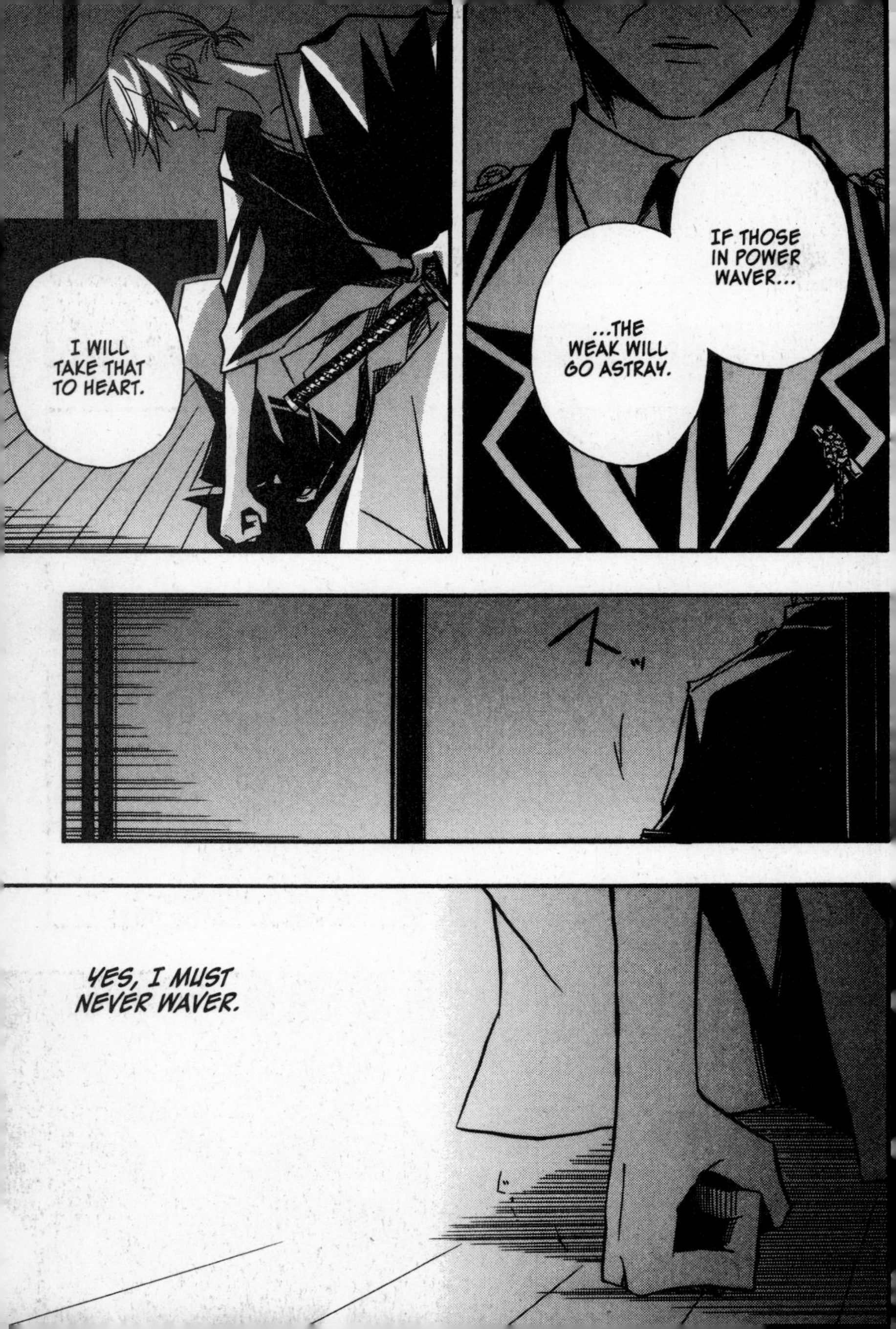
IF THOSE IN POWER WAVER...
...THE WEAK WILL GO ASTRAY.
I WILL TAKE THAT TO HEART.
YES, I MUST NEVER WAVER.

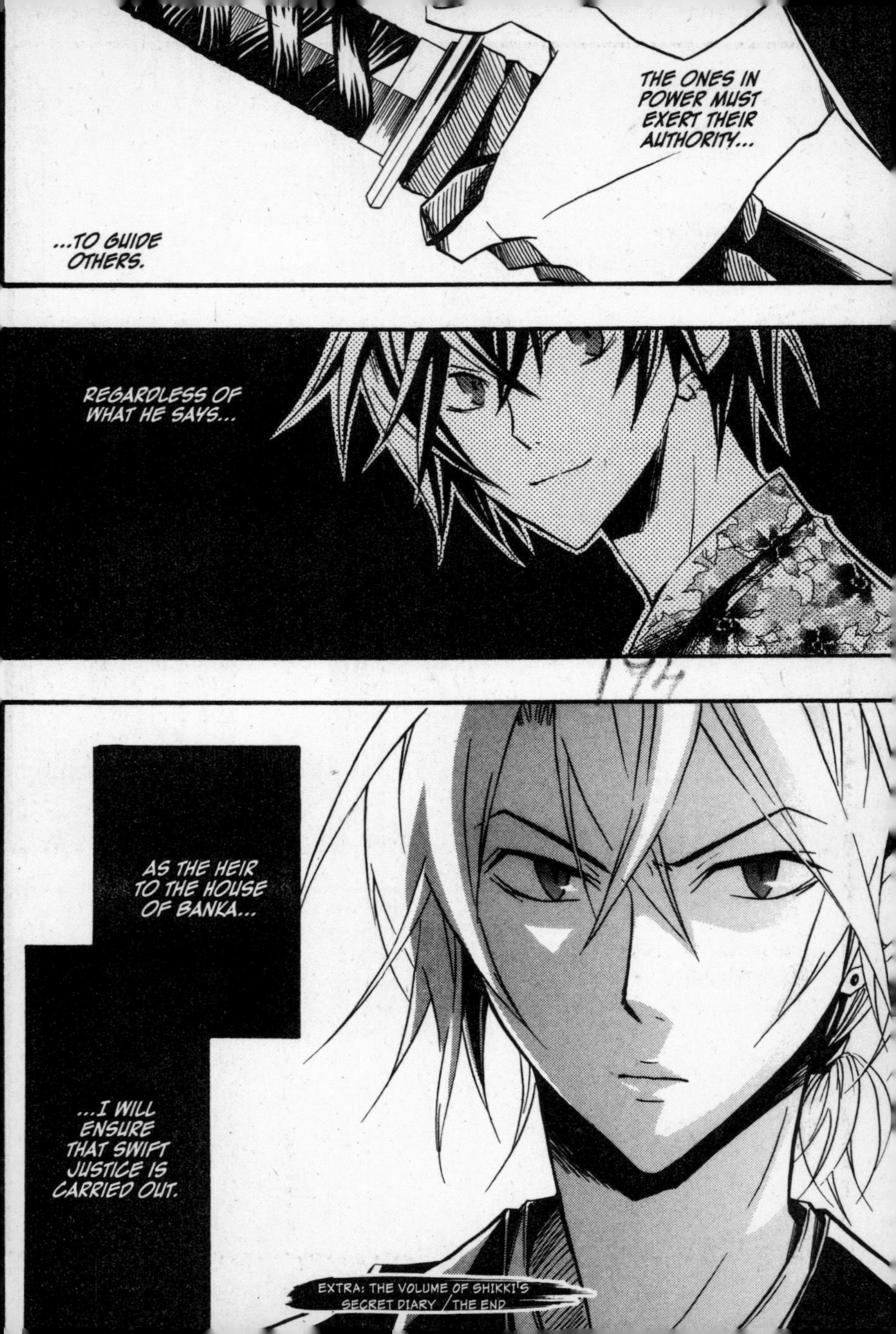
THE ONES IN POWER MUST EXERT THEIR AUTHORITY...
...TO GUIDE OTHERS.
REGARDLESS OF WHAT HE SAYS...
AS THE HEIR TO THE HOUSE OF BANKA...
...I WILL ENSURE THAT SWIFT JUSTICE IS CARRIED OUT.
EXTRA: THE VOLUME OF SHIKKI'S SECRET DIARY / THE END

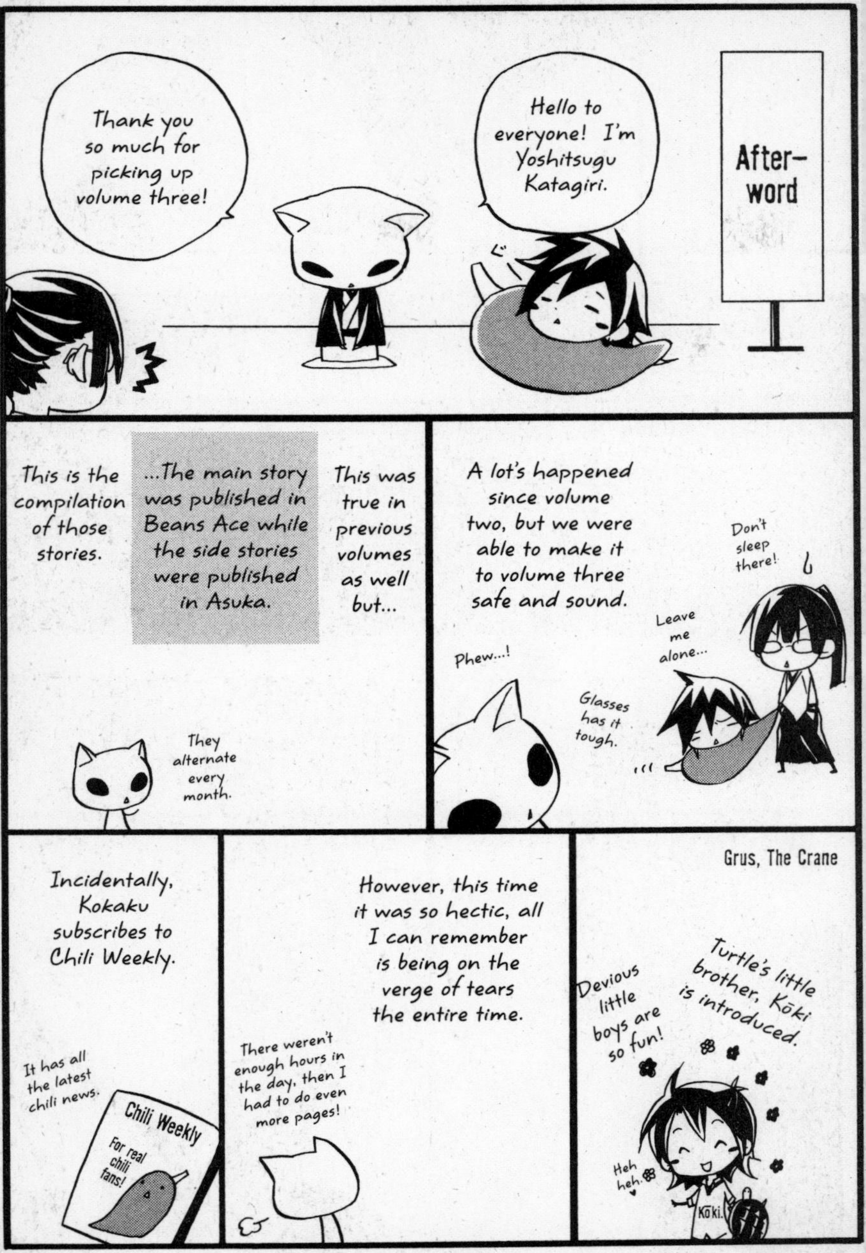
After-word
Hello to everyone! I'm Yoshitsugu Katagiri.
じ
Thank you so much for picking up volume three!
A lot's happened since volume two, but we were able to make it to volume three safe and sound.
Don't sleep there!
Leave me alone...
Phew...!
Glasses has it tough.
This was true in previous volumes as well but...
...The main story was published in Beans Ace while the side stories were published in Asuka.
This is the compilation of those stories.
They alternate every month.
Grus, The Crane
Turtle's little brother, Kōki is introduced.
Devious little boys are so fun!
Heh heh.
Kōki.
However, this time it was so hectic, all I can remember is being on the verge of tears the entire time.
There weren't enough hours in the day, then I had to do even more pages!
Incidentally, Kokaku subscribes to Chili Weekly.
It has all the latest chili news.
Chili Weekly
For real chili fans!

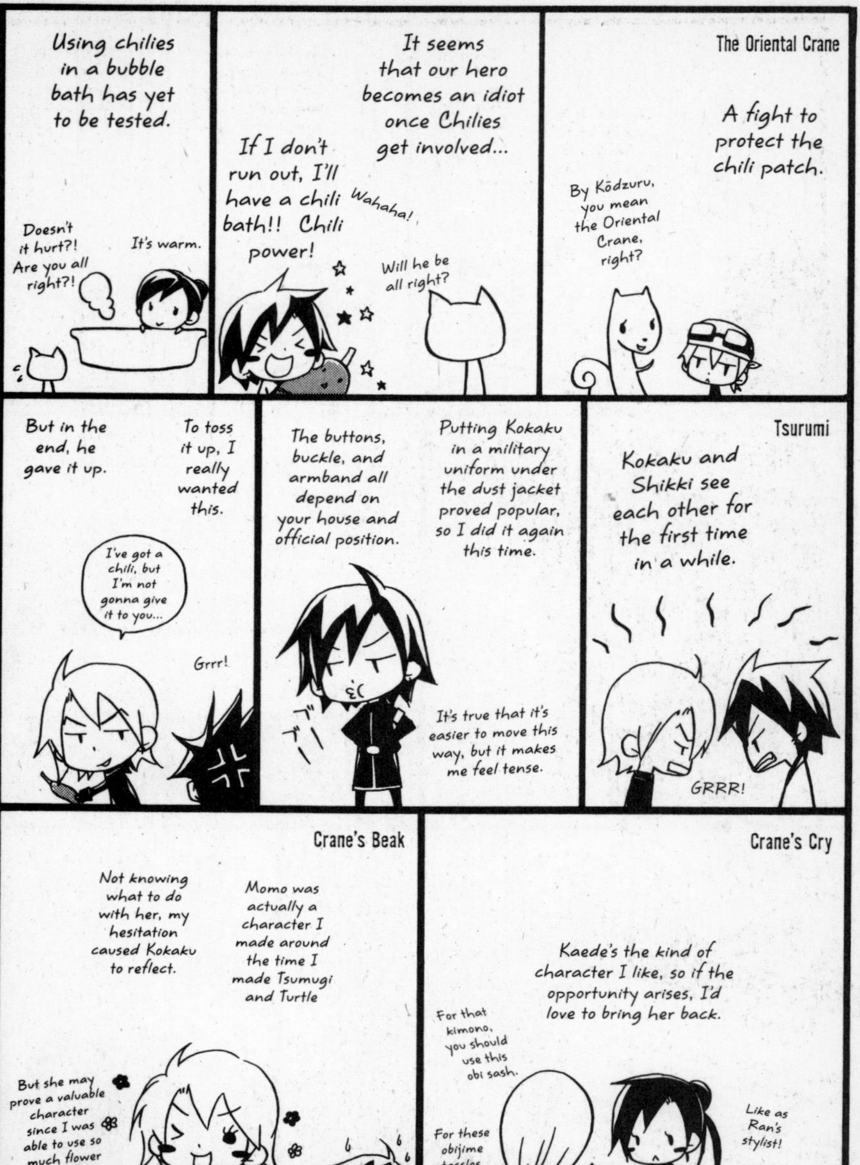
The Oriental Crane
A fight to protect the chili patch.
By Kōdzuru, you mean the Oriental Crane, right?
It seems that our hero becomes an idiot once Chilies get involved...
If I don't run out, I'll have a chili bath!! Chili power!
Wahaha!
Will he be all right?
Using chilies in a bubble bath has yet to be tested.
It's warm.
Doesn't it hurt?! Are you all right?!
Tsurumi
Kokaku and Shikki see each other for the first time in a while.
GRRR!
Putting Kokaku in a military uniform under the dust jacket proved popular, so I did it again this time.
The buttons, buckle, and armband all depend on your house and official position.
It's true that it's easier to move this way, but it makes me feel tense.
To toss it up, I really wanted this.
But in the end, he gave it up.
I've got a chili, but I'm not gonna give it to you...
Grrr!
Crane's Cry
Kaede's the kind of character I like, so if the opportunity arises, I'd love to bring her back.
Like as Ran's stylist!
For that kimono, you should use this obi sash.
For these obijime tassles, you should use this accessory.
Crane's Beak
Momo was actually a character I made around the time I made Tsumugi and Turtle
Not knowing what to do with her, my hesitation caused Kokaku to reflect.
But she may prove a valuable character since I was able to use so much flower screen tone.

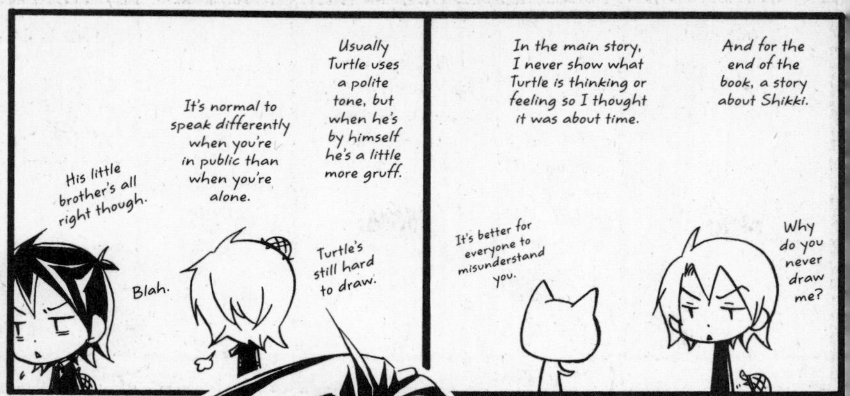
And for the end of the book, a story about Shikki.
In the main story, I never show what Turtle is thinking or feeling so I thought it was about time.
Why do you never draw me?
It's better for everyone to misunderstand you.
Usually Turtle uses a polite tone, but when he's by himself he's a little more gruff.
It's normal to speak differently when you're in public than when you're alone.
His little brother's all right though.
Turtle's still hard to draw.
Blah.

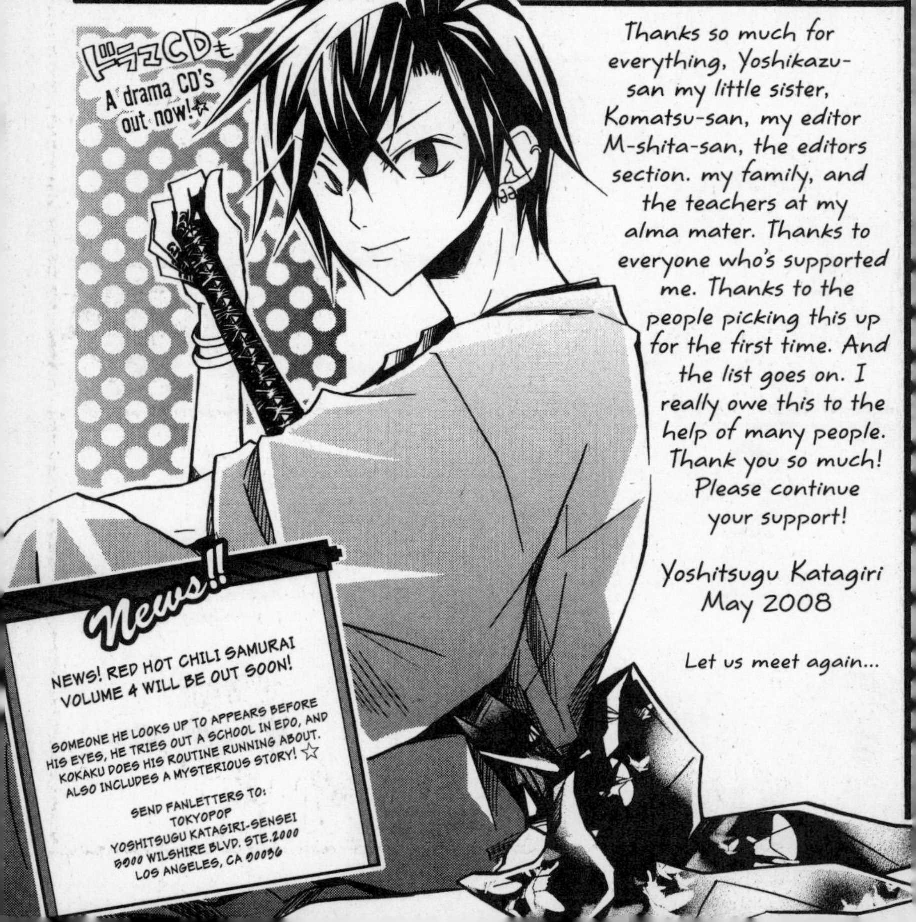
ドラマCDも
A drama CD's out now!☆
News!!
NEWS! RED HOT CHILI SAMURAI VOLUME 4 WILL BE OUT SOON!
SOMEONE HE LOOKS UP TO APPEARS BEFORE HIS EYES, HE TRIES OUT A SCHOOL IN EDO, AND KOKAKU DOES HIS ROUTINE RUNNING ABOUT. ALSO INCLUDES A MYSTERIOUS STORY! ☆
SEND FANLETTERS TO:
TOKYOPOP
YOSHITSUGU KATAGIRI-SENSEI
5900 WILSHIRE BLVD. STE.2000
LOS ANGELES, CA 90036

Thanks so much for everything, Yoshikazu-san my little sister, Komatsu-san, my editor M-shita-san, the editors section. my family, and the teachers at my alma mater. Thanks to everyone who's supported me. Thanks to the people picking this up for the first time. And the list goes on. I really owe this to the help of many people. Thank you so much! Please continue your support!

Yoshitsugu Katagiri
May 2008

Let us meet again...

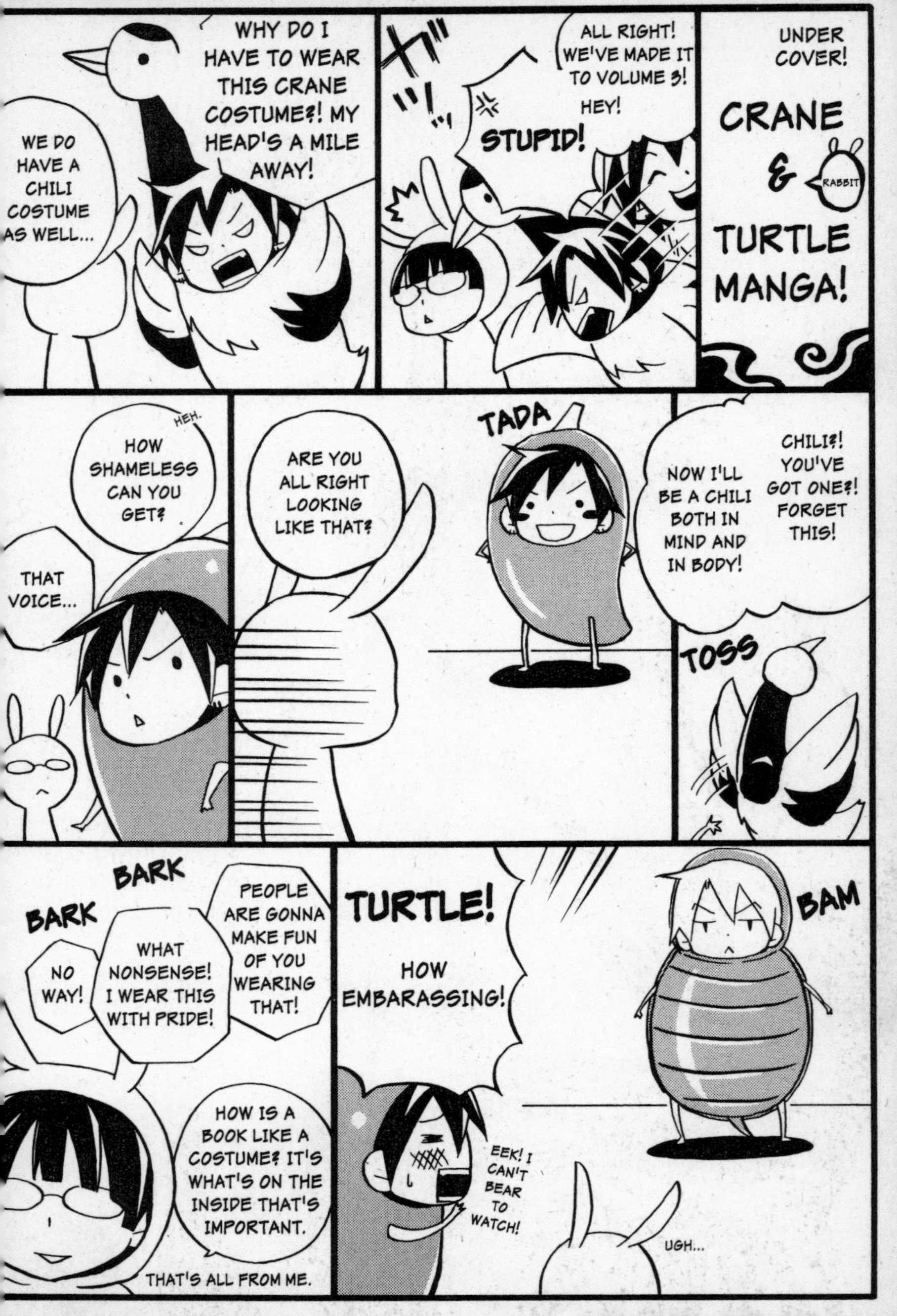
UNDER COVER!
CRANE & RABBIT TURTLE MANGA!
ALL RIGHT! WE'VE MADE IT TO VOLUME 3!
HEY!
STUPID!
WHY DO I HAVE TO WEAR THIS CRANE COSTUME?! MY HEAD'S A MILE AWAY!
WE DO HAVE A CHILI COSTUME AS WELL...
CHILI?! YOU'VE GOT ONE?! FORGET THIS!
NOW I'LL BE A CHILI BOTH IN MIND AND IN BODY!
TOSS
TADA
ARE YOU ALL RIGHT LOOKING LIKE THAT?
HEH.
HOW SHAMELESS CAN YOU GET?
THAT VOICE...
BAM
TURTLE!
HOW EMBARASSING!
EEK! I CAN'T BEAR TO WATCH!
UGH...
PEOPLE ARE GONNA MAKE FUN OF YOU WEARING THAT!
BARK
WHAT NONSENSE! I WEAR THIS WITH PRIDE!
BARK
NO WAY!
HOW IS A BOOK LIKE A COSTUME? IT'S WHAT'S ON THE INSIDE THAT'S IMPORTANT.
THAT'S ALL FROM ME.

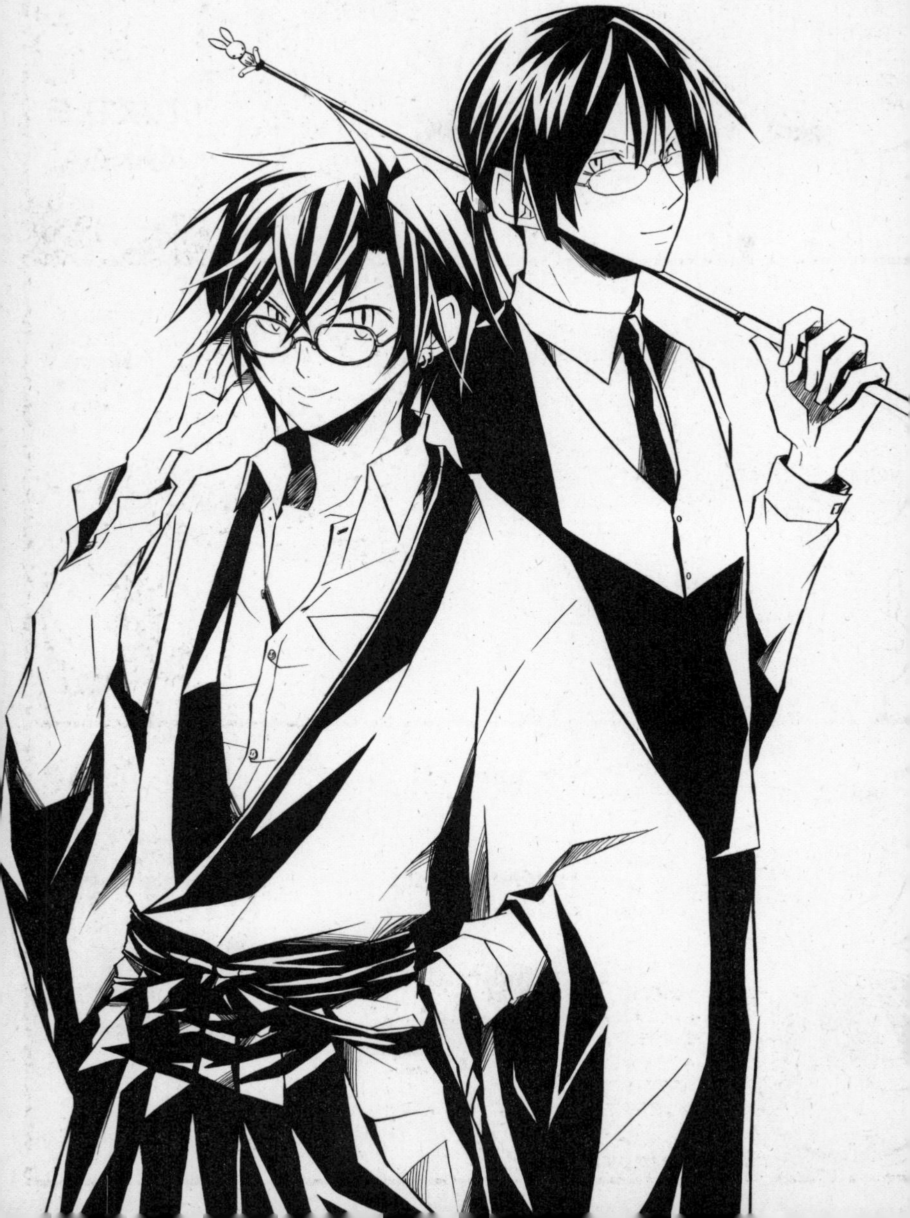

IN THE NEXT VOLUME OF...

ReD HoT CHiLI SaMuRai™

KOKAKU MUST RACE AGAINST TIME TO EXONERATE
AN OLD FRIEND BEFORE SHIKKI TAKES MATTERS
INTO HIS OWN HANDS! THEN THE TWO RIVALS MUST
PUT THEIR DIFFERENCES ASIDE WHEN THEY FIND
THEMSELVES IN THE MIDST OF A HOSTAGE CRISIS.
WILL KOKAKU LIVE UP TO HIS NOBLE IDEALS,
OR WILL THEY BE UNDERMINED BY GROWING
DOUBTS ABOUT WHY HE WIELDS THE SWORD?

VOLUME 4 COMING SOON!

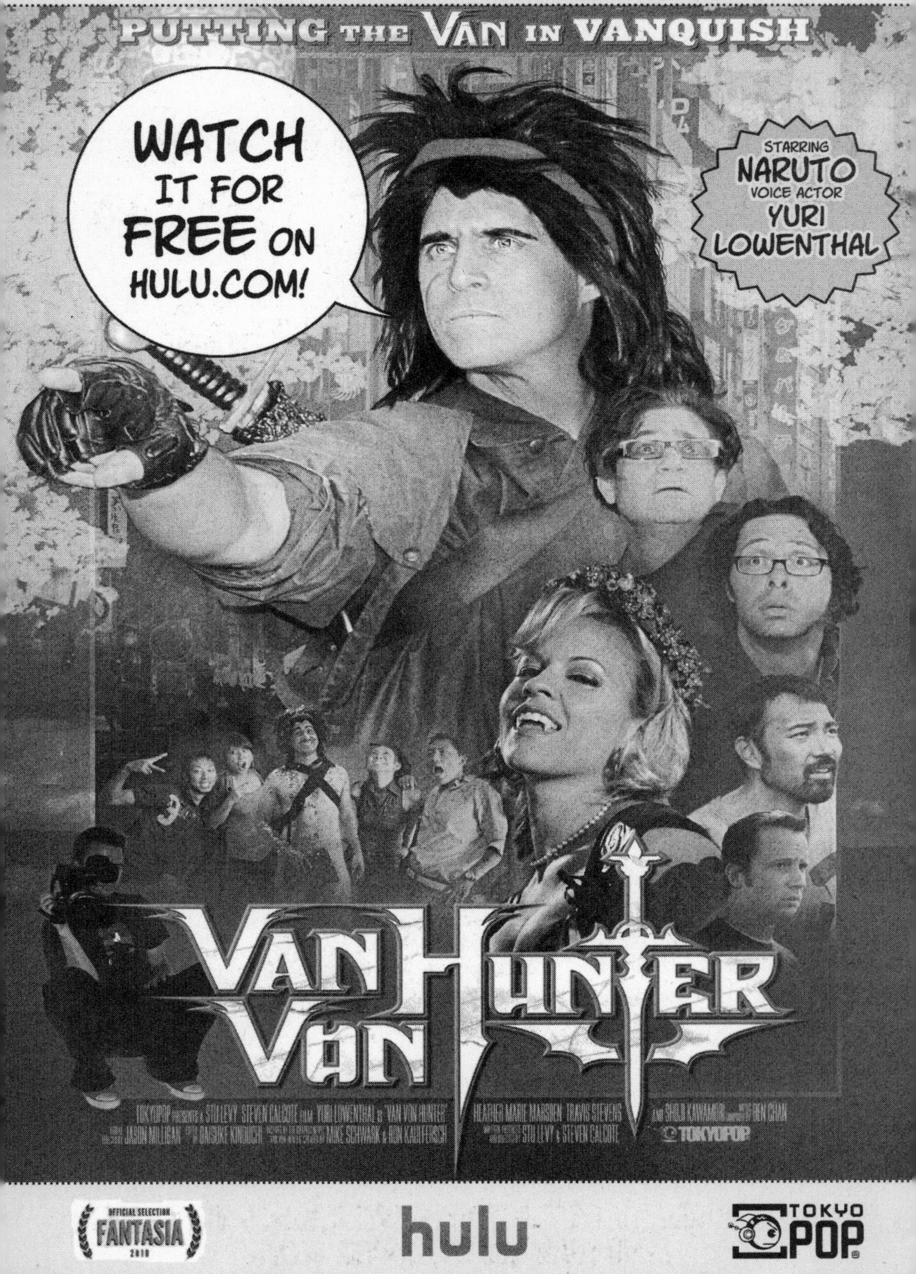
PUTTING THE VAN IN VANQUISH
WATCH IT FOR FREE ON HULU.COM!
STARRING NARUTO VOICE ACTOR YURI LOWENTHAL
VAN VON HUNTER
OFFICIAL SELECTION FANTASIA 2010
hulu
TOKYO POP

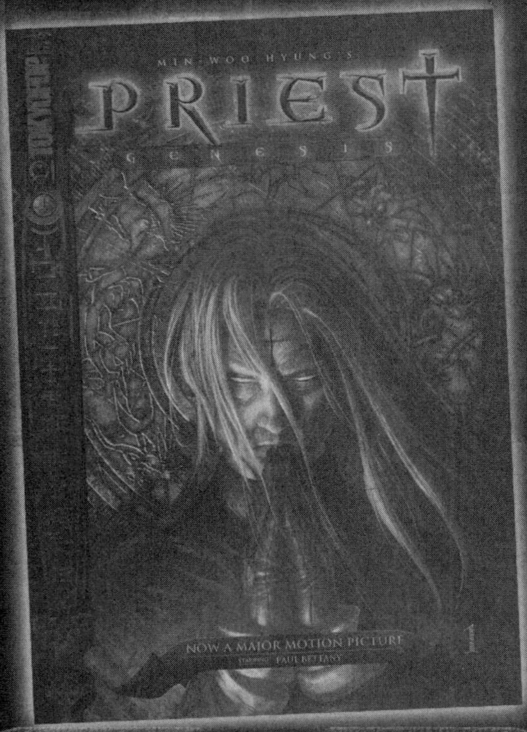
MIN-WOO HYUNG'S
PRIEST
GENESIS
NOW A MAJOR MOTION PICTURE
PAUL BETTANY
1